# Study Guide

## for

## Kalat's

# Biological Psychology

## Eighth Edition

**Elaine M. Hull**
*State University of New York at Buffalo*

THOMSON

WADSWORTH

Australia • Canada • Mexico • Singapore • Spain • United Kingdom • United States

For more information about our products, contact us at:
**Thomson Learning Academic Resource Center**
**1-800-423-0563**

**For permission to use material from this text, contact us by:**
Phone: 1-800-730-2214
Fax: 1-800-731-2215
Web: http://www.thomsonrights.com

**Wadsworth/Thomson Learning**
**10 Davis Drive**
**Belmont, CA 94002-3098**
**USA**

**Asia**
Thomson Learning
5 Shenton Way #01-01
UIC Building
Singapore 068808

**Australia/New Zealand**
Thomson Learning
102 Dodds Street
Southbank, Victoria 3006
Australia

**Canada**
Nelson
1120 Birchmount Road
Toronto, Ontario M1K 5G4
Canada

**Europe/Middle East/South Africa**
Thomson Learning
High Holborn House
50/51 Bedford Row
London WC1R 4LR
United Kingdom

**Latin America**
Thomson Learning
Seneca, 53
Colonia Polanco
11560 Mexico D.F.
Mexico

**Spain/Portugal**
Paraninfo
Calle/Magallanes, 25
28015 Madrid, Spain

# PREFACE

When a book is as well written as Kalat's *Biological Psychology*, everything fits together logically and "makes sense." It is easy to acquire a feeling of understanding. However, the sense of security produced by passive understanding is frequently shattered by an exam that requires recall and active reconstruction of the material. One of the earliest psychological principles of learning is that recognition is easier than recall and that passively following an argument is easier than actively reconstructing it. Unfortunately, passively understood material does not become part of us in the same way that actively manipulated material does.

The role of this study guide is to stimulate your active assimilation of the material in Kalat's textbook. The Introduction to each chapter in the Study Guide provides a brief review to refresh your memory at the beginning of a study session. Learning Objectives for each module provide goals for understanding. Key Terms and Concepts provide a quick overview of the material in outline form. Make sure that each term is familiar, and note its relationship to the overall structure of the chapter. Short-Answer Questions are designed to help you organize information pertinent to specific problems. These questions are listed under headings that refer to the main divisions of the chapter. If you have difficulty answering a question fully, refer to the appropriate section of the text to find the answer. The True/False, Fill-in-the-Blank, Matching, and Multiple-Choice Questions check your knowledge of detail and emphasize points that are easy to get confused. Some may seem picky, but it is better to encounter the confusing detail here rather than on an exam. Answers are listed at the end of the chapter. A number of chapters have graphics to be labeled or to be used in answering accompanying questions. Each graphic is adapted from or taken directly from the text; you can refer to the appropriate drawing in the text if you have difficulty labeling it. Some chapters have Helpful Hints that suggest analogies or mnemonic devices to help you understand or remember factual information. Finally, there are nine crossword puzzles, each covering one or two chapters. I hope that these provide an enjoyable way to solidify and test your knowledge of the information. The answers are given at the end of the Study Guide.

Biological psychology is full of detailed experimental knowledge and also of contradictions and perplexities. It has important general concepts and broad philosophical implications. A student once asked how anyone could stand to teach a course in which so much is unknown. However, the body does not work in a simple, stereotyped way. There is considerable orderliness about the body, but there is also a great deal of adaptability that gives rise to unresolved questions. The study of brain and behavior may well be the most exciting frontier of knowledge. In contrast to the dismay of the student who wanted knowledge handed out in tidy packets, many others have found that their biological psychology course did more to challenge and enrich their basic philosophy of life than did any other course. I hope that this text and study guide will help make your experiences with biological psychology more like those of the latter students than those of the former.

Thanks to James Kalat, author of *Biological Psychology*, to Victoria Knight, Psychology Publisher for Wadsworth Publishing, and Jennifer Wilkinson, Senior Assistant Editor for the Study Guide. My special thanks go to my husband, Richard T. Hull, a veteran crossword puzzle fan, for his help with the puzzles and many other aspects of this project.

Elaine M. Hull

# CONTENTS

# 1

## THE MAJOR ISSUES

### INTRODUCTION

Biological psychology is the study of the physiological, ontogenetic (developmental), evolutionary, and functional explanations of behavior. Bird song provides an example of the four types of explanation. Increased testosterone levels during mating season cause a brain area that is important for singing to increase in size, providing a physiological mechanism for singing. Ontogenetic explanations focus both on the genes that prepare for a behavior and on experience during a sensitive period, when a bird must hear the appropriate song. Evolutionary explanations discuss the selection of traits in terms of their adaptive value to the organism. Similar behavior patterns in two different species suggests that those species evolved from a common ancestor. Functional explanations describe the advantages conferred by each trait. For example, a male bird's song attracts a female and deters competition from other males.

Human behavior is also subject to biological explanation. There are a number of theories about the relationship of the mind to the brain. According to the dualist position, the mind and the brain exist independently, but somehow interact. However, that "somehow" causes a problem. Monism holds that there is only one kind of substance, though various theorists differ as to whether that substance is mental, physical, or some combination of the two. The materialist position (a form of monism) holds that everything that exists is material (physical). Mentalism suggests that only the mind really exists. The identity position (another form of monism) proposes that mental processes are the same thing as brain activity but are described in different terms.

David Chalmers proposed that there are "easy problems" concerning the specific application of the term consciousness to wakefulness vs. sleep, or to the focusing of attention, for example. However, the "hard problem" is how *any* kind of brain activity is associated with consciousness. He suggests that consciousness is a fundamental property of matter. On the other hand, Daniel Dennett argues that, once we understand all the easy problems, the hard problem will go away. Finally, Patricia Churchland and Murray Gell-Mann agree that physical terms are sufficient to explain consciousness. A major difficulty in studying consciousness is that it is not directly observable. This has led some to a solipsist position: I alone am conscious. However, while few people doubt that other people are conscious, they do question whether other animals, plants, or inanimate objects, including robots, are conscious. Neuroscience cannot resolve the issues of the essence and functional significance of the mind or of its relationship to the brain, but it can contribute relevant data.

Genes are the units of heredity; they maintain their structural identity from one generation to another. Chromosomes and the genes they contain come in pairs, one from each parent. An individual with identical genes of a given pair is said to be homozygous for that gene; an individual with an unmatched pair of genes is heterozygous for that gene. Genes may be dominant or recessive; dominant genes have strong effects in either homozygous or heterozygous individuals, whereas recessive genes have effects only in the homozygous condition. When chromosomes pair up during reproduction, they sometimes break apart and one part attaches to the other chromosome; this is called "crossing over." If two genes are close together on a chromosome, they are less likely to be separated by crossing over than if they are far apart. Sex-linked genes are usually found on the X chromosome; any characteristic produced by a recessive X-linked gene will be observed primarily in males, who do not have a second X chromosome to overrule the recessive gene. Sex-limited genes are found on autosomal chromosomes, and are therefore equally present in both sexes; however, their expression is activated by sex hormones that are more abundant in one sex than the other. Genetic variation is produced by recombination of genes during sexual reproduction and by random mutations. Most mutations are maladaptive and produce recessive genes. Such mutations are not likely to produce harmful effects unless both parents have the same mutant genes.

Heritability is a correlation coefficient that describes the extent to which variations in a characteristic are due to genetic, as opposed to environmental, variations. It is determined either by comparing the resemblance between monozygotic (identical) twins with that between dizygotic (fraternal) twins or by comparing the resemblance of adopted children to their adoptive vs. biological parents. Heritability may be overestimated if members of a population live in similar environments, if genetic and prenatal influences are confounded, and if the effects of a trait are magnified by their influence on the social environment. Even traits with high heritability in "standard" conditions may be influenced by environmental interventions. For example, phenylketonuria (PKU) results from a recessive gene that prevents metabolism of the amino acid phenylalanine. The resulting high levels of phenylalanine lead to brain malformations and mental retardation. However, a diet low in phenylalanine can greatly reduce the abnormalities.

DNA (deoxyribonucleic acid, the substance of genes) serves as a template for the synthesis of messenger RNA (ribonucleic acid), which in turn provides a template for the production of structural proteins and enzymes. Genetic influences on behavior may be either relatively direct, via control of brain chemicals, or indirect, by affecting height or physical activity, for example.

Evolution is a change over generations in the frequencies of various genes in a population. Genes that confer a reproductive advantage will become more prevalent in later generations. Neither use nor disuse of a given structure or behavior can cause an evolutionary increase or decrease in that feature, contrary to the theory of Lamarckian evolution. Furthermore, humans have not stopped evolving; medical treatments and welfare programs may increase survival, but may not enhance an individual's reproductive success. Evolution does not necessarily imply improvement, since previous success does not guarantee future success in a changing world. Evolution is based on the benefit for genes, not for individuals or species. Genes for altruistic behavior, for example, may be favored by reciprocal altruism or by kin selection. Sociobiology seeks functional explanations for the evolution of social behaviors. However, these explanations are often speculative. Furthermore, even if genes do predispose us towards certain behavior patterns, we still have flexibility in acting on those predispositions.

The issue of animal experimentation has become controversial. The usefulness of animal research rests both on the similarity across species of many biological functions and on the difficulty or impossibility of conducting such research on humans. In addition, we are interested in animals, both for their own sake and for the light they can shed on human evolution. Some animal rights activists, the "abolitionists", believe that all animals have the same rights as humans and should never be used by humans for any purpose. "Minimalists" believe that some animal research is necessary, but that it should be minimized. Valuable clinical treatments of human disorders have been gleaned from animal experiments. However, even though experimenters attempt to minimize pain, and even though animal care committees (which include veterinarians and community members as well as scientists) oversee the research, a certain amount of distress accompanies much animal experimentation. In this case, as in many other ethical issues, it is difficult to gain resolution of the competing values.

# LEARNING OBJECTIVES

## Module 1.1 The Mind-Brain Relationship

1. Be able to describe four kinds of biological explanations of behavior and give an example of each.
2. Understand the two major positions concerning the relationship between the brain and conscious experience.
3. Know which kinds of problems are thought to be "hard" or "easy."

## Module 1.2 The Genetics of Behavior

1. Understand the concept of Mendelian genetics.
2. Be able to describe the relationship between DNA, RNA, and proteins.
3. Understand the concepts of dominant and recessive genes, sex-linked and sex-limited genes, and sources of variation in the course of evolution.
4. Understand the concept of heritability and reasons why it can be overestimated.
5. Be able to discuss natural selection and the goals and criticisms of sociobiology.

## Module 1.3 The Use of Animals in Research

1. Understand the reasons for animal research.
2. Be able to discuss the ethical debate concerning the use of animals in research.
3. Be able to describe the regulatory committees that oversee animal research.

## Module 1.4 Prospects for Further Study

1. Be able to describe the professionals who conduct neuroscience research and who provide clinical treatment for psychological, neurological, and psychiatric disorders.

# KEY TERMS AND CONCEPTS

## Module 1.1 The Mind-Brain Relationship

1. Biological explanations of behavior
   No need for organism to understand function
   Physiological explanation
      Reduces a behavior to activity of the brain and other organ
      Testosterone and bird song: increase in size of a brain area
   Ontogenetic explanation
      Describes the development of a structure or behavior
      Song development: requires both genes and hearing song during early sensitive period
   Evolutionary explanation
      Examines a structure or behavior in terms of evolutionary history
      Common ancestor
   Functional explanation
      Describes why a structure or behavior evolved as it did
         Genetic drift within isolated community
      Male sings to attract mate and defend territory

2. The brain and conscious experience: mind-body or mind-brain problem
   Dualism: mind and body—different kinds of substance; exist independently but interact

3

Rene Descartes
    Pineal gland
    Conflict: law of conservation of matter and energy
  Monism: only one kind of existence
    Materialism
    Mentalism
    Identity
      Mental and brain processes described in different terms
Function of consciousness?
David Chalmers
    Easy problems: difference between wakefulness and sleep; mechanisms that focus
      attention
    Hard problem: how any brain activity is associated with consciousness
    Consciousness as unexplainable fundamental
Daniel Dennett
    Hard problem = a lot of easy problems
Patricia Churchland, Murray Gell-Mann
    Physical terms sufficient to explain consciousness
Solipsism: I alone exist.
    Problem of other minds
    Other mammals? Insects? Rocks?
    Atoms: protoconsciousness?
    Just-fertilized egg?
    Computers or robots?

## Module 1.2  The Genetics of Behavior

1.  Mendelian genetics
  Genes: units of heredity that maintain structural identity from one generation to another
    Chromosomes
    Deoxyribonucleic acid (DNA)
      Template for ribonucleic acid (RNA)
    Translation of mRNA
      Structural proteins or enzymes
    Homozygous vs. heterozygous
    Dominant vs. recessive
  Chromosomes and crossing over
    General independence of inheritance of genes on different chromosomes
    Crossing over: attachment of part of one chromosome on another
  Sex-linked and sex-limited genes
    Sex-linked: genes on sex chromosomes
    Autosomal genes
    X and Y chromosomes
    Sex-limited genes: genes activated by sex hormones
  Sources of variation
    Recombination
    Mutation

2. Heritability
    Ways of measuring human heritability
        Monozygotic (identical) twins
        Dizygotic (fraternal) twins
    Overestimating heritability
        Similar environments
        Monozygotic twins: usually share same chorion
        Dizygotic twins: separate chorions
        Multiplier effect: environment magnifies early tendencies
    Environmental modification of heritable behaviors
        Elevated plus maze
        Phenylketonuria (PKU)
            Inability to metabolize phenylalanine
            Brain malformations, mental retardation, irritablity
            Modified by low phenylalanine diet
    How genes affect behavior
        Increasing production of a protein
        Indirect effects
        Change in one behavior due to change in another behavior

3. The evolution of behavior
    Natural selection
        Evolutionary tree
        Genes associated with reproductive success
        Artificial selection
    Common misunderstandings about evolution
        Does use or disuse cause evolutionary change in that feature?
            Lamarckian evolution
        Have humans stopped evolving?
        Does evolution mean improvement?
        Does evolution benefit individual or species?
    Sociobiology
        Functional explanations
            Altruistic behavior
            Group selection
            Reciprocal altruism
            Kin selection
        Criticisms
            Explanations often speculative
            Assumption that every behavior must be adaptive
    In closing: Genes and behavior
        Flexibility in acting on predispositions

## Module 1.3  The Use of Animals in Research
1. Reasons for animal research
    Similar mechanisms of behavior and ease of studying animals
    Curiosity about animals
    Clues to human evolution
    Can't experiment on humans

2. The ethical debate
   Animal research → useful discoveries
   Minimalists vs. abolitionists
       Opposition to environmental protection groups
   European Science Foundation proposals
       Lab animals: both instrumental and intrinsic value
       Reduction, replacement, and refinement
       Research to improve animal welfare
       Evaluation by others
       Assumption: procedure painful to humans is painful to animals
       Training of investigators in animal care
       Publication policy on ethical treatment of animals
   Institutional Animal Care and Use Committees
   National laws and professional organization guidelines
   In closing: Humans and animals
       Difficulty of resolving moral issues

**Module 1.4  Prospects for Further Study**
1. Research
   Behavioral neuroscientist
   Neuroscientist
   Neuropsychologist
   Psychophysiologist
   Neurochemist
   Comparative psychologist
   Sociobiologist
2. Medicine
   Neurologist
   Neurosurgeon
   Psychiatrist
3. Primary research journals
4. Neuroscience journal for nonspecialists


**SHORT-ANSWER QUESTIONS**

**Module 1.1  The Mind-Brain Relationship**
1. *Biological explanations of behavior*
   a.  What are the four major types of explanation of behavior sought by biological psychologists?

1) physiological → relates a behavior to the activity of the brain and other organs.

2) ~~onto~~ Ontogenetic → describes the development of a structure or behavior.

3) evolutionary → examines in term of evolutionary history

4) functional → describes why a structure/behavior evolved as it did.

b. Discuss the singing of birds from each of these perspectives.

physiological → Brain influence by Testosterone

ontogenetical - young learn to sing from listening to an adult.

evolutionary

fonctional → in certain species only male birds sing

c. What is the effect of testosterone on the brain of male songbirds?

a certain area of the brain grows under the influence of Testosterone. enables a mature male to sing

d. What is an ontogenetic explanation?

Describes the development of a structure or a behavior.

Traces influences, of genes, nutrition, experiences.

e. What is an evolutionary explanation?

examines a structure or a behavior in terms of evolutionary **history**

ex, people, frightened, goose bumps.

f. What are the two functions of the male bird's song?

- Defend his territory

- find a mate

g. What is genetic drift, and under what circumstances does it occur?

(PG4)      b) where a gene can spread

• in a small community, one dominant male has an enormous # of offspring thereby spreading his genes

• Larger Pop.

7

h. What should we infer about an animal's or human's understanding of his or her behavior?

~~That of our conscious~~

2. *The brain and conscious experience*
   a. What are the two major positions regarding the mind-brain relationship? List the main variants of these major positions.

   Dualism → belief that mind + body are different kinds of substance that exists independantly, but interact.

   materialism
   mentalism → ~~monism~~ → the belief that the universe consists of only
   identity one kind of existence.
   position.
   b. Give a strength and a weakness of each of these positions.
   - Dualism: our thoughts control our actions, + the brain controls behavior.
     - conflicts w/ physicists law of conservation of matter + energy

   monism

   c. According to David Chalmers, what kinds of issues do "easy problems" deal with?

   deals with consciousness, such as wakefulness, sleep, and our ability to focus our attention.

   d. What is the main "hard problem"?

   how our brain activity is associated with consciousness.
   - hard because we do not know how to do the research.

   e. According to Daniel Dennett, what is the relationship of the "hard problem" to the "easy problems"?

   Argues that the hard prob really consists of an enormous number of easy prob. Once we solve the EP the HP will go away.

*Philisophical position*

*" I alone am "*

f.  What is the problem of other minds?  How does solipsism deal with that problem?

- everything is product of your mind.

- whether other people have conscious experiences

g.  How do non-solipsists deal with the problem of other minds in humans?  In animals, rocks, or computers?

## Module 1.2  Nature and Nurture

1. *The genetics of behavior*

a.  Briefly, what is a gene?

Units of hereditability maintain their structural Identity from one generation to another

b.  What is the relationship between DNA and RNA?   Between one type of RNA and protein molecules?

RNA → Single stranded, oxygenated version of DNA

DNA — lacks of Oxygen
  ↳ double stranded.
  ↳ encodes for RNA

c.  What are two major functions of protein molecules?

enzymes → catogolize functions in your body

ex. Turnss something on.

*describing what you have*

BB/bb

d. What does it mean for an individual to be homozygous for a particular gene? Heterozygous?

The Same

Bb

e. What is a dominant gene? When can the effects of a recessive gene be seen?

expresses a dominant

B

When you have

f. What is "crossing over"?

D      R

Same chromosome, ends switch. Depends what ~~crosses over~~ crossed over.

g. On which chromosome are almost all sex-linked genes?

X & Y Chromosome

h. What is a sex-limited gene? On which chromosomes may it occur? Why are its effects usually limited to one sex?

i. What are two sources of genetic variation?

j. How is heritability of a trait determined?

k. What three factors may lead to overestimation of heritability?

_ environment
- genes -> influence how other ppl treat _you_

l. What is phenylketonuria (PKU)? How can its effects be modified?

a form of mental
retardation caused by a
genetic inability to metabolize
the amino acid.

m. What are some of the ways in which genes may influence behavior?

2. *The evolution of behavior*
   a. What is evolution?

   is a Theory, which suggests that over generation
   In the frequencies of various genes in a pop.

   b. What is artificial selection?

   - choosing individuals with a desired trait & make
   them the parents of the next generation.

11

c. Does the use or disuse of a structure or behavior cause an evolutionary increase or decrease in that feature? What is Lamarckian evolution?

Inheritance of acquired characteristics.

d. Have humans stopped evolving?

 NO

e. Does evolution always imply improvement? Why or why not?

 NO

f. How can a gene that promotes altruistic behavior be maintained in evolution, if it places its possessor in danger?

g. What kinds of issues do sociobiologists seek to explain? What are two criticisms of sociobiological explanations?

how Social behaviors have evolved.

ex functional explanations

## Module 1.3 The Use of Animals in Research

1. *Reasons for animal research*
   a. What are four reasons biological psychologists study nonhuman animals?

   (Pg 20)

   1) The underlying mechanisms of behavior are similar across species.

   2) interested in animals for their own sake.

   3) what we learn shed light on human evolution

   4) Can't use human subjects cause of legal or ethical restriction

2. *The ethical debate*
   a. Compare the positions of the "minimalists" and the "abolitionists" with regard to the conduct of animal research.

   - length of life span shorter
   - can't tell us how they feel.

   b. What principles regarding animal research did the European Science Foundation propose?

   c. What is the role of Laboratory Animal Care Committees? What groups are represented in their membership?

## Module 1.4 Prospects for Further Study

1. *Research*
   a. Describe the main issues studied by neuroscientists, and specifically, behavioral neuroscientists?

13

b.   What is a neuropsychologist?  Where do they usually work?

c.   What does a psychophysiologist study?

d.   What issues do neurochemists investigate?

e.   Compare the main issues studied by comparative psychologists with those studied by sociobiologists.

2.   *Medicine*
   a.   Distinguish among neurologists, neurosurgeons, and psychiatrists.

**TRUE/FALSE QUESTIONS**

___F__ 1. Physiological explanations describe the development of a structure or behavior.

___T__ 2. The observation that a male bird sings to attract a mate and defend his territory is a functional explanation.

__T__ 3. Rene Descartes believed that the pineal gland was the site at which mind and brain interact.

x __T__ 4. According to David Chalmers, the hard problem is to discern the mechanisms that focus attention.

__T__ 5. DNA is the template for mRNA.

x __F__ 6. A sex-linked gene is one whose expression depends on the presence of sex hormones, which are more abundant in one sex or the other.

x __T__ 7. An autosomal gene is one located on the X or Y chromosome.

__T__ 8. Heritability may be overestimated in studies comparing mono- vs. dizygotic twins because monozygous twins usually share the same chorion, as well as the same genes.

__F__ 9. The mental retardation caused by PKU can be completely ameliorated by providing a low-phenylalanine diet for the first 10-12 years of life.

__T__ 10. A gene can affect behavior directly by increasing or decreasing the production of a structural protein or an enzyme or indirectly by influencing height, weight, or activity level.

__F__ 11. Humans have stopped evolving, thanks to our fabulous medical system and social support network.

x __T__ 12. The ethical treatment of animals depends solely on the good will and morals of individual researchers.

## FILL IN THE BLANKS

1. The observation that testosterone increases the size of a brain area that controls singing is a(n) ___physiological___ explanation.

2. The observation that bird song requires both genes and hearing song during the early sensitive period is a(n) ___onotogenetical___ explanation.

3. The observation that the tendency of humans to have "goose bumps" in frightening situations is related to the erection of hairs in our hairier ancestors, which made them look larger, is a (n) ___evolutionary___ explanation.

4. The spread of a gene within a small isolated community is called ___genetic___ ___Drift___.

5. Rene Descartes was a ___Dualist___, who believed that mind and body interact at the ___pineal___ ___gland___.

6. Three types of monism are ___materalism___, ___mentalism___, and ___identity___.

7. The search for neural mechanisms that distinguish waking and sleep is a pursuit of a(n) ___Easy___ problem.

8. The belief that "I alone exist" is referred to as ___Solipsism___.

9. The type of consciousness that has been ascribed to atoms is called ___protoconsciousness___.

10. The units of heredity that maintain structural identity from one generation to another are ___genes___.

11. The function of ___DNA___ is to serve as a template for mRNA, which in turn is translated into ___structural___ ___proteins___ or ___enzymes___.

12. An individual who has an identical pair of genes on the two matched chromosomes is said to be ___homozygotiz___ for that gene.

13. Two sources of genetic variation are ___recombination___ and ___mutation___.

14. The inability to metabolize phenylalanine is called _____ (___PKU___).

15. The proposal that use or disuse can cause evolutionary change in a feature is called ___Lamrackian___ ___evolution___.

16. The field of study that seeks functional explanations for how behavior evolved is called ___Sociobiology___.

17. People who believe that no animal should ever be used by humans for any purpose are called ___Abolistonists___.

18. People who believe that animal research is useful, but that it should be closely regulated, are called ___minimalists___.

19. Institutional Animal Care and Use Committees that oversee the use of animals in research include __Veterrarians__, __Community__ __members__, and __Scientists__ as members.

## MATCHING ITEMS

1. _H_ Dualist
2. _J_ Type of monism
3. _G_ Easy problem
4. _i_ Hard problem
5. _K_ Product of gene transcription
6. _A_ Dizogotic twin
7. _F_ Monozygotic twin
8. _D_ Sex-limited gene
9. _B_ Sex-linked gene
10. _C_ PKU
11. _e_ Lamarckian evolution

a. Fraternal twin
b. Gene on X chromosome that is expressed mostly in males
c. Inability to metabolize phenylalanine
d. Autosomal gene that depends on sex hormone for expression
e. Belief in evolutionary change caused by use or disuse
f. Identical twin
g. Difference between waking and sleeping
h. Rene Descartes
i. How any brain activity is associated with consciousness
j. Materialism
k. mRNA

## MULTIPLE-CHOICE QUESTIONS

1. Which of the following is not a major category of biological explanation?
   a. physiological explanations
   b. ontogenetic explanations
   c. evolutionary explanations
   d. mental explanations

17

2. Most adult male songbirds
   a. sing throughout the year and throughout wide territories.
   b. sing when testosterone levels are high enough to increase the size and activity of a brain area that is critical for singing.
   c. sing because they are consciously aware that their songs will attract females and deter male competitors.
   d. sing the correct song, even if they have never heard the song.

3. The dualist position
   a. is problematic because it does not fit with our commonsense notion of the mind.
   b. proposes that the mind is the same thing as brain activity.
   c. cannot explain how, if the mind is not a type of matter or energy, it could possibly alter the electrical and chemical activities of the brain.
   d. proposes that mind is just an illusion.

4. The view that everything that exists is physical, and that mental events either don't exist or can be explained in purely physical terms, is characteristic of which position?
   a. materialism
   b. dualism
   c. mentalism
   d. functionalism

5. David Chalmers proposed that the "hard problem" concerning consciousness
   a. is how neural mechanisms differentiate between wakefulness and sleep and allow us to focus our attention.
   b. is why and how *any* kind of brain activity is associated with consciousness.
   c. really consists of an enormous number of easy problems.
   d. is impossible to answer, under any circumstances.

6. A solipsist
   a. assumes that other people, animals, and computers are conscious because they look and/or act much like I do.
   b. assumes that other people are conscious, but animals and computers are not.
   c. assumes that I alone exist, or I alone am conscious.
   d. is frequently a member of an organization called Solipsists United.

7. The order of bases on DNA
   a. determines the order of bases on RNA, which in turn determines the order of amino acids in proteins.
   b. directly determines the order of amino acids in proteins, which in turn determines the order of bases in RNA.
   c. is less important for genetic function than is the total number of particular bases.
   d. is more important for determining the shapes of carbohydrates and fats than of proteins.

8. An individual with a pair of identical genes at a given site on a pair of chromosomes
   a. is homozygous for that gene.
   b. is heterozygous for that gene.
   c. must have crossing over at that gene.
   d. must not have the ability to taste phenylthiocarbamide.

18

9. Crossing over refers to
    a. chickens getting to the other side of the road.
    b. heterozygous genes now becoming homozygous.
    c. homozygous genes now becoming heterozygous.
    d. the breaking of paired chromosomes during reproduction, with a part of one chromosome now attaching to the paired chromosome.

10. Sex-linked genes are usually genes
    a. on autosomal chromosomes that are expressed only under hormonal conditions that are usually found only in one sex.
    b. on autosomal chromosomes that are expressed in both sexes.
    c. on the X chromosome, which cannot be overridden by a second X chromosome in males.
    d. that most frequently engage in crossing over.

11. Mutations
    a. result from the recombination of genes from the two parents.
    b. are random genetic changes that are usually maladaptive.
    c. are so extremely rare that they almost never affect inheritance.
    d. are unlikely to produce harmful effects in offspring if the two parents are closely related; therefore, people should marry their close relatives.

12. Heritability can be overestimated
    a. if populations are studied in extremely varied environmental conditions.
    b. because a democratic society treats all individuals similarly.
    c. because monozygotic twins share both their genetic heritage and a single chorion.
    d. all of the above.

13. Phenylketonuria (PKU)
    a. has high heritability under normal conditions.
    b. results from inability to metabolize phenylalanine, which results in high levels of that amino acid, which in turn results in brain damage and mental retardation.
    c. effects can be minimized by a low phenylalanine diet.
    d. all of the above.

14. The survival of genes for altruistic behavior can be explained by
    a. either reciprocal altruism or kin selection.
    b. the fact that altruism is only a little harmful to the individual.
    c. the fact that altruism benefits the species, though it may harm the individual.
    d. All of the above are equally good explanations.

15. Animal research
    a. yields no useful discoveries.
    b. is regulated by Institutional Animal Care and Use Committees, which are composed of veterinarians, community representatives, and scientists.
    c. depends entirely on the wisdom and good intentions of individual researchers for maintaining good care of the animals.
    d. all of the above.

16. "Abolitionist" animal advocates
    a. agree that some animal research is acceptable if an important goal can be achieved with minimal suffering.
    b. maintain that use of primates in experimentation should be abolished, but that "lower" animals may be used.
    c. maintain that all animal experimentation, as well as any other use of animals, should be totally eliminated.
    d. are also called "minimalists".

## Answers to True/False Questions

| | | |
|---|---|---|
| 1. F | 5. T | 9. F |
| 2. T | 6. T | 10. T |
| 3. T | 7. F | 11. F |
| 4. F | 8. T | 12. F |

## Answers to Fill-in-the-Blank Questions

1. physiological
2. ontogenetic
3. evolutionary
4. genetic drift
5. dualist, pineal gland
6. materialism, mentalism, identity
7. easy
8. solipsism
9. protoconsciousness
10. genes
11. DNA, structural proteins, enzymes
12. homozygous
13. recombination, mutation
14. phenylketonuria, PKU
15. Lamarckian evolution
16. sociobiology
17. abolitionists
18. minimalists
19. veterinarians, community members, scientists

## Answers to Matching Items

| | |
|---|---|
| 1. h | 7. f |
| 2. j | 8. d |
| 3. g | 9. b |
| 4. i | 10. c |
| 5. k | 11. e |
| 6. a | |

## Answers to Multiple-Choice Questions

| | | | |
|---|---|---|---|
| 1. d | 5. b | 9. d | 13. d |
| 2. b | 6. c | 10. c | 14. a |
| 3. c | 7. a | 11. b | 15. b |
| 4. a | 8. a | 12. c | 16. c |

**Please check the Exploring Biological Psychology CD-ROM.**

# 2

# NERVE CELLS AND NERVE IMPULSES

## INTRODUCTION

Neurons, like all animal cells, are bounded by a fatty membrane, which restricts the flow of chemicals into and out of the cell. Animal cells also contain structures, such as a nucleus, ribosomes, mitochondria, and an endoplasmic reticulum, that are important for various genetic, synthetic, and metabolic functions. A neuron is composed of (1) dendrites, which receive stimulation from other cells; (2) the soma or cell body, which contains the genetic and metabolic machinery and also conducts stimulation to the axon; and (3) the axon, which carries the nerve impulse to other neurons, frequently across long distances. Sensory neurons are highly sensitive to specific external stimuli; motor neurons stimulate muscles and glands; and local neurons have either no axon or a very short one and can convey information only to adjacent neurons. One can infer a great deal about a neuron's function from its shape. For example, a neuron that integrates input from many sources has many branching dendrites. It is now clear that experience can modify the shapes of neurons. The nervous system also contains many support cells called glia, which help synchronize the activity of axons, remove waste, build myelin sheaths, and guide neurons during development and during regeneration of peripheral axons.

A blood-brain barrier prevents many substances, including most viruses and bacteria and most forms of nutrition, from entering the brain. In most parts of the brain, glucose is the only nutrient that can cross the barrier in significant amounts. Therefore, the brain is highly dependent on glucose and on thiamine (vitamin $B_1$), which is needed to metabolize glucose. Fat soluble molecules and small uncharged molecules can cross the barrier freely. The barrier depends on tight junctions between endothelial cells lining the capillaries.

The ability of a neuron to respond quickly to stimulation depends on the resting potential. A metabolically active sodium-potassium pump establishes concentration gradients by transporting sodium ($Na^+$) ions out of the cell and potassium ($K^+$) ions into the cell. There is a resultant negative charge inside the cell, because three sodium ions are pumped out for every two potassium ions pumped in. Selective permeability of the membrane increases this potential by allowing potassium ions to flow out, down their concentration gradient; the loss of the positive potassium ions leaves the inside of the neuron even more negative. The relative impermeability of sodium results in minimal inflow of positive ions to offset the potassium outflow. The concentration and electrical gradients exert opposing influences on potassium. The electrical gradient (the negative charge inside the cell) attracts more potassium inside the cell than would be there if the concentration gradient were the only influence. Sodium ions, however, are attracted to the inside by both the electrical and concentration gradients. Therefore, when the sodium channels are opened, there is considerable impetus for sodium to flow into the cell.

A neuron may receive input that either hyperpolarizes it (makes the inside more negative) or depolarizes it (makes the inside less negative). If the membrane is depolarized to a threshold level, it briefly loses its ability to exclude sodium ions, and these ions rush in through voltage-activated sodium channels. They cause the inside of the neuron to become positive, at which point the membrane quickly becomes impermeable to sodium again. However, as the neuron becomes more depolarized, voltage-activated potassium channels open, resulting in even greater permeability than usual to potassium, which is repelled out of the neuron by both the positive electrical gradient and its own concentration gradient. The exit of the positively charged potassium ions returns the neuron approximately to its previous resting potential. This rapid exchange of ions is called the action

21

potential. All action potentials of a given axon are approximately equal in size, shape, and velocity, regardless of the size of the depolarization that gave rise to them. This principle is called the all-or-none law. Immediately after an action potential, a neuron is resistant to re-excitation. During the 1 millisecond absolute refractory period, no stimulus can initiate a new impulse; during the subsequent relative refractory period of about 2-4 milliseconds, slight hyperpolarization resulting from potassium outflow makes it difficult, but possible, to produce an action potential.

Once an action potential occurs, entering sodium ions spread to adjacent portions of membrane, thereby depolarizing these areas to their threshold and allowing sodium to rush in there. Thus the action potential is regenerated at each succeeding area of the axon until it reaches the end. The regenerative flow of ions across the membrane is slower than electrical conduction within the axon. In some axons, 1-mm-long segments of myelin (a fatty insulating substance) are wrapped around the axon, with short uncovered segments (nodes of Ranvier) in between. The action potential is conducted passively with some decrement under the myelin sheath. There is still sufficient potential to depolarize the next node of Ranvier to its threshold, and the action potential is regenerated at full strength at each node. The impulse appears to "jump" from node to node. This mode of transmission is called saltatory conduction and is much faster than transmission without myelin. It forces the action potential to use the faster electrical conduction within the axon for a longer distance before engaging in the slower regenerative flow across the membrane. Very small local neurons use only graded potentials, not action potentials, because they transmit information over very short distances.

## LEARNING OBJECTIVES

### Module 2.1  The Cells of the Nervous System
1.   Know the main structures of neurons and the structural differences among neurons.
2.   Know the main types of glia and their functions.
3.   Be able to describe the advantages and disadvantages of the blood-brain barrier.

### Module 2.2  The Nerve Impulse
1.   Understand why the neuron uses considerable energy to produce a resting potential.
2.   Understand the competing forces of the electrical and concentration gradients on potassium ions and how this competition produces the resting potential.
3.   Be able to describe the function and the molecular basis of the action potential.
4.   Understand how an action potential is conducted down an axon and how myelin sheaths contribute to this process.
5.   Know how local interneurons transmit information without benefit of action potentials.

## KEY TERMS AND CONCEPTS

### Module 2.1  The Cells of the Nervous System
1.   Anatomy of neurons and glia
     Santiago Ramon y Cajal, a pioneer of neuroscience
     The structures of an animal cell
          Membrane
               Two layers of fat molecules
               Protein channels
          Nucleus
          Mitochondria
          Ribosomes

Endoplasmic reticulum
The structure of a neuron
Motor neuron
Sensory neuron
Dendrites
Synaptic receptors
Dendritic spines
Cell body or soma
Nucleus, ribosomes, mitochondria
Axon
Myelin sheath, node of Ranvier
Presynaptic terminal, end bulb, or bouton
Afferent axon
Efferent axon
Interneuron, intrinsic neuron
Variations among neurons
Purkinje cell of cerebellum
Cells in retina
Shape modified by experience
Purvis and Hadley: dye technique
Glia (neuroglia)
Astrocytes
Encircle several presynaptic terminals
Take up, store, and transfer chemicals
Remove waste
Microglia
Remove waste, viruses, fungi
Oligodendrocytes (brain and spinal cord) and Schwann cells (periphery)
Form myelin sheaths
Radial glia (type of astrocyte): guide migrating neurons, growing axons and dendrites
during development
Schwann cells: guide peripheral axons during regeneration

2.  The blood-brain barrier
Why we need a blood-brain barrier
Virus-infected cells
How the blood-brain barrier works
Endothelial cells of capillaries
Small uncharged molecules
Fat-soluble molecules
Active transport system
Glucose
Amino acids
Vitamins
Certain hormones
Move some chemicals from brain to blood

3.  The nourishment of vertebrate neurons
Dependence on glucose
Due to blood-brain barrier

Ketones
Liver: converts carbohydrates, proteins, and fats into glucose
Requirement for thiamine (vitamin $B_1$)
Deficiency leads to Korsakoff's syndrome

4.  In closing: Neurons
Importance of communication among neurons

## Module 2.2  The Nerve Impulse
1.  The resting potential of the neuron
Phospholipid membrane with embedded proteins
Polarization
Resting potential
Negatively charged proteins inside
Microelectrode
Forces acting on sodium and potassium ions
Selective permeability
Ion channels
Concentration gradient
More sodium outside
More potassium inside
Sodium-potassium pump
Moves three sodium ions out for every two potassium ions in
Active transport
Electrical gradient vs. concentration gradient
Why a resting potential?  Strong, fast response

2.  The action potential
Hyperpolarization, depolarization
Threshold of excitation
The molecular basis of the action potential
Voltage-activated channels
Sodium inflow
Potassium outflow
Drug effects
Scorpion venom: opens sodium channels and closes potassium channels
Local anesthetic: blocks sodium channels
General anesthetic: opens potassium channels
The all-or-none law
The refractory period
Absolute refractory period
Relative refractory period

3.  Propagation of the action potential
Axon hillock
Successive depolarization of adjacent areas
Regenerative ion flow slower than current spread in axon

4.  The myelin sheath and saltatory conduction
Myelinated axons

Nodes of Ranvier
Saltatory conduction
  Increases speed by increasing distance current spreads within axon
  Conserves energy by decreasing sites of sodium inflow
Multiple sclerosis

5. Local neurons
  Graded potentials
   Depolarization
   Hyperpolarization
   Horizontal cell in retina
  Small neurons and big misconceptions
   Large neurons easier to study
   Small cells functionally important

6. In closing: Neural messages
  Communication based on multiple on/off messages

## SHORT-ANSWER QUESTIONS

### Module 2.1  The Cells of the Nervous System
1. *Neurons and glia*
  a. What did Ramon y Cajal demonstrate?

neurons don't physically merge into one another and that a narrow gap seperates one from the next.
          synapse

  b. List the major structures of animal cells and give the main function of each.

membrane → a structure that seperates the inside of the cell from the outside environment.

nucleus → structure that contains the chromosomes

mitochondrion → structure that performs metabolic activities

ribosomes → sites which the cell synthesizes new protein molecules (makes)

  c. What are the functional and structural differences between motor and sensory neurons?

motor neuron → recieves excitation from other neurons and conducts impulses from it's soma in the spinal cord to muscle or gland cells

Sensory neurons → is specialized at one end to be highly sensitive to a particular type of stimulation.

ex. Touch info from the skin

25

d.  What are the main subdivisions of the neuron and the function of each?

*Dendrites*
*cell body*
*axon*
*myelin sheath*
*node of Ranvier*
*presynaptic Terminal*

*(Pg 32)*

e.  List several anatomical distinctions between dendrites and axons.

f.  What is the myelin sheath?

*cover the axon used as a insulating material*

g.  What is the function of the presynaptic terminal or end bulb?

*The point from which the axon releases chemicals*

h.  Describe the structural and functional differences among sensory, motor, and local neurons.

i.  What do the terms afferent and efferent mean? Can an axon be both afferent and efferent? Explain.

*arrival    exit*

*brings info into a structure*    *carries info away from the structure*

j. What is an intrinsic neuron?

~~is a cell~~
If a cell's dendrites + axon are entirely within a single structure

k. How do glia cells differ from neurons?

glia cells
- don't transfer info over long distances
~~exchange~~

l. What are four functions of glia?

hold neurons together
exchange chemicals with adjacent neurons

m. What are two functions of astrocytes?

- wrap around the presynaptic terminals of several axons, presumably a functionally related group. ✱ Take up chemicals released by the axons + later release those chemicals back to the axon. helps synchronize the activity of the axons, enable them to send messages in waves.
- Removes waste material, particularly waste when neurons die.

n. What two kinds of glia form myelin sheaths?

- Schwann cells
- Oligodendrocytes

o. What is the function of radial glia? What related function do Schwann cells perform?

guide the migration of neurons and the growth of their axons + dendrites during embryonic development.

build the myelin sheath that surround + insulate certain vertebrate axons.

2. *The blood-brain barrier*
   a. Why do we need a blood-brain barrier? Why don't we have a similar barrier around other body organs?

   Lets somethings thru not everything

   - protects the brain
     - all harmful ones out.
   Bad - caffine, heroine, nictone        also keeps out useful chemicals

   b. What happens if a virus does enter the nervous system?

   Brain attacks or slow reproduction but not kill
   if do, stay for life,

   c. Describe the arrangement of the endothelial cells that form the blood-brain barrier.

   Form the walls of the capillaries.
   Joined very tightly that most molecules can't pass them.

   d. What types of chemicals can cross the blood-brain barrier freely?

   - oxygen
   - carbon dixoide

   e. Give one reason why heroin produces stronger effects than does morphine.

   f. What is the role of the active transport system? What four types of chemicals are transported in this way?

   protein-mediated
   process that expends
   energy to pump chemicals from blood into the brain

   - glucose
   - amino acids

28

3. *The nourishment of vertebrate neurons*
   a. What is the major fuel of neurons?

   glucose ➡ a simple sugar.

   b. Why can't most parts of the adult brain use fuels other than glucose?

   c. Why is a shortage of glucose usually not a problem?

   d. Why is a diet low in thiamine a problem? What is Korsakoff's syndrome?

   ↳ Thiamine deficiency can lead
   to death of neurons.
   Severe memory impairments

## Module 2.2  The Nerve Impulse

1. *The resting potential*
   a. What is the composition of the membrane covering the neuron? Describe its structure.

   two layers
   phospholipid molecules (fatty acids + aphosphate group)
   cylindrical protein

   →microelectrode (P40)

   b. How is the electrical potential across the membrane measured?

   Resting potential → difference in voltage in a
   Resting neuron.

29

c. What is meant by selective permeability of the membrane? Which chemicals can cross the membrane and which ones cannot? How do a few biologically important ions cross?

    → Some chemicals can pass through it more freely than others.

    can't — electrically charge ions molecules

    can — $O_2$ urea $CO_2$ $H_2O$

    Through membrane channels.

d. What is the sodium-potassium pump? How does its exchange of sodium and potassium ions lead directly to an electrical potential across the membrane?

    → a protein complex that repeatedly transports 3 sodium ions out of the cell while drawing 2 potassiums ions into the cell.

e. How does the selective permeability of the membrane increase the electrical potential?

f. Describe the competing forces acting on potassium ions. Why don't all the potassium ions surrounding a neuron migrate inside the cell to cancel the negative charge there?

g. What is the advantage of expending energy during the "resting" state to establish concentration gradients for sodium and potassium?

2. *The action potential*
   a. What happens to the electrical potential of a cell if a negative charge is applied? What is this change called?

   b. What happens to the potential if a brief, small positive current is applied? What is this change called?

   c. What happens to the potential if a threshold depolarization is applied?

   d. What does the term "voltage-activated sodium channels" mean?

   e. What causes the initial rapid increase in positivity of the action potential? Why doesn't the potential stop at 0 rather than actually reversing polarity?

   f. What accounts for the ensuing repolarization? Why does the neuron hyperpolarize slightly, rather than stopping at the previous resting potential?

g. What effect does scorpion venom have on the membrane?

h. What is the effect of local anesthetic drugs like Novocain and Xylocaine?

They attach to the Sodium Channels of the membrane & Prevent Sodium ions from entering

i. What is the effect of general anesthetics?

decrease brain activity by opening certain potassium Channels wider than usual.

j. What is the all-or-none law? How may a neuron signal "greater than"?

The amplitude & velocity of an action potential are independant of the intensity of the stimulus that initiated it.

k. What is the absolute refractory period? What causes it?

l. What is the relative refractory period? What causes it?

3. *Propagation of the action potential*
   a. How does an action potential propagate down an axon?

4. *The myelin sheath and saltatory conduction*
   a. What is the major advantage of the myelin sheath, and how is this advantage conferred?

   b. What is a node of Ranvier? What would happen if the axon were wrapped with one long expanse of myelin, without any nodes of Ranvier?

   c. What is meant by saltatory conduction?

5. *Signaling without action potentials*
   a. In what ways is transmission by local neurons different from the usual conduction by axons? Why is this local transmission restricted to very short distances?

**TRUE/FALSE QUESTIONS**

_F_ 1. Ramon y Cajal demonstrated that neurons are continuous with one another, providing a basis for our sense of unified beings.

_F_ 2. The membrane of a cell consists of a bilayer of protein molecules, through which only electrically charged ions and molecules can pass.

_T_ 3. Neurons that are afferent to one structure can also be efferent from another structure.

_F_ 4. Dendrites carry information from one neuron to another, releasing neurotransmitter from their end bulbs (boutons).

T _F_ 5. Dendritic spines increase the surface area available for synapses.

_F_ 6. Intrinsic neurons typically have long axons that convey action potentials from one brain area to another.

T _F_ 7. Astrocytes are glia that wrap around the terminals of several axons and, by taking up and then releasing chemicals released by axons, may help to synchronize the activity of those axons.

_F_ 8. The major function of the blood-brain barrier is to keep the blood from spilling into the brain.

_T_ 9. The brain depends heavily on glucose, because the blood-brain barrier keeps out most other nutrients.

_T_ 10. The neuron expends considerable energy to produce a resting potential, based on unequal distributions of ions across the membrane, so that a small stimulus that opens ion channels can produce a large, rapid flow of ions.

_T_ 11. The sodium-potassium pump extrudes 3 sodium ions for every 2 potassium ions that it brings in.

_F_ 12. Hyperpolarization decreases the charge across the membrane.

_F_ 13. The absolute refractory period ensures that an action potential is conducted in both directions from a given site on the axon.

_F_ 14. Saltatory conduction increases the speed of conduction of an action potential down an axon.

_F_ 15. A node of Ranvier is the site of release of neurotransmitter from an axon terminal.

## FILL IN THE BLANKS

1. Some structures common to all cells are the ___nucleus___, ___mitochondria___, ___ribosomes___, and the ___endoplasmic___ ___reticulum___.

2. ___Dendrites___ carry information from other neurons toward the soma.

3. _myelin____Sheaths___ are fatty coverings that force the action potential to use faster electrical conduction within an axon for a longer distance before engaging in slower regenerative flow of ions across the membrane.

4. An ___Afferent___ axon carries information toward a structure.

5. Purvis and Hadley discovered that the shape of neurons can be modified by _experience_.

6. _Schwann cells_____ and __Oligodendrocytes____ form myelin sheaths.

7. ___Astrocytes_____ absorb, store, and release chemicals released from axons.

8. _Radial____glia__ guide neuron migration during early development.

9. The __Blood_-_Brain___Barriers_____ prevents most viruses, bacteria, harmful chemicals, and many nutrients from gaining access to the brain.

10. The cell membrane is composed of a double layer of ___phospholido_____, with embedded proteins.

11. There is an excess of sodium ions ___outside_____ the neuron, and an excess of potassium ions __inside____ the neuron.

12. The neuron expends energy to produce a resting potential in order to ensure a __Strong___ and _fast__ response to a stimulus.

13. A _hyperpolarization____ is an increase in the voltage across the membrane; it __decreases____ the likelihood of an action potential.

14. In many neurons an action potential begins at the _axon___hillock___.

15. A _node_ of _Ranvier____ is a break between myelin sheaths.

16. __Saltatory_____ conduction refers to the jumping of the action potential from node to node.

17. Local neurons are able to signal to adjacent neurons without the aid of _action____potential_.

# MATCHING ITEMS

___ 1. Dendrite      a. Carries action potentials away from soma

___ 2. Soma     b. Fatty covering on an axon

___ 3. Axon     c. Glia that produce myelin sheaths

___ 4. Efferent axon     d. Receiver of neural input to a neuron

___ 5. Afferent axon     e. Carries information toward a neural structure

___ 6. Myelin sheath     f. Location of nucleus, ribosomes, endoplasmic reticulum

___ 7. Astrocytes     g. Ion actively transported out of the cell

___ 8. Oligodendrocytes     h. Carries information away from a neural structure

___ 9. Radial glia     i. Generated by sodium/potassium pump

___ 10. Sodium     j. Glia that absorb, store, and release chemicals

___ 11. Potassium     k. Slower than electrical conduction within axon

___ 12. Action potential     l. Rapid inflow of sodium and slower outflow of potassium

___ 13. Resting potential     m. Glia that guide neural migration during development

___ 14. Regenerative ion flow     n. Ion actively transported into the cell

## MULTIPLE-CHOICE QUESTIONS

1. The membrane of a cell consists primarily of
   a. two layers of protein molecules.
   b. two layers of fat molecules.
   c. two layers of carbohydrate molecules.
   d. one layer of fat molecules adjacent to a layer of protein molecules.

2. Which of the following is the site of protein synthesis in cells?
   a. ribosomes
   b. endoplasmic reticulum
   c. nucleus
   d. mitochondria

3. Which of the following is the site of chemical reactions that produce energy for the cell?
   a. ribosomes
   b. endoplasmic reticulum
   c. nucleus
   d. mitochondria

4. Which part of the cell consists of a network of thin tubes that transport newly synthesized proteins to other locations?
    a. ribosomes
    b. endoplasmic reticulum
    c. nucleus
    d. mitochondria

5. Which part of the cell contains the chromosomes?
    a. ribosomes
    b. endoplasmic reticulum
    c. nucleus
    d. mitochondria

6. Which part of the neuron is specialized to receive information from other neurons?
    a. dendrites
    b. soma
    c. axon
    d. end bulbs

7. Dendritic spines
    a. are structures inside the dendrite that give it rigidity.
    b. are the sites of all synapses on a neuron.
    c. increase the surface area available for synapses.
    d. are long outgrowths that stretch for several millimeters.

8. Sensory neurons
    a. are afferent to the rest of the nervous system.
    b. are highly sensitive to specific types of stimulation.
    c. sometimes have dendrites that merge directly into the axon, with the soma located on a stalk off the main trunk.
    d. all of the above.

9. Intrinsic neurons
    a. have multiple axons extending to numerous structures.
    b. have dendrites and axons confined within a structure.
    c. are afferent to a given structure.
    d. are efferent to a given structure.

10. Glia
    a. are larger as well as more numerous than neurons.
    b. are found in only a few areas of the brain.
    c. got their name because early investigators thought they glued neurons together.
    d. form synaptic connections with neurons and other glia.

11. Which of the following is not a function of glia?
    a. guiding the migration of neurons and the regeneration of peripheral axons
    b. exchanging chemicals with adjacent neurons
    c. forming myelin sheaths
    d. transmitting information over long distances to other cells

12. The blood-brain barrier
   a. allows some substances to pass freely, while others pass poorly or not at all.
   b. is formed by Schwann cells.
   c. is completely impermeable to all substances.
   d. keeps the blood from washing away neurons.

13. Which of the following is true of the blood-brain barrier?
   a. Electrically charged molecules are the only molecules that can cross.
   b. It results from tight junctions between endothelial cells.
   c. Fat soluble molecules cannot cross at all.
   d. An active transport system pumps blood across the barrier.

14. If a virus enters the brain,
   a. it survives in the infected neuron.
   b. a particle of it is exposed through the neuron's membrane so the infected cell can be killed.
   c. it is immediately removed by glia before it can enter a neuron.
   d. it is impossible for any virus ever to enter the brain.

15. Adult neurons
   a. are like all other cells of the body in depending heavily on glucose.
   b. depend heavily on glucose because they do not have enzymes to metabolize other nutrients.
   c. depend heavily on glucose because other nutrients cannot cross the blood-brain barrier in significant amounts.
   d. cannot use glucose because they do not receive enough oxygen or thiamine through the blood-brain barrier to metabolize it.

16. Potassium
   a. is found mostly outside the neuron.
   b. is pumped into the resting neuron by the sodium-potassium pump, but some flows out as a result of the concentration gradient.
   c. is actively pumped outside the neuron during the action potential.
   d. more than one of the above.

17. The sodium-potassium pump
   a. creates a negative potential inside the neuron by removing 3 sodium ions for every 2 potassium ions that it brings in.
   b. creates a negative potential inside the neuron by removing 2 sodium ions for every 3 potassium ions that it brings in.
   c. creates a positive potential inside the neuron by removing 3 sodium ions for every 2 potassium ions that it brings in.
   d. is basically a passive mechanism that requires no metabolic energy.

18. The resting potential
   a. prepares the neuron to respond rapidly to a stimulus.
   b. is negative inside the neuron relative to the outside.
   c. can be measured as the voltage difference between a microelectrode inside the neuron and a reference electrode outside the neuron.
   d. all of the above.

19. Sodium ions
   a.  are found largely inside the neuron during the resting state because they are attracted in by the negative charge there.
   b.  are found largely inside the neuron during the resting state because they are actively pumped in.
   c.  are found largely outside the neuron during the resting state because they are actively pumped out, and the membrane is largely impermeable to their reentry.
   d.  are actively repelled by the electrical charge of the neuron's resting potential.

20. Hyperpolarization
   a.  refers to a shift in the cell's potential in a more negative direction.
   b.  refers to a shift in the cell's potential in a positive direction.
   c.  can trigger an action potential if it is large enough.
   d.  occurs in an all-or-none fashion.

21. Depolarization of a neuron can be accomplished by having
   a.  a negative ion, such as chloride (Cl-), flow into the cell.
   b.  potassium (K+) ions flow out of the cell.
   c.  sodium (Na+) ions flow into the cell.
   d.  sodium ions flow out of the cell.

22. The all-or-none law
   a.  applies only to potentials in dendrites.
   b.  states that the size, shape, and velocity of the action potential are independent of the intensity of the stimulus that initiated it.
   c.  makes it impossible for the nervous system to signal intensity of a stimulus.
   d.  all of the above.

23. When a neuron receives a threshold depolarization
   a.  an action potential occurs, the size of which reflects the size of the stimulus that gave rise to it.
   b.  so much sodium comes in that it almost completely depletes the extracellular fluid of sodium.
   c.  sodium flows in only until the potential across the membrane is zero.
   d.  the membrane becomes highly permeable to sodium ions for a brief time.

24. The down slope of the action potential graph
   a.  is largely a result of sodium ions being pumped back out again.
   b.  is the result of potassium ions flowing in briefly.
   c.  is the result of sodium ions flowing in briefly.
   d.  usually passes the level of the resting potential, resulting in a brief hyperpolarization, due to potassium freely leaving the cell.

25. Which of the following is true?
   a.  Local anesthetics block nerve transmission by blocking sodium channels.
   b.  Scorpion venom also blocks sodium channels.
   c.  General anesthetics keep sodium channels open and close potassium channels.
   d.  All of the above are true.

26. The absolute refractory period is the time during which
    a. a stimulus must exceed the usual threshold in order to produce an action potential.
    b. a neuron is more excitable than usual.
    c. the sodium gates are firmly closed and no new action potentials can be generated.
    d. sodium and potassium ions are rapidly flowing.

27. Propagation of an action potential
    a. is analogous to the flow of electrons down a wire.
    b. is almost instantaneous.
    c. is inherently unidirectional because positive charges can flow only in one direction.
    d. depends on passive diffusion of sodium ions inside the axon, which depolarize the neighboring areas to their threshold.

28. Myelin sheaths
    a. would be much more efficient if they were not interrupted with a lot of leaky nodes.
    b. are interrupted about every 1 mm by a short unmyelinated segment.
    c. are much less effective in speeding transmission than a simple increase in axon size.
    d. are composed primarily of protein.

29. Saltatory conduction refers to
    a. the salt ions used in the action potential.
    b. sodium ions jumping into the neuron, once the sodium channels are opened.
    c. the impulse jumping from one node of Ranvier to the next.
    d. the impulse jumping from one myelin sheath to the next.

30. Myelin sheaths
    a. slow conduction of the impulse by blocking sodium's entry to the cell; their advantage lies in making the impulse all-or-none.
    b. are destroyed in multiple sclerosis.
    c. are found on dendrites.
    d. are found on cell bodies.

31. Nodes of Ranvier
    a. are interruptions of the myelin sheath at about 1 mm intervals.
    b. are sites of abundant sodium channels.
    c. are sites where an action potential is regenerated.
    d. all of the above.

32. Local neurons utilize
    a. graded potentials to convey information over short distances.
    b. graded potentials to convey information over long distances.
    c. action potentials to transmit information over long distances.
    d. action potentials to transmit information over short distances.

## Answers to True/False Questions

| | | | |
|---|---|---|---|
| 1. | F | 9. | T |
| 2. | F | 10. | T |
| 3. | T | 11. | T |
| 4. | F | 12. | F |
| 5. | T | 13. | F |
| 6. | F | 14. | F |
| 7. | T | 15. | F |
| 8. | F | | |

## Answers to Fill-in-the-Blank Questions

1. nucleus, mitochondria, ribosomes, endoplasmic reticulum
2. Dendrites
3. Myelin sheaths
4. afferent
5. experience
6. Oligodendrocytes, Schwann cells
7. Astrocytes
8. Radial glia
9. blood-brain barrier
10. phospholipids
11. outside, inside
12. strong, fast
13. hyperpolarization, decreases
14. axon hillock
15. node, Ranvier
16. Saltatory
17. action potentials

## Answers to Matching Items

| | | | | | | | | | |
|---|---|---|---|---|---|---|---|---|---|
| 1. | d | 4. h | 7. j | 10. g | 13. i |
| 2. | f | 5. e | 8. c | 11. n | 14. l |
| 3. | a | 6. b | 9. m | 12. k | |

## Answers to Multiple-Choice Questions

| | | | | | |
|---|---|---|---|---|---|
| 1. b | 7. c | 13. b | 19. c | 25. a | 31. d |
| 2. a | 8. d | 14. a | 20. a | 26. c | 32. a |
| 3. d | 9. b | 15. c | 21. c | 27. d | |
| 4. b | 10. c | 16. b | 22. b | 28. b | |
| 5. c | 11. d | 17. a | 23. d | 29. c | |
| 6. a | 12. a | 18. d | 24. d | 30. b | |

## Helpful Hints

1. To remember the relative locations of sodium and potassium ions during the resting potential, remember that sodium ($Na^+$) is "Not allowed" inside the neuron and potassium ($K^+$) is labeled "Keep".

2.   To appreciate the difference between fast electrical conduction inside the membrane and slow regenerative potentials across the membrane, think of ions simply elbowing their like-charged neighbors a short distance away inside the membrane, while sodium and potassium ions have to swim their equivalent of the length of a pool to cross the membrane.

**Please check the Exploring Biological Psychology CD-ROM.**

### Diagrams

1.   Label the following structures on the diagram of a motor neuron below:  axon, axon hillock, dendrites, myelin sheath, node of Ranvier, nucleus, soma, presynaptic terminals, muscle fiber.

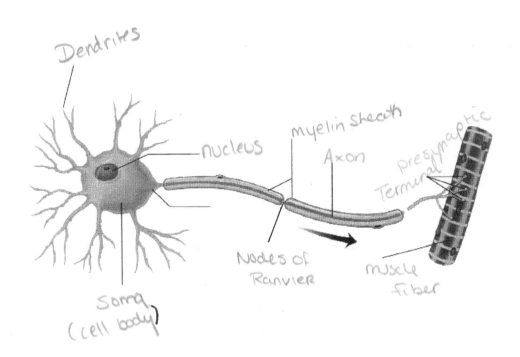

2.   In the diagram of neurons A and B below, label the directions as either afferent or efferent.

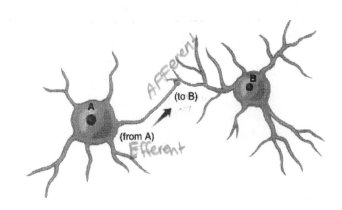

3. Label the five types of glia cells.

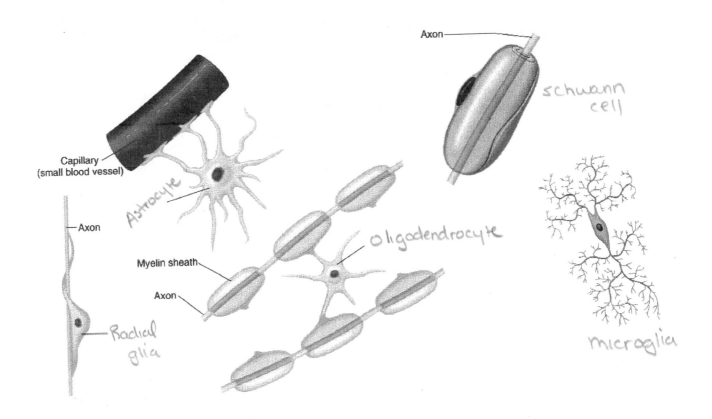

Axon

Capillary
(small blood vessel)

*schwann cell*

Axon

*Astrocyte*

Myelin sheath

*Oligodendrocyte*

Axon

*Radial glia*

*microglia*

4. Label the blanks below as either Na+ or K+.

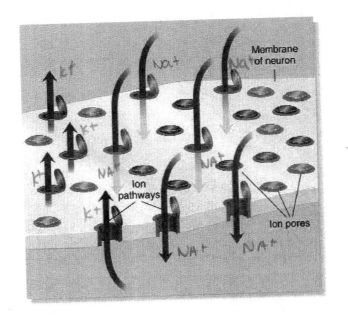

K+

Na+

Na+

Membrane
of neuron

K+

K+

Na+

Na+

Ion
pathways

K+

Na+

Ion pores

Na+

Na+

Depolarizing
potassium ↓
Sodium ↑

repolarizat
potassium ↑
Sodium ↓

# Genes, Neurons, and Behavior

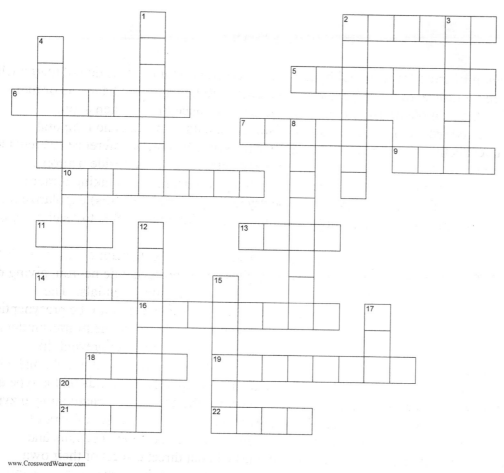

**ACROSS**

2 Type of glia that guides neurons in development
5 Part of neuron that receives input
6 Part of axon where action potentials start
7 Fatty sheaths covering some axons
9 Unit of heredity
10 Direction toward a structure
11 ____ selection: explanation for altruistic behavior
13 Problem of how any kind of brain activity is associated with consciousness
14 Small neuron using only graded potentials
16 Refractory period in which no new action potential can be started
18 Support cells
19 Theory that mental processes are the same as brain activity
21 With 2 Down, segment of axon not covered by myelin
22 Template for protein synthesis (abbr.)

**DOWN**

1 Major nutrient for brain
2 See 21 Across
3 ____ potential: rapid, "all-or-none" exchange of ions
4 Part of dendrite that increases area for synapses
8 Direction away from a structure
10 Type of acid that makes up proteins
12 Refractory period in which it is more difficult, but possible, to start an action potential
15 Main ion producing EPSPs
17 Major component of membranes
20 Substance of genes (abbr.)

# 3

# COMMUNICATION AT SYNAPSES

## INTRODUCTION

C. S. Sherrington inferred from careful behavioral observations that neurons do not merge with each other but communicate across tiny gaps called synapses. Reflex arcs that have one or more synapses are slower than simple transmission along the same distance of unbroken axon. Sherrington also inferred that complex integration of stimuli, including spatial and temporal summation of both excitation and inhibition, occurs at synapses. Most of his inferences were later confirmed by electrophysiological recordings using microelectrodes inserted inside neurons. Inhibitory postsynaptic potentials (IPSPs) hyperpolarize the postsynaptic cell, making it more difficult to produce an action potential. Excitatory postsynaptic potentials (EPSPs) depolarize the postsynaptic neuron and may summate spatially and temporally with other EPSPs to reach triggering threshold for an action potential.

EPSPs and IPSPs result from the release of neurotransmitters from presynaptic terminals. The neurotransmitter diffuses to and combines with receptor sites on the postsynaptic neuron, giving rise to either ionotropic or metabotropic changes that produce the postsynaptic potentials. The neurotransmitter then detaches from its receptor and is either transported back into the presynaptic terminal and reused or broken by enzymes into inactive components. Different neurotransmitters have different modes of inactivation, but some form of inactivation is critical to prevent the neurotransmitter from having a prolonged effect on the postsynaptic neuron, which would make it incapable of responding to new stimuli. The effect on the postsynaptic cell depends on the type and amount of neurotransmitter, the nature and number of receptors, the amount of deactivating enzyme present at the synapse, the rate of reuptake, and probably other factors. A number of peptide neurotransmitters are referred to as neuromodulators. They act at metabotropic receptors and modulate the effects of other neurotransmitters, sometimes without direct effects of their own. Hormones are different from neurotransmitters in that they are released from various organs into the blood, which carries them throughout the body. However, some hormones act like metabotropic neurotransmitters, binding to receptors on the cell membrane and activating an enzyme. Each neuron is thought to release the same neurotransmitter or combination of neurotransmitters at all of its terminals. Although each particular synapse is always excitatory or always inhibitory, each neuron receives many synapses, some of which are excitatory and some of which are inhibitory. Some synaptic mechanisms involve a brief flow of ions; others affect metabolic processes and are of slower onset and longer duration. However, all neurotransmitters must be inactivated, either by reuptake into presynaptic terminals or by enzymes. The most widely studied neurotransmitter systems are those of acetylcholine, dopamine, norepinephrine, epinephrine, serotonin, glutamate, glycine, gamma-aminobutyric acid (GABA), beta-endorphin, the enkephalins, purines (especially adenosine), and nitric oxide. Levels of some neurotransmitters can be affected by diet.

Drugs typically either impede or facilitate chemical transmission at a given type of synapse. It may seem surprising that many drugs are derived from plants. Plants may use these chemicals to communicate from one part of the plant to another, or they may have evolved them to entice or repel insects or other animals. Indeed, many of the same chemicals are used for communication throughout both the plant and animal kingdoms. Drugs may either block or activate a certain type of receptor, or they may affect release, reuptake, or enzyme inactivation of the neurotransmitter. Since different neurotransmitters have different behavioral and physiological effects, we can frequently predict the effect of a drug on behavior or physiology if we know its synaptic effect. However, there are individual differences in the effectiveness and side effects of drugs, due in part to differences in the numbers and distributions of the subtypes of receptors affected by the drug. Genetic differences in the forms of receptor subtypes may contribute to certain personality characteristics, such as a tendency toward risky behaviors, novelty seeking, and even schizophrenia. However, the statistical associations between the alternative receptors and the behavioral tendencies are weak.

## LEARNING OBJECTIVES

### Module 3.1  The Concept of the Synapse
1. Be able to describe Sherrington's inferences concerning the speed of a reflex and temporal and spatial summation.
2. Understand the mechanisms underlying the excitatory and inhibitory postsynaptic potentials.
3. Understand how synaptic potentials contribute to the firing rates of neurons and the integration of information.

### Module 3.2  Chemical Events at the Synapse
1. Be able to describe the contributions of T.R. Elliott and O. Loewi to the question of whether most synaptic transmission is electrically or chemically mediated.
2. Be able to list the six major types of neurotransmitters.
3. Understand the role of diet in the synthesis of neurotransmitters.
4. Understand the processes of transport, release, and diffusion of neurotransmitters.
5. Understand the differences between ionotropic and metabotropic effects on neurotransmitters.
6. Understand why inactivation of neurotransmitters is important and the two major ways in which this is achieved.
7. Understand how drugs affect synaptic activity and behavior.

## KEY TERMS AND CONCEPTS

### Module 3.1  The Concept of the Synapse
1. The properties of synapses
   Charles Sherrington's inferences
        Reflex arc
        Coordinated flexing and extending
   Speed of a reflex and delayed transmission at the synapse
   Temporal summation
        John Eccles
        Microelectrode
        Excitatory postsynaptic potential (EPSP)
   Spatial summation
   Inhibitory synapses
        Inhibitory postsynaptic potential (IPSP)

2. Relationship among EPSP, IPSP, and action potential
   Combination of temporal and spatial summation
   Spontaneous firing rate

3. In closing: The neuron as decision maker
   Integration of information
   Disinhibition

# Module 3.2  Chemical Events at the Synapse

1. The discovery that most synaptic transmission is chemical
    T. R. Elliott
        Adrenalin
        Sympathetic nervous system
    O. Loewi
        Vagus nerve
        Accelerator nerve

2. The sequence of chemical events at a synapse
    Types of neurotransmitters
        Amino acids
            Glutamate, GABA, glycine, aspartate, maybe others
        Peptides
            Endorphins, substance P, neuropeptide Y, many others
        Acetylcholine
            A modified amino acid
        Monoamines
            Indoleamine: serotonin
            Catecholamines: dopamine, norepinephrine, epinephrine
        Purines
            Adenosine, ATP, maybe others
        Gases
            Nitric oxide, maybe others
    Synthesis of transmitters
        Role of diet
            Acetylcholine
                Choline
                Lecithin
            Catecholamines
                Dopamine, norepinephrine, epinephrine
                Precursors: phenylalanine, tyrosine
            Serotonin
                Tryptophan
                Role of insulin
    Transport of transmitters
        Peptides
            Times of hours or days to transport to axon terminal
        Small neurotransmitters
            Synthesized in terminals, no problem with transport
    Release and diffusion of transmitters
        Vesicles
        Voltage-dependent calcium gates
        Exocytosis
            Combination of transmitters
        Ability to respond to numerous neurotransmitters, though it releases only a few
    Activation of receptors of the postsynaptic cell
        Multiple receptor subtypes
        Ionotropic effects (rapid, short-lived)
            Acetylcholine (nicotinic)

47

Glutamate

GABA

Glycine

Metabotropic effects and second messenger systems (slow, long-lasting)

G-protein (coupled to guanosine triphosphate, GTP)

Second messenger

Cyclic AMP

Neuromodulators, mainly peptides

Hormones

Released in larger quantities than transmitters, travel via blood

Inactivation and reuptake of neurotransmitters

Acetylcholinesterase

Reuptake

Transporters

Conversion to inactive chemicals

COMT (catechol-o-methyltransferase)

MAO (monoamine oxidase)

3. Synapses and drug effects

Why are our brains sensitive to plant chemicals?

Plants evolved chemicals to affect animals' receptors

Plants use the same "neurotransmitters"

How drugs affect synapses

Antagonist

Agonist

Mixed agonist-antagonist

Ways to influence synaptic activity

Increase or decrease synthesis of neurotransmitter

Cause neurotransmitter to leak from vesicles

Increase neurotransmitter release

Decrease neurotransmitter reuptake

Block neurotransmitter breakdown

Directly stimulate or block receptors

Affinity: ability to bind to a receptor

Efficacy: tendency to activate a receptor

Ratio of different kinds of receptors activated by a drug

Synapses and personality

Alternative form of dopamine $D_2$ receptor: alcoholism and reward deficiency

Alternative form of dopamine $D_4$ receptor: "novelty seeking" or schizophrenia

4. In closing: Neurotransmitters and behavior

Multiple receptor subtypes

# SHORT-ANSWER QUESTIONS

## Module 3.1  The Concept of the Synapse

1. *The properties of synapses*
    a.  What is a reflex?



    b.  What experimental evidence did Sherrington have for synaptic delay?  For temporal summation?



    c.  What evidence did he have for spatial summation?  For coordinated excitation and inhibition?



    d.  Describe John Eccles's experimental support for Sherrington's inferences.



    e.  What is an EPSP, and what ionic flow is largely responsible for it?

f.   What is an IPSP, and what ionic flows can produce it?

2.   *The relationship among EPSP, IPSP, and action potential*
    a.   What influence do EPSPs and IPSPs have on neurons with a spontaneous rate of firing?

3.   *In closing: The neuron as decision maker*
    a.   What factors influence a cell's "decision" whether or not to produce an action potential?

    b.   Describe a way in which inhibitory effects on neurons could result in excitation of a behavior.

**Module 3.2  Chemical Events at the Synapse**
1.   *The discovery that most synaptic transmission is chemical*
    a.   What did T. R. Elliott propose?

b. Describe Loewi's experiment with the two frogs' hearts.

2. *The sequence of chemical events at a synapse*
   a. What are the major events, in sequence, at a synapse?

   b. List the major neurotransmitters.

   c. How is nitric oxide unlike most other neurotransmitters?

   d. How is the synthesis of peptide neurotransmitters different from that of most other neurotransmitters?

   e. List the three catecholamines in the order of their synthesis. What is their amino acid precursor?

f. How might one increase the amount of acetylcholine in the brain? Serotonin?

g. How quickly can peptide neurotransmitters be transported to the terminal? Why is this not a problem for smaller neurotransmitters?

h. Describe the process of exocytosis.

i. What generalization can be drawn regarding the release of neurotransmitter(s) at the terminals of a given neuron?

j. Contrast ionotropic and metabotropic synaptic mechanisms. List three ionotropic neurotransmitter receptors.

k. Discuss the role of second messengers in producing the metabotropic effects of neurotransmitters. What kinds of changes can they exert?

l.     What is a G-protein?  What is the "first messenger"?  What is one common second messenger?

m.     What is a neuromodulator?  How may some neuromodulators differ from most neurotransmitters? Through what type of receptor (ionotropic or metabotropic) are neuromodulator's effects produced?

n.     What is a major difference between the function of neurotransmitters and hormones? Through what kind of receptor (ionotropic or metabotropic) do many hormones act?

o.     How are ACh, 5-HT, and the catecholamines inactivated?  Why is inactivation important?

p.     Why should there be multiple receptor types for each neurotransmitter?

3. *Synapses and drug effects*
   a. What are two possible explanations for why our brains are sensitive to plant chemicals? How common are neurotransmitter molecules throughout the animal kingdom?

   b. List six ways in which drugs may affect synaptic function.

   c. What is an agonist? An antagonist?

   d. How can one drug be an agonist at a given receptor, while another drug, with similar affinity for that receptor, is an antagonist?

   e. What sorts of behaviors have been linked with alternative forms of genes for the $D_2$ and $D_4$ dopamine receptors? How strong is the association?

## TRUE/FALSE QUESTIONS

F 1. Reflex arcs always consist of activation of motor neurons by sensory neurons within a single segment of the spinal cord.

_T_ 2. C. S. Sherrington discovered the concepts of spatial and temporal summation in simple experiments involving pinching a dog's foot.

_T F_ 3. EPSPs and action potentials are similar in that both result from the influx of sodium ions.

_F_ 4. IPSPs and EPSPs are also similar in that both result from the influx of sodium ions.

_T_ 5. The process of disinhibition can explain how an inhibitory synapse can result in activation of another neuron.

_F_ 6. Otto Loewi discovered that synaptic conduction is almost always electrical in nature.

_F_ 7. The three catecholamine neurotransmitters are dopamine, epinephrine, and serotonin.

_T_ 8. Brain levels of acetylcholine may be increased by eating a lot of milk, cauliflower, egg yolks, peanuts, and several other foods.

_T_ 9. Nitric oxide is a gaseous transmitter that is synthesized at the time it is needed, rather than being stored in vesicles; it is different from "laughing gas."

_F_ 10. Potassium, flowing in through voltage-dependent potassium channels in axon terminals, directly stimulates the release of vesicles containing neurotransmitter.

_T_ 11. Each neuron is responsive to many neurotransmitters, although it releases only one or a few neurotransmitters.

_T_ 12. Ionotropic effects result from ions crossing the membrane through cylindrical channels; these effects are faster, but more short-lived than metabotropic effects.

_F_ 13. Inactivation of neurotransmitters is accomplished almost exclusively by enzymes that convert them into inactive chemicals.

_F_ 14. Affinity and efficacy are really just two different words for the same factor—the ability of a drug to bind to a receptor.

## FILL IN THE BLANKS

1. Ramon y Cajal, in the late 1800s, showed that neurons do not physically merge with one another.

2. Charles Sherrington discovered the properties of spatial and temporal summation using behavioral experiments on dogs' reflexes.

3. Temporal summation in single cells was demonstrated by John Eccles, using microelectrodes inserted into neurons.

4. EPSPs and action potentials are similar in that they both result from an inflow of __Na+__ ions.

5. EPSPs and IPSPs are similar in that they are both __grade__ __potentials__.

6. IPSPs result from the outflow of __K+__ ions and/or the inflow of __Cl Chloride__ ions.

7. The periodic production of action potentials without synaptic input is referred to as a __Spontaneous__ __fire__ __Rating__.

8. Otto Loewi found that when he stimulated the vagus nerve of one frog and then placed fluid collected from around that heart onto a second frog's heart, the second heart __slowed__.

9. Amino acid neurotransmitters include __glutamate__, __GABA__, __glycine__, and __asparate__.

10. Monoamine neurotransmitters include __dopamine__, __norepinephrine__, __epinephrine__, and __Serotonin__.

11. Some peptide neurotransmitters are __endorphines__, __substance P__, and __nueopeptide Y__.

12. Insulin release, as a result of eating carbohydrates, can increase the production of __Serotonin__ in the brain.

13. Enzyme-mediated effects that emerge about 30 ms or more after the release of a neurotransmitter are referred to as __metabotropic__ effects.

14. The enzyme that inactivates acetylcholine is __acetylcholinerase__.

15. Symptoms of __acetylcholine erase__ can be alleviated by drugs that block acetylcholinesterase.

16. Serotonin and the catecholamines are inactivated primarily by __reuptake__, which occurs through membrane proteins called __transporters__.

17. The degree to which a drug binds to a receptor is called its __Affinity__; the degree to which the drug is able to activate the receptor is called its __efficacy__.

18. Alternative forms of the __D2__ receptor may be associated with alcoholism and other risky behaviors; alternative forms of the __D4__ receptor may be associated with a novelty-seeking tendency or schizophrenia. However, the statistical correlations for both associations are weak.

## MATCHING ITEMS

_h_ 1. Sherrington

_j_ 2. Eccles

_q_ 3. Loewi

_o_ 4. EPSP

_k_ 5. IPSP

_n_ 6. amino acid

_i_ 7. indoleamine

_d_ 8. catecholamine

_m_ 9. peptide

_A_ 10. gaseous transmitter

_R_ 11. modified amino acid

_P_ 12. ionotropic effect

_f_ 13. metabotropic effect

_b_ 14. treatment for myasthenia gravis

_e_ 15. affinity

_g_ 16. efficacy

_C_ 17. agonist

_g_ 18. antagonist

a. nitric oxide

b. acetylcholinesterase inhibitor

c. mimics or increases effects of transmitter

d. dopamine

e. ability to bind to a receptor

f. transmitter activation of G protein, enzyme

g. blocks effects of transmitter

h. inferred major properties of synapses

i. serotonin

j. showed temporal summation in single neurons

k. graded potential due to potassium out or chloride in

l. ability to activate a receptor

m. endorphin

n. glutamate

o. graded potential due to sodium influx

p. opening of ion channel by transmitter

q. showed synaptic conduction is chemical

r. acetylcholine

# MULTIPLE-CHOICE QUESTIONS

1. C. S. Sherrington
   a. did extensive electrophysiological recording of synaptic events.
   b. inferred the existence and properties of synapses from behavioral experiments on reflexes in dogs.
   c. was a student of John Eccles.
   d. found that conduction along a single axon is slower than through a reflex arc.

2. Which of the following was **not** one of Sherrington's findings?
   a. The speed of conduction through a reflex arc was significantly slower than the known speed of conduction along an axon.
   b. Repeating a subthreshold pinch several times in rapid succession elicited leg flexion.
   c. Simultaneous subthreshold pinches in different parts of the foot elicited flexion.
   d. Reflex arcs are limited to one limb and are always excitatory.

3. Electrophysiological recording from a single neuron
   a. utilizes a microelectrode inserted into the neuron.
   b. supported Sherrington's inferences.
   c. is a field pioneered by John Eccles.
   d. all of the above.

4. IPSPs
   a. may summate to generate an action potential.
   b. are always hyperpolarizing under natural conditions.
   c. are characterized mainly by a large influx of potassium ions.
   d. are characterized mainly by a large influx of sodium ions.

5. Which of the following is true?
   a. The size of EPSPs is the same at all excitatory synapses.
   b. The primary means of inactivation for all neurotransmitters is degradation by an enzyme.
   c. The size, duration, and direction (hyperpolarizing or depolarizing) of a postsynaptic potential are functions of the type and amount of transmitter released, the type and number of receptor sites present, and perhaps other factors.
   d. A given neuron may release either an excitatory or an inhibitory transmitter (at different times), depending on whether it was excited or inhibited by a previous neuron.

6. EPSPs and action potentials are similar in that
   a. sodium is the major ion producing a depolarization in both.
   b. sodium is the major ion producing a hyperpolarization in both.
   c. potassium is the major ion producing a depolarization in both.
   d. both decay as a function of time and space, decreasing in magnitude as they travel along the membrane.

7. EPSPs
   a. result from a flow of potassium ($K^+$) and chloride ($Cl^-$) ions.
   b. are always depolarizing in natural conditions.
   c. are always large enough to cause the postsynaptic cell to reach triggering threshold for an action potential; otherwise there would be too much uncertainty in the nervous system.
   d. are the same as action potentials.

8. EPSPs and IPSPs
   a. may alter a neuron's spontaneous firing rate.
   b. are always the same size.
   c. usually occur one at a time, so that the neuron does not get confused.
   d. all of the above.

9. T. R. Elliott discovered that
   a. adrenalin slowed a frog's heart.
   b. synaptic transmission is electrical rather than chemical.
   c. adrenalin could mimic the effects of the sympathetic nervous system.
   d. all of the above.

10. Otto Loewi discovered that a substance collected from the vagus nerve innervating one frog's heart and transferred to a second frog's heart
   a. slowed the second frog's heart.
   b. speeded the second frog's heart.
   c. either speeded or slowed the second frog's heart, depending on the quantity applied.
   d. had no effect, thereby showing that synaptic transmission is not chemically mediated.

11. The level of acetylcholine in the brain can be increased by increasing dietary intake of
   a. acetylcholine.
   b. tyrosine.
   c. choline.
   d. tryptophan.

12. Serotonin levels in the brain can be increased by eating a meal that has protein and is high in
   a. choline.
   b. tyrosine.
   c. fat.
   d. carbohydrates.

13. The speed of transport of substances down an axon
   a. is fast enough that even the longest axons require only a few minutes for substances synthesized in the nucleus to reach the terminal.
   b. limits the availability of small neurotransmitters more than that of peptides.
   c. limits the availability of peptides more than that of small neurotransmitters.
   d. is a severe limitation on the availability of all neurotransmitters.

14. Calcium
   a. is kept outside the neuron by voltage-dependent calcium gates during the resting state.
   b. enters the terminal when an action potential opens voltage-dependent calcium gates.
   c. causes the release of neurotransmitter.
   d. all of the above.

15. Vesicles
   a. are tiny nearly-spherical packets filled with neurotransmitter.
   b. are especially important for storing nitric oxide.
   c. are the only places where transmitter is found in axon terminals.
   d. store only excitatory neurotransmitters; inhibitory neurotransmitters are never stored in vesicles.

Each terminal of a given axon
- a. releases a different neurotransmitter, thus providing a rich repertoire of effects.
- b. releases the same neurotransmitter or combination of neurotransmitters at every terminal of that axon.
- c. releases only one neurotransmitter, so as not to "confuse" the postsynaptic cell.
- d. releases all of the neurotransmitters known to exist in the brain.

17. Ionotropic synaptic mechanisms
- a. have slow-onset, long-lasting effects.
- b. use a cyclic AMP second messenger response.
- c. are exemplified by glutamate, GABA, and nicotinic acetylcholine receptors.
- d. frequently use hormones as transmitters.

18. Metabotropic synapses
- a. may have effects that significantly outlast the release of the transmitter.
- b. are activated when a neurotransmitter binds to its receptor site and thereby induces a change in an intracellular part of the receptor that is coupled to a G-protein.
- c. are characterized by initiation of changes in proteins by cyclic AMP, which in turn open or close ion gates or alter the structure or metabolism of the cell.
- d. all of the above.

19. Neuromodulators
- a. are usually peptides that diffuse widely enough to affect several cells.
- b. are carried in the blood throughout the entire body.
- c. are usually monoamine neurotransmitters.
- d. usually have ionotropic effects.

20. Hormones
- a. are released in small quantities close to the target cells.
- b. may exert their effects through metabotropic receptors on the surface of cells.
- c. usually exert their effects through ionotropic receptors on the surface of cells.
- d. none of the above.

21. Acetylcholinesterase
- a. promotes reuptake of ACh into cholinergic terminals, thereby inactivating it.
- b. is the enzyme that produces ACh.
- c. is the enzyme that cleaves ACh into two inactive parts.
- d. blocks reuptake of choline into cholinergic terminals.

22. Reuptake of neurotransmitters
- a. is the major method of inactivation of ACh.
- b. is the major method of inactivation of serotonin and the catecholamines.
- c. is speeded up by COMT.
- d. is completely blocked by MAO.

23. An antagonist is a drug that
- a. has no affinity for a receptor.
- b. changes EPSPs into IPSPs.
- c. mimics or strengthens the effects of a neurotransmitter.
- d. blocks the effects of a neurotransmitter.

24. Which of the following is true?
    a.   Some plant-derived drugs are chemicals that are used by the plants to communicate from one part of the plant to another.
    b.   There is a great deal of specificity in neurotransmitters across species; most transmitters used in humans have no counterpart in other species.
    c.   A drug with high affinity for a given receptor will always elicit a response from that receptor.
    d.   The presence of alternative forms of certain dopamine receptors can explain most cases of alcoholism, novelty-seeking, and schizophrenia.

## Answers to True/False Questions

| | | | |
|---|---|---|---|
| 1.  F | 5.  T | 9.  T | 13. F |
| 2.  T | 6.  F | 10. F | 14. F |
| 3.  T | 7.  F | 11. T | |
| 4.  F | 8.  T | 12. T | |

## Answers to Fill-in-the-Blank Questions

1.   Ramon y Cajal
2.   Charles Sherrington
3.   John Eccles
4.   $Na^+$ (sodium)
5.   graded potentials
6.   $K^+$ (potassium), $Cl^-$ (chloride)
7.   spontaneous firing rate
8.   slowed
9.   glutamate, GABA, glycine, aspartate
10.  dopamine, norepinephrine, epinephrine, serotonin
11.  endorphins, substance P, and neuropeptide Y
12.  serotonin
13.  metabotropic
14.  acetylcholinesterase
15.  acetylcholinesterase
16.  reuptake, transporters
17.  affinity, efficacy
18.  $D_2$, $D_4$

## Answers to Matching Questions

| | | | |
|---|---|---|---|
| 1.  h | 6.  n | 11. r | 16. l |
| 2.  j | 7.  i | 12. p | 17. c |
| 3.  q | 8.  d | 13. f | 18. g |
| 4.  o | 9.  m | 14. b | |
| 5.  k | 10. a | 15. e | |

## Answers to Multiple-Choice Questions

| | | | |
|---|---|---|---|
| 1.  b | 4.  b | 7.  b | 10. a |
| 2.  d | 5.  c | 8.  a | 11. c |
| 3.  d | 6.  a | 9.  c | 12. d |

# Diagrams

1. Label the electrical potentials shown in the graph below.

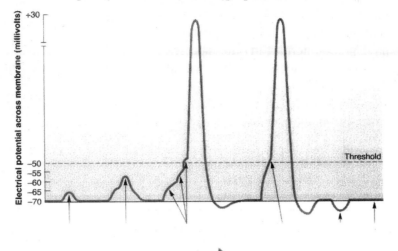

1._____    4._____

2._____    5._____

3._____    6._____

2. In the diagram below list the major events in neurotransmission.

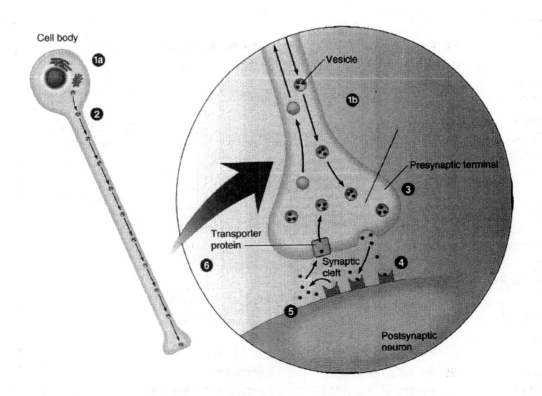

# Synaptic Symphony

10 Temporary depolarization (abbr.)

11 Negative ion that enters through GABA receptors

12 Monoamine transmitter made from tryptophan

13 He used microelectrodes to study neural electrical potentials

14 Type of summation in which inputs from separate locations exert a cumulative effect

18 Space between axon terminal and dendrite

20 Type of summation in which rapidly repeated stimuli have a cumulative effect

21 Cyclic _____, a common second messenger

24 Precursor of acetylcholine

26 Ability to bind to a receptor

27 Drug that increases activity at a given type of synapse

## ACROSS

3 Positive ion that produces EPSP

6 Kind of animal whose reflexes were studied by Sherrington

7 A peptide transmitter

9 Storage packet for neurotransmitters

15 Temporary hyperpolarization (abbr.)

16 Major means of inactivating released transmitters

17 Tendency to activate a receptor

19 Excitatory amino acid transmitter

22 Type of acid used as transmitter or as building blocks of peptides and proteins

23 A protein that synthesizes or metabolizes transmitters (and other chemicals)

25 Inhibitory amino acid transmitter (abbr.)

28 A type of receptor that opens ion channels

29 An automatic muscular response to a stimulus

30 Receptor activated by acetylcholine

## DOWN

1 Enzyme that metabolizes monoamines (abbr.)

2 He stimulated a frog's vagus nerve, showed synaptic transmission is chemical

4 Nitric _____, a gaseous transmitter

5 A chain of amino acids

8 Monoamine transmitter important for reward or activation

# 4

# ANATOMY OF THE NERVOUS SYSTEM

## INTRODUCTION

Describing the structure of the brain can be tedious, but understanding the functions of the various structures is daunting. Light and electron microscopes provide descriptions of cellular structures, and images of the whole brain can be obtained by computerized axial tomography (CAT or CT scans). The functions of brain areas can be inferred from accidental (in humans) or deliberate (in animals) damage or temporary inactivation. Such inferences can be compared with those from electrical or magnetic stimulation of those areas in an intact brain. In addition brain activity can be recorded during a task, using electrodes or positron emission tomography (PET), which detects radioactivity from labeled chemicals taken up by the most active brain areas. A variant of PET is the regional cerebral blood flow (rCBF) method, which measures the amount of radioactivity from a chemical carried to the areas of greatest activity. A less expensive and less dangerous method is functional magnetic resonance imaging (fMRI), which detects changes in hemoglobin molecules as they release oxygen to the most active brain areas. One problem with inferences about the function of a brain area from correlations between its size or activity and behavior is that correlation does not imply causation. Also, previous experience with a task may alter the brain's activity during a task.

The vertebrate nervous system consists of two major divisions, the central (CNS) and the peripheral (PNS) nervous systems. The CNS is composed of the brain and the spinal cord. The PNS is divided into the somatic and the autonomic nervous systems. The somatic system consists of sensory nerves that convey information from sense organs to the spinal cord, and motor nerves carrying messages from the spinal cord to muscles and glands. A pair of sensory nerves enters (one from each side) and a pair of motor nerves exits from the spinal cord through each pair of openings in the vertebral canal. The sensory nerves enter the spinal cord from the dorsal direction, and the motor axons leave from the ventral aspect. Cell bodies of sensory neurons lie in the dorsal root ganglia; those of the motor neurons are in the spinal cord. The autonomic nervous system also sends neurons through the vertebral openings; they synapse in ganglia outside the spinal cord. Ganglia of the sympathetic division of the autonomic nervous system are arranged in an interconnected chain along the thoracic and lumbar sections of the spinal cord. Ganglia of the parasympathetic division of the autonomic nervous system receive input from the cranial nerves and the sacral section of the cord and are located near the organs they innervate. The interconnections of the sympathetic system promote unified action by the body in a fight-or-flight situation, whereas the relative independence of the parasympathetic innervations allows for more discrete energy-saving responses. Most of the final synapses of the sympathetic nervous system use the neurotransmitter norepinephrine, while the final parasympathetic synapses use acetylcholine.

The brain is divided into the hindbrain, the midbrain, and the forebrain. The hindbrain is composed of the medulla, the pons, and the cerebellum. The medulla contains numerous nuclei that control life-preserving reflexes. The pons has many fibers that cross from right to left (and vice versa), going to the cerebellum, which is directly behind the pons. The cerebellum helps control movement and may be important for shifting attention and for timing. The reticular formation and the raphe system, which increase and decrease, respectively, the brain's readiness to respond to stimuli, have diffusely branching neurons throughout the medulla, pons, and midbrain and send diffusely branching axons throughout the brain. The midbrain is composed of the tectum (or roof), on which are the two superior colliculi and the two inferior colliculi, involved in sensory processing; and the tegmentum, containing extensions of neural systems of the hindbrain and also the substantia nigra, degeneration of which causes Parkinson's disease. The forebrain includes the limbic system, a number of interlinked structures important for motivational and emotional behaviors; the thalamus, which is the main source of sensory input to the cerebral cortex; the hypothalamus, important for motivational and hormonal regulation; the pituitary or "master gland"; the basal ganglia, which influence motor movements, emotional expression, memory, and reasoning; the hippocampus, important in memory functions; and the cerebral cortex, which surrounds the rest of the brain and is responsible for complex sensory analysis and integration, language processing, motor control, and social awareness. The ventricles are fluid-filled cavities within the brain.

The cerebral cortex consists of up to six laminae, or layers, of cell bodies parallel to the surface of the brain. The cells are organized into columns, perpendicular to the laminae; each column contains cells with similar response properties. The occipital lobe of the cerebral cortex is the site of primary visual processing. The parietal lobe processes somatosensory information and contributes to our sense of location relative to visual or auditory stimuli. The temporal lobe processes auditory information and is important for perception of complex visual patterns and comprehension of language. The frontal lobe contains the motor cortex, which controls fine movements, and prefrontal cortex, which contributes to social awareness, the expression of emotion, memory for recent details (working memory), and calculation of actions and their outcomes.

Each part of the brain accomplishes a set of more or less specific functions; yet, a sense of unified experience emerges from these separate operations. The question of how the brain integrates various kinds of sensory information into the perception of a unified object is known as the binding problem. How are the various aspects bound together? One possibility is that binding depends on precisely simultaneous activity (gamma waves) in the different brain areas. The inferior temporal cortex may coordinate this activity. However, we still do not understand how synchronized gamma waves bind the different aspects into a unified perception.

## LEARNING OBJECTIVES

**Module 4.1  Research Methods**
1. Understand the uses of and principles underlying the techniques of computerized axial tomography (CAT), positron emission tomography (PET), regional cerebral blood flow (rCBF), and functional magnetic resonance imaging (fMRI).
2. Be able to identify the major ways of inactivating parts of the brain, temporarily or permanently, and of stimulating parts of the brain.
3. Understand the problems of interpretation of the effects of lesions.

**Module 4.2  Structure of the Vertebrate Nervous System**
1. Be able to identify the directional terms for anatomical structures.
2. Be able to describe the structure of the spinal cord and the locations of its sensory inputs and motor outputs.
3. Know the functions, locations, and organization of the two main branches of the autonomic nervous system.
4. Know the three main divisions of the hindbrain and both their unique and their shared functions.
5. Know the two divisions of the midbrain and the major structures in each.
6. Be able to identify the main structures and functions of the diencephalons, the limbic system, the basal ganglia, and the basal forebrain.

**Module 4.3  The Cerebral Cortex**
1. Know the locations and functions of the four lobes of the cerebral cortex.
2. Understand the "binding problem" and a possible means of coordinating neural activity throughout a large portion of the brain to form a unified perception.

# KEY TERMS AND CONCEPTS

## Module 4.1  Research Methods
1.  Observation of brain structure
    Light and electron microscopes
        Chemicals stain certain cells or parts of cells
    Computerized axial tomography (CAT or CT scan)
        Pass x-rays through the head

2.  Effects of brain damage
    Paul Broca
        Part of left frontal lobe: Broca's area: ability to speak
    Disruption of local activity by intense, prolonged magnetic field
    Chemical inactivation or electrode-induced lesion in animals
    Gene knockout approach: directed mutation of a gene
    Difficulty of determining exact function

3.  Effects of brain stimulation
    Electrical stimulation: Rare in humans
    Brief, moderate intensity magnetic fields
    Injection of chemical that stimulates one kind of receptor

4.  Recording brain activity
    Positron emission tomography (PET)
        Radioactive chemical absorbed by most active neurons
        Regional cerebral blood flow (rCBF)
        Dangerous because of radioactivity
    Functional magnetic resonance imaging (fMRI)
        Changes in hemoglobin molecules as they release oxygen in active areas
        Less dangerous and less expensive that PET
        Problem with interpretation of results
            What is comparison task?
            Experience alters results

5.  Correlating brain activity with behavior
    Phrenology
    Experience-induced increase in brain area devoted to a process
    Problems
        Correlation doesn't indicate causation
        Small sample size

6.  In closing:  Methods and their limits

## Module 4.2  Structure of the Vertebrate Nervous System
1.  Nervous system terminology
    Central nervous system (CNS):  Brain and spinal cord
    Peripheral nervous system (PNS): Somatic and autonomic nervous systems
    Dorsal (toward the back)
    Ventral (toward the stomach)
    Dorsal-ventral axis of human brain at right angles to dorsal-ventral axis of spinal cord

2.  The spinal cord
    Sensory nerves: Enter dorsally
    Motor nerves: Exit ventrally
    Bell-Magendie Law
    Dorsal root ganglia: Clusters of cell bodies of sensory neurons
    Gray matter: Cell bodies and dendrites
    White matter: Myelinated axons

3.  The autonomic nervous system
    Sympathetic nervous system ("fight or flight")
        Sympathetic chains of ganglia
        Thoracic and lumbar regions
        Norepinephrine
    Parasympathetic nervous system (energy conserving)
        Cranial and sacral regions (craniosacral system)
        Ganglia near organs
        Acetylcholine

4.  The hindbrain (rhombencephalon): Medulla, pons, cerebellum
    Brain stem (medulla, pons, midbrain, some forebrain structures)
    Medulla
        Vital reflexes
        Cranial nerves
        Reticular formation
        Raphe system
    Pons ("bridge")
        Fibers crossing
        Cranial nerves
        Reticular formation
        Raphe system
    Cerebellum
        Control of movement
            Balance and coordination
        Shifting attention
        Timing

5.  The midbrain (mesencephalon)
    Tectum
        Superior and inferior colliculi
    Tegmentum
        Cranial nerves
        Reticular formation
        Substantia nigra

6.  The forebrain (prosencephalon)
    Limbic system: Border around brain stem
        Olfactory bulb
        Hypothalamus
        Hippocampus

Amygdala
Cingulate gyrus of cerebral cortex
Thalamus (part of diencephalon)
Transmit sensory information (except olfaction) to cortex
Hypothalamus (part of diencephalon, ventral to thalamus)
Motivated behaviors
Control of pituitary gland
Pituitary gland
Controls other glands
Basal ganglia
Caudate nucleus
Putamen
Globus pallidus
Connections with frontal cortex
Control of movement
Aspects of memory and emotional expression
Parkinson's disease
Huntington's disease
Basal forebrain
Nucleus basalis: acetylcholine to cortex
Arousal, wakefulness, attention
Parkinson's disease
Alzheimer's disease
Hippocampus
Storing new memories
Fornix: hippocampus to hypothalamus

7.  The ventricles
Central canal
Cerebrospinal fluid (CSF)
Cushion, buoyancy, reservoir of hormones and nutrition
Choroid plexus: Forms CSF
Meninges
Subarachnoid space: Reabsorption of CSF into blood vessels
Hydrocephalus

8.  In closing: Learning neuroanatomy

## Module 4.3  The Cerebral Cortex
1.  Hemispheric interconnections
Corpus callosum
Anterior commissure

2.  Organization of the cerebral cortex
Laminae and columns

3.  The occipital lobe (posterior, or caudal, end of cortex)
Primary visual cortex
Striate cortex
Cortical blindness

4. The parietal lobe (between occipital lobe and central sulcus)
   Central sulcus
   Postcentral gyrus
   Primary somatosensory cortex: four bands parallel to central sulcus
       Two light-touch bands
       One deep-pressure band
       One light-touch and deep-pressure band
   Interpretation of visual and auditory input

5. The temporal lobe (lateral, near temples)
   Primary auditory cortex
   Language comprehension
   Complex visual patterns
   Kluver-Bucy syndrome

6. The frontal lobe (from central sulcus to anterior end of brain)
   Precentral gyrus
       Primary motor cortex
   Prefrontal cortex
       Prefrontal lobotomies
           Lack of initiative
           Failure to inhibit unacceptable impulses
       Modern view of functions of the prefrontal cortex
           Working memory: Memory for recent events
               Delayed-response task
           Modify behavior according to context

7. How do the parts work together?
   Operation as a whole vs. collection of parts
       Role of central amygdala in feeling and recognizing fear
   The binding problem
       How brain areas influence one another to produce perception of single object
       "Association area"
           Advanced processing on a particular sensory system, not combining 2 systems
       Synchronized gamma waves (30-80 action potentials/second)
       Inferior parietal cortex and pulvinar nucleus
           Facilitate ability of cortex to maintain synchrony

8. In closing: Functions of the cerebral cortex
   Elaborating sensory material

# SHORT-ANSWER QUESTIONS

**Module 4.1  Research Methods**

1. *Observation of brain structure*
    a. Describe two methods of observing the structure of the brain.

2. *Effects of brain damage*
    a. What did Paul Broca discover?

    b. What are four methods of deliberately inactivating brain activity?

    c. What is the main problem with inferences about function based on these approaches?

3. *Effects of brain stimulation*
    a. Compare the magnetic stimulation used to stimulate certain brain areas with that used to inactivate brain areas.

b. What is a problem with inferences about the functions of brain areas based on localized stimulation?

4. *Recording brain activity*
   a. What is the principle on which positron emission tomography (PET) is based? How is this adapted for studying regional cerebral blood flow (rCBF)?

   b. What are two advantages of functional magnetic resonance imaging (fMRI) over PET and rCBF? What is the physical basis for fMRI?

   c. What are two problems with inferring function from records of brain activity?

5. *Correlating brain activity with behavior*
   a. What are two limitations of inferences of function from correlations with measurable features of the brain?

**Module 4.2  Structure of the Vertebrate Nervous System**
1.  *The spinal cord*
    a.  Draw a cross section of the spinal cord, including sensory and motor nerves, dorsal root ganglia, and dorsal and ventral directions.

    b.  What is the Bell-Magendie Law?

    c.  What makes up gray matter?  White matter?

2.  *The autonomic nervous system*
    a.  Of what two parts does the autonomic nervous system consist?  Give the location and basic function of each.

    b.  Which transmitter is used by the postganglionic parasympathetic nerves?  Which is used by most sympathetic postganglionic nerves?

3. *The hindbrain*
   a. What are the three components of the hindbrain? Give one "specialty" of each.

   b. What are cranial nerves? Where are their nuclei?

   c. What are the anatomical locations and functions of the reticular formation and the raphe system?

4. *The midbrain*
   a. What are the two major divisions of the midbrain? Name two structures in each division.

5. *The forebrain*
   a. What are the major structures comprising the limbic system? What are the general functions of this interconnected system?

   b. Describe the relationship of the thalamus to the cerebral cortex.

c. Where is the hypothalamus, and what kinds of behavior does it help regulate?

d. Where is the pituitary?  What is its function?  What structure largely controls it?

e. Where are the basal ganglia?  Which structures make up the basal ganglia?  Briefly describe their function.

f. Where is the hippocampus?  To what psychological process has it been linked?

6. *The ventricles*
   a. What are the ventricles?  Where is cerebrospinal fluid (CSF) formed?  In which direction does it flow?  Where is it reabsorbed into blood vessels?

   b. What are the functions of CSF?

# Module 4.3  The Cerebral Cortex

1. *Organization of cerebral cortex*

   a. What is the relationship of gray matter to white in the cortex?  Compare this relationship to that in the spinal cord.

   b. How many layers (laminae) does human neocortex have?  Describe the input to lamina IV and the output from lamina V.

   c. What is the relationship of columns to laminae?  What can be said about all the cells within one column?

2. *The occipital lobe*

   a. What are the location and functions of the occipital lobe?

3. *The parietal lobe*

   a. What are the location and functions of the parietal lobe?

4. *The temporal lobe*
    a. Where is the temporal lobe? What are some temporal lobe functions?

5. *The frontal lobe*
    a. What are the location and functions of the frontal lobe? Distinguish between the precentral gyrus and the prefrontal cortex.

    b. What were the results of prefrontal lobotomies?

    c. What is the difference between working memory and reference memory? Which shows greater impairment after prefrontal lesions?

    d. What is the delayed response task, and how is it affected by prefrontal lesions? Is this primarily a test of working or reference memory?

6. *How do the parts work together?*
   a. How would you answer the question of whether the brain operates as an undifferentiated whole or a collection of independent parts?

   b. What is the binding problem?

   c. What are gamma waves? What may be the role of the inferior temporal cortex in binding the different aspects of sensory objects?

## TRUE/FALSE QUESTIONS

_____ 1. PET scans are safer and less expensive than fMRI scans.

_____ 2. Paul Broca discovered that people who had lost their ability to speak usually had damage to a part of the left frontal lobe.

_____ 3. Sensory nerves enter the spinal cord from the dorsal side, and motor nerves exit from the ventral side.

_____ 4. Ganglia of the sympathetic nervous system lie along the cervical and sacral parts of the spinal cord.

_____ 5. The postganglionic transmitter of the parasympathetic nervous system is norepinephrine.

_____ 6. The reticular formation and raphe system system are found in the pons and medulla; they regulate arousal and the readiness to respond, respectively.

_____ 7. The substantia nigra is found in the tectum of the midbrain and controls vital reflexes.

_____ 8. The limbic system comprises the olfactory bulb, the hypothalamus, the hippocampus, the amygdala, and the cingulate gyrus of the cerebral cortex.

_____9. The main function of the hypothalamus is to transmit information to the cortex.

_____10. The basal ganglia are concerned with the control of movement and also some aspects of memory and emotional expression.

_____11. A major function of the hippocampus is control of the pituitary gland.

_____12. The ventricles contain cerebrospinal fluid (CSF) that is produced by the choroid plexus and provides cushioning and buoyancy to the brain.

_____13. Laminae of the cerebral cortex are the same thing as columns.

_____14. The occipital lobe is the site of primary auditory cortex.

_____15. The temporal lobe is essential for the understanding of spoken language and also contributes to complex visual perceptions.

_____16. The prefrontal cortex is the primary motor cortex.

## FILL IN THE BLANKS

1. Paul Broca discovered that loss of speech was frequently correlated with brain damage in the

   _____  _____  _____.

2. Different intensities and durations of magnetic fields can be used either to

   _____ or to _____ localized brain areas.

3. The method of recording brain activity that measures changes in hemoglobin molecules as they

   release oxygen in active brain areas is _____  _____

   _____  _____  (_____).

4. The Bell-Magendie Law states that sensory neurons enter the spinal cord from the

   _____ direction, and motor neurons exit the spinal cord from the _____

   direction.

5. The autonomic nervous system consists of the _____ nervous

   system, with ganglia located _____, and the

   _____ nervous system, with ganglia located _____

   _____.

78

6. The hind brain consists of the _____, the _____, and the

_____.

7. In addition to containing the reticular formation and the raphe system, the medulla contains

cranial nuclei that control _____ _____.

8. The pons gets its name (Latin for "bridge") from _____

_____.

9. The cerebellum was originally thought to be important only for controlling _____;

however, we now know that it also contributes to _____ and _____

_____.

10. The _____ of the midbrain contains the superior and inferior colliculi;

the _____ of the midbrain contains nuclei of cranial nerves, part of the

reticular formation, and the substantia nigra.

11. The main structures that comprise the limbic system are the _____ _____,

the _____, the _____, the

_____, and the _____ _____ of the cerebral

cortex.

12. The main function of the _____ is to transmit sensory information (except

olfaction) to the cerebral cortex.

13. The hypothalamus sends hypothalamic hormones to the _____ gland, and also

helps to regulate various _____ behaviors.

14. The basal ganglia comprise the _____ _____, the

_____, and the _____ _____.

15. The basal ganglia have important connections with the _____ _____

and are important for the control of _____ and aspects of

_____ and _____ _____.

16. The _____ _____ in the basal forebrain sends acetylcholine to the cortex and promotes arousal, wakefulness, and attention.

17. The main function of the _____ is storing new memories.

18. The _____ _____ forms cerebrospinal fluid.

19. The _____ of the cerebral cortex are layers of cell bodies that lie parallel to the surface of the cortex; the _____ of the cortex are perpendicular to the laminae and contain neurons that have similar properties.

20. Primary visual cortex is located in the _____ lobe.

21. The parietal lobe contains the postcentral gyrus, which is the primary _____ cortex.

22. A tumor in the temporal lobe may give rise to _____ or _____ hallucinations.

23. The main divisions of the frontal lobe are the _____ _____, which serves as the primary motor cortex, and the _____ _____, which contributes to working memory and modifies behavior according to the context.

24. The question of how the various areas of the brain work together to form a unitary perception is known as the _____ _____. This function may be mediated by _____ waves of neural firing throughout much of the cortex.

## MATCHING ITEMS

____ 1. CAT scans

____ 2. Intense, prolonged magnetic fields

____ 3. Brief, moderate intensity magnetic fields

____ 4. PET scans

____ 5. fMRI

____ 6. dorsal root ganglia

____ 7. motor axons

____ 8. sympathetic nervous system

____ 9. medulla

____ 10. pons

____ 11. midbrain

____ 12. thalamus

____ 13. hypothalamus

____ 14. basal ganglia

____ 15. occipital lobe

____ 16. temporal lobe

____ 17. parietal lobe

____ 18. frontal lobe

a. contains "vital nuclei"

b. site of axons crossing to other side

c. contains primary motor cortex

d. x-rays used to show brain structure

e. exit through the ventral horn

f. hemoglobin molecules releasing oxygen

g. relays information to cerebral cortex

h. method of temporarily inactivating an area

i. movement, memory, emotional expression

j. primary visual cortex

k. "fight or flight" system

l. cell bodies of sensory neurons

m. primary somatosensory cortex

n. site of tectum and tegmentum

o. primary auditory cortex

p. method of stimulating a brain area

q. motivated behaviors, controls pituitary

r. radioactive chemicals in most-active areas

## MULTIPLE-CHOICE QUESTIONS

1. CAT scans
   a. use intense magnetic fields to inactivate brain areas temporarily.
   b. use x-rays to describe brain structure.
   c. use changes in hemoglobin as it releases oxygen to areas with high metabolic activity.
   d. use brief, moderate magnetic fields to stimulate brain areas.

2. A problem in trying to infer behavioral function from measures of brain structure or activity is:
   a. Correlation does not imply causation.
   b. Cases of brain damage often are not specifically localized to one area.
   c. It is difficult to determine which aspect of a complex task is controlled by the brain area that was inactivated.
   d. All of the above are true.

3. Which is true concerning the spinal cord?
   a. Sensory neurons enter on the ventral side; motor neurons exit on the dorsal side.
   b. Cell bodies of sensory neurons lie outside the CNS in the dorsal root ganglia.
   c. Cell bodies of motor neurons lie outside the CNS in the ventral root ganglia.
   d. All of the above are true.

4. The parasympathetic nervous system
   a. is sometimes called the "fight or flight" system.
   b. has a chain of interconnected ganglia along the thoracic and lumbar parts of the spinal cord.
   c. uses norepinephrine as its transmitter to end organs, whereas the sympathetic system uses acetylcholine.
   d. is an energy-conserving system.

5. Concerning the cranial nerves,
   a. nuclei for the first four enter the forebrain and midbrain; nuclei for the rest are in the medulla and pons.
   b. nuclei for all twelve are in the medulla and pons.
   c. all have both sensory and motor components.
   d. all have only sensory or only motor components.

6. The hindbrain
   a. consists of four parts: the superior and inferior colliculi, the tectum, and the tegmentum.
   b. contains the reticular formation and raphe system.
   c. controls the pituitary gland.
   d. consists of the pons, which is adjacent to the spinal cord; the medulla, which is rostral to the pons; and the cerebellum, which is anterior to the pons.

7. The medulla
   a. contains prominent axons crossing from one side of the brain to the other.
   b. is part of the limbic system.
   c. contains nuclei that control vital functions.
   d. is especially important for working memory.

8. The cerebellum
   a. contributes to the control of movement, shifting of attention, and timing.
   b. is concerned mostly with visual location in space.
   c. is located immediately ventral to the pons.
   d. all of the above.

9. The components of the midbrain include
   a. the superior and inferior colliculi in the tectum, involved in sensory processing.
   b. the tegmentum, containing nuclei of the third and fourth cranial nerves, part of the reticular formation, and pathways connecting higher and lower structures.
   c. the substantia nigra, origin of a dopamine-containing pathway that deteriorates in Parkinson's disease.
   d. all of the above.

10. The limbic system
    a. is a set of isolated areas that are important for different aspects of memory.
    b. is a set of interlinked structures that are important for motivated and emotional behaviors.
    c. is another term for the basal ganglia.
    d. gets its name from the Latin word for bridge.

11. The hypothalamus
    a. contains parts of the reticular formation and raphe system.
    b. is part of the basal ganglia.
    c. is important for motivated behaviors and hormonal control.
    d. is connected only with the brain stem.

12. The basal ganglia
    a. are composed primarily of the caudate nucleus, putamen, and globus pallidus.
    b. control movement directly via axons to the spinal cord.
    c. are primarily concerned with sensory processing.
    d. all of the above.

13. The hippocampus
    a. controls breathing, heart rate, and other vital reflexes.
    b. provides the major control for the pituitary gland.
    c. is part of the basal ganglia.
    d. none of the above.

14. The thalamus contains
    a. the superior and inferior colliculi.
    b. nuclei that project to particular areas of cerebral cortex.
    c. nuclei that regulate the pituitary.
    d. nuclei having to do with motivated behaviors, such as eating, drinking, sex, fighting, arousal level, and temperature regulation.

15. Cerebrospinal fluid
    a. is formed by cells lining the four ventricles.
    b. flows from the lateral ventricles to the third and fourth ventricles, and from there either to the central canal of the spinal cord or to the subarachnoid space, where it is reabsorbed into the blood vessels.
    c. cushions the brain and provides buoyancy.
    d. all of the above.

16. The laminae of the cortex
    a.   usually consist of only two layers, one of axons and one of cell bodies.
    b.   are the same thickness throughout the brain of a given species, but differ across species.
    c.   consist of up to six layers, which vary in thickness across the various brain areas.
    d.   are present only in humans; other mammals have cortical cells and axons mixed together.

17. Which of the following is true of cortical columns?
    a.   Columns run parallel to the laminae, across the surface of the cortex.
    b.   There are six columns in the human brain, and only one or two in other mammals.
    c.   Cells within a column have similar response properties.
    d.   The properties of cells within a column change systematically from top to bottom; cells at the top may respond to one stimulus, while those at the bottom respond to a different one.

18. Which is true of the occipital lobe?
    a.   It is located at the posterior end of the cortex and contains primary visual cortex.
    b.   It is located at the sides of the brain and is concerned mostly with perception of complex visual patterns.
    c.   It is located immediately behind the central sulcus and contains the postcentral gyrus.
    d.   It is located at the top of the brain and contributes to somatosensory processing.

19. Which is true of the parietal lobe?
    a.   It contains the primary receiving area for axons carrying touch sensations and other skin and muscle information.
    b.   It has 4 bands on the postcentral gyrus representing different sensory qualities.
    c.   It contributes to our sense of our body in space, relative to visual and auditory stimuli.
    d.   All of the above are true.

20. The temporal lobe
    a.   is located immediately in front of the central sulcus.
    b.   is involved in some complex aspects of visual processing as well as auditory processing.
    c.   has as its only function the processing of simple auditory information.
    d.   none of the above.

21. Damage to the frontal lobe
    a.   may cause losses of initiative and of social inhibitions and produce difficulties with delayed response tasks.
    b.   is still a widely used surgical technique for mental patients because of its remarkable calming and normalizing tendencies without noticeable side effects.
    c.   produces drastic impairments in intelligence.
    d.   all of the above.

22. Gamma waves
    a.   are synchronized waves of activity (30 to 80 per second) in various brain areas, which may reflect binding of sensory aspects into a unified perception.
    b.   are synchronized by the prefrontal cortex, indicating that prefrontal cortex is the site of unified experience.
    c.   are seen in the central amygdala during fearful experiences, and therefore are the basis for our sense of fear.
    d.   are synchronized waves of activity localized within a specific brain area, and are important for shifting attention to the sensory aspect that is processed by that area.

# Answers to True/False Questions

| | | | |
|---|---|---|---|
| 1. F | 5. F | 9. F | 13. F |
| 2. T | 6. T | 10. T | 14. F |
| 3. T | 7. F | 11. F | 15. T |
| 4. F | 8. T | 12. T | 16. T |

# Answers to Fill-in-the-Blank Questions

1. left frontal lobe
2. inactivate, stimulate
3. regional cerebral blood flow (rCBF)
4. dorsal, ventral
5. sympathetic, along the spinal cord, parasympathetic, near the organs they innervate
6. medulla, pons, cerebellum
7. vital reflexes
8. axons crossing from right to left
9. movement, timing, shifting attention
10. tectum, tegmentum
11. olfactory bulb, hypothalamus, hippocampus, amygdala, cingulate gyrus
12. thalamus
13. pituitary, motivated
14. caudate nucleus, putamen, globus pallidus
15. frontal lobe, movement, memory, emotional expression
16. nucleus basalis
17. hippocampus
18. choroid plexus
19. laminae, columns
20. occipital
21. somatosensory
22. auditory, visual
23. precentral gyrus, prefrontal cortex
24. binding problem, gamma

# Answers to Matching Items

| | | | |
|---|---|---|---|
| 1. d | 6. l | 11. n | 16. o |
| 2. h | 7. e | 12. g | 17. m |
| 3. p | 8. k | 13. q | 18. c |
| 4. r | 9. a | 14. i | |
| 5. f | 10. b | 15. j | |

# Answers to Multiple-Choice Questions

| | | | |
|---|---|---|---|
| 1. b | 7. c | 13. d | 19. d |
| 2. d | 8. a | 14. b | 20. b |
| 3. b | 9. d | 15. d | 21. a |
| 4. d | 10. b | 16. c | 22. a |
| 5. a | 11. c | 17. c | |
| 6. b | 12. a | 18. a | |

**Please check the Exploring Biological Psychology CD-ROM**

## Helpful Hints

1. To remember the 12 cranial nerves, use this mnemonic device:

   | | | | | |
   |---|---|---|---|---|
   | 1. On | (Olfactory) | 7. Firm, | (Facial) |
   | 2. Old | (Optic) | 8. Staid | (Statoacoustic) |
   | 3. Olympia's | (Oculomotor) | 9. German | (Glossopharyngial) |
   | 4. Towering | (Trochlear) | 10. Viewed | (Vagus) |
   | 5. Tops, | (Trigeminal) | 11. A lot of | (Accessory) |
   | 6. A | (Abducens) | 12. Hops | (Hypoglossal) |

2. To remember the functions of the hypothalamus, think of the "4 Fs": Fighting, Fleeing, Feeding, and Reproductive Behavior.

## Diagrams

1. In the following diagram of a sagittal section through the human brain, label the following structures: cerebral cortex, parietal lobe, occipital lobe, frontal lobe, cingulate gyrus, corpus callosum, thalamus, hypothalamus, superior and inferior colliculi, midbrain, cerebellum, pons, pituitary gland, tissue dividing the lateral ventricles, medulla, spinal cord, central canal of the spinal cord.

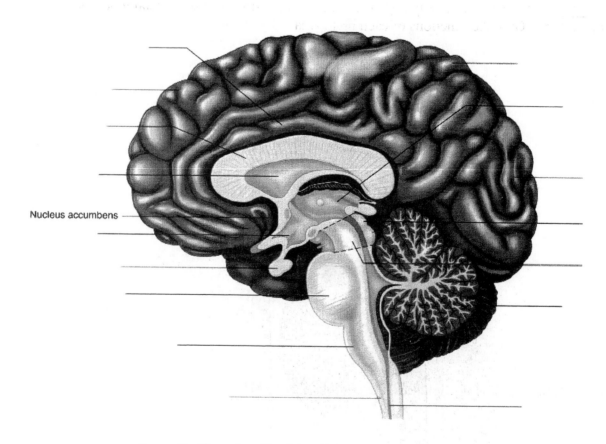

Nucleus accumbens

*Source: After Nieuwenhuys, Voogd, & vanHuijzen 1988*

2. In the following diagram of a cross section through the spinal cord, label the following directions or structures: dorsal, ventral, sensory nerve, dorsal root ganglion, motor nerve, white matter, gray matter, central canal.

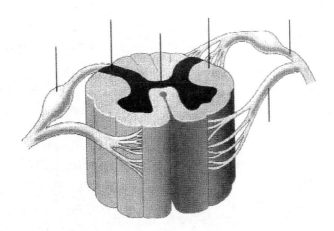

3. In the following diagram of the human cerebral cortex, label the following structures: central sulcus, precentral gyrus, postcentral gyrus, occipital lobe, frontal lobe, parietal lobe, and temporal lobe. Give the functions of each brain area.

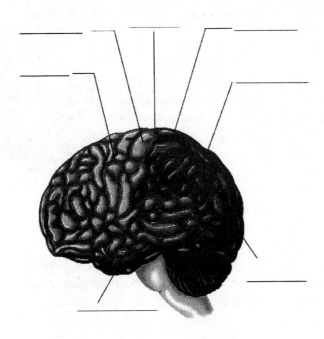

# 5

## DEVELOPMENT AND
## PLASTICITY OF THE BRAIN

### INTRODUCTION

The central nervous system develops from two long thin lips on the surface of the embryo that merge to form a fluid-filled tube. The forward end of the tube enlarges to become the forebrain, midbrain, and hindbrain; the rest becomes the spinal cord. Cerebrospinal fluid continues to fill the central canal of the spinal cord and four hollow ventricles of the brain.

There are five major stages in the development of neurons: proliferation, migration, differentiation, myelination, and synaptogenesis. During proliferation, cells lining the ventricles divide. Some of the new cells remain in place and continue dividing, whereas others migrate to their new destinations. Differentiation includes formation of the axon and dendrites and determination of shape and chemical components. Myelination is the formation, by glial cells, of insulating sheaths around axons, which increase the speed of transmission. Synaptogenesis, the formation of functional synapses, continues throughout life.

There is an initial overproduction of neurons; those that fail to form synapses with appropriate target cells die. The process of programmed cell death, or apoptosis, can be prevented if the neuron receives a neurotrophin from the target cell. Rita Levi-Montalcini discovered the first neurotrophin, nerve growth factor (NGF), which promotes survival of neurons of the sympathetic nervous system. Several additional neurotrophins have been discovered, including brain-derived neurotrophic factor (BDNF). In addition to preventing apoptosis, neurotrophins also attract axons during development, enhance axonal branching during memory formation, and promote regrowth of axons after injury. During maturation of the prefrontal cortex and parts of parietal and temporal cortex in adolescence, white matter increases, but the number of neurons decreases. Thus, more successful neurons and connections survive at the expense of less successful ones.

As the brain grows, axons must travel long distances to reach their appropriate targets. They are guided by concentration gradients of chemicals, such as the protein $TOP_{DV}$, which guides retinal axons to the appropriate part of the tectum. Axons are attracted by some chemicals and repelled by others. After axons reach the general area of their target, they begin to form synapses with postsynaptic cells. These target cells receive an overabundance of synapses; they gradually strengthen some synapses and reject others. Initially, there are many tentative connections between axons and target cells; later, fewer but stronger attachments develop. The overproduction of neurons and subsequent pruning of unsuccessful connections provide a process of selection of the fittest or most informative connections.

Environmental enrichment results in a thicker cortex, more dendritic branching, and enhanced performance on learning tasks. Effects of enrichment, or of sensory deprivation, have been observed in several species, including fish, rats, and humans, although it is sometimes difficult to determine cause and effect relationships. The traditional view that vertebrates do not generate any new neurons in adulthood has been shown to be inaccurate in at least some cases. Undifferentiated stem cells in the interior of the brain migrate to the olfactory bulb and become glia or neurons. New neurons also have also been found in the song control areas of songbirds and in the hippocampus of birds and mammals. There have been reports of new neurons in human cortex, but some of those supposedly new neurons may have been glia or neurons undergoing DNA repair. Extensive training may increase the amount of cortical area devoted to a skill. In professional musicians one area in the right temporal lobe was larger than in nonmusicians. However, cause and effect relationships are not clear. There was also a larger representation of the fingers of left hand in the right postcentral gyrus of people who play stringed instruments. While such an increase in cortical representation is usually beneficial, it can produce problems if the representations of two fingers overlap.

There are remarkable similarities of location, function, and detailed anatomy of brain areas across species. However, in primates the cerebral cortex occupies a larger proportion of the brain, and the medulla and midbrain, a smaller proportion, than in other mammals. Increases in brain size may be due to a longer time of neuron proliferation and to an increase in the number of neurons produced per day. Small changes in the genes governing neuron proliferation can produce large changes in the sizes of brain areas.

Developing brains are not only more responsive to environmental stimuli, they are also more vulnerable to malnutrition, toxic chemicals, and disease. For example, fetal alcohol syndrome is characterized by decreased alertness, hyperactivity, mental retardation and other physical and mental abnormalities. Children with fetal alcohol syndrome have neurons with smaller, less branching dendrites. Alcohol decreases the release of glutamate and neurotrophins and increases activity at inhibitory GABA synapses; as a result more neurons undergo apoptosis. Prenatal exposure to cocaine and to the effects of cigarette smoking also result in physical and intellectual deficits.

Brain damage can be caused by a variety of factors, including closed head injury and stroke. Stroke can result either from ischemia due to a blood clot that obstructs an artery, or from hemorrhage, caused by rupture of an artery. Strokes kill neurons either by depriving them of oxygen and glucose or by overexcitation, which allows excess sodium, calcium, and zinc ions to enter the neuron, resulting in swelling or bursting of the membrane and interfering with normal processes. Cell death can be minimized by the use of drugs that break up clots and perhaps those that block glutamate receptors, if given early after the stroke. Blocking calcium channels or opening potassium channels may also help. However, after the immediate injury, drugs that reduce excitation may result in neural death from understimulation. Potential new treatments include cooling the brain, food restriction, and the administration of neurotrophins, cannabinoids, or drugs that trap free radicals.

Very old people have less potential for recovery after brain damage than do young adults. This suggests that damage to infant brains should be less debilitating than similar damage to adult brains. Under some circumstances this is true, and the infant's brain development can be modified to compensate for damage. On the other hand, damage to an infant brain may be more disruptive than that to an adult brain, depending on the age, brain area affected, and type of damage. Although young brains are more plastic than adult brains, they are also more vulnerable to forces that interfere with brain development and organization.

Recovery from brain damage depends on a number of physiological mechanisms. Learned adjustments in behavior allow an individual to make better use of abilities unaffected by the damage and to improve abilities that were impaired by the damage, but not lost. Diaschisis, or decreased activity of neurons after loss of input, contributes to impairment following brain damage. It can be reduced by administration of stimulant drugs during the recovery phase. Regrowth of axons can be guided by myelin sheaths in the periphery. However, axons in the central nervous system do not regenerate, in part because of formation of scar tissue and in part because of growth-inhibiting chemicals from myelin. Sprouting of axons occurs in response to normal cell death, as well as after brain damage; axons from undamaged neurons develop new terminals that occupy the vacant synapses. Denervation supersensitivity refers to the increased sensitivity to a neurotransmitter by a postsynaptic cell that is deprived of synaptic input. Reorganization of sensory representations can occur by postsynaptic adjustments of synaptic strength or by collateral sprouting, sometimes over surprisingly long distances. However, these reorganizations may not be beneficial, as in the case of phantom-limb sensations. Therapies for brain damage include behavioral interventions that help people to reaccess memories or skills or to make better use of their unimpaired abilities. More recently, researchers have experimented with brain grafting and with drug treatments, such as calcium channel blockers, gangliosides, and progesterone. While these treatments are still in experimental stages, there is optimism for future improvements.

## LEARNING OBJECTIVES

### Module 5.1 Development of the Brain

1. Understand the processes of growth and differentiation of the brain.
2. Understand why there is initial overproduction of neurons and how axons follow chemical paths to their destinations and make functional connections, thereby allowing them to survive.
3. Be able to describe the effects of experience on the brain.
4. Be able to describe the methods of studying brain anatomy and function.
5. Understand the reasons why the developing brain is vulnerable to chemical insults.

### Module 5.2 Plasticity after Brain Damage

1. Be able to describe the processes by which strokes damage the brain and the means of lessening the damage.
2. Understand the mechanisms of recovery after brain damage and how various therapies promote recovery.

## KEY TERMS AND CONCEPTS

### Module 5.1 Development of the Brain

1. Growth and differentiation of the vertebrate brain
   Early development of the nervous system
      Neural tube → hindbrain, midbrain, forebrain, spinal cord
      Cavity of neural tube → central canal of spinal cord, ventricles of brain
         Cerebrospinal fluid (CSF)
   Growth and development of neurons
      Proliferation of new cells
      Migration toward eventual destinations
      Differentiation, forming axon first and then dendrites
      Myelination of some axons, continuing for years
      Synaptogenesis, continuing throughout life
   Determinants of neuron survival
      Nerve growth factor (NGF)
         Sympathetic nervous system
         Rita Levi-Montalcini
         Promotes survival and growth, not neuronal birth
         Apoptosis vs. necrosis
      Other neurotrophins
         Brain-derived neurotrophic factor (BDNF) and others
      Functions of neurotrophins
         Prevent apoptosis
         Increase branching of incoming axons → store memories
         Increase axon regrowth after injury
      Overproduction of neurons and massive cell death
         Release of neurotransmitter plus neurotrophin
            Neurotrophins needed from both incoming axons and target cells

90

Error correction
Match incoming axons to number of recipient cells

2.  Pathfinding by axons
    Chemical pathfinding by axons
        Specificity of axon connections
        Axons to extra leg of salamander
        Optic tract axons to tectum of newts
    Chemical gradients
        TOP$_{DV}$
    Competition among axons as a general principle
        Neural Darwinism

3.  Fine-tuning by experience
    Effects of experience on dendritic branching
        Enriched environment
            Thicker cortex
            More dendritic branches
            Improved learning
            Extensive education in humans
    Generation of new neurons
        Olfactory receptors
        Stem cells
            Undifferentiated, in interior of brain
            Daughter cells→olfactory bulb
        New neurons in hippocampus of song birds
        Unclear whether new neurons form in adult human cortex
    Effects of experience on human brain structure
        Early music training
            Larger area in right temporal cortex
        Playing stringed instruments (fingering with left hand)
            Larger area in right postcentral gyrus
                Usually beneficial
                Focal hand dystonia ("musician's cramp"): due to overlap of cortical
                    representation of two fingers
    Methods 5.1: Magnetoencephalography
        Magnetic fields generated by brain activity
        Good temporal resolution, poor spatial resolution
    Combinations of chemical and experiential effects
        Two-stage process
            Chemical gradients guide axons to approximate target
            Strengthen some connections, discard others in response to experience
                Spontaneous action potentials
        Simultaneous activity of axons from nearby retinal areas
            Lateral geniculate

4.  Proportional growth of brain areas
    Similarities of location, function, & detailed anatomy across species
        Primates
            Larger cerebral cortex relative to rest of brain

Smaller medulla and midbrain, relative to rest of brain

Cerebellum remarkably constant

Size of brain areas

Number of days of neuron proliferation

Longer in humans than in chimpanzee

Number of neurons produced per day

Small genetic change → large difference in outcome

Methods 5.2: MRI scans: magnetic resonance imaging

Atoms with odd-numbered atomic weights: inherent rotation

Magnetic field → alignment of axes of rotation

Brief radio frequency field → tilt axes

Turn off radio frequency field → atomic nuclei relax and release electromagnetic energy

Advantage: good spatial resolution without radioactivity

Disadvantage: lie motionless in confining, noisy apparatus

5. The vulnerable developing brain

Greater vulnerablilty to malnutrition, toxic chemicals, infections

Impaired thyroid function in infancy: Permanent mental retardation and slow body growth

Anesthetics: Death of neurons in infants

Diabetes in mother: Oxygen & glucose deprivation of fetus → memory & attention deficits

Fetal alcohol syndrome

Short, less branched dendrites

Alcohol: Inhibits glutamate & neurotrophin release; increases GABA activity

Maternal cocaine or cigarette smoking

6. In closing: Brain Development

Many ways to disrupt development; wonder that it ever works normally

**Module 5.2 Plasticity after Brain Damage**

1. Causes of brain damage

Closed head injury

Rotational force

Blood clots

Reducing the harm from a stroke (cerebrovascular accident)

Ischemia (blood clot closes artery)

Area of direct damage: loss of oxygen and glucose

Penumbra: loss of much, but not all, oxygen and glucose

Hemorrhage (rupture of artery)

Area of direct damage: loss of oxygen and glucose

Penumbra: excess oxygen, calcium, blood products

Penumbra, following both ischemia and hemorrhage

Waste from dead cells in area of direct damage

Extracellular potassium

Edema

Glutamate actively transported out of cells →

Overstimulation →

Accumulation of sodium, calcium, and zinc →

Block metabolism in mitochondria →

Neurons die, glia proliferate

Means of lessening damage

Tissue plasminogen activator (tPA): breaks up blood clots
Open potassium channels
Glutamate antagonists and calcium channel blockers: mixed results
Deficient glutamate and calcium → apoptosis
Time course of MK-801 (glutamate NMDA receptor antagonist)
Useful in early stages, harmful during recovery
Animal studies
Neurotrophins
Drugs that trap free radicals
Food restriction
Cannabinoids
Cooling brain—most effective
Effects of age on recovery
Older people: Other cells dying; remaining cells less plastic than before
Kennard principle: more extensive recovery after early damage
Applies only to certain kinds of damage
Young brain more plastic, also more vulnerable
Effects on still-developing neurons
Remove one hemisphere: increased thickness of other hemisphere
Remove anterior cortex: less development of posterior cortex

2. Mechanisms of recovery after brain damage
Learned adjustments in behavior
Deafferented limbs
One deafferented limb: Lack of spontaneous use
Two deafferented limbs: Monkey learns to use both
Diaschisis
Amphetamine (releases dopamine and norepinephrine): Enhanced recovery
Haloperidol (blocks dopamine receptors): Impaired recovery
Tranquilizers (decrease dopamine and norepinephrine release): Impair recovery
Methods 5.3: Lesions
Lesion: Damage to a brain area
Ablation: Removal of part of the brain
Stereotaxic instrument
Stereotaxic atlas
Sham lesion
The regrowth of axons
Myelin sheaths as guides
Scar tissue
Mechanical barrier
Growth-inhibiting chemicals: chondroitin sulphate proteoglycans
Myelin
Inhibits axon regrowth in CNS
Stimulates axon regrowth in periphery
Hemiplegia
Sprouting
Collateral sprouts
Locus coeruleus
Normal condition, not just response to damage
Cut connections from left entorhinal cortex to left hippocampus →

Right entorhinal cortex sprouts → recovery
Then cut path from right entorhinal cortex → impairs recovery
Therefore, sprouting was beneficial
Denervation supersensitivy
Disuse supersensitivity
6-OHDA (6-hydroxydopmine)
Amphetamine: Increased release of dopamine mostly on intact side of brain
Apomorphine: Stimulated supersensitive dopamine receptors on brain-injured side
Methods 5.4: Autoradiography
Application of radioactive chemicals to thin brain sections
Sections placed against film → records amount of radioactivity in various brain areas
Reorganized sensory representations and the phantom limb
Based on collateral sprouting or increased receptor sensitivity
Amputation of finger: Cortical responsiveness to adjacent fingers
Deafferentation of forelimb: Cortical responsiveness to face
Phantom limb sensations in humans
Touch face → feel phantom hand
Sexual activity → feel phantom foot
Use mirror to reduce phantom pain
Methods 5.5: Histochemistry
Horseradish peroxidase: Transported from axon terminal to cell body

3.  Therapies
Behavioral interventions
Reinforcement for appropriate behaviors
Reaccess lost skills or memories
Practice impaired skills
Remove distracting stimuli
Drugs
Nimodipine
Calcium channel blocker
Prevent damage due to excess NMDA stimulation
Gangliosides (glycolipids)
Progesterone
Brain grafts
Stem cells from embryos, infants, adults, or recently deceased bodies


**SHORT-ANSWER QUESTIONS**


**Module 5.1  Development of the Brain**
1.  *Growth and differentiation of the vertebrate brain*
    a.  Describe the formation of the central nervous system in the embryo.  What happens to the fluid-filled cavity?

b.  What are the three main divisions of the brain?

c.  What are the five stages in the development of neurons?  Describe the processes in each.

d.  Who discovered nerve growth factor?  What happens if a neuron in the sympathetic nervous system does not receive enough nerve growth factor?

e.  What is apoptosis?  What type of chemical can prevent apoptosis?

f.  What is another neurotrophin besides nerve growth factor.  What three functions do neurotrophins serve?

2.  *Pathfinding by axons*
    a.  What did Weiss observe in his experiments on salamanders' extra limbs?  What principle did he conclude directed the innervation of the extra limb?  Is this principle still thought to be correct?

b.  What did Sperry observe when he damaged the optic nerve of newts? What happened when he rotated the eye by 180 degrees? How did the newt with the rotated eye see the world?

c.  What conclusion did these results suggest?

d.  What is $TOP_{DV}$? What is its role in directing retinal axons to the tectum?

e.  What happens to axons that form active synapses? What happens to axons that do not form active synapses?

f.  Describe the principle of neural Darwinism. How does this relate to the initial overproduction and subsequent death of large numbers of neurons?

3.  *Fine-tuning by experience*
    a.  Describe the effects of environmental "enrichment".

b.   How may exercise contribute to the development of axons and dendrites?

c.   In what brain areas have new neurons been found in adult vertebrates? What are stem cells?

d.   What brain area is larger in professional musicians? What can we conclude about cause and effect in the relationship of brain size, musical ability, and experience?

e.   What area is larger in people who had extensive experience playing stringed instruments? What is focal hand dystonia, and what is its physiological basis?

f.   How does a lateral geniculate neuron "know" which axons originated near one another in the retina?

4.  *Proportional growth of brain areas*
    a.   What two factors determine the size of each brain area?

b.  Compare the relative ratios of cerebral cortex, medulla, midbrain, and cerebellum to total brain size in primates and in insectivores.

5.  *The vulnerable developing brain*
    a.  What are the effects of thyroid deficiency in adulthood?  Compare these with the effects of thyroid deficiency in infancy.

    b.  Describe fetal alcohol syndrome.  How are dendrites affected?  What effects of alcohol on synaptic activity may explain the neural deficits.

    c.  What are the effects of prenatal cocaine exposure?  Cigarette smoking during pregnancy?

**Module 5.2  Plasticity after Brain Damage**
1.  *Causes of brain damage*
    a.  What is the most common cause of brain damage in young people? What actually produces the brain damage in these cases?

b.  What are the two types of stroke and the cause of each?

c.  In what two ways does a stroke kill neurons?  Describe the sequence of destructive processes in the penumbra.

d.  What are six treatments that may minimize damage from stroke?

e.  Why is recovery from brain damage more difficult in old age?

f.  What is the Kennard principle?  What evidence supports or refutes it?

g.  What are some factors that may determine whether an infant brain is better or less able to recover from brain damage, compared to an adult brain?

2. *Mechanisms of recovery after brain damage*
   a. List six potential mechanisms for recovery from brain damage.

   b. How may learned adjustments in behavior be promoted?

   c. What is diaschisis? How is recovery from diaschisis affected by amphetamine or haloperidol?

   d. How may crushed, but not cut, axons in the peripheral nervous system form appropriate connections when they regenerate? Why don't axons in the central nervous system regenerate? How might this lack of regeneration be overcome?

   e. Under what conditions is sprouting most likely to be useful? What evidence suggests that sprouting produces beneficial results?

f.  What is denervation supersensitivity? What are two mechanisms of supersensitivity?

g.  What are the effects of 6-OHDA?  Explain the differential effects of amphetamine and apomorphine after 6-OHDA lesions.

h.  What evidence is there that sensory representations may be reorganized during recovery? What surprised investigators about the brain of a monkey whose limb had been deafferented 12 years earlier?

i.  What are some sources of sensory input that can give rise to phantom limbs?  What is the relationship between reorganization of somatosensory cortex and the likelihood of phantom sensations?

3.  *Therapies*
    a.  How may behavioral interventions facilitate recovery from brain damage?

b.  What are three potential drug therapies for brain damage?  How may they work?

c.  What are some sources of brain grafts? How well established is this approach to therapy?

4.  *Methods boxes*
    a.  What does the magnetoencephalograph (MEG) measure?  What is an advantage and a disadvantage of the MEG?

    b.  What is the principle behind magnetic resonance imaging (MRI)?  What is an advantage and a disadvantage of this technique?

    c.  What is a stereotaxic instrument?  Why is important to compare sham lesions with actual lesions?

    d.  How is autoradiography used?  What kind of data does it provide?

e. How can histochemistry be used?

## TRUE/FALSE QUESTIONS

_____ 1. The cavity of the neural tube fills in with neural tissue as the brain develops.

_____ 2. The five stages of neural development are proliferation, migration, differentiation, myelination, and synaptogenesis.

_____ 3. Nerve growth factor (NGF) primarily promotes neuronal birth.

_____ 4. Apoptosis is the process of increasing the branching of dendrites.

_____ 5. In addition to preventing programmed cell death, neurotrophins increase the branching of incoming axons and increase axon growth after injury.

_____ 6. Massive cell death early in development is a sign of profound disorder.

_____ 7. Axons follow chemical gradients to get to the area where they can make functional synaptic connections.

_____ 8. Rats that were reared in an enriched environment had thicker cortex, more dendritic branching, and improved learning.

_____ 9. Mammals are born with all the neurons they will ever have.

_____10. Professional musicians have a larger area in the right temporal lobe than do non-musicians.

_____11. Magnetoencephalography is a technique that detects the electromagnetic energy given off after atoms with odd numbers of electrons relax after a strong radiofrequency field is turned off.

_____12. Fetuses are generally more likely to recover from physical damage than from malnutrition, toxic chemicals, and infections.

_____13. The two kinds of stroke are ischemic and hemorrhagic.

_____14. The penumbra is the area of most direct damage from a stroke; neurons in the penumbra are killed almost immediately.

_____15. One way to decrease damage immediately after a stroke is to administer a glutamate antagonist; however, this may be harmful if administered later, during recovery.

103

_____16. Tissue plasminogen activator (tPA) should be administered after a hemorrhagic stroke, but not after an ischemic stroke.

_____17. Heating the brain, mimicking a fever, is the most effective treatment for a stroke.

_____18. After one limb was deafferented, the monkey stopped using it; if both arms were deafferented, the monkey learned how to use both arms.

_____19. A stereotaxic instrument is used to direct electrodes to a precise area of the brain.

_____20. Scar tissue inhibits the growth of axons both by providing a physical barrier and by releasing growth-inhibiting chemicals.

_____21. 6-OHDA is an effective treatment for diaschisis.

_____22. In studies of laboratory animals males typically recover better than females, because the higher levels of progesterone in females impede recovery.

## FILL IN THE BLANKS

1. Early in development the _____ _____ differentiates into the hindbrain, the midbrain, the forebrain, and the spinal cord.

2. The five stages of neural development are _____, _____, _____, _____, and _____.

3. _____ _____ discovered the first neurotrophin, _____ _____ _____.

4. Programmed cell death, also called _____, occurs if neurons do not receive sufficient neurotrophins.

5. The principle of competition among axons is referred to as _____ _____.

6. The cells that give rise to new neurons in the adult brain are called _____ _____.

7. An area in the _____ lobe of the _____ hemisphere was larger in professional musicians. An area of the _____ gyrus of the _____ hemisphere was larger in people who play stringed instruments.

104

8. The technique of _____ records magnetic fields generated by brain activity. It has good _____ resolution, but poor _____ resolution.

9. The technique of _____ _____ _____ (_____) uses the inherent rotation of atoms with odd-numbered atomic weights. A powerful magnetic field aligns the axes of rotation, which are tilted by a radiofrequency field. When the radiofrequency field is turned off, the atoms release electromagnetic energy as they relax. This technique has good _____ resolution.

10. The developing brain is more plastic in response to physical damage than is the adult brain, but is more vulnerable to _____, _____ _____, and _____.

11. The two types of stroke are _____ and _____.

12. The area surrounding the direct damage from a stroke is called the _____.

13. Some potential means of lessening the damage, if applied immediately after a stroke are _____ antagonists, drugs that open _____ channels or block _____ channels; however, these may be harmful if applied during recovery

14. The _____ principle states that there is more extensive recovery after damage to a developing brain than after damage to an adult brain.

15. _____ refers to the decreased activity of surviving neurons after other neurons are damaged. A treatment for this condition may be administration of _____ during recovery.

16. Myelin sheaths in the _____ nervous system inhibit axon growth; myelin sheaths in the _____ nervous system stimulate growth.

17. Denervation _____ is a mechanism of recovery after damage.

18. Phantom limb sensations arise because of collateral _____ of axons or

increased receptor _____.

19. Three drugs that may be used during therapy for brain damage are _____

(a calcium channel blocker), _____, and

_____.

## MATCHING ITEMS

_____ 1.  Cavity of neural tube             a.  Cell death due to injury or toxic chemical

_____ 2.  Rita Levi-Montalcini             b.  A cause of damage several days after a stroke

_____ 3.  Apoptosis                        c.  Stroke caused by ruptured blood vessel

_____ 4.  Necrosis                         d.  A cause of damage immediately after a stroke

_____ 5.  Neural Darwinism                 e.  Programmed cell death

_____ 6.  Stem cells                       f.  Stroke caused by blood clot

_____ 7.  Ischemic                         g.  Cerebral ventricles and spinal central canal

_____ 8.  Hemorrhagic                      h.  Discovered nerve growth factor

_____ 9.  Overexcitation                   i.  Undifferentiated cells that can become neurons

_____10.  Underexcitation                  j.  Axons competing for synapses and survival

## MULTIPLE-CHOICE QUESTIONS

1. The neural tube
   a. arises from a pair of long thin lips that merge around a fluid-filled cavity.
   b. develops into the spinal cord; the brain arises from a separate structure.
   c. eventually merges to form a solid structure, squeezing out the primitive cerebrospinal fluid.
   d. none of the above.

2. The five major stages in the development of neurons, in order, are
   a. proliferation, differentiation, migration, myelination, synaptogenesis.
   b. proliferation, growth, synaptogenesis, myelination, migration.
   c. proliferation, migration, myelination, synaptogenesis, growth.
   d. proliferation, migration, differentiation, myelination, synaptogenesis.

3. Which of the following is true?
   a. Myelination is complete by the end of the first year in humans.
   b. Neurons experimentally transplanted from one site to another at an intermediate stage of development may keep some properties of cells in the old location and develop some that are characteristic of their new location.
   c. Dendrites usually form before axons, and are usually fully formed before migration begins.
   d. Neurons are incapable of conducting action potentials until they are fully myelinated.

4. Apoptosis
   a. is caused by an excess of neurotrophin.
   b. occurs in only a few areas of the brain.
   c. is the "suicide program" of the cell.
   d. was the first neurotrophin to be discovered.

5. Nerve growth factor
   a. was discovered by Roger Sperry.
   b. is important for the survival and growth of sympathetic neurons.
   c. determines the number of neurons that will be formed.
   d. all of the above.

6. When Paul Weiss grafted an extra leg onto a salamander
   a. the extra leg received no neurons and therefore could not move.
   b. the extra leg moved in the opposite direction from the normal adjacent leg.
   c. the extra leg moved in synchrony with the normal adjacent leg.
   d. the leg degenerated because the immune system rejected it.

7. Sperry's work with the eyes of newts led him to conclude that
   a. neurons attach to postsynaptic cells randomly, and the postsynaptic cell confers specificity.
   b. axons follow a chemical trail that places them in the general vicinity of their target.
   c. innervation in the sensory system is guided by specific genetic information, whereas that in the motor system is random.
   d. neurons follow specific genetic information that directs each of them to precisely the right postsynaptic cell.

8. TOP$_{DV}$
   a. is a trophic factor necessary for the survival of neurons of the sympathetic nervous system.
   b. is a protein that guides axons to the developing legs of newts.
   c. is a protein that causes a group of neurons that possess it to fire together, thereby increasing their chance of survival.
   d. is a protein that is more concentrated in neurons of the dorsal retina and the ventral tectum than in the ventral retina and dorsal tectum.

9. Massive cell death early in development
   a. would be so maladaptive that it hardly ever occurs.
   b. occurs only with sensory deprivation or when the fetus has been exposed to toxins.
   c. occurs as a result of genetic mistakes, which fail to direct the cells to their genetically programmed target. As a result the neurons wander aimlessly until they die.
   d. is a normal result of unsuccessful competition for synapses and growth factors.

10. Neural Darwinism
   a. was formulated by Roger Sperry.
   b. has recently been shown to be false.
   c. proposes that synapses form somewhat randomly at first; those that work best are kept, while the others degenerate.
   d. all of the above.

11. Environmental enrichment
   a. produces greater dendritic branching and a thicker cortex.
   b. produces changes in the structure of neurons, but no changes in neural function.
   c. produces changes in the function of neurons, but no changes in neural structure.
   d. has beneficial effects only in primates.

12. Stem cells
   a. are hippocampal neurons that are especially resistant to damage.
   b. are undifferentiated cells in the interior of the brain that sometimes generate daughter cells that migrate to the olfactory bulb and become glial cells or neurons.
   c. are glial cells that guide neurons during migration.
   d. are neurons that develop especially long axons that resemble the stems of plants.

13. Which of the following is true?
   a. Professional musicians have a larger area in the right temporal lobe than do nonmusicians.
   b. Exercise generates waste products that are harmful to neural survival.
   c. During early development the lateral geniculate neurons become responsive to inputs that are active out of phase with each other, in order to maximize the diversity of inputs.
   d. All of the above are true.

14. Which of the following is true?
   a. The increase in representation of the left hand in the right postcentral gyrus of stringed instrument players is always beneficial.
   b. Embryonic neurons do not produce action potentials until they are ready to participate in complex, patterned sensory or motor processing.
   c. Primates have a larger medulla, midbrain, and cerebellum, relative to the rest of the brain, than do insectivores.
   d. Differences in brain structure across species probably depend on a small number of genes that determine the duration of neurogenesis and the number of neurons produced per day.

15. Mental retardation
   a. can be caused by thyroid deficiency during adulthood.
   b. can be caused by thyroid deficiency in infancy.
   c. is not due to lack or excess of chemicals during development, because the young brain is very plastic and can repair itself easily.
   d. all of the above.

16. Fetal alcohol syndrome
    a. results in decreased alertness, hyperactivity, varying degrees of mental retardation, motor problems, heart defects, and facial abnormalities.
    b. occurs because alcohol increases glutamate release and decreases GABA release.
    c. results from excessively long, heavily branched dendrites.
    d. all of the above.

17. Children of mothers who smoked during pregnancy have greater risk for
    a. low birth weight and many illnesses early in life.
    b. Sudden Infant Death Syndrome (SIDS).
    c. intellectual deficits, ADHD, and impairments of the immune system.
    d. all of the above.

18. The most common cause of brain damage in young adults is
    a. stroke.
    b. disease.
    c. a sharp blow to the head.
    d. a brain tumor.

19. Which of the following occurs in the penumbra around the area of direct damage from stroke?
    a. It is invaded by waste products from the dead or dying cells in the area of direct damage.
    b. Potassium ions and fluid accumulate outside the neurons.
    c. Glutamate released by reverse transport overstimulates neurons, resulting in sodium, calcium, and zinc ions accumulating in the cells, which in turn block metabolism in the mitochondria.
    d. All of the above are true.

20. Damage from strokes can be minimized by
    a. activating glutamate synapses immediately after the stroke.
    b. giving tissue plasminogen activator, if the stroke is due to ischemia.
    c. creating a fever, which will increase the temperature of the brain and enhance repair processes.
    d. all of the above.

21. Aging is associated with
    a. shrinking of dendrites in certain brain areas in senile people, but not in alert older people.
    b. impaired recovery from brain damage, in part because remaining neurons modify their branching less readily than in younger people.
    c. continuing loss of neurons.
    d. all of the above.

22. The Kennard principle
    a. states that infants have less ability than adults to recover from brain damage, since their brains are more fragile.
    b. is true only for the peripheral nervous system.
    c. is only partly correct, since fetal and infant brains are actually more vulnerable than adults' brains to the effects of malnutrition, toxic chemicals, and infections.
    d. is entirely correct, since infants always have greater ability to recover from any sort of brain damage.

23. Which of the following statements about recovery from damage in infant brains is **not** true?
    a. Young children can always recover language fully after left hemisphere damage.
    b. Removal of the anterior portion of the infant cortex results in less development of the posterior cortex, because the posterior neurons require interaction with the anterior neurons.
    c. Removal of one hemisphere of an infant rat brain results in increased thickness in the opposite side.
    d. Rats recover better from amygdala damage that occurs at 10 days of age than from damage occurring at 40 days.

24. Research on recovery from brain damage has shown that
    a. recovery can occur when an individual is forced to make full use of remaining capabilities.
    b. a person has to completely relearn the skills and memories that were lost.
    c. the primary means of recovery is having some other area of the brain take over the function of the damaged area.
    d. injections of transmitters is the best way to restore lost memories.

25. Amphetamine administered during practice improves recovery by
    a. producing denervation supersensitivity.
    b. reducing diaschisis.
    c. relieving stress.
    d. stimulating regrowth of axons.

26. Adequate regrowth of an axon does not occur if
    a. the damaged axon is in the spinal cord of fish.
    b. an axon in the peripheral nervous system of mammals is crushed.
    c. the damaged axon is in the central nervous system of mammals.
    d. all of the above.

27. Research on regrowth of axons in mammals has shown that
    a. administration of chondroitin sulphate proteoglycans will stimulate growth of axons.
    b. myelin in the peripheral, but not central, nervous system helps axons regenerate.
    c. the mammalian central nervous system has evolved advanced chemical stimuli to promote better axon regrowth than that seen in fish.
    d. the reason that neurons in the central nervous system fail to regenerate is that there are no myelin sheaths there.

28. Sprouting
    a. occurs only in response to traumatic brain damage.
    b. is always maladaptive, since the wrong axons make connections.
    c. may be adaptive if sprouts come from closely related axons.
    d. is enhanced by haloperidol.

29. Denervation supersensitivity is the result of
    a. increased output from other presynaptic cells adjacent to the one that has been damaged.
    b. postsynaptic neurons producing receptors for a different transmitter.
    c. changes in the chemical composition of the transmitter, making it more potent.
    d. an increased number of receptors on the postsynaptic cell and increased effectiveness of the receptors.

30. After 6-OHDA lesions were made on the left side of a rat's brain
    a. amphetamine increased the release of dopamine mostly on the intact right side and thereby caused the rat to turn left.
    b. amphetamine directly stimulated supersensitive postsynaptic receptors on the intact right side, causing the rat to turn to the right.
    c. both amphetamine and apomorphine stimulated postsynaptic receptors on both sides of the brain, causing the animal to walk in a straight line.
    d. the primary means of recovery was collateral sprouting of neurons containing acetylcholine.

31. After amputation of one finger of an owl monkey
    a. neurons that had previously responded to it died because of lack of input.
    b. neurons that had previously responded to it became responsive to other parts of the hand.
    c. reorganization caused the adjacent fingers to feel like the lost one.
    d. no reorganization could occur because connections become permanently fixed during the early critical period.

32. Nimodipine
    a. is a type of ganglioside that can decrease the amount of damage caused by a stroke.
    b. is an immune suppressant that stops rejection of brain grafts.
    c. is a neurotoxin that destroys catecholamine neurons.
    d. is a calcium channel blocker that can decrease the amount of damage caused by a stroke, if administered soon after the stroke.

33. Brain grafting
    a. has a problem in obtaining suitable donor cells to graft.
    b. is currently a very successful treatment for Alzheimer's disease, but cannot be used in other diseases.
    c. cannot be used, because the brain has such an effective immune system that the transplants never live.
    d. is by now a well established way of treating numerous disorders.

## Answers to True/False Questions

| | | | |
|---|---|---|---|
| 1. F | 7. T | 13. T | 19. T |
| 2. T | 8. T | 14. F | 20. T |
| 3. F | 9. F | 15. T | 21. F |
| 4. F | 10. T | 16. F | 22. F |
| 5. T | 11. F | 17. F | |
| 6. F | 12. T | 18. T | |

## Answers to Fill-in-the-Blank Questions

1. neural tube
2. proliferation, migration, differentiation, myelination, synaptogenesis
3. Rita Levi-Montalcini, nerve growth factor
4. apoptosis
5. neural Darwinism
6. stem cells
7. temporal, right, postcentral, right
8. magnetoencephalography, temporal, spatial

9.  magnetic resonance imaging, MRI, spatial
10. malnutrition, toxic chemicals, infections
11. ischemic, hemorrhagic
12. penumbra
13. glutamate, potassium, calcium
14. Kennard
15. Diaschisis, amphetamine
16. central, peripheral
17. supersensitivity
18. sprouting, sensitivity
19. nimodipine, gangliosides, progesterone

## Answers to Matching Items

1.  g
2.  h
3.  e
4.  a
5.  j
6.  i
7.  f
8.  c
9.  d
10. b

## Answers to Multiple-Choice Questions

1.  a
2.  d
3.  b
4.  c
5.  b
6.  c
7.  b
8.  d
9.  d
10. c
11. a
12. b
13. a
14. d
15. b
16. a
17. d
18. c
19. d
20. b
21. d
22. c
23. a
24. a
25. b
26. c
27. b
28. c
29. d
30. a
31. b
32. d
33. a

**Please check the Exploring Biological Psychology CD-ROM**

# Brain Parts and Development

## ACROSS

1 "Hole in the brain" filled with cerebrospinal fluid

3 Stage of development in which neurons move to their final destination

6 Nucleus that is part of basal ganglia

9 Substantia ____: midbrain structure, degeneration of which causes Parkinson's disease

11 ____ problem: How we construct a single object out of many aspects

13 Roof of midbrain

14 Neural "suicide program"

16 Cortex lobe that processes somatosensory input

17 Area surrounding site of direct stroke damage

19 Fluid that fills the ventricles and cushions the brain

20 "Fight or flight" system

## DOWN

2 Units of cortex

4 Type of matter composed mostly of cell bodies and dendrites

5 Forebrain structure important for motivation and hormone control

7 Chemical gradient that guides retinal axons to proper area of tectum

8 ____ channel blockers: drugs used after a stroke to prevent damage due to excess NMDA stimulation

10 Forebrain structure important for memory

12 Portion of brainstem that controls vital reflexes

15 ____ cells: type of cell that lines the ventricles and produces new neurons and glia

18 Imaging system based on use of a magnetic field to tilt rotation axes of atoms with odd-numbered atomic weights

113

# 6

## VISION

### INTRODUCTION

Sensory systems, including vision, are concerned with reception (absorption) of physical energy and transduction of that energy into neural activity that encodes some aspect of the stimulus. The structure of each kind of sensory receptor allows it to be stimulated maximally by one kind of energy, and little or not at all by other forms of energy. The brain interprets any information sent by nerves that synapse with those receptors as being about that form of energy. This principle was described by Müller as the law of specific nerve energies. A recent test of this principle showed that ferrets whose optic nerve was redirected to the auditory area of the thalamus on one side of the brain reprogrammed the auditory thalamus and cortex to produce visual responses.

The retina contains two kinds of receptors. Cones are most densely packed in the fovea, an area in the center of the retina with the most acute (detailed) vision. This acuity is largely the result of the small number of cones that synapse with each bipolar cell. Rods are located more peripherally in the retina than are cones and are more sensitive to low levels of light. Furthermore, each bipolar cell receives input from a large number of rods. This improves sensitivity to dim light but sacrifices acuity.

All mammalian photopigments contain 11-cis-retinal bound to one of several opsins. Light converts 11-cis-retinal to all-trans-retinal, which in turn activates second-messenger molecules. Cones mediate color vision because three different photopigments are found in three types of cones. Each photopigment is maximally sensitive to one wavelength of light but responds less readily to other wavelengths. Thus, each wavelength produces a certain ratio of responses from the three receptor types; the ratio remains essentially constant regardless of brightness. Rods, in contrast to cones, contain only one photopigment and therefore do not contribute directly to our perception of colors. Processing of color vision beyond the receptor level depends on an opponent-process mechanism, in which a given cell responds to one color with increased firing and to another color with a decrease below its spontaneous rate of firing. In addition, color constancy, the ability to recognize the color of an object despite changes in lighting, depends on an area of the cortex that compares colors across all the objects in the visual field. Color vision deficiency occurs when an individual lacks, or has low numbers of, long-, medium-, and/or short-wavelength cones.

A receptive field of a neuron in the visual system is that area of the visual field in which the presence or absence of light affects that neuron's activity. A receptive field beyond the receptor level represents a composite of the receptive fields of neurons that provide its input. Many contain both excitatory and inhibitory regions. The receptive fields of bipolar, ganglion, and geniculate cells are concentric circles. For some cells light in the center is excitatory, and for other cells it is inhibitory; light in the surround has the opposite effect. Cells in the visual cortex (occipital lobe) have bar shaped receptive fields as a result of summing the receptive fields of their lateral geniculate cell inputs.

Visual input is processed neurally in order to provide an organized, useful representation of the environment. To understand the more complex processing later in the system, we begin with the retina. A visual receptor is able not only to stimulate its own bipolar(s) but also to inhibit activity in neighboring bipolars. It accomplishes this feat through the cooperation of horizontal cells, which receive input from a number of receptors and synapse with a number of bipolars. Electrical activity can flow in all directions in horizontal cells. The advantage of this arrangement is that borders are enhanced at the expense of redundant input. The process is called lateral inhibition.

Ganglion cells have been divided into two major types. Parvocellular neurons are relatively small cells, located in or near the fovea, that respond differentially to colors. Because they have small receptive fields, they are highly sensitive to details. Magnocellular neurons are larger, are spread evenly across the retina, and respond best to moving stimuli. Because their receptive fields are large, they are not sensitive to small details; they also do not respond differentially to colors. A smaller group of cells, koniocellular neurons, respond weakly to light and are poorly understood. At the lateral geniculate nucleus of the thalamus, most parvocellular ganglion cell axons synapse with parvocellular geniculate neurons, and most magnocellular ganglion cell axons synapse with magnocellular geniculate neurons, although a few have connections with other visual areas of the thalamus. Koniocellular neurons send axons to the lateral geniculate nucleus, other parts of the thalamus, and the superior colliculus.

Most of the input from the lateral geniculate goes to the primary visual cortex (area V1), which in turn projects to secondary visual cortex (area V2). From area V2, information branches out to numerous additional areas. At the cortex, the parvocellular and magnocellular systems split into three pathways. One pathway processes shape information from the parvocellular system. Another processes movement information from the magnocellular system. The third pathway processes brightness input from the magnocellular system and color information from the parvocellular system. Beyond the occipital cortex, shape information is sent to the inferior temporal cortex, which responds preferentially to highly complex shapes such as hands or faces. This path is referred to as the ventral stream, or the "what" pathway. Cells in this area are specialized to recognize objects. Other neurons project to a part of the parietal cortex, referred to as the dorsal stream, or the "where" or "how" pathway. It primarily helps the motor system to find objects and manipulate them.

David Hubel and Torsten Wiesel received the Nobel Prize for their pioneering work on feature detectors in the visual cortex. They distinguished three categories of neurons: simple, complex, and end-stopped, or hypercomplex. Simple cells respond maximally to a bar oriented in a particular direction and in a particular location on the retina. Their receptive fields can be mapped into fixed excitatory and inhibitory areas. Complex cells, on the other hand, have larger receptive fields, respond to correctly oriented bars located anywhere within the field (i.e., they do not have fixed excitatory and inhibitory areas), and respond best to stimuli moving perpendicular to the receptive field axis. End-stopped, or hypercomplex, cells are like complex cells, except for an area of strong inhibition at one end of the field. Cortical cells with similar properties are grouped in columns perpendicular to the surface.

It has been suggested that neurons in areas V1 are feature detectors. However, although each neuron has a preferred stimulus, it will respond to other similar stimuli. Therefore, the response of any cell must be compared with responses of many other cells. Furthermore, many cells in V1 respond best to sine wave gratings; however, it is obvious that we do not perceive the world as an assembly of sine waves. Therefore, the role of V1 in visual perception is probably to provide preliminary analyses for other areas that actually identify objects.

After V1, receptive fields become even larger and more specialized. Some cells in V2 respond best to lines, edges, and sine wave gratings; however, others prefer circles, right angles, or other complex patterns. In V4 some cells respond best to a slanted line in a three-dimensional space. Additional processing of shape information is accomplished by the inferior temporal cortex (in the ventral stream, or "what" pathway), which responds preferentially to highly complex shapes such as hands or faces. Cells in this area ignore changes in location, size, and perspective; they may contribute to our capacity for shape constancy. Damage to the pattern pathway results in visual agnosia, the inability to recognize visual objects. Some people have difficulty identifying almost all objects; others experience agnosia for only one or a few classes of stimuli. An area in the inferior temporal lobe (the fusiform gyrus) and part of the prefrontal cortex are activated during recognition of faces and, to a lesser degree, other complex figures.

Area V4, or a nearby area, is especially important for color constancy. Animals with damage to this area retain some color vision, but lose the ability to recognize the color of an object across lighting conditions. Area V4 receives input from the "blobs" of area V1, which in turn receive input from parvocellular color processing cells and magnocellular brightness cells. Area V4 also contributes to visual attention.

Some cells in the magnocellular system are specialized for depth perception. They are sensitive to the amount of discrepancy between the images from the two eyes. Another branch of the magnocellular system detects motion. It projects to area V5 (middle temporal cortex, or MT) and an adjacent area (medial superior temporal cortex, MST). Neurons in these areas respond preferentially to different speeds and directions of movement, without analyzing the object that is moving. Many cells in MT respond best to moving borders of single objects, while cells in the dorsal part of MST prefer expanding, contracting, or rotating large scenes. These two types of cells send their output to the ventral part of MST, which allows us to perceive the motion of an object against a stationary field. Damage to MT can result in motion blindness.

The shifting of visual attention from one object to another is correlated with increased activity in parts of the frontal and parietal lobes. As a result, neural activity in visual cortex is altered, so that areas most relevant to the focused stimulus show increased activity. Much of the processing of visual information is unconscious. Furthermore, there appears to be no single area of the brain that puts together all the information about a given object. Perhaps simultaneous synchronized activity in the various areas is sufficient to bind the multiple aspects of an object into a unified perception.

Cells in the mammalian visual cortex are endowed at the individual's birth with certain adultlike characteristics. However, normal sensory experience is necessary to develop these characteristics fully and to prevent them from degenerating. If only one eye is deprived of vision during an early sensitive period, the brain becomes unresponsive to that eye. Input from the active eye displaces the early connections made by the inactive eye. It is likely that axons from the active eye compete successfully for neurotrophins provided by the postsynaptic cells. If both eyes are kept shut, cortical cells remain at least somewhat responsive to both eyes, though their responses are sluggish. Visual experience after the sensitive, or critical, period does not restore responsiveness to the previously inactive eye, unless the previously active eye is covered for a prolonged time. Other aspects of vision that require early experience for proper development are stereoscopic depth perception, ability to see lines of a given direction, and motion perception. If there is a total lack of visual stimulation throughout the sensitive period, the cortical areas that would have analyzed visual stimuli may become responsive to auditory or touch stimuli.

## LEARNING OBJECTIVES

### Module 6.1  Visual Coding and the Retinal Receptors
1.  Be able to describe the parts of the eye and its connections to the brain.
2.  Understand the process by which three types of cones, and the neurons they connect with, can produce a rich spectrum of perceived color.
3.  Understand the trade-off between acuity for detail and sensitivity to dim light.

### Module 6.2  The Neural Basis of Visual Perception
1.  Understand the concept of receptive fields and how they change from the retina to the various areas of the visual cortex.
2.  Understand how the parvocellular and magnocellular pathways branch into three pathways in the cerebral cortex and what each of those pathways analyzes.
3.  Know the contributions of areas V1, V2, V4, and inferior temporal cortex to shape perception.
4.  Be able to describe the brain areas that process color and motion.

## Module 6.3  Development of the Visual System
1.  Be able to describe the effects of early experiences and of visual deprivation of the development of the visual system.


## KEY TERMS AND CONCEPTS

### Module 6.1  Visual Coding and the Retinal Receptors
1.  General principles of perception
    From neuronal activity to perception
        Receptor potential: A local depolarization or hyperpolarization of a receptor membrane
        Coding does not duplicate shape of object in brain
    Law of specific nerve energies: Activity by a given nerve always sends same kind of information to brain
    Reorganization of auditory cortex by visual input in immature ferrets


2.  The eye and its connections to the brain
    The route within the retina
        Receptors → bipolar cells → ganglion cells
        Amacrine cells
        Blind spot
        Optic nerve
    Fovea and periphery of the retina
        Macula
        Fovea (pit): Center of macula
            Blood vessels and ganglion cell axons nearly absent
            Midget ganglion cells: Input from single cone
            Good acuity: Sensitivity to detail
            Poor sensitivity to dim light
        Periphery
            More receptors converge on bipolar and ganglion cells
                Better sensitivity to dim light
                Poorer acuity
        Birds: Two foveas per eye


3.  Visual receptors: Rods and cones
    Rods
        Most abundant in periphery
        Responsive to faint light, bleached out by bright light
    Cones
        Most abundant in and around fovea
        Essential for color vision, less active in dim light
    Photopigments
        11-cis-retinal
        Opsins
        Conversion of 11-cis-retinal to all-trans-retinal releases energy


4.  Color vision
    Dependent on patterns of responses by different neurons

The trichromatic theory (Young-Helmholtz)
> Psychophysical color matching
> More long- and medium-wavelength than short-wavelength cones
> Random distribution of cones in central area of retina

The opponent-process theory (Hering)
> Negative color afterimage
> Color opponent

The retinex theory
> Color constancy
> Edwin Land

Color vision deficiency
> Most common form: Difficulty distinguishing red from green
>> Red and green cones make same photopigment
>> Sex linked (gene on X chromosome)

## Module 6.2  The Neural Basis of Visual Perception

1.  An overview of the mammalian visual system
> Retina
>> Receptors (rods and cones)
>> Horizontal cells
>> Bipolar cells
>> Amacrine cells
>> Ganglion cells
>>> Axons form optic nerve
>>> Optic chiasm
> Lateral geniculate nucleus of the thalamus
> Superior colliculus
> Hypothalamus
> Cerebral cortex: many visual areas with distinct functions
>> Axons from cortex back to thalamus

2.  Mechanisms of processing in the visual system
> Receptive fields
>> That part of visual field to which a given neuron responds
>> Receptive field of ganglion cell: Composite of receptive fields of its inputs
> Lateral inhibition
>> Horizontal cells (local cells)
>> Bipolar cells

3.  Concurrent pathways in the visual system
> In the retina and lateral geniculate
>> Parvocellular
>>> Small cell bodies
>>> Small receptive fields
>>> Located in or near fovea
>>> Good acuity and color discrimination
>> Magnocellular
>>> Larger cell bodies
>>>> Larger receptive fields
>>>> Even distribution

Best response to moving stimuli

No color discrimination

Koniocellular: least responsive, least understood

Project to several areas of thalamus and superior colliculus

Lateral geniculate

Parvocellular geniculate cells: Input from parvocellular ganglion cells

Magnocellular geniculate cells: Input from magnocellular ganglion cells

Some input from koniocellular cells

In the cerebral cortex

Primary visual cortex, striate cortex (V1)

Secondary visual cortex (V2)

30-40 brain areas receiving visual input in monkeys

Three pathways

Mostly parvocellular: Details of shape

Mostly magnocellular

Ventral branch: Movement

Dorsal branch: Integrating vision with action

Mixed parvocellular and magnocellular: Brightness and color

Some sensitivity to shape

Beyond occipital cortex

Ventral stream ("what" pathway): Temporal cortex

Input from shape, movement, and brightness/color pathways

Dorsal stream ("where" or "how" pathway): Parietal cortex

Coordinates with motor system

4.  The cerebral cortex: The shape pathway

Methods 6.1: Microelectrode recordings

Electrode types

Thin metal wire, insulated except for tip

Narrow glass tube, filled with salt solution and a metal wire

Hubel and Wiesel's cell types in the primary visual cortex

Bar- or edge-shaped receptive fields

Simple cells (V1)

Fixed excitatory and inhibitory zones in receptive fields

Complex cells (V1 and V2)

Larger receptive fields

Cannot be mapped into excitatory and inhibitory zones

Response to moving bar of light

Input from simple cells

End-stopped or hypercomplex cells

Strong inhibitory area at one end of bar-shaped receptive field

Largest receptive field

The columnar organization of the visual cortex

Columns perpendicular to surface

Similar response properties within a column

Are visual cortex cells feature detectors?

Prolonged exposure: Decreased sensitivity to feature

Ambiguity of response of a single cell

Spatial frequencies, sine-wave gratings

Shape analysis beyond area V1

Area V2
   Lines, bars, sine wave gratings
   Circles, right angles, other complex patterns
Area V4
   Slant of line in three-dimensional space
Inferior temporal cortex
   Huge receptive fields, always include fovea
   Shape constancy
Disorders of object recognition
   Visual agnosia
   Prosopagnosia
   Fusiform gyrus in inferior temporal cortex
   Part of prefrontal cortex
   Some specialization and some overlap of function
Methods 6.2: fMRI scans (functional magnetic resonance imaging)
   Hemoglobin: different response in magnetic field after releasing oxygen
   Good spatial and temporal resolution
   No radiation hazard

5. The cerebral cortex: The color, motion, and depth pathways
   Structures important for color perception
      Area V1 "blobs"
         Input from parvocellular (color) and magnocellular (brightness) pathways
         Output to V2, V4, and posterior inferior temporal cortex
      Area V4
         Color constancy
         Visual attention
      Stereoscopic depth perception
         Magnocellular pathway
   Structures important for motion perception
      Area V5 (middle temporal cortex, MT)
         Cells respond best to moving borders
      Medial superior temporal cortex (MST)
         Cells in dorsal MST: best response to expansion, contraction, or rotation of large scene
         Cells in ventral MST: best response to movement of an object relative to its
            background
      Input to both MT and MST
         Most from magnocellular path (overall patterns)
         Some from parvocelular path (disparity between left and right eyes)
      Area near MT: Biological motion
   Suppressed vision during eye movements
      Suppression of visual cortex activity
   Motion blindness

6. Visual attention
      Feedback from other areas to enhance responsiveness of V1 to specific stimulus
      Similar facilitation of response to specific color or motion

7. The binding problem revisited: Visual consciousness
   Synchronized activity in left and right hemispheres

Blindsight
    Superior colliculus
    Islands of healthy tissue in otherwise damaged cortex

8.  In closing: Coordinating separate visual pathways
    Simultaneous processing of different aspects by different brain areas

## Module 6.3  Development of the Visual System

1.  Infant vision
    More time looking at patterns
    Difficulty shifting attention

2.  Effects of experience on visual development
    Effects of early lack of stimulation of one eye
        Binocular input to cortex, normally
        Blindness in deprived eye
    Effects of early lack of stimulation of both eyes
        Cortical cells
            Sluggish response to both eyes
            No sharp receptive fields
        Difficulty identifying objects visually
        Sensitive, or critical, period
            Depends on availability of GABA
    Restoration of response after early deprivation of vision
        Lazy eye, or amblyopia
    Uncorrelated stimulation in both eyes
        Stereoscopic depth perception
        Retinal disparity
        Strabismus
        Synchronous messages
        Nerve growth factor (NGF) and other neurotrophins, including NT-4
    Effects of early exposure to a limited array of patterns
        Astigmatism
    Lack of seeing objects in motion
        Stroboscopic illumination
        Motion blindness
    Effects of blindness on the cortex
        Kittens: visual part of parietal lobe became responsive to sound or touch
        Humans: parts of visual cortex became responsive to sound or touch

3.  In closing: The nature and nurture of vision
    Some visual abilities at birth
    Require experience to maintain and refine them

**Module 6.1  Visual Coding and the Retinal Receptors**
1.  *General principles of perception*
    a.  What is a receptor potential?

    b.  State the law of specific nerve energies.  Who formulated it?

    c.  Describe the results of the experiment in which one optic nerve of an immature ferret was attached to the auditory cortex.

2.  *The eye and its connections to the brain*
    a.  What is the fovea?  How did it get its name?

    b.  How have many bird species solved the problem of getting detailed information from two different directions?

c.  Trace the path of visual information from a receptor to the optic nerve.  What is the blind spot?

3.  *Visual receptors:  Rods and cones*
    a.  Compare foveal and peripheral vision with regard to acuity, sensitivity to dim light, and color vision.

    b.  What is the specific role of light in the initiation of a response in a receptor?  What is a photopigment?

    c.  What is the relationship of 11-cis-retinal to all-trans-retinal?  What is an opsin?

    d.  What kind of electrical response is produced in the receptor, and how does this affect the bipolars with which it synapses?

4. *Color vision*
   a. Why does the presence of cones in the retina of a given species not guarantee color vision? Why does color vision necessarily depend on the pattern of responses of a number of different neurons?

   b. How did Young and Helmholtz propose to account for color vision? On what kind of data was their theory based?

   c. What kind of theory did Hering propose? What observations supported his theory?

   d. What is the current relationship between the three-receptor and the opponent-process theories?

   e. What visual ability does the retinex theory explain?

f.   What is the genetic basis for the most common form of color vision deficiency?  Why do more males than females have this form of color deficiency?

## Module 6.2  The Neural Basis of Visual Perception
1.  *An overview of the mammalian visual system*
   a.   Draw a diagram showing the relationships among the rods and cones, the bipolar and horizontal cells, and the ganglion and amacrine cells.

   b.   Axons of which kind of cell form the optic nerve?  What is the name of the site where the right and left optic nerves meet?  What percentage of axons cross to the opposite side of the brain in humans?  In species with eyes far to the sides of their heads?

   c.   Where do most axons in the optic nerve synapse?  Where do some other optic nerve axons synapse?

   d.   What is the destination of axons from the lateral geniculate nucleus?

2. *Mechanisms of processing in the visual system*
   a. What is the definition of the receptive field of a neuron in the visual system?

   b. What is lateral inhibition? How does it enhance contrast?

   c. How is lateral inhibition accomplished in the vertebrate retina?

   d. If several bipolar cells provide input to a certain ganglion cell, what can be said about the location of their receptive fields relative to that of the ganglion cell?

3. *Concurrent pathways in the visual system*
   a. Describe the characteristics of parvocellular ganglion cells.

   b. How do they differ from magnocellular ganglion cells?

c.   What happens to the parvocellular and magnocellular pathways in the cortex?  What type of information does each of the three main concurrent visual pathways process?

d.   In what cortical area does the ventral stream of visual input end?  What is its specialty?

e.   In what cortical area does the dorsal stream of visual input end?  What is its specialty?

4.   *The cerebral cortex:  The shape pathway*
   a.   For what accomplishment did David Hubel and Torsten Wiesel share the Nobel Prize?

   b.   Describe the receptive fields of simple cells.

   c.   What is the major difference between responses of simple and complex visual cortical cells?

d.   Describe the receptive field of an end-stopped, or hypercomplex, cell?

e.   What can be said about the receptive fields of neurons in a column in the visual cortex?

f.   What is a feature detector?

g.   What evidence suggests that neurons in area V1 are feature detectors?

h.   What are the problems with that interpretation?

i.   What is the evidence for spatial frequency detectors?  What is the problem with the view that neurons in V1 are primarily spatial frequency detectors?

j.   Which areas, beyond V1, are important for shape analysis?  What are their major contributions?

k.   Describe the symptoms of visual agnosia.  What is prosopagnosia?

l.   Which area in the inferior temporal lobe increases its activity when people with intact brains recognize faces?

5.  *The cerebral cortex: The color, motion, and depth pathways*
    a.   What are the sources of input to the "blobs" of area V1?  Where do the "blobs" send their output?

    b.   What appears to be the special function of area V4?

    c.   What might the magnocellular pathway, which does not analyze color information directly, contribute to color constancy?

d.  To what other function does area V4 contribute?




e.  Cells of which pathway are specialized for stereoscopic depth perception?  To what aspect of the visual stimulus are they highly sensitive?




f.  Which two areas of the cortex are specialized for motion perception?  How "picky" are cells in these areas to the specific characteristics of the stimulus that is moving?




g.  Describe the response characteristics of some cells in area MT.




h.  Describe the preferred stimuli for many cells in the dorsal part of area MST.




i.  What is the role of cells in the ventral part of MST?

j.  Why don't we see a blur when we move our eyes?

k.  Describe the symptoms of motion blindness. Damage to what area might cause motion blindness?

l.  What cortical areas may be important for shifting visual attention?  How does activity in the visual cortex change when attention is shifted?

m.  What is blindsight?  What are two potential explanations for it?

## Module 6.3  Development of the Visual System
1.  *Infant vision*
    a.  What is the evidence that newborn infants can perceive complex stimuli?

    b.  How easy is it for infants to shift their attention to other visual stimuli?

131

2. *Effects of experience on visual development*
   a.   What is the effect of depriving only one eye of pattern vision during the critical period?




   b.   What happens if both eyes are kept shut early in life?




   c.   What is a sensitive or critical period?  What neurotransmitter is important for establishing organization during the critical period?




   d.   For what human condition does deprivation of visual experience in one eye have relevance? What is the usual treatment for this condition?  Why is it important to begin treatment as early as possible?




   e.   Define retinal disparity.  How does the brain use this information to produce stereoscopic depth perception?

f.   What is strabismus? Does surgical correction in adulthood improve depth perception in people with this disorder?

g.   What chemicals may normally promote survival of synapses from the most active eye?

h.   What is the effect of supplying excess neurotrophins during the time when one eye is closed?

i.   What happens to the response characteristics of visual cortical cells in a kitten exposed to only horizontal lines early in life?

j.   What is astigmatism? What happens if a child has severe, uncorrected astigmatism during the first few years of life?

k.   What was the effect of rearing kittens in an environment illuminated only by a strobe light?

1.  What changes occur in the cortex of kittens or people who have been blind since birth?

## TRUE/FALSE QUESTIONS

_____ 1.  In order to perceive the shape of an object, the pattern of activity in the cortex must duplicate that shape in the brain.

_____ 2.  The law of specific nerve energies states that the activity of a given nerve always sends the same kind of information to the brain.

_____ 3.  The order of information transmission in the retina is receptor → ganglion cell → bipolar cell → amacrine cell.

_____ 4.  The fovea is the site at which ganglion cell axons exit the retina.

_____ 5.  The reason that peripheral vision has relatively low acuity, but good sensitivity to dim light, is that many receptors send input to each bipolar, and many bipolars synapse with each ganglion cell.

_____ 6.  Conversion of all-trans-retinol to 11-cis-retinal releases energy that controls the receptor's activity.

_____ 7.  The trichromatic theory was proposed by Young and Helmholst on the basis of psychophysical color matching experiments.

_____ 8.  A likely physiological basis for the opponent-process theory is the depolarization of bipolar cells by some wavelengths and their hyperpolarization by other wavelengths.

_____ 9.  The retinex theory was proposed by Herring to explain negative color afterimages.

_____ 10. The receptive field of a ganglion cell is composed of the receptive fields of the cells that send input to it.

_____ 11. Lateral inhibition is produced by horizontal cells, which inhibit nearby bipolar cells.

_____ 12. Parvocellular neurons are large cells that are especially important for motion detection.

_____ 13. The parvocellular and magnocellular pathways remain completely separate throughout the visual cortex.

_____ 14. The ventral stream ("what") pathway terminates in the temporal cortex.

_____15. The dorsal stream ("where" or "how") pathway also terminates in the temporal lobe, but more dorsally than the ventral stream.

_____16. Hubel and Wiesel received the Nobel Prize for discovering that cells in the primary visual cortex respond preferentially to bars or edges, rather than spots of light.

_____17. Complex cells have receptive fields that can be mapped into excitatory and inhibitory areas, but those areas form complex shapes, such as triangles, squares, or faces.

_____18. Columns in the visual cortex are spread across the surface of the cortex and have response characteristics that vary systematically across the column.

_____19. Sine wave gratings of specific spatial frequencies elicit even greater responses from cells in primary visual cortex than do bars and edges; however, we don't perceive the world as a series of gratings, suggesting that these neurons provide an early stage of analysis.

_____20. Area V1 "blobs" receive input from both parvocellular (color) and magnocellular (brightness) pathways.

_____21. Cells in the inferior temporal cortex respond primarily to movement, regardless of what is moving.

_____22. Area V4 is especially important for color constancy and visual attention.

_____23. Cells in the MT and MST respond primarily to faces.

_____24. Early lack of stimulation of one eye usually is not problematic, because stimulation at any later time can release neurotrophins that cause the visual cortex to be responsive to the previously deprived eye.

## FILL IN THE BLANKS

1. The _____ _____ is a local depolarization or hyperpolarization of a receptor membrane.

2. The _____ cells receive input from the retinal receptors and send input to the _____ cells.

3. The _____ is an area in the center of the macula that provides the most acute vision, as a result of tight packing of receptors and near absence of _____ _____ and _____ _____ _____ in front of it.

4. Compared to the fovea, the periphery has _____ sensitivity to dim light, both because rods are _____ sensitive than cones and because ganglion cells there have _____ receptive fields than in the fovea.

5. _____ - _____ - retinal is converted to _____ - _____ - retinal by light; this releases energy that leads to a receptor potential.

6. Helmholtz proposed the _____ theory, based on psychophysical experiments.

7. Hering proposed the _____ - _____ theory, based on negative color afterimages.

8. Land proposed the _____ theory to account for color constancy.

9. Axons of _____ cells form the optic nerve, which exits the retina at the _____ _____.

10. The _____ _____ _____ receives input from ganglion cell axons and sends its output to the primary visual cortex.

11. Lateral inhibition is produced by _____ cells; it is useful for _____ contrast.

12. _____ ganglion cells in the retina have small cell bodies and small receptive fields and are located in or near the fovea.

13. _____ ganglion cells have larger cell bodies and larger receptive fields and are located more evenly across the retina.

14. In the cortex the parvocellular and magnocellular pathways split into three pathways: a mostly parvocellular pathway provides _____ information, a mostly magnocellular pathway has a ventral branch that is sensitive to _____ and a dorsal branch that integrates vision with _____, and a mixed

parvocellular and magnocellular pathway that is specialized for

_____ and _____ .

15. The brain area that confers shape constancy is the _____

_____ cortex.

16. The brain area that confers color constancy is area _____ .

17. The area of the cortex that responds best to moving borders and may record the movement of

single objects is _____ _____ cortex ( ___ ___ ).

18. The cortical area that responds best to expansion, contraction, or rotation of large scenes is

_____ _____ _____ cortex.

19. Blindsight may be mediated by the _____ _____ or

by islands of healthy tissue in otherwise damaged cortex.

20. The neurotransmitter that is important for establishing neural connections during the early

critical period is _____ .

21. A human condition similar to that of animals that were deprived of vision in one eye for several

days is _____ .

22. Animals that were deprived of vision in one eye during the early critical period, but had extra

_____ _____ supplied to the brain, the visual system

retained responsiveness to both eyes.

23. Animals raised with uncorrelated stimulation of the two eyes lacked

_____ _____ perception.

24. Animals that were raised with only stroboscopic lighting had _____

blindness.

## MATCHING ITEMS

_____ 1. Horizontal cells

_____ 2. Blind spot

_____ 3. Ganglion cells

_____ 4. Fovea

_____ 5. Rods

_____ 6. Cones

_____ 7. Parvocellular neurons

_____ 8. Magnocellular neurons

_____ 9. Columns of cortex

_____ 10. Simple cells

_____ 11. Hypercomplex cells

_____ 12. Area MST

_____ 13. Area MT

_____ 14. Area V4

_____ 15. Inferior temporal lobe

_____ 16. Superior colliculus

a. Small cells, small receptive fields → detailed vision

b. Detects movement of simple objects

c. Detects expansion, contraction, or rotation of field

d. Possible mediator of blindsight

e. Color constancy

f. Cells with similar responses, perpendicular to surface

g. Site where ganglion cells exit the retina

h. Cells in V1 with fixed excitatory & inhibitory areas

i. Lateral inhibition

j. Large receptive field w/ inhibitory area at 1 end

k. Receptors more sensitive to dim light

l. Shape constancy

m. Cells that send axons to lateral geniculate nucleus

n. Receptors with 3 different pigments → color vision

o. "pit" in retina, all cones, most acute vision

p. Large cells, large receptive fields, detect movement

## MULTIPLE-CHOICE QUESTIONS

1. The law of specific nerve energies
   a. was proposed by Herring.
   b. states that any activity of a given nerve always conveys the same kind of information to the brain.
   c. states that the information carried by a given nerve changes, depending on the kind of stimulus that gave rise to the nerve's activity.
   d. is no longer thought to be true, and is now only of historical interest.

2. The fovea
   a. is completely blind because axons from ganglion cells exit from the retina there.
   b. covers approximately half the retina.
   c. contains no rods and is bypassed by most blood vessels and axons of distant ganglion cells.
   d. is color blind because it contains no cones but has good sensitivity to dim light.

3. Which of the following is true?
   a. The fovea is more sensitive to dim light than is the periphery.
   b. The fovea has more detailed vision because few receptors synapse with each bipolar.
   c. Cones mediate more detailed vision because of their shape.
   d. Cones are situated peripherally in the retina, rods more centrally, though there is overlap.

4. A photopigment molecule absorbs a photon of light whose energy converts
   a. all-trans-retinal to 11-cis-retinal.
   b. opsin to all-trans-retinal.
   c. 11-cis-retinal to all-trans-retinal.
   d. 11-cis-retinal to opsin.

5. The opponent-process theory
   a. is now thought to describe color processing by neurons after the receptor level, whereas the trichromatic theory describes responses of three kinds of cones.
   b. is now thought to describe color processing at the receptor level, whereas the trichromatic theory describes processing at higher levels.
   c. states that each receptor is sensitive only to a narrow band of wavelengths of light and that wavelength bands of different receptor groups do not overlap.
   d. is true only for rods, not cones.

6. The most common form of color vision deficiency
   a. is more common in women than in men.
   b. has been well known since the earliest civilizations.
   c. is characterized by difficulty distinguishing blue from yellow.
   d. is characterized by difficulty distinguishing red from green.

7. Which of the following best describes the main route of visual information in the retina?
   a. receptor→ganglion cell→bipolar cell
   b. receptor→bipolar cell→ganglion cell
   c. receptor→ganglion cell→amacrine cell
   d. receptor→horizontal cell→amacrine cell

8. Which of the following is true concerning receptive fields?
   a. They are always defined as an area surrounding "their" neuron; the receptive field for a simple cortical cell is itself in the cortex.
   b. The presence of both excitatory and inhibitory areas in the same receptive field is maladaptive and is a holdover from an earlier, inefficient way of processing information.
   c. Receptive fields of simple cortical cells are circular.
   d. For mammalian ganglion cells, they are generally doughnut-shaped, with the center being either excitatory or inhibitory and the surround being the opposite.

9. Lateral inhibition
   a. increases sensitivity to dim light.
   b. ordinarily decreases contrast at borders.
   c. ordinarily heightens contrast at borders.
   d. interferes with processing of color information.

10. Horizontal cells
    a. send axons out of the retina through the blind spot.
    b. send graded inhibitory responses to neighboring bipolar cells.
    c. are located behind the receptors so that they are out of the way of incoming light.
    d. all of the above.

11. Parvocellular ganglion cells
    a. are highly sensitive to both detail and color.
    b. are located primarily in the periphery of the retina.
    c. are among the largest ganglion cells in the retina.
    d. respond only weakly to visual stimuli.

12. The parvocellular and magnocellular systems
    a. merge in area V1 and remain one system for subsequent analysis.
    b. remain as two systems throughout visual processing.
    c. divide into three systems, with much of the parvocellular system continuing to analyze details of shape, most of the magnocellular system analyzing movement, and the third system containing parvocellular cells that analyze color and magnocellular cells that analyze brightness.
    d. divide into many concurrent pathways, each analyzing a different color, direction of movement, or shape, but then converge in one master area, where all of these aspects are put together into a unified perception.

13. Simple cells in the visual cortex
    a. respond maximally to bars of light oriented in one direction but not to bars of light oriented in another direction.
    b. respond to "correctly" oriented bars of light only when the bars are in the "correct" part of the retina.
    c. were first described by Hubel and Wiesel.
    d. all of the above.

14. Simple and complex cells differ in that
    a. the receptive field of a simple cell is larger than that of a complex cell.
    b. the receptive field of a complex cell cannot be mapped into fixed excitatory and inhibitory zones, but that of a simple cell can.
    c. a simple cell does not respond at all to small spots of light, whereas complex cells respond best to small spots of light.
    d. all of the above.

15. Simple and complex cells are similar in that
    a. most of them receive at least some input from both eyes.
    b. most respond maximally to bars of light oriented in a particular direction.
    c. both may be found in the striate cortex.
    d. all of the above.

16. End-stopped, or hypercomplex, cells
    a. have extremely small receptive fields.
    b. are similar to complex cells, except for an inhibitory area at one end of the receptive field.
    c. respond only to very complex stimuli, such as faces.
    d. respond best to small spots of light.

17. Neurons along the track of an electrode inserted perpendicular to the surface of visual cortex
    a. have response characteristics that vary widely, but systematically, from the top to the bottom.
    b. have a random distribution of response characteristics.
    c. have certain response characteristics in common.
    d. cannot have their responses recorded, since the electrode damages them severely.

18. The hypothesis that neurons in the visual cortex are feature detectors
    a. is supported by the observation that prolonged exposure to a given feature seems to fatigue the relevant detectors.
    b. is supported by the finding that each cell in the primary visual cortex responds only to one very precise stimulus, so its response is not at all ambiguous.
    c. is disproved by the observation that visual cortical cells respond only to sine-wave gratings, and not at all to bars and edges.
    d. is now known to be true for cells in area V1, but not for any other visual processing area.

19. The inferior temporal cortex
    a. has receptive fields that always include the fovea.
    b. is concerned with advanced pattern analysis and complex shapes.
    c. may provide our sense of shape constancy.
    d. all of the above.

20. A person with visual agnosia
    a. may have lost recognition only for a few kinds of stimuli, such as faces, as in prosopagnosia.
    b. has lost the ability to read.
    c. is blind.
    d. has had damage limited to the primary visual cortex (area V1).

21. Area V4
    a. seems to be especially important for face recognition.
    b. seems to be especially important for color constancy.
    c. seems to be especially important for shape constancy.
    d. receives input only from the parvocellular system.

22. Occipital area V5 (MT, middle-temporal cortex) analyzes
    a. complex shapes.
    b. colors.
    c. speed and direction of movement.
    d. stereoscopic depth cues.

23. Cells in the dorsal part of MST that respond to expansion, contraction, or rotation of a large visual scene
    a. probably help to record the movement of the head with respect to the world.
    b. probably help to keep track of a single object.
    c. are very particular about the specific objects in their receptive field.
    d. receive input primarily from the parvocellular system.

24. Cells in the ventral part of MST
    a. receive input from cells in MT that respond best to moving borders.
    b. receive input from cells in dorsal MST that respond best to expansion, contraction, or rotation of a large visual scene.
    c. respond whenever an object moves relative to its background.
    d. all of the above.

25. Which of the following is true?
    a. Shifting visual attention is associated with activity in the frontal and parietal cortex.
    b. Recognition of complex objects, especially faces, is associated with activity in the fusiform gyrus of the inferior temporal cortex.
    c. The dorsal stream, ending in the parietal cortex, helps the motor system find objects, move toward them and grasp them.
    d. All of the above are true.

26. Human infants
    a. are unable to see patterns for at least several weeks.
    b. spend more time looking at patternless displays that at faces.
    c. have trouble shifting their attention before about 6 months of age.
    d. all of the above.

27. If a kitten's eyelid is sutured shut for the first 6 weeks of life, and the sutures are then removed, the kitten
    a. is totally blind in the inactive eye only if the other eye had normal visual input.
    b. is totally blind in the inactive eye regardless of the other eye's visual experience.
    c. is able to see horizontal and vertical lines, but not diagonal lines or curves.
    d. sees normally out of the eye, since all of its connections were formed before birth.

28. Children with lazy eye (amblyopia)
    a. should have the active eye covered continuously until adulthood.
    b. should have the active eye covered as early as possible, but only until the lazy eye becomes functional.
    c. should have the active eye covered only after they have reached normal adult size, in order to avoid reorganization of connections.
    d. should not be treated at all, since they will eventually outgrow the condition.

29. Retinal disparity
    a. is an abnormal condition that should be treated as early as possible.
    b. is a cue for depth perception only in people with strabismus.
    c. can be used as a cue for depth perception regardless of the organism's early experience.
    d. can normally be used for stereoscopic depth perception because cortical cells respond differentially to the degree of retinal disparity.

30. Neurotrophin NT-4, if injected in large amounts into the brains of infant rats while one eye was surgically closed,
    a. decreased responsiveness to the closed eye, so that even extensive visual experience while the previously active eye was covered could not restore vision to the previously closed eye.
    b. cortical cells that received the NT-4 remained responsive to both eyes.
    c. cortical cells that received the NT-4 became unresponsive to either eye.
    d. resulted in astigmatism in the previously closed eye.

31. Experiments on abnormal sensory environments have shown that
    a.  if kittens are reared in an environment in which they see only horizontal lines, at maturity all cells are completely normal, because receptive field characteristics are fully determined at birth.
    b.  if kittens are reared with only horizontal lines, they will become so habituated to that stimulus that they soon lose their ability to see horizontal lines.
    c.  if kittens are reared with only horizontal lines, they will lose the ability to see vertical lines.
    d.  if the environment is illuminated only with a strobe light during development, kittens lose their ability to see either horizontal or vertical lines.

32. Astigmatism
    a.  is caused by asymmetric curvature of the eyes and results in blurring of vision for lines in one direction.
    b.  is caused by strabismus and results in color blindness.
    c.  is caused by amblyopia and results in loss of binocular cells in the cortex.
    d.  is caused by too much retinal disparity and results in loss of depth perception.

33. Blindness from birth
    a.  in kittens, resulted in supersensitivity to visual stimuli when vision was restored in adulthood.
    b.  in people, resulted in increased responsiveness of visual cortex to auditory and touch stimuli.
    c.  in all mammalian species, results in inability to see colors when vision is restored in adulthood, but otherwise vision is normal.
    d.  can be restored in adulthood by infusions of neurotrophins.

## Answers to True/False Questions

| | | | |
|---|---|---|---|
| 1.  F | 7.  T | 13. F | 19. T |
| 2.  T | 8.  T | 14. T | 20. T |
| 3.  F | 9.  T | 15. T | 21. F |
| 4.  F | 10. T | 16. T | 22. T |
| 5.  T | 11. T | 17. F | 23. F |
| 6.  F | 12. F | 18. F | 24. F |

## Answers to Fill-in-the-Blanks Questions

| | |
|---|---|
| 1.  receptor potential | 13. Magnocellular |
| 2.  bipolar, ganglion | 14. shape, movement, action, brightness, color |
| 3.  fovea, blood vessels, ganglion cell axons | 15. inferior temporal |
| 4.  greater, more, larger | 16. V4 |
| 5.  11-cis, all-trans | 17. middle temporal, MT, or V5 |
| 6.  trichromatic | 18. medial superior temporal |
| 7.  opponent-process | 19. superior colliculus |
| 8.  retinex | 20. GABA |
| 9.  ganglion, blind spot | 21. amblyopia |
| 10. lateral geniculate nucleus | 22. neurotrophin, NT-4 |
| 11. horizontal, enhancing | 23. stereoscopic depth |
| 12. Parvocellular | 24. motion |

## Answers to Matching Items

| | | | |
|---|---|---|---|
| 1. i | 5. k | 9. f | 13. b |
| 2. g | 6. n | 10. h | 14. e |
| 3. m | 7. a | 11. j | 15. 1 |
| 4. o | 8. p | 12. c | 16. d |

## Answers to Multiple-Choice Questions

| | | | |
|---|---|---|---|
| 1. b | 10. b | 19. d | 28. b |
| 2. c | 11. a | 20. a | 29. d |
| 3. b | 12. c | 21. b | 30. b |
| 4. c | 13. d | 22. c | 31. c |
| 5. a | 14. b | 23. a | 32. a |
| 6. d | 15. d | 24. d | 33. b |
| 7. b | 16. b | 25. c | |
| 8. d | 17. c | 26. c | |
| 9. c | 18. a | 27. a | |

**Please check the Exploring Biological Psychology CD-ROM**

### Helpful Hint

Here is an analogy of the selective absorption of different wavelengths by the three types of cones. Think of three tennis nets with different sized holes. The one with the largest holes will easily "catch" a red foam-rubber ball about the same size as its holes. Larger or smaller balls will tend to either bounce back off the net or to go through it, though if they are hit just right, they may be caught in the net. A net with medium-sized holes will easily catch a yellow tennis ball, and a net with even smaller holes will catch a blue golf ball.

### Diagrams

1. In the diagram below label the parts of the eye.

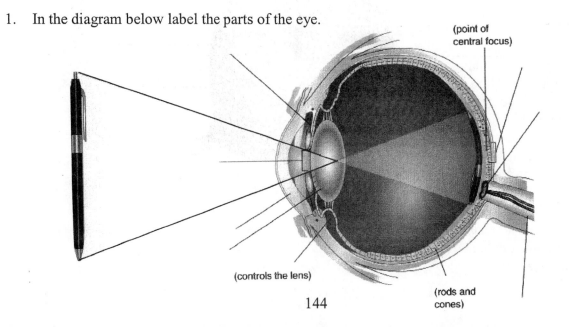

(point of central focus)

(controls the lens)

(rods and cones)

144

2. Label the cells in the following diagram: R for receptors; B for bipolar cells; G for ganglion cells; H for horizontal cells; and A for amacrine cells.

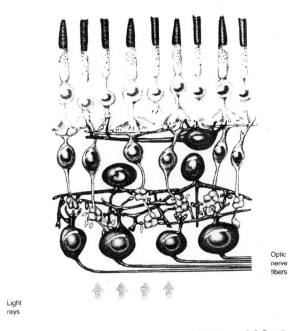

Optic
nerve
fibers

Light
rays

Source: Based on "Organization of the Primate Retina," by J. E. Dowling and B. B. Boycott, Proceedings of the Royal Society of London, B. 1966, 166, p. 80-111. Used by permission of the Royal Society of London and John Dowling.

3. Label the following components of the vision pathways on this horizontal section of the brain: optic nerve, optic chiasm, lateral geniculate nucleus, primary visual cortex, superior colliculus.

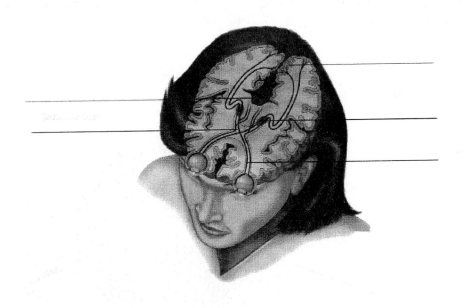

4. Does the following diagram represent the response characteristics of a retinal ganglion cell, a lateral geniculate cell, a "simple" cortical cell, or a "complex" cortical cell?

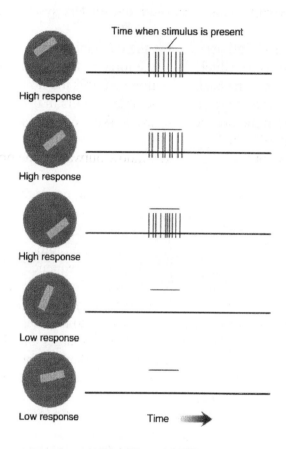

# 7
# THE OTHER SENSORY SYSTEMS AND ATTENTION

## INTRODUCTION

Sensory systems have evolved to provide information most useful for each species. Although humans can perceive a relatively wide range of stimuli, our sensory systems also show certain specializations.

The sense of hearing uses air vibrations to move the tympanic membrane and three middle ear bones (the hammer, anvil, and stirrup), which focus the force of the vibrations so that they can move the heavier fluid inside the cochlea. The basilar membrane forms the floor of a tunnel, the scala media. Receptor cells are embedded in the basilar membrane; hairs in the top of the receptors are in contact with the overlying tectorial membrane. Inward pressure of the stirrup on the oval window increases pressure in scala vestibuli, which presses down on scala media, which in turn bulges downward into scala tympani and pushes the round window outward. The opposite happens when the stirrup moves outward. The movement of the basilar membrane (the floor of scala media) relative to the tectorial membrane produces a shearing action that bends the hair cells, thereby generating a potential.

Pitch perception depends on a combination of three mechanisms. At low frequencies, neurons can fire with each vibration. At medium frequencies, neurons split into volleys, one volley firing with one vibration, another with the next, and so on. At higher frequencies the area of the basilar membrane with greatest displacement is used as a place code. The characteristics of the basilar membrane vary along the length of the cochlea. At the basal end a bony shelf occupies most of the floor of scala media, and the basilar membrane, which attaches to the shelf, is thin and stiff. At the apex, there is almost no bony shelf, and the basilar membrane is larger and floppier, even though the cochlea as a whole is smaller. The size and stiffness of the basilar membrane determine which part of the basilar membrane will respond to various frequencies of sound with the greatest-amplitude traveling wave. High-pitched tones cause maximal displacement near the base, and low-pitched tones cause maximal displacement closer to the apex. There is considerable overlap of pitches coded by frequency of firing and by place.

After passing through several subcortical structures, auditory information reaches the primary auditory cortex in the temporal lobes. Neurons in one area respond selectively to the location of sound, and those in another area respond selectively to tones. Neurons with similar preferred tones cluster together there. Damage to the primary auditory cortex does not impair responses to simple sounds but does impair responses to combinations or sequences of sounds.

There are two categories of hearing impairment. Conductive, or middle ear, deafness results from failure of the middle ear bones to transmit sound waves to the cochlea. It can be caused by diseases, infections, or tumorous growths in the middle ear. Nerve, or inner ear, deafness is caused by damage to the cochlea, the hair cells, or the auditory nerve. Prenatal infections or toxins, inadequate oxygen during birth, diseases, reactions to drugs, and exposure to loud noises are frequent causes of nerve deafness.

Sound localization is accomplished by two methods. The difference in loudness between the two ears is used for high-frequency sounds, while the phase difference for sound waves arriving at the two ears is used for low-frequency sounds. However, for animals with small heads, there is little phase difference in the sound waves reaching the two ears. Therefore, it is difficult for them to localize low-frequency tones. Furthermore, they can use loudness differences only for higher frequencies than humans can. These animals have evolved the ability to perceive sounds that they can localize easily.

Our auditory system may have evolved from the touch receptors of primitive animals. Vestibular sensation, based on the otolith organs and the semicircular canals in the inner ear, contributes to our sense of balance and guidance of our eye movements.

The sense of touch is composed of several modalities, some of which are fairly well correlated with activity in specific receptor types. For example, free nerve endings are involved in sensations of pain, warmth, and cold. Hair-follicle receptors respond to movement of hairs; Meissner's corpuscles and Pacinian corpuscles signal sudden displacement of skin. Merkel's disks produce a prolonged response to steady indentation of the skin, while Ruffini endings respond to skin stretching.

Sensory nerves enter and motor nerves exit the spinal cord through each of 31 openings in the vertebral canal. These nerves innervate overlapping segments of the body (dermatomes). Several well defined pathways ascend from the spinal cord to separate areas of the thalamus, and thence to appropriate areas of somatosensory cortex in the parietal lobe. Thus, the various aspects of somatosensation are at least partially separate, from the receptor level to the cerebral cortex. Bodily sensations are mapped onto four parallel strips, two of which respond mostly to touch and the other two, to deep pressure and movement of joints and muscles. In some patients damage to the somatosensory cortex may result in impairment of body perception.

Pain information is transmitted to the spinal cord by axons that use glutamate and substance P as their transmitters. Mild pain releases only glutamate; stronger pain releases both. Pain sensations can be inhibited by release of the brain's endogenous opiates (endorphins), including leu- and met-enkephalin, and beta-endorphin. According to the gate theory, various kinds of nonpain stimuli can modify pain sensations. Endorphins released in the periaqueductal gray area of the midbrain result in excitation of neurons that block the release of substance P in the spinal cord and brainstem.

Capsaicin, derived from hot peppers, elicits the release of substance P and thereby produces a sensation of pain or heat. However, following application of capsaicin, there is a prolonged decrease in pain sensations. Placebo procedures may decrease the emotional response to painful stimuli by inhibiting a pathway through the hypothalamus, amygdala, and cingulate cortex. Pain may be increased as a result of sensitization in damaged or inflamed tissue. Histamine, nerve growth factor, and other chemicals that promote healing also increase sodium gates in pain receptors and may thereby enhance pain sensitivity. Anti-inflammatory drugs, such as ibuprofen, and the neurotrophin GDNF decrease pain by reducing the release of chemicals from damaged tissue. Morphine administered for serious pain is almost never addictive. It is more effective at blocking thin axons that carry dull post-surgical pain than the larger axons that carry sharp pain. The sensation of itch is poorly understood. It is generated by the release of histamines in the skin that activate a very slow-conducting path in the spinal cord.

Taste and olfactory stimuli activate some receptors better than others; however, vertebrate sensory systems do not have any pure "labeled lines." Instead, the brain analyzes patterns of firing across populations of neurons. Studies of cross-adaptation suggest that we have at least four types of taste receptor: sweet, sour, salty, and bitter. There may also be a receptor for glutamate, termed umami by the Japanese, and additional receptors for bitter and sweet. The mechanisms of activation of some taste receptors have been discovered. Sodium ions activate salty receptors; acids close potassium channels in sour receptors; and sweetness, bitterness, and umami receptors respond to molecules that activate G proteins, which then release a second messenger within the cell. The anterior two-thirds of the tongue sends information via the chorda tympani, a branch of the seventh cranial nerve (facial nerve) to the nucleus of the tractus solitarius in the medulla. The posterior third of the tongue and the throat send input via branches of the ninth and tenth cranial nerves to different parts of the nucleus of the tractus solitarius. From there the information is sent to numerous areas, including the pons, lateral hypothalamus, amygdala, ventral-posterior thalamus, and two areas of the cerebral cortex. There are individual differences in sensitivity to tastes. "Supertasters" have more fungiform papillae near the tip of the tongue. Estradiol increases women's taste sensitivity at mid-cycle and during the early stages of pregnancy.

Olfactory cells have cilia that extend into the mucous lining of the nasal passages. Odorant molecules must diffuse through a mucous fluid in order to reach the receptor sites on the cilia. Humans have several hundred types of olfactory receptor proteins, whereas rats and mice have about 1000 olfactory receptor proteins, which operate on the same principles as some neurotransmitter receptors. When activated by an odorant molecule, the receptor triggers a change in a G protein, which in turn elicits chemical activities within the cell. People with specific anosmias lack one or more of these receptors. Because there are so many types of receptor, olfaction has more of a labeled-line system of coding than does, for example, color vision, which has only three types of cones. However, even in olfaction, each receptor responds to other odorants that are similar to its preferred stimulus. Therefore, a single receptor can provide an approximate classification of an odorant, but related receptors provide more exact information. A population of varied receptors can provide information about complex mixtures of odors. Pheromones are chemicals released by members of a species that affect the behavior of other members of that species. They are detected by the vomeronasal organ (VNO), located near, but separate from the olfactory receptors. Each VNO receptor responds to only one pheromone and is linked to a G-protein. The VNO in humans is vestigial; however, humans do respond to pheromones, perhaps via receptors in the main olfactory mucosa.

Attention is partly automatic ("bottom up") but can also be directed consciously ("top down"). Information may enter the nervous system and influence behavior even with conscious perception. Damage to various areas of the cortex may result in impairment attention to certain kinds of stimuli. Damage to auditory cortex decreases automatic attention to sounds, although people with such damage can consciously direct their attention to sounds. Widespread damage to the right hemisphere, especially the superior temporal gyrus, results in spatial neglect. People with spatial neglect are usually unaware of any stimuli on the right side of their environment. However, there are ways of increasing attention to the neglected side.

Attention-deficit hyperactivity disorder (ADHD) is characterized by attention deficits, hyperactivity, impulsivity, mood swings and other psychological problems. Several tasks can differentiate people with ADHD from other people. There are small differences in the brains of ADHD people and in forms of the dopamine D4 receptor; however, these differences are not consistent. The stimulant drugs methylphenidate (Ritalin) and amphetamine are able to increase attentiveness and improve school performance. They act by increasing the amount of dopamine available to receptors. Some behavioral treatments also improve the ability to attend to and perform tasks. However, neither ADHD nor attention, in general, is well understood.

## LEARNING OBJECTIVES

### Module 7.1  Audition
1. Be able to describe the physical structures of the ear and their contributions to hearing.
2. Understand the mechanisms of pitch perception and sound localization.
3. Know the types of hearing loss and the conditions that can cause them.

### Module 7.2  The Mechanical Senses
1. Understand the roles of the otolith organs and semicircular canals in vestibular sensation.
2. Be able to describe the somatosensory receptors and the stimuli they respond to.
3. Be able to describe the cortical processing of somatosensory information.
4. Understand the roles of the various neurotransmitters in the production and the alleviation of pain and itch sensations.

**Module 7.3 The Chemical Senses**
1. Understand the concepts of the labeled-line and across-fiber pattern principles and how they apply to each of the senses.
2. Understand the mechanisms of the taste receptors and be able to describe the pathways of taste coding in the brain.
3. Describe the operation and numbers of olfactory receptors, and the implications of the numbers of receptors for coding olfactory information.
4. Understand the physical operation of the vomeronasal organ and the types of stimuli that it responds to.

**Module 7.4 Attention**
1. Be able to describe the symptoms and physical causes of sensory neglect.
2. Be able to describe the symptoms, possible brain correlates, and treatments of attention-deficit hyperactivity disorder (ADHD).

**KEY TERMS AND CONCEPTS**

**Module 7.1 Audition**
1. Sound and the ear
   Physical and psychological dimensions of sound
       Amplitude (physical intensity)
           Loudness (perception of intensity)
       Frequency (compressions per second)
           Pitch (perception related to frequency)
   Structures of the ear
       Outer ear
           Pinna
       Middle ear
           Tympanic membrane (eardrum)
               Middle ear bones
                   Hammer (malleus)
                   Anvil (incus)
                   Stirrup (stapes)
       Inner ear
           Oval window
           Cochlea
               Scala vestibuli
               Scala tympani
               Scala media
                   Basilar membrane
                   Hair cells (auditory receptors)
                   Tectorial membrane
           Auditory nerve (part of eighth cranial nerve)

2. Pitch perception
   Frequency theory and place theory
       Action potentials in synchrony with sound
       Volley principle
       Base: thin, stiff basilar membrane

Apex: larger, floppier basilar membrane
Traveling wave
Pitch perception in the cerebral cortex
Primary auditory cortex (temporal lobes)
Major input from opposite ear
Part of auditory cortex responsive to location of sound
Part is tonotopic map
Important for combinations or sequences of sounds
Complex combination of sounds, such as speech

3.  Hearing loss
Conductive deafness (middle-ear deafness)
Certain diseases or infections
Tumorous bone growth in middle ear
Can hear sounds that bypass middle ear, including own voice
Nerve deafness (inner-ear deafness)
May be inherited
Prenatal exposure to rubella, syphilis, or other contagious diseases or to toxins
Inadequate oxygen to brain during birth
Inadequate thyroid activity
Diseases, including multiple sclerosis and meningitis
Childhood reactions to drugs, including aspirin
Repeated exposure to loud noises
Tinnitis: frequent or constant ringing in ears
Similarity to phantom limb

4.  Localization of sounds
Difference in intensity
Sound shadow
High frequencies
Difference in time of arrival
Sudden onset sounds
Useful for any frequency
Phase difference
Low frequencies
Size of head
Small heads—high frequencies
Large heads—low frequencies

5.  In closing: Functions of hearing

**Module 7.2  The Mechanical Senses**
1.  Vestibular sensation
Vestibular organ (adjacent to cochlea)
Otolith organs
Saccule
Utricle
Otoliths: calcium carbonate particles next to hair cells
Semicircular canals (three planes): Filled with jellylike substance, lined with hair cells
Eighth cranial nerve, vestibular component

151

Brain stem and cerebellum

2.   Somatosensation
Somatosensory receptors
    Bare (or free) nerve ending
        Pain, warmth, cold
    Hair-follicle receptors
        Movement of hairs
    Meissner's corpuscles
        Sudden displacement of skin, low frequency vibration
    Pacinian corpuscles
        Sudden displacement of skin, high frequency vibration
    Merkel's disks
        Indentation of skin
    Ruffini endings
        Stretch of skin
    Krause end bulbs
        Uncertain function
    Touch receptors (bare nerve endings, Ruffini endings, Meissner's corpuscles, Pacinian corpuscles):  Opening of sodium channels
    Heat receptors:  Also respond to capsaicin
    Cold receptors:  Also respond to menthol and mint
    Tickle: Poorly understood
        Can't tickle oneself
        Motor areas signal somatosensory areas
Input to the spinal cord and the brain
    31 sets of spinal nerves
    Dermatome
Somatosensory thalamus
Somatosensory cortex
    Parietal lobe
    Four parallel strips
        Two for touch
        Two for deep pressure and joint and muscle movement
    Most input from contralateral side, but some from opposite hemisphere via corpus callosum
    Damage to somatosensory cortex → impaired perception of body

3.   Pain
The neurotransmitters of pain
    Glutamate (mild pain)
    Substance P (strong pain)
    Opioid mechanisms: Inhibit pain
        Candace Pert and Solomon Snyder
        Inhibit effects of substance P
        Met-enkephalin and Leu-enkephalin
        β-endorphin (endogenous morphine)
        Gate theory: Nonpainful stimuli decrease pain
        Endorphins in periaqueductal gray area → medulla
            Both areas → spinal cord → block release of substance P
    Painful heat

Capsaicin (induces release of substance P, stimulates heat receptors)

     Depletes substance P → analgesia

     High doses → damage pain receptors

  Pain and emotion

    Placebo → relief of subjective distress of pain

    Somatosensory cortex → painful sensation

    Hypothalamus, amygdala, and cingulate cortex → emotional aspects

  Sensitization of pain

    Histamine, nerve growth factor → repair damage

     Also increase sodium gates → magnify pain response

     Facilitate activity at capsaicin receptors

    Nonsteroidal anti-inflammatory drugs → decrease release of these chemicals

    Neurotrophin GDNF → blocks pain sensitivity

  Pain control

    Morphine before surgery

     Rarely addicitve

     Blocks activity of thin, unmyelinated axons → blocks postsurgical pain

     Doesn't block acute pain carried by large-diameter axons

4. Itch

    Histamines in skin → slow-conducting pathway

    Mild pain (scratching) → blocks itch

    Opiates decrease pain, increase itch

5. In closing: The mechanical senses

**Module 7.3  The Chemical Senses**

1. General issues about chemical coding

  Labeled-line principle

  Across-fiber pattern principle

2. Taste

  Taste receptors (modified skin cells)

    Taste buds (about 50 receptors per taste bud)

    Papillae (0-10 taste buds per papilla)

  How many kinds of taste receptors?

    Adaptation and cross adaptation

    Four main types: sweet, sour, salty, bitter

    Other possibilities

    Monosodium glutamate

     Umami

  Miracle berries and modification of taste receptors

    Miraculin

     Acids → sweet

    Gymnena sylvestre

    Theophylline

    Sodium laurel sulfate

  Mechanisms of taste receptors

    Salty:  Sodium influx

     Amiloride: blocks sodium entry → decreases salty taste

    Sour:  Acid closes potassium channels → depolarize membrane

Sweet, bitter, umami:  G protein and second messenger
    Multiple bitter receptors
Taste coding in the brain
    Pattern across fibers
    Information from anterior two-thirds of tongue
        Chorda tympani: Branch of seventh cranial nerve (facial nerve)
    Information from posterior third of tongue and throat
        Ninth and tenth cranial nerves
        Anesthetize chorda tympani
            Lose taste in anterior tongue
            Increase bitter and salt sensitivity in posterior tongue
            "Phantoms"
    Nucleus of the tractus solitarius (NTS, in medulla)
    Pons, lateral hypothalamus, amygdala, ventral-posterior thalamus, two areas of cerebral
        cortex (taste and touch)
    Ipsilateral input
Individual differences in taste
    Phenylthiocarbamate (PTC)
        Bitter, very bitter, or little taste
        Supertasters: most fungiform papillae
    Women's taste sensitivity correlated with estrogen


3.   Olfaction
    Olfactory receptors
        Olfactory cells: replaceable
        Olfactory epithelium
        Cilia
        Rapid adaptation
        Olfactory bulb
            Coding by area of olfactory bulb excited
        Several parts of cortex
    Behavioral methods of identifying olfactory receptors
        Specific anosmias
        Isobutyric acid
        Musky, fishy, urinous, spermous, malty
        Up to 26 others
    Biochemical identification of receptor types
        Similar to neurotransmitter receptors
            Seven transmembrane sections
            G proteins
        One receptor type per cell
        About 1000 receptor proteins in rodents
        Hundreds in humans
    Implications for coding
        Each receptor: Identify approximate nature of molecule
        Receptor population: More precise; identify complex mixture
        Variety of airborne chemicals, not on single dimension
        Space for many receptors not a problem

4. Vomeronasal sensation and pheromones
    Vomeronasal organ (VNO): Receptors located near, but separate from, olfactory receptors
        7-transmembrane receptor proteins
        Fewer receptor types
            Each receptor responds to one pheromone
        Nonadapting
        Vestigial in humans
            Pheromone receptors in olfactory mucosa
    Pheromones: Chemicals released by animals, affect conspecifics
        Human pheromones
            Skin secretions → increased activity in hypothalamus
            Unconscious effects
            Synchronized menstrual cycles
            Man's pheromones → more regular cycles in partner

5. In closing: Different senses offer different ways of knowing the world
        Odors more important than we realize


## Module 7.4 Attention
1. Conscious and unconscious, attended and unattended experience
    Subliminal stimuli → subtle behavioral effects
    Bottom up: Stimulus increases brain activity
    Top down: Brain areas increase attention to stimulus

2. Neglect
    Brain damage → widespread neglect
        Top-down processes from prefrontal cortex → increase attention
    Spatial neglect: Damage to right hemisphere
        Ignore left side of body and its surroundings
        Right superior temporal gyrus
            Input from ventral ("what") and dorsal ("where") visual pathways
            Output to basal ganglia → attention and movement
        Not due to loss of sensation
        Difficulty perceiving two visual or auditory items present at same time

3. Attention-deficit hyperactivity disorder (ADHD)
    Distractibility, impulsivity, sensitivity to stress, mood swings, short temper, deficit in planning
    3-10% of children, especially males
    Difficult diagnosis
    Measurements of ADHD behavior
        Choice-delay task: Smaller reward now vs. larger later
        Stop signal task: Disregard previous signal
        Attentional blink task: Miss probe letter after blue letter
    Possible causes and brain differences
        Fairly high heritability
            Dopamine D4 receptor form
        95% of normal brain volume
            Smaller right prefrontal cortex and cerebellum
    Treatments

Methylamphetamine (Ritalin) or amphetamine
    Increase attentiveness in children and adults
    Increase dopamine availability to postsynaptic receptors
        Max effect in 1 hour, when dopamine levels highest
Behavioral treatments
    Reduce distraction
    Use lists, schedules
    Pace oneself
    Learn to relax

4.  In closing: What little we know about attention
        Devoting limited abilities to most important information


## SHORT-ANSWER QUESTIONS

**Module 7.1  Audition**
1.  *Sound and the ear*
    a.  What is the relationship between amplitude and loudness? Between frequency and pitch?

    b.  What is the role of the tympanic membrane and the hammer, anvil, and stirrup?

    c.  Where are the auditory receptors located?  How are they stimulated?

2.  *Pitch perception*
    a.  What led to the downfall of the frequency theory of pitch discrimination in its simple form?

b.  What is the volley theory?




c.  What observation led to the downfall of the place theory as originally stated?




d.  What is the current compromise between the place and frequency theories of pitch discrimination?




e.  At which end of the cochlea is the basilar membrane stiffest?




f.  Describe the location of the primary auditory cortex. To what two aspects of auditory stimuli do parts of primary auditory cortex respond?




g.  What are the effects of damage to the primary auditory cortex?

3. *Hearing loss*
   a. For which type of deafness can one hear one's own voice, though external sounds are heard poorly?

   b. For what type of deafness is hearing impaired for a limited range of frequencies?

   c. What are some causes of nerve deafness? Of conductive deafness?

4. *Localization of sounds*
   a. For which frequencies is the "sound shadow" method of localization best? Why?

   b. What characteristic of sound is necessary to be able to localize sounds on the basis of difference in time of arrival? Are some frequencies easier to localize on this basis than others?

c.   Describe the basis of localization on the basis of phase difference.  For which frequencies is it most effective?

d.   Which method of sound localization is best for a species with a small head?  Why?

## Module 7.2  The Mechanical Senses

1.   *Vestibular sensation*
   a.   What are the main parts of the vestibular organ?  What are otoliths?  What is their function?

   b.   What are the semicircular canals?  How do they differ from the otolith organs?

2.   *Somatosensation*
   a.   List the somatosensory receptors and their probable functions.

   b.   How many sets of spinal nerves do we have?

c.  What is a dermatome?

d.  Describe briefly the cortical projections of the somatosensory system.

e.  Describe the loss of body sense that may accompany Alzheimer's disease.

3.  *Pain*
    a.  What is the role of glutamate in pain sensation? What is substance P? What sensation would be produced by an injection of substance P into the spinal cord?

    b.  What is capsaicin? How does it work? What food contains capsaicin?

    c.  What theory did Melzack and Wall propose to account for variations in pain responsiveness? What is its main principle?

d. What are endorphins? How was the term derived?

e. Where are endorphin synapses concentrated? What is their function there?

f. What is a placebo? What aspect of pain does it sometimes relieve? Which areas of the brain are important for this effect?

g. Describe the process by which tissue damage results in pain sensitization. Which drugs or natural chemicals can decrease pain sensitization?

h. In which type of axons does morphine decrease activity? How addictive is morphine when used for pain relief in hospital settings?

4. *Itch*
   a. What is the physiological mechanism of itch sensation?

**Module 7.3  The Chemical Senses**

1. *General issues about chemical coding*
   a. Describe the labeled-line type of coding.  Give an example.

   b. Describe the across-fiber pattern type of coding.  Give an example.

2. *Taste*
   a. Where are the taste receptors located?  What is the relationship between taste buds and papillae?

   b. How can cross-adaptation be used to help determine the number of taste receptors?

   c. What are the four major kinds of taste receptor?  What additional kinds may we have?

   d. What are the mechanisms of activation of salty, sour, sweet, bitter, and umami receptors? How does amiloride affect salty tastes?

e.  Describe the changes in taste sensitivity that occur if the chorda tympani is anesthetized.

f.  Which structures in the brain process taste information? Is taste analysis primarily ipsilateral or contralateral?

g.  Describe the individual differences in taste of phenylthiocarbamate (PTC).  What is the physiological basis of increased sensitivity in supertasters?

3.  *Olfaction*
    a.  Describe the olfactory receptors.  Where do their axons project.

    b.  What is a specific anosmia?  What can we conclude about the number of olfactory receptors, based on information about specific anosmias?

c. How are olfactory receptors similar to neurotransmitter receptors? How many olfactory receptor proteins are estimated to exist in rodents, based on isolation of these proteins? in humans?

d. What can we say about the labeled-line theory vs. the across-fiber pattern theory for smell?

e. What is the vomeronasal organ? What type of molecules does it detect?

f. What are some functions of pheromones in mice?

g. What are two functions of pheromones that have been demonstrated in humans?

**Module 7.4 Attention**
1. *Conscious and unconscious, attended and unattended experience*
   a. Explain the difference between "bottom up" and "top down" processes.

b.   What is the relationship between brain activity and consciousness?

2.  *Neglect*
    a.   Describe the effects of bilateral stroke damage in the auditory cortex. How can responsiveness be restored under certain circumstances?

    b.   Describe spatial neglect. What types of brain damage results in spatial neglect?

    c.   What types of input and output may explain the important role of the superior temporal gyrus in processing spatial attention?

    d.   How may the attention of a person with spatial neglect be directed to objects on his or her left side?

3.  *Attention-deficit hyperactivity disorder*
    a.   List the symptoms of attention-deficit hyperactivity disorder (ADHD).

b.  Briefly describe three tests that may be used to diagnose ADHD.

c.  How heritable is ADHD? What is one gene that has been implicated in ADHD? How likely is it that this gene accounts for most cases of ADHD?

d.  What are some physical differences that have been noted between people with and without ADHD? How consistent are these differences?

e.  Which drugs have been used to treat ADHD? What is their mechanism of action?

f.  What behavioral techniques have been used to treat ADHD?

## TRUE/FALSE QUESTIONS

_____ 1.  The function of the middle ear bones is to focus the force of vibrations of the eardrum onto the smaller oval window, in order to move the viscous fluid behind the oval window.

_____ 2. The basilar membrane at the base of the cochlea is larger and floppier than at the smaller apex of the cochlea.

_____ 3. Two areas of the primary auditory cortex are sensitive to location and frequency of sounds.

_____ 4. Extensive damage to the primary auditory cortex results in profound deafness for all sounds.

_____ 5. People with inner-ear deafness can hear their own voices.

_____ 6. Localization of high-frequency sounds depends mainly on a sound shadow created by the head.

_____ 7. Pacinian corpuscles are the primary receptors for heat and pain.

_____ 8. A dermatome is an area on the cortex that receives input from a peripheral structure, such as an arm.

_____ 9. The somatosensory cortex receives input primarily from the contralateral side of the body, although many neurons also receive input via the corpus callosum from the ipsilateral side.

_____ 10. Mild pains release only glutamate in the spinal cord; intense pain releases both glutamate and substance P.

_____ 11. Endorphins in the periaqueductal gray lead to the activation of neurons that decrease the release of substance P in the spinal cord.

_____ 12. Capsaicin is an endorphin that that is released in the spinal cord and immediately decreases the release of substance P.

_____ 13. A placebo decreases the emotional response to pain by decreasing activity in a pathway through the hypothalamus, amygdala, and cingulate cortex.

_____ 14. Histamine, nerve growth factor, and other chemicals released from inflamed tissue inhibit pain in the area.

_____ 15. Opiates are even more effective at inhibiting itch than at inhibiting pain.

_____ 16. Saltiness receptors permit sodium ions on the tongue to cross their membrane and depolarize the neuron.

_____ 17. Sweet, bitter, and umami receptors close potassium channels, keeping more of the positive ions inside the cell and thereby depolarizing it.

_____ 18. Taste nerves project to the nucleus of the tractus solitarius in the medulla, which in turn projects to the pons, lateral hypothalamus, amygdala, ventral-posterior thalamus, and two areas of cerebral cortex.

_____19. Each olfactory axon branches widely to provide input to a large percentage of the olfactory bulb.

_____20. Vomeronasal receptors respond to species-specific pheromones that regulate sexual interest, and, in humans, timing of the menstrual cycle.

_____21. Spatial neglect results from extensive damage to the right hemisphere, especially the right superior temporal gyrus.

_____22. Drugs such as Ritalin and amphetamine rarely help children with ADHD, and should no longer be used.

## FILL IN THE BLANKS

1. The three middle ear bones are the _____, the _____, and the _____.

2. The basilar membrane in located in the scala _____.

3. Pitch perception depends on aspects of both the _____ theory and the _____ theory.

4. The two kinds of deafness are _____ and _____ _____ deafness.

5. Phase differences are most useful for localizing _____-frequency sounds.

6. The vestibular organs consist of the _____, the _____, and the _____ _____.

7. Bare (or free) nerve endings convey information about _____, _____, and _____. Stimulation of these neurons opens _____ channels.

8. The transmitters that convey pain information are _____ and _____ _____.

9. According to the _____ theory, nonpainful stimuli can decrease the intensity of pain by releasing endorphins in the _____ _____ of the midbrain.

10 _____ is a chemical found in red peppers that activates pain and heat receptors.

11. A drug or procedure that has no pharmacological effect, but that can ease the psychological distress of pain is called a _____.

12. Sensitization of pain occurs when _____, _____ _____ _____, and other chemicals that promote healing also increase the number of _____ gates in pain neurons.

13. Itch is occasioned by release of _____ in the skin.

14. Taste buds are located in _____ on the surface of the tongue.

15. _____ receptors are activated by sodium on the tongue; _____ receptors respond by closing potassium gates; _____, _____, and _____ receptors activate G-proteins that release second messengers within the cell.

16. Olfactory receptors are located on _____ that extend into the mucus surface of the nasal passage.

17. Olfactory coding relies more on a _____ - _____ principle than does taste coding, because there are so many types of receptor proteins, and each receptor projects to a specific area of the olfactory bulb.

18. Receptors sensitive to pheromones are located in the _____ organ.

19. Spatial neglect is often the result of extensive damage to the right hemisphere, especially the _____ _____ _____.

20. Some children with ADHD have smaller than average brain areas, including the right _____ cortex and the _____.

# MATCHING ITEMS

_____ 1. Amplitude            a. Localize low-frequency sounds

_____ 2. Frequency           b. Localize high-frequency sounds

_____ 3. Sound shadow       c. Localize sudden onset sounds

_____ 4. Time of arrival        d. Stimulates heat and pain receptors

_____ 5. Phase difference      e. Marker for ADHD

_____ 6. Capsaicin           f. Pitch

_____ 7. Endorphins          g. Loudness

_____ 8. Histamine           h. Decrease pain

_____ 9. Substance P         i. Major transmitter for intense pain

_____ 10. Pheromone         j. Increases both healing and pain in sensitization

_____ 11. Dopamine D4 receptor gene    k. Vomeronasal organ

# MULTIPLE-CHOICE QUESTIONS

1. Which of the following is true of auditory perception?
   a. Loudness is the same thing as amplitude.
   b. Pitch is the perception of intensity.
   c. Perception of low frequencies decreases with age.
   d. Perception of high frequencies decreases with age.

2. The function of the tympanic membrane and middle-ear bones is to
   a. directly stimulate the auditory receptors.
   b. move the tectorial membrane to which the stirrup is connected.
   c. focus the vibrations on a small area, so that there is sufficient force to produce pressure waves in the fluid-filled cochlea.
   d. none of the above.

3. The auditory receptors
   a. are called hair cells.
   b. are embedded in the basilar membrane below and the tectorial membrane above.
   c. are stimulated when the basilar membrane moves relative to the tectorial membrane; displacement of the hair cells by about the diameter of one atom opens ion channels in the membrane of the neuron.
   d. all of the above.

170

4. The frequency theory
   a. in its simplest form cannot describe coding of very high-frequency tones because the refractory periods of neurons limit their firing rates.
   b. can be modified by the volley principle to account for pitch discrimination of all frequencies, up to 20,000 Hz.
   c. is now thought to be valid for high-frequency tones, whereas the place theory describes pitch coding of lower tones.
   d. is a form of labeled-line theory.

5. The place theory
   a. received experimental support from demonstrations that the basilar membrane was composed of a series of separate strings.
   b. has been modified so that a given frequency produces a greater displacement at one area of the basilar membrane than at others.
   c. cannot be true at all, because the basilar membrane is the same throughout its length and therefore cannot localize vibrations.
   d. cannot be true at all, because the basilar membrane is too loose and floppy to show any localization.

6. The basilar membrane
   a. is smallest and stiffest at the apex (farthest, small end) of the cochlea.
   b. is smallest and stiffest at the base (large end) of the cochlea.
   c. has the same dimensions and consistency throughout its length.
   d. shows maximum displacement for low tones near its base.

7. Pitch discrimination
   a. depends on a combination of mechanisms: frequency coding for low pitches, place coding for high pitches, and both mechanisms for intermediate pitches.
   b. depends on a combination of mechanisms: frequency coding for high pitches, place coding for low pitches, and both mechanisms for intermediate pitches.
   c. cannot be satisfactorily explained by any theory.
   d. is accomplished only by place coding.

8. Damage to primary auditory cortex results in
   a. inability to hear anything.
   b. inability to hear high tones, but not low tones.
   c. inability to hear low tones, but not high tones.
   d. inability to recognize combinations or sequences of sounds, as in music or speech.

9. Inner-ear deafness
   a. is frequently temporary; if it persists, it can usually be corrected by surgery.
   b. is characterized by total deafness to all sounds.
   c. may result from exposure of one's mother to rubella or other contagious diseases during pregnancy.
   d. is characterized by being able to hear one's own voice but not external sounds.

10. A "sound shadow"
    a. is useful for sound localization only for low-pitched sounds.
    b. is useful for sound localization only for wavelengths shorter than the width of the head (that is, higher pitches).
    c. is a means of sound localization that uses differences in time of arrival between the two ears.
    d. cannot be used at all by small-headed species such as rodents.

11. Vestibular sensation
    a. arises from free nerve endings in the inner ear.
    b. is produced by a pressure wave along a membrane in the otolith organs.
    c. arises from hair cells in the otolith organs and the semicircular canals.
    d. plays only a minor role in balance and coordination.

12. Which of the following pairs of receptors and sensations is most correct?
    a. free nerve endings: pain, warmth, cold
    b. Merkel's disks: sudden movement across skin
    c. Pacinian corpuscles: steady indentation of skin
    d. Ruffini endings: movement of hairs

13. Dermatomes
    a. are sharply defined, nonoverlapping areas innervated by single sensory spinal nerves.
    b. are overlapping areas innervated by single sensory spinal nerves.
    c. are symptoms of a skin disorder, much like acne.
    d. are found only on the trunk of the body, not the arms, legs, or head.

14. Somatosensory information
    a. travels up a single pathway to one thalamic nucleus, which projects to one strip in the parietal lobe.
    b. travels up different pathways to separate thalamic areas, which project to four parallel strips in the parietal lobe.
    c. travels directly from the spinal cord to the parietal lobe, without any synapses on the way.
    d. travels to separate thalamic areas, which project to four parallel strips in the temporal lobe.

15. Substance P
    a. is an endogenous opiate.
    b. activates receptors that are normally blocked by capsaicin.
    c. is a neurotransmitter that signals intense pain.
    d. none of the above.

16. The gate theory of pain
    a. was proposed by Melzack and Wall.
    b. states that nonpain input can close the "gates" for pain messages.
    c. may explain why athletes and soldiers may report little pain from a serious injury.
    d. all of the above.

17. Leu- and met-enkephalin
    a. have chemical structures virtually identical to morphine.
    b. are transmitters that produce a sensation of pain.
    c. are peptide neurotransmitters, consisting of five amino acids each, that have opiate-like effects.
    d. all of the above.

18. Which of the following is true of the periaqueductal gray area?
    a. Stimulation of enkephalin receptors there leads to blockade of substance P release in pain pathways.
    b. It is an area in the spinal cord where substance P is released to cause pain.
    c. Stimulation of it reduces sharp pain, but not slow, dull pain.
    d. It is a major site for the induction of pain sensitization.

19. The labeled-line principle
    a. states that each receptor responds to a wide range of stimuli and contributes to the perception of each of them.
    b. states that each receptor responds to a narrow range of stimuli and sends a direct line to the brain.
    c. describes color coding better than does the across-fiber pattern principle.
    d. describes most sensory systems in vertebrates.

20. Which of the following is true concerning taste receptors?
    a. There are about 50 receptor cells in each taste bud, and 0 to 10 or more taste buds in each papilla.
    b. Each receptor has its own taste bud.
    c. Taste receptor cells are true neurons that send axons directly to the thalamus.
    d. In adult humans taste buds are located mainly in the center of the tongue.

21. Cross-adaptation studies have suggested that
    a. there are at least four kinds of taste receptors.
    b. there may be a separate receptor for monosodium glutamate.
    c. there may be more than one kind of receptor for both bitter and sweet tastes.
    d. all of the above.

22. Which of the following is an appropriate pairing of receptor type with its method of activation?
    a. salty: sodium inflow
    b. sweet: closing potassium channels
    c. sour: activation of G protein
    d. bitter: sodium outflow

23. Amiloride
    a. facilitates sodium flow across the membrane and intensifies salty tastes.
    b. blocks sodium flow across the membrane and intensifies salty tastes.
    c. blocks sodium flow across the membrane and reduces the intensity of salty tastes
    d. facilitates potassium flow across the membrane and intensifies sweet tastes

24. The across-fiber pattern principle of taste
    a. assumes that there are seven basic taste qualities.
    b. holds that taste is coded in terms of a pattern of neural activity across many neurons.
    c. has been disproven by the finding that every receptor responds only to one taste.
    d. none of the above.

25. The nucleus of the tractus solitarius (NTS)
    a. is located in the medulla and sends taste information to the pons, lateral hypothalamus, amygdala, thalamus, and cerebral cortex.
    b. is responsible for analyzing pheromones.
    c. is located in the medulla and sends its output primarily to cranial nerves.
    d. is located in the cerebral cortex and projects to the medulla.

26. Olfactory receptors
    a. are not replaceable, once they die.
    b. each responds to only one specific odor.
    c. respond equally well to a great many odors.
    d. are located on cilia that extend into the mucous surface of the nasal passage.

27. Specific anosmias
    a. are usually very debilitating.
    b. have shown that there are only 4 kinds of olfactory receptors.
    c. suggest that there are probably a fairly large number of kinds of olfactory receptors.
    d. suggest that identification of odors depends entirely on an across-fiber pattern code.

28. Which of the following is true of olfactory receptors?
    a. They are similar to neurotransmitter receptors in that they have seven transmembrane sections and trigger changes in a G protein, which then provokes chemical activities inside the cell.
    b. There are as many as 1000 olfactory receptor proteins in mice and hundreds in humans.
    c. They send their axons to specific areas of the olfactory bulb.
    d. all of the above are true.

29. Pheromones
    a. are detected by standard olfactory receptors, which have an especially rapid adaptation.
    b. can synchronize or regularize women's menstrual cycles.
    c. are used in lower mammals, but not in humans.
    d. are especially important for locating sources of food.

30. Consciousness
    a. is correlated with increased brain activity.
    b. can be deliberately directed to certain stimuli by a top-down process.
    c. is the opposite of sensory neglect.
    d. all of the above.

31. ADHD
    a. has been associated with smaller brain size.
    b. shows little or no heritability.
    c. is best treated with sedative drugs.
    d. can be treated only with drugs; behavioral treatments are ineffective.

## Answers to True/False Questions

| | | | | | | | |
|---|---|---|---|---|---|---|---|
| 1. | T | 7. | F | 13. | T | 19. | F |
| 2. | F | 8. | F | 14. | F | 20. | T |
| 3. | T | 9. | T | 15. | F | 21. | T |
| 4. | F | 10. | T | 16. | T | 22. | F |
| 5. | F | 11. | T | 17. | F | | |
| 6. | T | 12. | F | 18. | T | | |

## Answers to Fill-in-the-Blank Questions

1. hammer (malleus), anvil (incus), stirrup (stapes)
2. media
3. frequency, place
4. conductive (middle-ear), nerve (inner-ear)
5. low
6. saccule, utricle, semicircular canals
7. pain, heat, cold, sodium
8. glutamate, substance P
9. gate, periaqueductal gray
10. Capsaicin
11. placebo
12. histamine, nerve growth factor, sodium
13. histamine
14. papillae
15. saltiness, sourness, sweetness, bitterness, umami
16. cilia
17. labeled-line
18. vomeronasal
19. superior temporal gyrus
20. prefrontal, cerebellum

## Answers to Matching Items

| | | | | | |
|---|---|---|---|---|---|
| 1. | g | 5. | a | 9. | i |
| 2. | f | 6. | d | 10. | k |
| 3. | b | 7. | h | 11. | e |
| 4. | c | 8. | j | | |

## Answers to Multiple-Choice Questions

| | | | | | | | |
|---|---|---|---|---|---|---|---|
| 1. | d | 9. | c | 17. | c | 25. | a |
| 2. | c | 10. | b | 18. | a | 26. | d |
| 3. | d | 11. | c | 19. | b | 27. | c |
| 4. | a | 12. | a | 20. | a | 28. | d |
| 5. | b | 13. | b | 21. | d | 29. | b |
| 6. | b | 14. | b | 22. | a | 30. | c |
| 7. | a | 15. | c | 23. | c | 31. | a |
| 8. | d | 16. | d | 24. | b | | |

# Diagram

Label the following structures of the inner ear: scala vestibuli, scala media, scala tympani, basilar membrane, hair cells, cochlear neuron, tectorial membrane.

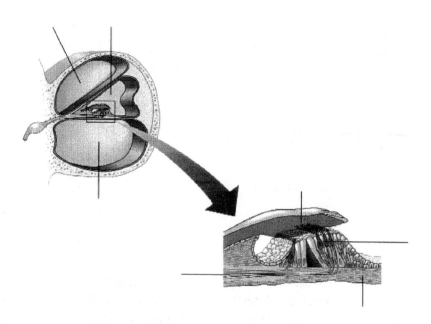

# Sensational Senses

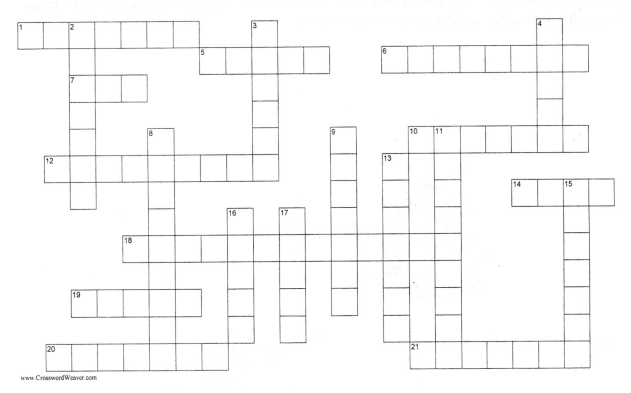

www.CrosswordWeaver.com

**ACROSS**

**1** Organ consisting of 3 canals and containing auditory receptors

**5** ____ spot: site where ganglion cell axons leave retina

**6** Type of retinal cell whose axons go to LGN or tectum

**7** Cortex area responding to expansion, contraction, or rotation of large scene (abbr.)

**10** Neural stream (path) of visual input to inferior temporal lobe

**12** Portion of body innervated by a nerve

**14** Type of information processed by ventral stream (See 10 Across)

**18** Small cell in visual system, sensitive to color and detail

**19** Quality of tone determined by frequency of vibration of sound waves

**20** 11-cis____: part of photopigments in dark-adapted state

**21** Inability to smell a substance

**DOWN**

**2** Type of visual cortex cell responding to specific line of light anywhere in its receptive field

**3** Type of visual cortex cell whose receptive field can be mapped with spot of light

**4** Area of retina with no rods and high acuity

**8** Chemical in hot peppers that stimulates pain receptors

**9** Retinal neuron between receptor and ganglion cell

**11** Endogenous opiate

**13** Calcium carbonate particle next to hair cell

**15** Inability to recognize particular objects

**16** Visual receptors mediating color vision

**17** Scala ____: one of 3 cochlear canals, the floor of which is the basilar membrane

# 8

# MOVEMENT

## INTRODUCTION

All movements of the body result from muscle contractions. Acetylcholine is the neurotransmitter released at the neuromuscular junction; it always results in contraction of the recipient muscle. Myasthenia gravis is a disease characterized by weakness and fatigue. It results from autoimmune destruction of acetylcholine receptors on muscle fibers. It may be treated either with immune-suppressant drugs or with drugs that inhibit the enzyme acetylcholinesterase, which breaks down acetylcholine. We manage to move our limbs in two opposite directions by alternately contracting antagonistic muscles, such as flexors and extensors. There are three categories of muscle: smooth, skeletal (or striated), and cardiac. Skeletal muscles may be either fast or slow. Fish have three types of muscle: red, slow, fatigue-resistant; pink, intermediate-speed, moderately fatigue-resistant; and white, fast, easily fatigued. Mammals have muscles composed of mixed fast-twitch and slow-twitch fibers. Muscles consist of many fibers, each of which is innervated by one axon; however, each axon can innervate more than one fiber. Greater precision of movement can be achieved if each axon innervates few muscle fibers.

Two kinds of receptors signal change in the state of muscle contraction. The muscle spindle is a stretch receptor located in fibers parallel to the main muscle. Whenever the main muscle and spindle are stretched, the spindle sends impulses to the spinal cord that excite the motor neurons innervating the main muscle. This results in contraction of the main muscle, opposing the original stretch. The Golgi tendon organ is located at both ends of the main muscle and responds to increased tension in the muscle, as when the muscle is contracting or being actively stretched by an external stimulus. Its impulses to the spinal cord inhibit the motor neuron, leading to relaxation of the muscle. Combinations of activity in these two receptors allow one to maintain steady positions, to resist external forces, and to monitor voluntary movement.

Most behaviors are complex mixtures of voluntary and involuntary, or reflexive, components. Some movements are ballistic, which means that they proceed automatically once triggered. Other movements require constant sensory feedback. Central pattern generators control rhythmic movements, such as wing flapping and scratching. Motor programs are fixed sequences of movements; they may be learned or innate, rhythmic or not.

The cerebral cortex coordinates complex plans of movement. The primary motor cortex sends axons to the medulla and spinal cord, which in turn innervate the muscles. It has overlapping areas that control different parts of the body. The posterior parietal cortex responds to visual and somatosensory input and to future or current movements; it is important for converting perception into action. The primary somatosensory cortex provides the primary motor cortex with sensory information and also sends axons directly to the spinal cord. Several other cortical areas guide the preparation for movement. Prefrontal cortex responds mostly to sensory stimuli that lead to movement; premotor cortex is active before a movement; supplementary motor cortex is active before a rapid series of movements.

Output from the cortex to the spinal cord can be divided into two tracts. The dorsolateral tract controls movements in the periphery of the opposite side of the body. It includes axons from the primary motor cortex and adjacent areas and from the red nucleus, all of which cross from one side to the other in bulges in the medulla called the pyramids. These axons extend without synapsing to targets in the medulla and spinal cord. The ventromedial tract controls movements near the midline of the body that require bilateral control. It consists of some axons from primary and supplementary motor cortex, others from widespread areas of cortex, and those from the midbrain tectum, reticular formation, and vestibular nucleus. None of them cross within the brain, although some axons branch to both sides of the cord. They control muscles of the neck, shoulders, and trunk, whose movements are necessarily bilateral.

The cerebellum is important for learning, planning and coordinating complex movements, especially rapid ballistic sequences that require accurate timing and aiming. It also contributes to sensory and cognitive processes, especially those that guide movement and integrate several problem-solving steps into a smooth sequence. Damage to the cerebellum impairs rapid alternating movements, saccades, the ability to touch one's nose with one's finger, and the ability to shift attention. Parallel fibers in the cerebellar cortex activate Purkinje cells, which in turn inhibit the cerebellar and vestibular nuclei. Inhibiting these nuclei for shorter or longer times determines the duration and distance of a movement. Information from these nuclei is then sent to the midbrain and thalamus.

The basal ganglia are a group of subcortical structures that contribute to the selection and organization of movements and to habit learning. The caudate nucleus and putamen receive sensory input from the thalamus and cerebral cortex and send information to the globus pallidus, which in turn sends output to the thalamus, which finally sends the output to motor and prefrontal cortex. The basal ganglia may synchronize outputs from the cortex by activating certain movements and inhibiting others.

The symptoms of Parkinson's disease include muscle rigidity and tremor, slow movement, difficulty initiating physical or mental activity, depression, and cognitive deficits. Parkinson's disease results from degeneration of dopamine neurons ascending from the substantia nigra in the midbrain to the caudate nucleus and putamen, which are part of the basal ganglia. Loss of dopamine in the basal ganglia results ultimately in less excitation of the cortex. Therefore, the cortex is less able to initiate movements. Genetic factors contribute to early-onset Parkinson's disease, but play less of a role in late-onset disease. One gene that has been implicated in early-onset Parkinson's disease leads to increased accumulation of α-synuclein. One possible cause of this disease is MPTP in the environment, possibly in the form of herbicides and pesticides. MPTP is converted in the body to MPP+, which accumulates in dopamine neurons and destroys them. On the other hand, nicotine and caffeine may decrease risk of the disease. The symptoms of Parkinson's disease can be lessened with L-dopa, the precursor of dopamine, although such treatment frequently results in undesirable side effects. Furthermore, L-dopa does not prevent, and may even hasten, the further loss of neurons. Other possible treatments include antioxidants, drugs that stimulate dopamine receptors or inhibit glutamate receptors, drugs that decrease apoptosis, and inactivation of the globus pallidus. Brain grafts of fetal substantia nigra tissue have produced promising results in laboratory animals, but have produced only modest benefits in humans. Research is continuing on the possible use of genetically altered stem cells, substantia nigra tissue from other species, and neurotrophins.

Whereas Parkinson's disease results from degeneration of the dopaminergic input to the basal ganglia, Huntington's disease results from degeneration of the postsynaptic neurons there and in the cortex. Symptoms begin with a facial twitch and progressively lead to tremors in other parts of the body and to writhing movements and psychological disorders. An autosomal dominant gene on chromosome 4 has been identified as the ultimate cause of the disease. In people with Huntington's disease this gene contains extra repetitions of a sequence of bases in the genetic code for a protein called huntingtin. Huntingtin is found inside neurons and interferes with the expression of numerous genes.

KEY TERMS AND CONCEPTS

**Module 8.1  The Control of Movement**
1.  Muscles and their movements
    Categories of muscle
        Smooth
        Skeletal or striated
        Cardiac
    Precise movements: Few muscle fibers innervated by each axon
    Neuromuscular junction
        Acetylcholine
        Muscle contraction
    Antagonistic muscles
        Flexor
        Extensor
    Myasthenia gravis
        Autoimmune attack on acetylcholine receptors at neuromuscular junctions
        Progressive weakness and rapid fatigue
        Depletion of acetylcholine after several action potentials in rapid succession
        Treatment
            Drugs that suppress immune system
            Drugs that inhibit acetylcholinesterase (enzyme that breaks down acetylcholine)
                Prolongs action of acetylcholine
    Fast and slow muscles
        Fish
            Red, slow, resistant to fatigue
            Pink, intermediate speed, moderately resistant to fatigue
            White, fast, forceful, fatigue quickly
        Humans and other mammals: Mixed fibers in each muscle
            Fast-twitch fibers
                Anaerobic→lactate & phosphate→muscle fatigue
            Slow-twitch fibers
                Aerobic→slow to fatigue
            Goldfish: Anaerobic→ethanol→diffuses away→no fatigue
    Muscle control by proprioceptors
        Proprioceptor: Receptor that detects position or movement
        Stretch reflex
        Muscle spindle
            Stretch receptor parallel to muscle
            Causes muscle to contract: Decreases stretch
        Golgi tendon organ
            In tendons at opposite ends of muscle
            Inhibits muscle: Brake against too vigorous contraction

2.  Units of movement
    Voluntary and involuntary movements
        Reflexes: Consistent automatic responses to stimuli
            Involuntary
            Infant reflexes
                Grasp reflex

Babinski reflex

Rooting reflex

Cerebral cortex damage in adults → infant reflexes released from inhibition

Allied reflexes: Several reflexes elicited together

Many behaviors: mixture of voluntary and involuntary influences

Movements with different sensitivity to feedback

Ballistic movement: Executed as a whole; cannot be altered after initiated

High sensitivity to feedback

Threading needle

Singing

Delayed auditory feedback

Sequences of behaviors

Central pattern generators

Rhythmic movements

Frequency of repetition governed by spinal cord

Motor program: Fixed sequence of movements

Learned or built in

Birds: Wing extension when dropped

Humans: Yawning

3. In closing: Categories of movement

Spinal motor neuron: Final common path

Many brain areas control different patterns

## Module 8.2  Brain Mechanisms of Movement

1. The role of the cerebral cortex

Primary motor cortex: Precentral gyrus

General movement plans

Specific movements controlled by medulla and other subcortical areas

Brief electrical stimulation of cortex → twitches

Longer (.5 sec) stimulation → complex movements

Areas near the primary motor cortex

Posterior parietal cortex

Position of body relative to the world

Converting perception into action

Primary somatosensory cortex

Sensory information to motor cortex

Direct output to spinal cord

Prefrontal cortex

Response to sensory signals that lead to a movement

Premotor cortex

Preparation for movement

Supplementary motor cortex

Preparation for rapid series of movements

Connections from the brain to the spinal cord

Dorsolateral tract of spinal cord

Axons from primary motor cortex and surrounding areas and from red nucleus of midbrain

Direct connection to spinal cord

Cross in pyramids of medulla

Controls peripheral movements on opposite side of body
Ventromedial tract of spinal cord
Uncrossed axons from primary and supplementary motor cortex, other cortical areas, tectum, reticular formation and vestibular nucleus
Axons branch to both sides of spinal cord
Controls midline movements requiring bilateral influence

2. The role of the cerebellum ("little brain")
More neurons than rest of brain combined
Rapid ballistic movements
Effects of damage to the cerebellum
Inability to link motions rapidly and smoothly
Tests of cerebellar functioning
Saccades
Finger-to-nose test
Move function: Cerebellar cortex
Hold function: Cerebellar nuclei
Slow movement: Not dependent on cerebellum
Evidence of a broad role
Response to sensory stimuli that direct movement
Programming sequence of actions as a whole
Precise timing of brief intervals
Aspects of attention
Cellular organization
Input from spinal cord, sensory cranial nerve nuclei, and cerebral cortex
Cerebellar cortex: Precise geometrical pattern with multiple repetitions of same units
Parallel fibers (axons parallel to each other) activate Purkinje cells (flat cells in sequential planes)
Purkinje cells inhibit cerebellar nuclei and vestibular nuclei of brain stem
These then send information to midbrain and thalamus
Controls duration of response

3. The role of the basal ganglia
Component structures
Caudate nucleus
Putamen
Globus pallidus
Input from sensory thalamus and cortex to caudate nucleus and putamen
Output from globus pallidus to thalamus, which projects to motor and prefrontal cortex
Functions
Organize action sequences into automatic units
Select correct movement and inhibit other movements
Obsessive-compulsive disorder: Excessive activity in caudate nucleus and prefrontal cortex

4. In closing: Movement control and cognition
Selecting and organizing a movement: Intertwined with sensory and cognitive processes

## Module 8.3  Disorders of Movement
1. Parkinson's disease
Symptoms

Rigidity
Muscle tremors
Slow movements
Difficulty initiating physical and mental activity
Depression and cognitive deficits
Less problem if external stimuli guide action
Degeneration of dopamine projections from substantia nigra to caudate nucleus and putamen
Decreased excitation of cerebral cortex
Possible causes
Early-onset Parkinson's disease: Accumulation of α-synuclein
Low heritability of late-onset Parkinson's disease
Higher heritability of early-onset Parkinson's disease
Five genes slightly more common in those with Parkinson'd disease
Exposure to toxins
Heroin-like drug: MPTP, MPP$^+$
Postsynaptic neurons increase dopamine receptors
Compensation for loss of dopamine
Result in over-responsiveness
Herbicides, pesticides
Cigarette smoking, caffeine: Decreases risk
L-dopa treatment
Precursor to dopamine
Effectiveness varies
Does not prevent, and may increase, loss of dopamine neurons
Side effects: Nausea, restlessness, sleep problems, low blood pressure, repetitive
movements, hallucinations, delusions
Therapies other than L-dopa
Antioxidant drugs
Drugs that stimulate dopamine receptors
Drugs that block glutamate
Neurotrophins
Drugs that decrease apoptosis
Inactivation of globus pallidus by electrical stimulation
Surgical damage to globus pallidus or parts of thalamus
Brain grafts
Patient's adrenal gland
Brain tissue from aborted fetuses together with neurotrophins
Genetically altered fetal cells: Produce much L-dopa
Stem cells
Fetal tissue from other species
Transplanted tissue that produces neurotrophins

2. Huntington's disease (Huntington's chorea)
Symptoms
Twitches and tremors
Writhing movements
Impaired ability to learn new movements
Extensive brain damage, especially in caudate nucleus, putamen, globus pallidus, and cortex
Psychological symptoms: Depression, memory impairment, anxiety, hallucinations and
delusions, poor judgment, alcoholism, drug abuse, sexual disorders

Stimulating environment may delay onset of symptoms
Heredity and presymptomatic testing
  Autosomal dominant gene on chromosome #4
  Extra repetitions of sequence of bases (CAG): The more repetitions, the earlier the onset
  Protein encoded: huntingtin
    Mutant form: Interferes with gene expression
      No release of BDNF
Methods 8.1  PET scans
  High resolution image of brain activity
  Radioactive chemicals made in cyclotron → positron collides with electron → gamma rays
  Gamma ray detectors

3.  In closing:  Heredity and environment in movement disorders


## SHORT-ANSWER QUESTIONS

**Module 8.1  The Control of Movement**
1.  *Muscles and their movements*
    a.  List the three categories of muscle.




    b.  What is the transmitter at the neuromuscular junction?  What is its effect?  How do we move our limbs in two opposite directions?




    c.  Describe the symptoms and cause of myasthenia gravis.




    d.  What are two kinds of treatment for this disease?

e. List the types and functions of skeletal muscle in fish.

f. How are mammalian muscles different from those of fish? Contrast the muscles of sprinters and marathon runners.

g. What is a proprioceptor? A stretch reflex?

h. What is a muscle spindle? What is its effect on the spinal motor neuron that innervates its associated muscle?

i. Explain the knee-jerk reflex in terms of the above mechanism.

j. What is a Golgi tendon organ? What is its effect on the spinal motor neuron that innervates its associated muscle? What is its functional role?

2. *Units of movement*
   a. What is a reflex?

   b. Describe some of the involuntary components of "voluntary" behaviors, such as walking or talking.

   c. What is a ballistic movement?

   d. What is the effect of delayed auditory feedback on a singer's ability to hold a single note for a long time?

   e. What is a motor program? Give examples of "built-in" and learned motor programs.

   f. Do humans have any built-in motor patterns?

## Module 8.2  Brain Mechanisms of Movement

1. *The role of the cerebral cortex*

   a. Describe the role of the primary motor cortex in the control of movement.

   b. To what two processes do neurons in the posterior parietal cortex respond? What is the result of damage there?

   c. Describe the roles of the prefrontal, premotor, and supplementary motor cortex.

   d. Where does the dorsolateral tract begin? Where does it cross from one side to the other?

   e. From what structures does the ventromedial tract originate? What is the relationship between this tract and the two sides of the spinal cord?

f. Which movements are controlled by the dorsolateral tract, and which by the ventromedial tract?

2. *The role of the cerebellum*
   a. What kinds of movements are especially affected by cerebellar damage?

   b. What are saccades? Describe the effect of cerebellar damage on the control of saccades?

   c. Describe the motor control required to touch one's finger to one's nose as quickly as possible.

   d. Why may a police officer use the finger-to-nose test to check for alcohol intoxication?

   e. Describe the evidence for a broad role for the cerebellum, beyond motor performance.

f.   From what sources does the cerebellum receive input?  To which structures do its output fibers project?

g.   Describe the relationship between the Purkinje cells and the parallel fibers.  How does this affect movement?

3.   *The role of the basal ganglia*
     a.   What structures comprise the basal ganglia?

     b.   Which are the main receptive areas?  the main output area?  Where does the sensory input come from, and where does the output go?

     c.   What is the role of the basal ganglia in the learning of motor patterns?

     d.   How does cerebellar function compare with that of the basal ganglia?

## Module 8.3  Disorders of Movement

1. *Parkinson's disease*
   a. Describe the symptoms of Parkinson's disease.

   b. What is its immediate cause?  How does loss of dopamine in the caudate nucleus and putamen affect activity in the cortex?

   c. How strong is the evidence for a genetic predisposition for Parkinson's disease?

   d. How did the experience with a heroin substitute lead to suspicion of an environmental toxin as a cause of this disease?

   e. How may herbicides and pesticides be implicated?

   f. What is a problem with the toxin-exposure hypothesis?

g.  What was the unexpected finding concerning cigarette smoking and Parkinson's disease? What may be the basis for this effect?

h.  What is the rationale for treatment of Parkinson's disease with L-dopa?  What are the side effects of this treatment?

i.  List some other possible treatments for Parkinson's disease?

j.  How successful have brain grafts been in treating Parkinson's disease in humans?  What are some of the problems with the use of fetal tissue?  From where in the brain is fetal tissue taken?

k.  What kinds of tissue have been used for brain grafts to treat Parkinson's disease? What are some potential additional sources for tissue for such grafts?

2. *Huntington's disease*
   a. What are the physical and psychological symptoms of Huntington's disease?

   b. Which neurons degenerate in Huntington's disease?

   c. Discuss the role of genetics in Huntington's disease. On which chromosome is the gene for Huntington's disease located?

   d. What is huntingtin? What do we know about the base sequence of the gene that codes for it? What may it do inside the cell?

## TRUE/FALSE QUESTIONS

_____ 1. Acetylcholine is the transmitter at all neuromuscular junctions; however, it has excitatory effects at some muscles, and inhibitory effects at others, depending on the type of receptor on the muscle.

_____ 2. Myasthenia gravis can be treated with drugs that block the immune system or with drugs that inhibit acetylcholinesterase activity.

_____ 3. Muscle spindles are receptors at opposite ends of a muscle; activation of them inhibits muscle contraction.

_____ 4. Ballistic movements are those that have especially high sensitivity to feedback while they are being executed.

_____ 5. Primary motor cortex is located in the precentral gyrus, at the posterior end of the frontal lobe.

_____ 6. The posterior parietal cortex is important for preparation for a rapid series of movements.

_____ 7. The prefrontal cortex responds to signals that lead to a movement.

_____ 8. The dorsolateral tract descends from primary motor cortex and surrounding cortical areas and from the red nucleus; its axons cross in the pyramids of the medulla.

_____ 9. The ventromedial tract controls peripheral movements on the opposite side of the body.

_____ 10. The cerebellum is especially important for linking motions rapidly and smoothly, especially ballistic movements. However, it is also important for aspects of attention.

_____ 11. Purkinje cells in the cerebellar cortex inhibit parallel fibers, which are the main output cells of the cerebellum.

_____ 12. The globus pallidus is the main receiver of input to the basal ganglia; the caudate nucleus and the putamen provide the main output.

_____ 13. Parkinson's disease results from degeneration of dopamine projections from substantia nigra to the caudate nucleus and putamen.

_____ 14. L-dopa provides some relief from symptoms of Parkinson's disease, but may also hasten the loss of dopamine neurons.

_____ 15. Only the earliest-onset form of Huntington's disease shows any heritability.

_____ 16. Huntington's disease is characterized by excessively long repeats of CAG in the gene that codes for huntingtin.

## FILL IN THE BLANKS

1. The three categories of muscle are _____, _____, and

_____.

2. Antagonistic skeletal muscles are _____ and _____.

3. Myasthenia gravis results from the loss of _____ receptors, as a

result of autoimmune attack.

4. In humans a high ratio of _____-_____ to _____-_____ fibers is more characteristic of sprinters than marathon runners.

5. A stretch receptor located in parallel to a muscle, and that causes the muscle to contract, is called a _____ _____.

6. A receptor located in tendons at opposite ends of a muscle, and that inhibits muscle contraction, is called a _____ _____ _____.

7. A movement executed as a whole, without intervening feedback, is a _____ movement.

8. A fixed sequence of movements is called a _____ _____.

9. The primary motor cortex is located in the _____ gyrus.

10. The brain area that helps to convert perception into action is the _____ _____ cortex.

11. The brain area in front of primary motor cortex that responds to sensory signals that lead to a movement is the _____ cortex.

12. The _____ tract controls peripheral movements on the opposite side of the body; the _____ tract controls midline movements that require bilateral influence.

13. The brain area that controls ballistic movements, links movements rapidly and smoothly, and contributes to aspects of attention is the _____.

14. The three structures that comprise the basal ganglia are the _____ _____, the _____, and the _____ _____.

15. Excessive activity in the caudate nucleus and prefrontal cortex is one characteristic of _____-_____ disorder.

16. Parkinson's disease results from degeneration of the tract from the _____ _____ to the _____ _____ and _____.

17. The usual treatment for Parkinson's disease is ___-_____; however, this may hasten the loss of dopamine neurons.

18. _____ disease is characterized by twitches and tremors, writhing movements, and impaired ability to learn new movements.

19. This disorder results from mutation in the gene on chromosome _____ that codes for the protein called _____; as a result a mutant form of the protein is produced, which interferes with gene expression and with the release of _____.

## MATCHING ITEMS

_____ 1.   Acetylcholinesterase

_____ 2.   Golgi tendon organ

_____ 3.   Muscle spindle

_____ 4.   Primary motor cortex

_____ 5.   Posterior parietal cortex

_____ 6.   Primary somatosensory cortex

_____ 7.   Dorsolateral tract

_____ 8.   Ventromedial tract

_____ 9.   Cerebellum

_____ 10.  Caudate nucleus, putamen

_____ 11.  Globus pallidus

_____ 12.  Parkinson's disease

_____ 13.  L-dopa

_____ 14.  Hunington's disease

a.   Causes associated muscle to contract

b.   Precentral gyrus

c.   Receive dopamine from substantia nigra

d.   Disease with excessive CAG repeats in a gene

e.   Treatment for Parkinson's disease

f.   Contains Purkinje cells and parallel fibers

g.   Inhibits contraction of associated muscle

h.   Converts perception into action

i.   Provides sensory information to motor cortex

j.   Degeneration of dopamine neurons

k.   Enzyme that breaks down acetylcholine

l.   Crosses in the pyramids of medulla

m.  Main output from basal ganglia

n.   Controls midline movements

# MULTIPLE-CHOICE QUESTIONS

1. Which of the following is true of nerves and muscles?
   a. There is always a one-to-one relationship between axons and muscle fibers.
   b. Each axon innervates several or many muscle fibers.
   c. Each muscle fiber receives many axons.
   d. Some muscle fibers are not innervated by any axons.

2. Acetylcholine
   a. has only inhibitory effects on skeletal muscles.
   b. has excitatory effects on some skeletal muscles and inhibitory effects on others.
   c. has only excitatory effects on skeletal muscles.
   d. is released only onto smooth muscles, never onto skeletal muscles.

3. Myasthenia gravis
   a. results from destruction of acetylcholine receptors at neuromuscular junctions by an autoimmune process.
   b. is helped by drugs that increase the effect of acetylcholinesterase.
   c. is helped by drugs that enhance the function of the immune system.
   d. all of the above.

4. Which of the following is a type of skeletal muscle in fish?
   a. slow, white, fatigue-resistant
   b. fast, white, fatigue-resistant
   c. slow, pink, fatigue-prone
   d. slow, red, fatigue-resistant

5. Mammalian muscles
   a. can be classified as red, pink, and white, as in fish.
   b. contain either fast-twitch or slow-twitch fibers, but not both.
   c. contain both fast-twitch and slow-twitch fibers in the same muscles.
   d. show only genetic, and not any environmental, determination of the ratio of fast-twitch to slow-twitch fibers.

6. The muscle spindle
   a. is a stretch receptor located in parallel to the muscle.
   b. inhibits the motor neuron innervating the muscle when it is stretched; this leads to relaxation of the muscle.
   c. responds only when the muscle contracts.
   d. synapses onto the muscle to excite it directly.

7. The Golgi tendon organ
   a. is also located in the muscle spindle.
   b. affects the motor neuron in the same way as the muscle spindle, thereby enhancing its effect.
   c. responds when the muscle contracts.
   d. excites the motor neuron that innervates the muscle.

8. Ballistic movements
   a. are required when a singer holds a note for a long time.
   b. require feedback as they are being executed.
   c. are controlled largely by the basal ganglia.
   d. proceed automatically once triggered.

9. The frequency of repetition of a cat's scratch reflex
   a. varies, and is controlled by pattern generators in the brain.
   b. is constant at three to four scratches per second, and is determined by cells in the lumbar spinal cord.
   c. is constant and is determined by pattern generators in the brain.
   d. is an example of feedback control.

10. Which of the following is true?
    a. Feedback control must be at the root of all movements; otherwise we would be unable to modify our behavior.
    b. Singing a single note does not require feedback, although singing several notes in a sequence does require feedback.
    c. Even ballistic movements are in reality feedback controlled.
    d. There are involuntary components of many voluntary behaviors.

11. Which of the following is true of motor programs?
    a. Grooming behavior of mice is an example of a built-in motor program.
    b. Grooming behavior of mice is an example of a learned motor program.
    c. Species of birds that have not used their wings for flight for millions of years still extend their wings when dropped.
    d. Humans have only learned, and not built-in, motor programs.

12. The primary motor cortex
    a. sends axons to the basal ganglia, the brainstem and the spinal cord.
    b. includes the somatomotor, prefrontal, premotor, and supplementary motor cortex, as well as the basal ganglia.
    c. controls isolated movements of individual muscles.
    d. all of the above.

13. The order of activity in preparing for and executing a movement is
    a. primary motor, premotor, prefrontal cortex.
    b. prefrontal, premotor, primary motor cortex.
    c. premotor, prefrontal, primary motor cortex.
    d. primary motor, prefrontal, premotor cortex.

14. The posterior parietal cortex
    a. is the main receiving area for somatosensory information.
    b. helps us to program a series of rapid movements.
    c. helps us to convert perception into action.
    d. is part of the primary motor cortex.

15. The dorsolateral tract of the spinal cord
    a. originates mostly in the primary motor cortex and adjacent areas and in the red nucleus of the midbrain.
    b. controls movements in the periphery of the body.
    c. controls movements on the side of the body opposite the brain area where the fibers originate.
    d. all of the above.

16. The ventromedial tract of the spinal cord
    a. contains crossed fibers from the primary motor cortex and adjacent areas and from the red nucleus of the midbrain.
    b. controls movements near the midline of the body that are necessarily bilateral.
    c. controls movements on the side of the body opposite the brain area where the fibers originate.
    d. works independently from the dorsolateral tract.

17. The pyramids of the medulla
    a. contain the cell bodies of the dorsolateral tract.
    b. contain the cell bodies of the ventromedial tract.
    c. are the site where axons of the dorsolateral tract cross from one side to the other.
    d. are the site where axons of the ventromedial tract cross from one side to the other.

18 The cerebellum
    a. is especially important for performance of rapid ballistic movement sequences that require accurate aiming and timing.
    b. is large and critical for the behavior of sloths.
    c. is important only for innate, not learned, motor responses.
    d. more than one of the above.

19. Damage to the cerebellum produces
    a. Parkinson's disease.
    b. Huntington's disease.
    c. deficits in saccadic movements of the eyes.
    d. deficits in slow feedback-controlled movements.

20. In executing the "finger-to-nose" movement quickly
    a. the cerebellar cortex is important in the initial rapid movement.
    b. the cerebellar nuclei are important in maintaining the brief hold pattern.
    c. other structures are important in the final slow movement.
    d. all of the above.

21. Purkinje cells in the cerebellum
    a. receive input from parallel fibers.
    b. send output to parallel fibers.
    c. excite cells in the cerebellar nuclei.
    d. send output to the basal ganglia and cerebral cortex.

22. The cerebellum
    a.  shows most activity during purely motor tasks.
    b.  contributes to any behavior that requires careful timing of brief intervals.
    c.  is now thought to contribute only to cognitive tasks, and not to motor tasks.
    d.  is especially important for controlling muscle force.

23. The basal ganglia consist of
    a.  the caudate nucleus, the cerebellum, and the thalamus.
    b.  the cerebellum, the putamen, and the thalamus.
    c.  the putamen, the globus pallidus, and the pyramids of the medulla.
    d.  the caudate nucleus, the putamen, and the globus pallidus.

24. The basal ganglia are important for
    a.  rapid ballistic movements.
    b.  selecting and organizing responses.
    c.  wing flapping in birds.
    d.  fine control of movement.

25. Parkinson's disease
    a.  results from too much dopamine in the basal ganglia.
    b.  results from too little acetylcholine at the neuromuscular junction.
    c.  results from too little dopamine in the basal ganglia.
    d.  is almost completely determined genetically.

26. MPTP
    a.  has been used with some success in treating Parkinson's disease.
    b.  may be an environmental cause of Parkinson's disease.
    c.  may be an environmental cause of myasthenia gravis.
    d.  has been used with some success in treating myasthenia gravis.

27. Which of the following is **not** a current or potential treatment for Parkinson's disease?
    a.  dopamine pills.
    b.  L-dopa.
    c.  nicotine.
    d.  antioxidants.

28. Brain grafts
    a.  are currently the best treatment for Parkinson's disease.
    b.  are most effective if they use tissue from the patient's own adrenal gland in order to prevent rejection.
    c.  are able to produce behavioral recovery only if the implanted tissue survives and makes functional synapses.
    d.  currently use fetal substantia nigra tissue, but may someday use stem cells genetically altered to produce large quantities of L-dopa.

29. Huntington's disease
    a.  results from destruction of dopaminergic input to the basal ganglia.
    b.  is characterized by great weakness.
    c.  is caused by a dominant gene on human chromosome number 4.
    d.  is caused by a recessive gene on human chromosome number 10.

30. Which of the following are not symptoms of Huntington's disease?
    a. weakness and difficulty initiating movements
    b. depression, anxiety, memory impairment, hallucinations, and delusions
    c. poor judgment, alcoholism, and drug abuse
    d. facial twitch and tremors

31. The gene associated with Huntington's disease
    a. in its normal form, contains a sequence of bases repeated at least 40 times; many of those repeats are lost in patients with Huntington's disease.
    b. in its normal form, does not contain any repeated sequences of bases.
    c. is now known to code for acetylcholine receptors.
    d. is now known to code for huntingtin, a protein, the mutant form of which interferes with the expression of many genes.

### Answers to True/False Questions

| | | | | | | | |
|---|---|---|---|---|---|---|---|
| 1. | F | 5. | T | 9. | F | 13. | T |
| 2. | T | 6. | F | 10. | T | 14. | T |
| 3. | F | 7. | T | 11. | F | 15. | F |
| 4. | F | 8. | T | 12. | F | 16. | T |

### Answers to Fill-in-the-Blank Questions

1. smooth, skeletal (striated), cardiac
2. flexors, extensors
3. acetylcholine
4. fast-twitch, slow-twitch
5. muscle spindle
6. Golgi tendon organ
7. ballistic
8. motor pattern
9. precentral
10. posterior parietal
11. premotor
12. dorsolateral, ventromedial
13. cerebellum
14. caudate nucleus, putamen, globus pallidus
15. obsessive, compulsive
16. substantia nigra, caudate nucleus, putamen
17. L-dopa
18. Huntington's
19. 4, huntingtin, BDNF

### Answers to Matching Items

| | | | | | | | |
|---|---|---|---|---|---|---|---|
| 1. | k | 5. | h | 9. | f | 13. | e |
| 2. | g | 6 | i | 10. | c | 14. | d |
| 3. | a | 7. | l | 11. | m | | |
| 4. | b | 8. | n | 12. | j | | |

## Answers to Multiple-Choice Questions

| | | | |
|---|---|---|---|
| 1. b | 9. b | 17. c | 25. c |
| 2. c | 10. d | 18. a | 26. b |
| 3. a | 11. a | 19. c | 27. a |
| 4. d | 12. a | 20. d | 28. d |
| 5. c | 13. b | 21. a | 29. c |
| 6. a | 14. c | 22. b | 30. a |
| 7. c | 15. d | 23. d | 31. d |
| 8. d | 16. b | 24. b | |

**Please check the Exploring Biological Psychology CD-ROM.**

## Diagram

Label the principal areas of the motor cortex in the human brain: posterior parietal cortex, prefrontal cortex, premotor cortex, primary motor cortex, primary somatosensory cortex, supplementary motor cortex.

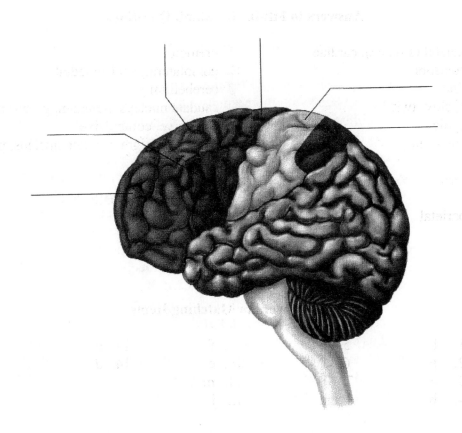

# 9

# WAKEFULNESS AND SLEEP

## INTRODUCTION

Animals ranging from insects to humans exhibit endogenous rhythms of behavior. Circannual (approximately year-long) cycles govern hibernation, migration, and seasonal mating in some species. Circadian (approximately 24-hour) cycles regulate activity and sleep as well as other bodily functions. The "clock" governing these cycles generates the rhythm internally, although the external light cycles affect the specific settings. The mechanism of the clock is not understood; however, the length of the rhythm may be altered by genetic mutation. The protein products of two genes in fruit flies build up during the day and produce sleepiness; high levels then feed back to decrease production of the proteins. Similar genes have been found in mice and humans. Light appears to act on the suprachiasmatic nucleus (SCN) of the hypothalamus. If the SCN is isolated from the rest of the brain, it continues to generate a circadian rhythm of approximately 24 hours. Melatonin, a hormone produced by the pineal gland, may be one means by which the SCN regulates sleeping and waking. Increased melatonin secretion begins 2 to 3 hours before the onset of sleepiness. The SCN can be reset by various stimuli, including light, tides, exercise, noises, meals, etc. Light is the most important stimulus (zeitgeber: time giver) for most mammals. Some axons in the optic nerve form the retinohypothalamic path, which innervates the SCN. Even animals with little or no vision can use retinal ganglion cells with their own photopigment to regulate the biological clock. People traveling across several time zones suffer from jet lag, which is worse traveling east than traveling west. People who work night shifts are also stressed and are plagued by more errors and injuries than people who work during their normal waking period. Very bright lights during the new day time and complete darkness during the new night help travelers and shift workers adapt to their schedules.

Relaxed wakefulness (with the eyes closed) is characterized by alpha waves at a frequency of 8 - 12 per second. Stage 1 of sleep is signaled by irregular, low-voltage waves, after which progression through stages 2, 3, and 4 is correlated with increasingly slow, large-amplitude waves. Throughout the night, there is a cyclic progression back and forth through the four stages. However, after the first period of stage 1, each return to stage 1 is correlated with rapid eye movements, relaxed muscles, and rapid and variable heart rate and breathing. Rapid eye movement (REM) sleep has also been called paradoxical sleep, because the EEG shows fast, low amplitude waves, as during wakefulness, and the heart rate and breathing are variable, but the postural muscles are completely relaxed. Dreams during REM sleep tend to be more intense than those during non-REM (NREM) sleep.

Wakefulness and behavioral arousal depend, in part, on the reticular formation, a group of large, branching neurons running from the medulla into the forebrain. The pontomesencephalon is the part of the reticular formation that contributes to cortical arousal. It receives input diffusely from many sensory systems and generates spontaneous activity of its own. It sends output to the thalamus and basal forebrain. There are different types of arousal, requiring many brain areas. The locus coeruleus, in the pons, is active in response to meaningful events and may help to form memories. It sends widely branching axons containing norepinephrine to the cortex. The basal forebrain is the site of nuclei that send acetylcholine-containing axons to widespread areas of the thalamus and cortex; these neurons also promote wakefulness. Finally, two paths from the hypothalamus increase arousal by releasing the neurotransmitter histamine.

Sleep results in part from reductions of sensory input and of activity in arousal systems. Adenosine accumulates during wakefulness and shuts off the basal forebrain neurons that produce arousal. Prostaglandins also increase during the day and inhibit hypothalamic cells that increase arousal. In addition, some brain areas actively promote sleep. Clusters of GABA-containing neurons in the basal forebrain send widespread axons that promote the onset of sleep. These neurons receive much of their input from the anterior and preoptic areas of the hypothalamus, which also regulate temperature.

During REM sleep, high-amplitude potentials can be recorded in the pons, geniculate, and occipital cortex (PGO waves). Animals maintain nearly constant amounts of PGO waves. If deprived of REM, PGO waves intrude into other sleep stages and even wakefulness. Animals compensate for lost PGO waves when allowed to sleep freely. Cells in the pons also inhibit the motor neurons that control postural muscles. Other sites that are active during REM are the limbic system and parts of parietal and temporal cortex; other cortical areas, including the primary visual, motor, and dorsolateral prefrontal cortex, become less active during REM. Acetylcholine induces the onset of REM, and serotonin and norepinephrine interrupt or shorten it.

There are three categories of insomnia: onset, maintenance, and termination. Causes of insomnia include abnormalities of biological rhythms, withdrawal from tranquilizers, and periodic limb movements. Sleep apnea, the inability to breathe during sleep, may be caused by obesity or impairment of brain mechanisms for respiration. Narcolepsy refers to periods of extreme sleepiness during the day. Additional symptoms of narcolepsy are cataplexy (extreme muscle weakness while awake), sleep paralysis (inability to move during transition into or out of sleep), and hypnagogic hallucinations (dreamlike experiences that are difficult to distinguish from reality). All of these symptoms can be interpreted as intrusions of REM sleep into wakefulness. Narcolepsy may result from excessive acetylcholine input to areas of the pons that suppress muscle activity during dreams. It may also result from a deficit in orexin (hypocretin), which in turn stimulates acetylcholine neurons that promote wakefulness. In REM behavior disorder people appear to act out their dreams, possibly as a result of damage to the neurons in the pons that inhibit movement during REM. Nightmares are unpleasant dreams that occur during REM sleep; night terrors are experiences of extreme anxiety, occurring during NREM sleep, from which a person wakens in terror. Sleep talking occurs with similar probability in REM and NREM sleep, whereas sleepwalking occurs mostly during stages 3 and 4 slow-wave sleep.

Sleep serves two major functions. The repair and restoration theory stresses that restorative functions occur mostly during sleep, especially for the brain. The evolutionary theory proposes that sleep is basically an energy-conserving mechanism employed during times when activity would be either inefficient or dangerous. These two theories are complementary and compatible.

The function of REM sleep is not well understood. In general, the percentage of sleep spent in REM correlates positively with the total amount of sleep. REM deprivation has resulted in increased irritability, anxiety, and appetite, impaired concentration, and increased REM time on subsequent uninterrupted nights. REM may facilitate the consolidation of motor skills; whereas NREM sleep may strengthen verbal memories. The eye movements that characterize REM may also increase oxygen supply to the corneas. Dreams may result from the brain's attempt to make sense of its increased activity during REM episodes (activation-synthesis hypothesis). A clinico-anatomical hypothesis rests in part on the observations that during REM, neural activity in primary visual, motor, and prefrontal cortex is suppressed. Therefore, normal visual input cannot compete with self-generated stimulation, and motor activity is suppressed. Also, working memory and "use of knowledge," functions of prefrontal cortex, are inhibited. On the other hand, increased activity in inferior parietal cortex and higher visual areas may increase spatial perception and visual imagery. Finally, increased activity in the hypothalamus, amygdala, and other areas may increase the emotional intensity of dreams.

# LEARNING OBJECTIVES

**Module 9.1  Rhythms of Waking and Sleeping**
1. Understand the functions of endogenous rhythms and our difficulty with altered rhythms.
2. Be able to describe the anatomical location of the biological clock and its biochemical and hormonal signals.
3. Be able to explain how light can reset the biological clock.

**Module 9.2  Stages of Sleep and Brain Mechanisms**
1. Know the characteristics of the stages of slow-wave and REM sleep.
2. Know the brain areas and neurotransmitters that promote wakefulness, slow-wave sleep and REM sleep.
3. Know the various sleep disorders, their possible causes, and their treatments.

**Module 9.3  Why Sleep, Why REM? Why Dreams?**
1. Understand the proposed functions of sleep, REM sleep, and dreaming.

# KEY TERMS AND CONCEPTS

**Module 9.1  Rhythms of Waking and Sleeping**
1. Endogenous cycles
   Endogenous circannual and circadian rhythms
      Bird migration
      Squirrel food storage and fat deposition
      Animal mating
   Duration of the human circadian rhythm
      Difficulties with experiments
      Constant light → rhythms faster than 24 hours
      Constant dark → rhythms slower than 24 hours
      Ability to adapt to 23- or 25-hour days, but not 22- or 28-hour days
      Lighting of choice → almost 25 hour cycle
      28-hour light cycle → 24.2 hour wake/sleep cycle

2. Mechanisms of the biological clock
      Interfering with the biological clock
         Curt Richter
            Lack of effect of most procedures
      The suprachiasmatic nucleus (SCN)
         Main control of rhythms of sleep and temperature
         Endogenous rhythm
            Disconnected SCN still generates rhythms
            Single SCN cells generate rhythm
               Less steady than group of cells
            Genetic mutation that produces 20-hour rhythm
               Transplantation of mutant or normal SCN: Animals followed rhythm of SCN
      The biochemistry of the circadian rhythm
         Drosophila genes
            *Period (per)*
            *Timeless (tim)*
            Proteins Per and Tim build up during day

Interact with Clock protein → sleepiness
Negative feedback → reset
Similar genes in mice and humans
Mutations → altered rhythms
Melatonin
Pineal gland
Peak 2 to 3 hours before sleepiness
Melatonin pill in afternoon → phase advance
Melatonin pill in morning → phase delay
Antioxidant
Increased movement deficits in Parkinsonian rats
Impaired reproduction in rats

3. Setting and resetting the biological clock
Free-running rhythm
Zeitgeber
Light, tides, exercise, noises, meals, temperature
Hamsters in constant light → two hemispheres out of phase
Jet lag
Worse going east
Phase-delay going west
Phase-advance going east
Stress of jet lag → cortisol → degeneration of hippocampus neurons
Shift work
Exposure to bright lights
How light resets the SCN
Retinohypothalamic path
Axons from optic nerve
Animals with little or no vision: Light still resets rhythms
Mice with genetic defects
Blind mole rats
Retinal ganglion cells with own photopigment
Respond slowly to average amount of light

4. In closing: Sleep-wake cycles
Sleepiness not voluntary
Work when sleepy → errors and injuries

**Module 9.2 Stages of Sleep and Brain Mechanisms**
1. The stages of sleep
Alpha waves (8 - 12 per second): Relaxed wakefulness
Stage 1 sleep
Irregular, low-voltage EEG waves
Stage 2 sleep
Sleep spindle
K-complex
Stages 3 and 4 slow-wave sleep
Synchronized EEG: Slow, large amplitude waves
Sense organs responsive; thalamus doesn't relay input to cortex
Cycling back through stages 3 and 2

2. Methods 9.1: Electroencephalography
    Electrodes attached to scalp
    Record average activity of population of cells under electrode
    Can determine: asleep, awake, dreaming, excited
    Abnormalities: epilepsy, tumor, other medical problems

3. Paradoxical or REM sleep
    Characteristics
        Paradoxical sleep
            In some ways deepest and in some ways lightest sleep
        Rapid eye movements (REM)
        Irregular, low-voltage fast (desynchronized) EEG
        Postural relaxation
        Variable heart rate and breathing
        Penile erection or vaginal moistening
        Facial twitches
        Polysomnograph: EEG and eye movement records
        Sleep cycles
            90-minute cycles
            Stages 3 and 4 predominant early in night
            REM predominant late in night
            REM sleep and dreaming
                Dement & Kleitman: Dreams reported on 80 to 90% of awakenings from REM
                Some kind of thought process during non-REM sleep (NREM)
                REM: intensifies dreams but not synonymous with dreaming

4. Brain mechanisms of wakefulness and arousal
    Brain structures of arousal
        Cut through midbrain → prolonged sleep
            Not due to loss of sensory input
        Reticular formation: Interconnected network
        Pontomesencephalon
            Widespread sensory input
            Spontaneous activity
            Axons to thalamus and basal forebrain
                Acetylcholine and glutamate → excitatory effects
                Arousal then relayed to cortex
        Arousal not a unitary process
            Four kinds of attention
                Waking up
                Directing attention to a stimulus
                Storing a memory
                Increasing goal-directed effort
            Locus coeruleus ("dark blue place") in pons
                Bursts of impulses in response to meaningful events
                Norepinephrine
                May aid in memory formation
            Basal forebrain nuclei (anterior and dorsal to hypothalamus)
                Provides input to thalamus and cortex

Main transmitter: acetylcholine → mostly excitatory effects
Some neurons: GABA → inhibitory effects
Damage (including Alzheimer's disease) → impairments of arousal, learning and attention, increased NREM sleep
Paths from hypothalamus
Histamine → arousal
Getting to sleep
Decrease temperature
Shift blood to periphery
Decrease stimulation
Gentle rocking may help
Inhibit arousal systems
Adenosine inhibits basal forebrain arousal systems
Metabolism: Adenosine monophosphate (AMP) → adenosine → second messengers → gene activity for hours → sustains sleep
Caffeine → inhibits adenosine → wakefulness
Prostaglandins
Build up during day, decline during sleep
Increased by immune system during infection
Inhibit hypothalamic neurons that increase arousal
Basal forebrain and hypothalamic nuclei that induce sleep
Transmitter: GABA → inhibitory effects
Input from anterior and preoptic hypothalamus
Temperature regulation
Fever increases output to sleep-related cells

5.  Brain function in REM sleep
Increased activity in pons and limbic system
Decreased activity in primary visual, motor, and dorsolateral prefrontal cortex
PGO (pons-geniculate-occipital) waves
Compensation for lost PGO waves
Pons → spinal cord → inhibition of motor neurons
Neurotransmitters
Acetylcholine → REM onset
Carbachol
Important for both waking and REM → activate brain
Serotonin → interrupts or shortens REM
Norepinephrine from locus coeruleus → blocks REM

6.  Abnormalities of sleep
Insomnia
Onset insomnia
Possible cause: Phase-delayed temperature rhythm
Maintenance insomnia
Possible cause: Circadian rhythm irregularity
Termination insomnia
Possible cause: Phase-advanced temperature rhythm
Early onset of REM sleep
Depression
Withdrawal from tranquilizers

Sleep apnea
    Sudden infant death syndrome
    Obesity
Narcolepsy
    Attacks of daytime sleepiness
    Cataplexy
    Sleep paralysis
    Hypnagogic hallucinations
    May be due to intrusion of REM into wakefulness
        Overactive acetylcholine synapses
    Orexin (hypocretin)
        Peptide neurotransmitter
        Cells in hypothalamus project widely to forebrain and brainstem
        Stimulate acetylcholine-releasing cells → increase arousal
    Treated with stimulants
        Pemoline (Cylert) or methylphenidate (Ritalin)
Periodic limb movement disorder (mostly during NREM sleep)
REM behavior disorder
    Acting out dreams
    Damage in pons
    Motor neurons no longer inhibited
Night terrors, sleep talking, and sleepwalking
    Night terrors different from nightmares
        Occur in NREM sleep
    Sleep talking
        Occurs in REM or NREM sleep
    Sleepwalking
        Most common in children
        Mostly in Stages 3 and 4 (not during REM)

7.  In closing: Stages of sleep
        Usefulness of EEG recordings in identifying internal experiences


## Module 9.3  Why sleep?  Why REM?  Why dreams?
1.  The functions of sleep
    The repair and restoration theory of sleep
        Effects of sleep deprivation
            Human (voluntary) experiments: Dizziness, impaired concentration, irritability, hand
                tremors, hallucinations, increased immune function
            Animal (nonvoluntary) experiments
                Few days deprivation → increased temperature, metabolism, and appetite
                Longer deprivation → decreased immune function, decreased brain activity
        Little effect of physical exertion
        Variability of requirements
    The evolutionary theory
        Hibernation
        Energy conservation
        Hibernation → retards aging
        Time required for food search
        Safety from predators

2. The functions of REM sleep
  Individual and species differences
    Percent of time in REM correlated with length of sleep
  The effects of REM deprivation
    Humans
      Increased anxiety and irritability
      Decreased concentration
      Increased appetite
      REM rebound (increased REM in uninterrupted nights)
    Paradoxical sleep deprivation in nonhumans (up to 70 days)
      Severe impairments of behavior and health
        Maybe due in part to falling into cold water
  Hypotheses
    Memory storage
      Differential effects on types of learning
      NREM also important for learning
    Deprivation of sleep early in night (mostly SWS) → impaired verbal learning
    Deprivation of sleep late in night (much REM) → impaired consolidation of motor skills
    Increase oxygen to eyeballs

3. Biological perspectives on dreaming
  The activation-synthesis hypothesis
    Cortex synthesizes story from stimuli processed in activated areas of cortex and amygdala
    Primary visual cortex and prefrontal cortex inactivated
      No sensory input to interfere
      Can't remember dreams
    Vague and hard to test
  A clinico-anatomical hypothesis
    Arousing stimuli processed in unusual ways
    Suppression of activity in primary visual, motor, and prefrontal cortex
      No normal visual stimuli or motor responses
      Inhibited working memory and "use of knowledge"
    Increased activity in inferior parietal cortex
      Damage there → poor spatial perception and no dreams
    Increased activity in "higher" visual areas
      Damage there → dreams with no visual content
    Increased activity in hypothalamus, amygdala, and other areas that process emotions
    Also vague and hard to test

4. In closing: Our limited self-understanding
    No need for conscious understanding of evolutionary reasons for behavior

## Module 9.1  Rhythms of waking and sleeping

1. *Endogenous cycles*
    a.  What do we know about the factors that do, or do not, initiate migration in birds?

    b.  What are endogenous circannual rhythms?  endogenous circadian rhythms?  How consistent are circadian rhythms within individuals in a given environment?  between individuals?

    c.  How can circadian rhythms be demonstrated experimentally?  What are some bodily and behavioral changes that occur in circadian rhythms?

    d.  How easily can humans adapt to a new cycle length?  What are the limits of adaptation?

2. *Mechanisms of the biological clock*
    a.  What sorts of attempted interference with the biological clock were not effective?

b.  What structure is the source of the circadian rhythms?  What is its relationship to the visual system?

c.  What is the evidence that the suprachiasmatic nucleus (SCN) generates rhythms itself?

d.  What happened when SCN tissue from hamsters with a mutant gene for a 20-hour rhythm were transplanted into normal hamsters?

e.  What two genes, discovered in Drosophila (fruitflies), govern circadian rhythms?  How do they work?  How common is this mechanism in other animals?

f.  What is melatonin?  From which gland is it secreted?  When does increased secretion of melatonin occur?

g.  From what pathway does the SCN get its input from the visual system?  How are blind mice and mole rats able to use light to reset their SCN?

3. *Setting and resetting the biological clock*
   a. What is a Zeitgeber? What is the most effective Zeitgeber for land animals? for many marine animals?

   b. Is it easier to cross time zones going east or west? Why?

   c. What is the best way to reset the biological clock when working a night shift?

   d. By what path does the retina influence the SCN? What is unusual about the ganglion cells whose axons make up this path? How rapidly do they respond to light?

## Module 9.2  Stages of Sleep and Brain Mechanisms
1. *The stages of sleep*
   a. Describe the usual behavioral correlate of alpha waves. What is their frequency?

   b. Describe the EEG in stage 1 sleep.

c.  What are the EEG characteristics of stage 2 sleep?

d.  Which stages of sleep are classed as slow-wave sleep (SWS)?

2.  *Methods 9.1  Electroencephalography*
    a.  What is an electroencephalogram?

    b.  What accounts for rapid, low-voltage EEG activity?  slow, high-voltage activity?

3.  *Paradoxical or REM sleep*
    a.  Why is REM sleep sometimes called paradoxical sleep?  What are its characteristics?

    b.  What is a polysomnograph?

c. What is the typical duration of the sleep cycle? During which part of the night is REM predominant? During which part are stages 3 and 4 SWS predominant?

d. How good is the correlation between REM and dreaming?

4. *Brain mechanisms of wakefulness and arousal*
   a. What is the effect of a cut through the midbrain on sleep and waking cycles? Was this result due simply to loss of sensory input or to damage to a particular brain structure?

   b. Describe the input, output, and interconnections of the pontomesencephalon. What is its relation to the reticular formation?

   c. Name four kinds of attention.

   d. Give the location, neurotransmitter, and a major function of the locus coeruleus.

e.  What is the major neurotransmitter released by neurons in the basal forebrain that contribute to arousal?

f.  What is the neurotransmitter of two paths from the hypothalamus that stimulate arousal? What is the implication of this for allergy treatments?

g.  What is a good indicator of how fast a person will get to sleep? Explain this finding.

h.  How does adenosine contribute to sleepiness? How does caffeine increase arousal?

i.  What are prostaglandins? How do they provoke sleep?

j.  What neurotransmitter is released by neurons of the hypothalamus and basal forebrain that promote sleep? What is a major source of input to those neurons? What is another function of that source?

5. *Brain function in REM sleep*

    a. What are PGO waves? Where are they recorded? What happens to PGO waves after a period of REM deprivation?

    b. Describe the mechanism for inhibiting motor activity during REM sleep.

    c. Which neurotransmitter is important for REM onset? Which two neurotransmitters interrupt or shorten REM? What is one effect of the drug carbachol?

6. *Abnormalities of sleep*

    a. List and describe the characteristics of the three categories of insomnia. What circadian rhythm disorders may cause each category?

    b. What are the pharmacological effects of most tranquilizers that are used as sleeping pills? How may sleeping pills contribute to insomnia?

c. Describe the symptoms of sleep apnea. What are three factors that may contribute to sleep apnea?

d. What four symptoms are commonly associated with narcolepsy?

e. Define cataplexy. What tends to trigger it? What is one explanation for cataplexy?

f. Define hypnagogic hallucinations.

g. Describe the symptoms of periodic limb movement disorder.

h. What are the symptoms and a possible cause of REM behavior disorder?

i. How do night terrors differ from nightmares? During which type of sleep are night terrors most common?

j. During which stages does sleep talking occur? sleepwalking?

**Module 9.3 Why sleep? Why REM? Why Dreams?**
1. *The functions of sleep*
   a. Describe the repair and restoration theory of sleep.

   b. What are some effects of sleep deprivation in humans? in rats?

   c. Describe the evolutionary theory of the need for sleep. What evidence supports it?

   d. How compatible are these two theories?

2.  *The functions of REM sleep*
    a.  What is the relationship between percentage of time in REM and total sleep time?

    b.  What kinds of behavioral changes occur if people are selectively deprived of REM sleep? How does this compare with the effects on nonhuman animals?

    c.  Describe the apparent relationship between learning and paradoxical sleep. For what kind of learning does paradoxical sleep seem to be most important? To what kind of learning does NREM contribute?

    d.  How may REM contribute to oxygen supply for the cornea?

4.  *Biological perspectives on dreaming*
    a.  What is the current view of Freud's assumptions concerning dreaming?

    b.  State the activation-synthesis hypothesis. What evidence supports this hypothesis?

c.  Describe the controversy concerning the role of the pons in dreaming.  What is another criticism of the theory.

d.  Summarize the basic ideas of the clinico-anatomical hypothesis.

e.  What three cortical areas are suppressed during dreams?  What would be the effects of these suppressions?

f.  What two cortical areas are active during dreams?  What would they contribute to dreams?

g.  Which subcortical areas are active during dreams? What do these areas contribute?

## TRUE/FALSE QUESTIONS

_____  1.  Day length is the most powerful stimulus for bird migration; if birds are kept in a constant environment, they would eventually migrate, but only after a delay of months.

_____  2.  Humans can adapt to 23- or 25-hour days, but not to 22- or 28-hour days.

_____  3.  The suprachiasmatic nucleus can generate circadian rhythms, even if it is disconnected from the rest of the brain.

220

_____ 4. The genes *per* and *tim* produce proteins, high levels of which interact with the Clock protein to induce wakefulness.

_____ 5. Melatonin is a hormone produced by the pituitary gland that induces sleepiness within minutes after being introduced into the body.

_____ 6. A zeitgeber resets the circadian rhythm, but is not the actual generator of the rhythm.

_____ 7. Jet lag is worst going east.

_____ 8. The SCN receives branches of the same axons that project to the lateral geniculate nucleus of the thalamus and carry normal visual information.

_____ 9. Sleep spindles and K-complexes are characteristic of REM sleep.

_____10. Sleep stages 3 and 4 predominate early in the night, and REM periods take up more time late in the night.

_____11. GABA-containing neurons of the basal forebrain produce arousal.

_____12. Acetylcholine triggers the onset of REM sleep, and serotonin and norepinephrine inhibit REM sleep.

_____13. Termination insomnia may be caused by a phase-delayed temperature rhythm.

_____14. Narcolepsy may result either from excessive acetylcholine input to the neurons in the pons that inhibit motor neurons or from deficient orexin activity from the hypothalamus to the forebrain and brainstem.

_____15. REM deprivation may impair primarily verbal learning.

_____16. Activity in primary visual cortex is increased in REM sleep, thereby giving rise to the visual content of dreams.

## FILL IN THE BLANKS

1. The site of the biological clock is the _____ _____.

2. The drosophila genes _____ (___) and _____ (___) produce proteins that

   interact with the _____ protein to induce sleepiness.

3. Melatonin is produced by the _____ gland and peaks _____

   before the onset of sleepiness.

4. A stimulus that resets the circadian rhythm is called a _____.

5. The tract that carries input concerning light to the biological clock is the

_____ path, which arises from _____

cells with their own photopigment.

6. The EEG waves characteristic of relaxed wakefulness are _____ waves.

7. Sleep cycles last approximately _____ minutes.

8. The _____ is a part of the reticular formation that sends

axons to the thalamus and basal forebrain that release _____ and

_____ to produce arousal.

9. Two chemicals that build up during waking and induce sleepiness are_____

and _____.

10. REM sleep is associated with high-amplitude electrical potentials called _____ _____.

11. The transmitter that stimulates REM onset is _____; two that

inhibit REM are _____ and _____.

12. _____ is a peptide neurotransmitter that stimulates acetylcholine neurons

that, in turn, produce wakefulness.

13. The theory that dreams are caused by the brain's attempt to make sense out of neural activity is

the _____-_____ theory.

14. The clinico-anatomical hypothesis observes that suppressed activity in primary _____,

_____ and _____cortex leaves the brain without normal sensory

input and motor output and without normal working memory and "use of knowledge."

# MATCHING ITEMS

_____ 1.   Suprachiasmatic nucleus

_____ 2.   Pineal gland

_____ 3.   Zeitgeber

_____ 4.   Retinohypothalamic path source

_____ 5.   Alpha waves

_____ 6.   Sleep spindle

_____ 7.   Pontomesencephalon

_____ 8.   Locus coeruleus

_____ 9.   Basal forebrain GABA neurons

_____ 10.  PGO waves

_____ 11.  Acetylcholine

_____ 12.  Serotonin

_____ 13.  Adenosine

_____ 14.  Onset insomnia

_____ 15.  Termination insomnia

_____ 16.  Orexin

a.   EEG sign of REM sleep

b.   A transmitter that inhibits REM

c.   EEG sign of stage 2 sleep

d.   A transmitter that → waking & REM

e.   Site of norepinephrine neurons→memory store

f.   EEG sign of relaxed wakefulness

g.   Ganglion cells with own photopigment

h.   Site of biological clock

i.   Phase-delayed temperature rhythm

j.   Peptide transmitter that → arousal

k.   Phase-advanced temperature rhythm

l.   Part of reticular formation that → arousal

m.   Structure that releases melatonin

n.   Stimulus that resets circadian rhythm

o.   Neurons that induce sleep

p.   Chemical that builds up to → sleepiness

# MULTIPLE-CHOICE QUESTIONS

1. Curt Richter suggested the revolutionary idea that
   a.   nearly all behavior is a reaction to a stimulus.
   b.   the body generates its own cycles of activity and inactivity.
   c.   temperature fluctuations are the best zeitgeber.
   d.   animals wait till the first frost before preparing for winter so that they can enjoy summer longer.

2. Migratory birds
   a.   respond only to temperature signals to begin migration.
   b.   respond only to the ratio of light to dark, especially in spring.
   c.   respond only to the availability of food.
   d.   become more active in the spring, even in the absence of external cues, and fly north if released from captivity.

223

3. Circadian rhythms
   a. cannot be demonstrated if lights are always on or always off.
   b. always average within a minute or two of 24 hours in length, regardless of the light cycle.
   c. include cycles of waking and sleeping, eating and drinking, temperature, hormone secretion, and urine production.
   d. are very flexible and can be changed as soon as a different light cycle is established.

4. Which of the following can totally disrupt the biological clock?
   a. food or water deprivation
   b. anesthesia
   c. lack of oxygen
   d. none of the above

5. The suprachiasmatic nucleus (SCN)
   a. is located in the brain stem.
   b. no longer generates a rhythm if it is disconnected from input from the optic nerve.
   c. if transplanted from fetal hamsters that have a mutant gene producing a 20-hour cycle, into normal hamsters, will produce 20-hour cycles in the recipients.
   d. is concerned only with the resetting of the clock, not with generating the rhythm.

6. Two genes in Drosophila known as *period* (*per*) and *timeless* (*tim*)
   a. produce proteins that are present in only small amounts early in the day, but increase throughout the day.
   b. produce proteins that make the fly sleepy, when present in high levels.
   c. are similar to genes found in mice.
   d. all of the above.

7. Melatonin
   a. is secreted by the pituitary gland.
   b. is secreted primarily at the time of sleep onset.
   c. is secreted 2 - 3 hours before the time of sleep onset.
   d. has now been tested extensively and is known to have no side effects.

8. The human circadian rhythm
   a. can easily adjust to 22- or 28-hour days, but not to 20- or 30-hour days.
   b. has a mean of 24.2 hours, but can adjust to 23- or 25-hour days.
   c. can be most easily reset by using only dim lights in the evening.
   d. cannot be reset at all.

9. Which of the following is true?
   a. It is easier to adjust our biological rhythms to longer cycles and to travel across time zones going west.
   b. It is easier to adjust our biological rhythms to shorter cycles and to travel across time zones going east.
   c. People on irregular shifts tend to sleep the longest when they go to sleep in the morning or early afternoon.
   d. People on night shifts that were exposed to normal levels of room lighting found it easy to adjust their cycles.

10. Alpha waves are characteristic of
    a. REM sleep.
    b. alert mental activity.
    c. relaxed wakefulness.
    d. slow-wave sleep.

11. Stages 3 and 4 sleep
    a. are characterized by sleep spindles and K-complexes.
    b. together are known as slow-wave sleep.
    c. are characterized by irregular, jagged, low-voltage waves.
    d. are the stages during which REM occurs.

12. Which of the following is **not** a sign of REM sleep?
    a. tenseness in postural muscles
    b. extreme relaxation of postural muscles
    c. variable heart and breathing rates
    d. irregular, low-voltage, fast EEG activity

13. Paradoxical sleep is paradoxical because brain waves suggest
    a. slow-wave sleep, when one is really dreaming.
    b. dreaming, when one is really in slow-wave sleep.
    c. sleep, when one is really awake.
    d. activation, when one's postural muscles are most relaxed.

14. REM sleep occurs
    a. only early in a night's sleep.
    b. cyclically, about every 90 minutes.
    c. randomly throughout the night.
    d. only after a period of physical exercise.

15. Dreams
    a. are highly correlated with sleep talking.
    b. are of greater duration and frequency during the early part of the night.
    c. may occur in NREM, but are more likely to include vivid visual imagery during REM.
    d. all of the above.

16. A cut through the midbrain
    a. produced prolonged sleep because an area that promotes wakefulness was cut off from the rest of the brain.
    b. left the animal sleeping constantly because most sensory input was cut off from the brain.
    c. left the animal sleeping and waking normally, since structures that control these functions are anterior to the midbrain.
    d. left the animal more wakeful than usual because much of the reticular formation was still connected to the brain, but a sleep-promoting system had been damaged.

17. The pontomesencephalon, a part of the reticular formation,
    a. is very discretely organized, with few interconnections.
    b. is important in generating slow-wave sleep.
    c. is primarily concerned with sensory analysis.
    d. none of the above.

18. The locus coeruleus
    a. is very active during REM sleep.
    b. is very active during slow wave sleep.
    c. is very active during meaningful events, and may be important for storing information.
    d. got its name from its dark red color.

19. Neurons in the basal forebrain that promote arousal
    a. use acetylcholine as their transmitter in most cases.
    b. use norepinephrine as their transmitter in most cases.
    c. use prostaglandin as their transmitter in most cases.
    d. are focused only on waking up and are not related to learning, attention, or any other processes.

20. Adenosine
    a. is a major neurotransmitter producing arousal.
    b. builds up during wakefulness until it reaches a sufficient level to shut off arousal neurons in the basal forebrain and thereby produce sleepiness.
    c. is the component of coffee that keeps us awake.
    d. is produced by neurons in the cortex during REM sleep.

21. Sleep-inducing nuclei in the basal forebrain and hypothalamus
    a. use GABA as their neurotransmitter.
    b. use acetylcholine as their neurotransmitter.
    c. have very restricted projections to specific cortical areas.
    d. are inhibited during a fever, resulting in prolonged wakefulness.

22. PGO waves
    a. occur during REM sleep.
    b. are recorded in the pons, lateral geniculate, and occipital cortex.
    c. are compensated, if "lost" due to REM deprivation.
    d. all of the above.

23. Neurons that are more active during REM sleep are located in
    a. primary visual, motor, and dorsolateral prefrontal cortex.
    b. parts of the parietal and temporal cortex.
    c. neurons in the basal forebrain that release GABA as their neurotransmitter.
    d. the locus coeruleus.

24. Inhibition of motor neurons during REM is induced by neurons in
    a. the dorsolateral prefrontal cortex.
    b. the reticular formation.
    c. the pons.
    d. the amygdala.

25. Which of the following is true?
    a. Acetylcholine promotes the onset of REM sleep.
    b. Acetylcholine promotes slow-wave sleep.
    c. Carbachol inhibits REM sleep.
    d. Serotonin promotes the onset of REM sleep.

26. People with phase-delayed temperature rhythms who try to fall asleep at the normal time may experience
    a.  excess sleep.
    b.  maintenance insomnia.
    c.  termination insomnia.
    d.  onset insomnia.

27. Which of the following is a cause of insomnia?
    a.  narcolepsy
    b.  cataplexy
    c.  repeated use of tranquilizers
    d.  hypnagogic hallucinations

28. Which of the following is more closely associated with REM sleep than NREM sleep?
    a.  nightmares
    b.  night terrors
    c.  sleep walking
    d.  all of the above

29. When people are deprived of sleep for a week or more,
    a.  they usually suffer severe consequences, including death.
    b.  some report dizziness, irritability, and difficulty concentrating, but no drastic consequences.
    c.  they actually fall asleep early in the deprivation period and only appear to be awake, because their sleepwalking and sleep talking appear to be very realistic.
    d.  they report no symptoms whatever.

30. The evolutionary theory of sleep
    a.  states that species regulate their sleep time according to how much repair and restoration their bodies need.
    b.  states that species evolved a mechanism to promote energy conservation at times when they are relatively inefficient.
    c.  is incompatible with other theories concerning repair and restoration.
    d.  is currently very well established.

31. Comparisons of sleep patterns across individuals and across species indicate that
    a.  percentage of time spent in REM remains the same, no matter how long the individual sleeps.
    b.  percentage of time in REM decreases as total amount of sleep increases.
    c.  percentage of time in REM increases as total amount of sleep increases..
    d.  percentage of time spent in REM is extremely variable, and shows no relationship to the total amount of sleep.

32. After about a week of REM deprivation, at least some subjects
    a.  reported increased anxiety, irritability and impaired concentration.
    b.  experienced increased appetite and weight gain.
    c.  spent more sleep time on subsequent nights in REM sleep.
    d.  all of the above.

33. The activation-synthesis hypothesis proposes that dreams result from
    a. unconscious wishes struggling for expression.
    b. the ego's attempt to gain control of the id.
    c. the brain's attempt to make sense of its activity.
    d. the brain's attempt to wake up.

34. The clinico-anatomical hypothesis is based on observations that during dreaming
    a. there is increased activity in the inferior parietal cortex, which contributes to visuo-spatial perception; in visual cortex outside V1, which provides visual imagery; and in the hypothalamus and amygdala, which contribute emotional intensity.
    b. there is increased activity in prefrontal cortex, which contributes to the fantasy-like experience of dreams.
    c. there is increased activity in primary visual cortex, which contributes to visual dreams.
    d. there is also increased activity in primary auditory cortex, which provides rich auditory content.


**Please check the Exploring Biological Psychology CD-ROM**


## Answers to True/False Questions

| | | | |
|---|---|---|---|
| 1. F | 5. F | 9. F | 13. F |
| 2. T | 6. T | 10. T | 14. T |
| 3. T | 7. T | 11. F | 15. F |
| 4. F | 8. F | 12. T | 16. F |


## Answers to Fill-in-the-Blank Questions

1. suprachiasmatic nucleus
2. *period, per, timeless, tim*, Clock
3. pineal, 2-3 hours
4. zeitgeber
5. retino-hypothalamic, ganglion
6. alpha
7. 90
8. pontomesencephalon, acetylcholine, glutamate
9. adenosine, prostaglandins
10. PGO waves
11. acetylcholine, serotonin, norephinephrine
12. Orexin
13. activation-synthesis
14. visual, motor, prefrontal


## Answers to Matching Items

| | | | |
|---|---|---|---|
| 1. h | 5. f | 9. o | 13. p |
| 2. m | 6. c | 10. a | 14. i |
| 3. n | 7. l | 11. d | 15. k |
| 4. g | 8. e | 12. b | 16. j |

# Answers to Multiple-Choice Questions

| | | | |
|---|---|---|---|
| 1. b | 10. c | 19. a | 28. a |
| 2. d | 11. b | 20. b | 29. b |
| 3. c | 12. a | 21. a | 30. b |
| 4. d | 13. d | 22. d | 31. c |
| 5. c | 14. b | 23. b | 32. d |
| 6. d | 15. c | 24. c | 33. c |
| 7. c | 16. a | 25. a | 34. a |
| 8. b | 17. d | 26. d | |
| 9. a | 18. c | 27. c | |

# Doing and Dreaming

## ACROSS

1 The biological clock (abbr.)
2 Tract from numerous cortical areas to spinal cord with multiple synapses
6 Slow, fatigue-resistant muscle in fish
8 Disorder in which person falls asleep during emotional excitement
12 Transmitter at neuromuscular junction and used in tracts that arouse brain
14 Stimulus that can reset the biological clock
15 Protein, mutation of which causes Huntington's disease
16 Hormone produced by pineal gland and promoting sleep

## DOWN

1 Type of muscle, connected to bones
3 Tract from motor cortex to spinal cord with no synapses
4 Precursor of dopamine
5 Type of EEG wave with 8-12 hertz rhythm
7 Tendon organ located at both ends of a muscle, responds to muscle contraction
9 ____ gravis: disorder caused by autoimmune destruction of acetylcholine receptors
10 Fast, easily-fatigued muscle in fish
11 Part of hindbrain important for ballistic movements and timing
13 Type of brain wave produced during rapid eye movement sleep (abbr.)

230

# 10

# INTERNAL REGULATION

## INTRODUCTION

Homeostatic drives are drives that tend to maintain certain biological conditions within a fixed range. Temperature regulation in mammals and birds is such a drive. Constant relatively high temperatures provide conditions in which chemical reactions can be regulated precisely and, by increasing the metabolic rate, increase capacity for prolonged activity. Several physiological mechanisms, including shivering, sweating, panting, and redirection of blood flow, raise and lower temperature appropriately. These are coordinated primarily by the preoptic area, which monitors both its own temperature and that of the skin and spinal cord. Behavioral regulation of temperature is used both by animals that are poikilothermic (body temperature matches that of environment) and by those that are homeothermic (body temperature is regulated within a few degrees of a constant setting). Fever is produced when leukocytes (white blood cells) release interleukin-1, which causes production of prostaglandins $E_1$ and $E_2$, which in turn cause the preoptic area to raise body temperature. Moderate fevers are helpful in combating bacterial infections.

Water balance is critical, both for regulating the concentration of chemicals in our bodily fluids (and therefore the rate of chemical reactions) and for maintaining normal blood pressure. If we have ample supplies of palatable fluids to drink, we may drink a great deal of them and let the kidneys discard the excess. If there is a shortage of fluids to drink, or a large loss of water, the posterior pituitary releases vasopressin (also known as antidiuretic hormone, or ADH), which increases both blood pressure and water retention by the kidneys. There are two major types of stimuli for thirst: decreased water content inside cells and decreased blood volume. When there are increased solutes in the blood, the blood and extracellular fluid become more concentrated. Water tends to flow out of cells into the area of higher osmotic pressure (extracellular fluid). The resulting loss of water from cells in the OVLT (organum vasculosum laminae terminalis) elicits neural responses that are relayed to several hypothalamic nuclei, including the supraoptic and paraventricular nuclei, which produce vasopressin (antidiuretic hormone, ADH), the hormone that is released from the posterior pituitary and that increases blood pressure and urine concentration. The OVLT also relays information to the lateral preoptic area, which gives rise to osmotic thirst. Thus, an increase in osmotic signals results in greater water retention, increased water intake, and higher blood pressure. If large amounts of whole blood are lost, the resulting hypovolemia (low volume of blood) is detected by baroreceptors in the large veins. The kidney also detects the hypovolemia and releases renin, which acts in the blood to produce angiotensin II. This hormone causes constriction of blood vessels to maintain blood pressure. It also stimulates neurons in the subfornical organ (SFO), which in turn relay the signal to neurons in the OVLT or SFO, which produce hypovolemic thirst. The signals from the baroreceptors and angiotensin II are synergistic.

Hypovolemic thirst is satisfied best by salt water. A hunger for sodium depends largely on two hormones, aldosterone and angiotensin II. Aldosterone, secreted by the adrenal glands, causes the kidneys, salivary glands, and sweat glands to conserve sodium; it also stimulates an increase in salt intake. Angiotensin II, as noted above, stimulates sodium hunger. The effects of aldosterone and angiotensin II are mediated by the nucleus of the tractus solitarius, which begins to respond to salt in nearly the same way as to sugar.

The factors regulating hunger, satiety, and the selection of specific foods are very complex. Food selection is influenced by the digestive system (including intestinal enzymes), cultural factors, taste, familiarity, and memories of the consequences of consuming a particular food. Hunger and satiety depend on stimuli from the mouth, stomach, and duodenum, as well as blood levels of glucose and other nutrients. Oral factors, stomach or duodenum distension, and nutrient contents of the stomach contribute to satiety. Cholecystokinin (CCK), released by the duodenum, inhibits stomach emptying. CCK also stimulates the vagus nerve, which activates neurons that release CCK in the brain. Blood glucose levels are maintained in a relatively narrow range by varying amounts of insulin, which enables glucose to enter cells, and glucagon, which converts stored glycogen into glucose. Damage to the lateral hypothalamus results in self-starvation, unless the animal is force-fed. The intact lateral hypothalamus contributes to feeding by modifying activity in the nucleus of the tractus solitarius (NTS), which influences taste sensations and salivation, and also by increasing insulin release and facilitating ingestion. It also sends axons to other brain structures that initiate and reinforce learned behaviors and that increase autonomic responses such as the release of digestive juices. Damage to the ventromedial hypothalamus results in obesity. This results from faster emptying of the stomach and increased release of insulin, which promotes fat storage and inhibits its release for use as fuel. As a result, the animal consumes more frequent normal-sized meals. Damage to the paraventricular nucleus (PVN) also results in overeating. However, rats with PVN damage eat larger meals, rather than more frequent meals.

Several chemicals have been found to influence eating and satiety. Leptin is a peptide produced by fat cells that increases energy expenditure and decreases feeding. However, leptin is not an effective treatment of obese people; apparently they produce leptin, but are insensitive to its effects. One means by which leptin decreases feeding is by inhibiting the release of neuropeptide Y (NPY), which normally increases feeding by inhibiting the PVN. Thus, the effect of NPY is similar to lesions of the PVN (failure to end meals appropriately), and leptin inhibits that effect. Several chemicals, including CCK and glucagon (similar to GLP-1 in the brain), have central and peripheral effects that are complementary. Some chemicals also influence behaviors other than feeding; for example, orexin increases both feeding and wakefulness. The multiple messengers and pathways that control food intake and digestion provide an effective system of checks and balances.

Genes control body weight in many ways, including metabolic rate. Other genetic influences include the sensitivity to peptides, such as melanocortin, that regulate eating. However, social and other environmental influences, as well as exercise and eating habits, are important determinants of body weight. Some appetite-suppressant drugs increase levels of norepinephrine, serotonin, and dopamine.

Anorexia nervosa is a disorder in which people eat much less than they need, sometimes starving themselves to death. They are usually perfectionistic, most frequently women, and often are depressed; however, antidepressant drugs are seldom effective in treating anorexia. People with bulimia nervosa alternate between overeating and dieting, frequently eating a huge meal and then purging. People with bulimia have higher than normal levels of peptide YY (a neuromodulator similar to NPY), low levels of CCK, and/or altered serotonin receptors. However, it is not clear whether transmitter abnormalities precede or result from the bulimia. Bulimia may have some similarities to drug addiction. Rats that consumed excessive glucose after a period of deprivation had increased release of dopamine and opiate-like chemicals in their brains; furthermore, withdrawal from the glucose resulted in some of the symptoms of drug withdrawal.

## LEARNING OBJECTIVES

### Module 10.1 Temperature Regulation

1. Understand the advantages of constant high body temperatures and the brain mechanisms that maintain temperatures.
2. Know the advantage of moderate fevers and the physiological mechanisms that produce fever.

## Module 10.2  Thirst
1.  Understand the concepts of osmotic and hypovolemic thirst and stimuli that give rise to each.
2.  Know the brain mechanisms that promote osmotic and hypovolemic thirst and salt appetite.

## Module 10.3  Hunger
1.  Know the functions of the various components of the digestive system and their roles in hunger and satiety.
2.  Understand the functions of the lateral and medial areas of the hypothalamus in the control of feeding.
3.  Know the various peripheral and central chemicals that contribute to satiety.
4.  Know the evidence for a genetic contribution to obesity and the effects of early under- or over-feeding on obesity.
5.  Be able to describe the characteristics of anorexia nervosa and bulimia nervosa and the physiological correlates of bulimia nervosa.

## KEY TERMS AND CONCEPTS

## Module 10.1  Temperature Regulation
1.  Homeostasis
    Walter R. Cannon
    Set range
    Set point
    Negative feedback
        Role of behavior
    Differences from simple homeostasis
        Anticipation of future needs
        Set points vary with conditions
        Nonhomeostatic influences, such as taste

2.  Controlling body temperature
    Poikilothermic: Body temperature same as environment
    Homeothermic: Body temperature almost constant
    Surviving in extreme cold
        Problem: Formation of ice crystals → tear blood vessels and cell membranes
        Some insects and fish: Glycerol and other antifreeze chemicals in blood
        Wood frogs: Do freeze
            Withdraw most fluid from organs and blood vessels, store it in extracellular space
            Chemicals that regulate ice crystal formation
            Increased blood-clotting
    The advantages of constant high body temperature
        Warmer muscles work better
        Easier to heat than to cool body
        $37^\circ$ C close to warmest environmental temperature
        Optimal temperatures for enzymes
        Reproductive cells: Cooler environment
    Physiological mechanisms
        Hypothalamus
        Preoptic area/anterior hypothalamus (POA/AH)
            Monitors own temperature

Monitors temperature of skin and spinal cord
Behavioral mechanisms
Fever
Leukocytes → interleukin-1 → prostaglandins $E_1$ and $E_2$ → POA/AH → fever
Moderate fevers helpful
Physiological and behavioral means

3.  In closing: Temperature and behavior
Redundancy of mechanisms

## Module 10.2  Thirst
1.  Mechanisms of water regulation
Increasing intake
Decreasing output
Vasopressin or antidiuretic hormone (ADH)

2.  Osmotic thirst
Osmotic pressure
Semipermeable membrane
Increase in solute concentration outside cell
Water leaves cells
Brain areas
OVLT (organum vasculosum laminae terminalis): Detects osmotic pressure
Input from stomach: High levels of sodium
Supraoptic and paraventricular nuclei: Vasopressin release from posterior pituitary
Lateral preoptic area: Drinking
Cell bodies and axons passing through
Input from mouth, stomach, intestines → inhibit thirst temporarily

3.  Hypovolemic thirst
Loss of blood volume
Satisfied best by salt water
Specific sodium hunger
Adrenal glands → aldosterone → salt retention and sodium hunger
Angiotensin II → sodium hunger
Nucleus of the tractus solitarius
Mechanisms
Baroreceptors in large veins → hypothalamus → thirst and vasopressin
Hormones from kidneys
Renin
Angiotensinogen in blood → Angiotensin II → constricts blood vessels
Angiotensin II → OVLT or subfornical organ (SFO) → thirst
Angiotensin II also neurotransmitter
Synergistic effects of angiotensin and baroreceptors

4.  In closing: The psychology and biology of thirst
Both behavioral and autonomic controls

**Module 10.3  Hunger**
1. How the digestive system influences food selection
    Mouth: Enzymes in saliva → carbohydrate digestion
    Stomach: Hydrochloric acid, enzymes → protein digestion
    Small intestine: Enzymes → protein, fat, and carbohydrate digestion
        Absorption of nutrients
    Large intestine
        Water and mineral absorption
        Lubrication
    Enzymes and consumption of dairy products
        Lactose, milk sugar
        Lactase enzyme
    Other influences on food selection
        Carnivore, herbivore, omnivore
        Culture, taste, familiarity, learning
            Conditioned taste aversions


2. How taste and digestion control hunger and satiety
    Oral factors
        Desire to taste or chew
        Sham feeding: Eat, pause, eat more
    The stomach and intestines
        Vagus nerve (cranial nerve X)
            Information about stretching of stomach: sufficient but not necessary for satiety
        Splanchnic nerves
            Information about nutrient contents
        The duodenum
            Also sufficient but not necessary for satiety
            Taste neurons in pons: Food in duodenum decreases responsiveness to sweet taste
            Sugars → satiety faster than fats
            The hormone CCK (cholecystokinin)
                CCK directly inhibits stomach emptying
                CCK also → vagus nerve → CCK released as neurotransmitter in brain
    Glucose, insulin, and glucagon
        Glucose: Main fuel for brain, one of several for rest of body
        Insulin: Facilitates glucose entry into cells
            In brain: Satiety hormone
            Migratory and hibernating species: Store fat and glycogen
            Diabetes: High blood glucose; little reaches cells, most is excreted
            Obese people: High blood glucose; much glucose stored as fat
        Glucagon → liver converts stored glycogen to glucose


3. The hypothalamus and feeding regulation
    The lateral hypothalamus
        Lesions: Starvation or weight loss
        Electrical stimulation: Eating
        Neurons vs. dopamine axons passing through
            Damage to dopamine axons with 6-OHDA → inactivity
            Damage to cell bodies or lesions in very young rats → loss of feeding

Mechanisms

 Axons to NTS (nucleus of the tractus solitarius in medulla) → taste, salivation

 Increase insulin secretion

 Axons to forebrain structures → facilitate ingestion

 Dopamine-containing axons → initiation and reinforcement of learned behaviors

 Stimulation of autonomic responses, including digestive secretions

Medial areas of the hypothalamus

 Ventromedial hypothalamus

  Lesions → weight gain to a new high set point

  Ventromedial hypothalamic syndrome: Includes damage to nearby cells and axons

  Ventral noradrenergic bundle

  Finickiness

  More normal-sized meals per day

  Increased stomach motility and secretions

  Faster stomach emptying

  Increased insulin and fat storage

 Paraventricular nucleus

  Critical for ending meals

4. Satiety chemicals and eating disorders

Leptin

 Produced by fat cells

 Decreases hunger, increases energy expenditure and immune function

 Obese people: More leptin than lean people; may be insensitive to it

Neuropeptide Y (NPY)

 Arcuate nucleus: Leptin inhibits neurons that release NPY

 NPY → inhibition of paraventricular nucleus (PVN), which would otherwise end the meal

Other neurotransmitters and hormones

 Microdialysis

 Similarity of function across species

  CCK → satiety in humans and snails

 Similarity of function in brain and periphery

  Glucagon and GLP-1 decrease feeding

  CCK in intestines and brain inhibits feeding

 Similarity of function for multiple behaviors

  Orexin → feeding and wakefulness

 Numerous chemicals affect feeding

  Obesity in rodents due to deficiencies in leptin, CCK, melanocortin; excess
   corticosterone

Genetics and human body weight

 High heritability of obesity

 Melanocortin receptor

  Mutation → obesity

 Gene on chromosome 4 linked to obesity in women, not men

 Multiple gene influences

 Environment

  Early under- or over-feeding → interaction with genes in vulnerable people

  Native American Pimas: Typical American diet → obesity

Weight loss techniques

 Increase exercise

Restraint of eating
Appetite suppressant drugs
"Fen-phen"
Fenfluramine →increase serotonin release and decrease reuptake
Phentermine → block norepinephrine and dopamine reuptake
Medical complications
Sibutramine (Meridia)
Blocks reuptake of serotonin and norepinephrine
Experimental drugs: block fat absorption
Anorexia and bulimia
Anorexia nervosa
Hardworking perfectionists (obsessive-compulsive)
Depression
Antidepressant drugs seldom effective
Bulimia nervosa
Eat enormous meal, then purge
High levels of peptide YY (PYY)
Low levels of CCK
Altered serotonin receptors
Similar to drug addiction
Food-deprive rats for first 4 hours of day, then offer glucose → great increase in eating
Increased dopamine and opiate-like compounds in brain (similar to abused drugs)
Deprived of glucose → withdrawal symptoms

5. In closing: The multiple controls of hunger
Checks and balances


## SHORT-ANSWER QUESTIONS


**Module 10.1  Temperature Regulation**
1. *Homeostasis*
   a.  What is a homeostatic process?




   b.  What are some of the physiological processes that are controlled near a set point?  What are some homeostatic processes that anticipate future needs or that change under various conditions?

c. Why does the scrotum of most male mammals hang outside the body? Why should pregnant women avoid hot baths?

2. *Controlling body temperature*
   a. Define the terms poikilothermic and homeothermic.

   b. What is two advantages of a constant relatively high body temperature? What is the cost to the animal for maintaining homeothermy?

   c. What two kinds of stimuli does the preoptic area monitor for temperature control?

   d. What prevents the temperature of fish, amphibians, and reptiles from fluctuating wildly?

   e. What are interleukin-1 and prostaglandins $E_1$ and $E_2$? What are their roles in producing a fever?

f.   Of what benefit is a moderate fever?

**Module 10.2   Thirst**

1.   *Mechanisms of water regulation*
    a.   Describe the different mechanisms of maintaining water balance that have been developed by desert animals and by animals with an abundant water supply.

    b.   What are the two functions of vasopressin when body fluids are low?  What is its other name?

2.   *Osmotic thirst*
    a.   What is osmotic pressure?

    b.   How does the body "know" when its osmotic pressure is low?

c.    What are the roles of the OVLT, the supraoptic and paraventricular nuclei, and the lateral preoptic area in osmotic thirst?

3.   *Hypovolemic thirst*
    a.   Why is hypovolemia dangerous?

    b.   Under what circumstances does hypovolemic thirst occur?

    c.   Will an animal with hypovolemic thirst drink more pure water or more salt water with the same concentration as blood? Why?

    d.   What two effects of aldosterone are beneficial in cases of sodium deficiency? What other hormone contributes to salt hunger? On what brain area do these two hormones act to increase salt hunger?

    e.   What is the role of baroreceptors in hypovolemic thirst?

f.   Describe the steps leading to the production of antiotensin II.  What are its two main effects?

g.   Which brain structures seem to mediate hypovolemic thirst?

h.   How may the effects of angiotensin II be enhanced?

**Module 10.3  Hunger**
1.   *How the digestive system influences food selection*
     a.   Enzymes for the digestion of what type of nutrient(s) are present in saliva?  In the stomach? In the small intestine?

     b.   From which structure is digested food absorbed?

     c.   Why do newborn mammals stop nursing as they grow older?

d.  Discuss the evidence that humans are a partial exception to the principle of lactose intolerance in adults.

e.  List the factors that may influence food selection.

2.  *How taste and digestion control hunger*
    a.  Summarize the evidence for the importance of oral factors in hunger and satiety. What is the evidence that these factors are not sufficient to end a meal normally?

    b.  How did Deutsch et al. demonstrate the importance of stomach distension in regulating meal size?

    c.  Which two nerves convey the stomach's satiety signals?

    d.  What is CCK? In what two places is it produced? What is one mechanism by which it induces satiety?

e.  What is the effect of insulin on blood glucose?  In what ways does insulin affect hunger?  Compare the effects of glucagon with those of insulin.

f.  Why do people with untreated diabetes eat a lot but gain little weight?  How is this similar to, and how is it different from, the effects of high levels of insulin?

3.  *The hypothalamus and feeding regulation*
    a.  Describe the evidence that the lateral hypothalamus is important for hunger.

    b.  What is 6-hydroxydopamine?  What kind of neuronal damage does it inflict when injected into the lateral hypothalamus?  What are the behavioral results of such damage?

    c.  What is the result of damage to lateral hypothalamic cell bodies?

d. By what five mechanisms may the lateral hypothalamus contribute to feeding?

e. Describe the various behavioral changes produced by lesions of the ventromedial hypothalamus, ventral noradrenergic bundle, and surrounding areas.

f. To what factors can we attribute the obesity induced by ventromedial hypothalamus lesions?

g. What are the effects of damage to the paraventricular nucleus (PVN)? How are these effects different from those of ventromedial hypothalamus damage?

4. *Satiety chemicals and eating disorders*
   a. What type of cells produce leptin? What message does leptin convey? Is there any evidence that overweight humans produce too little leptin?

b.   What brain area is inhibited by neuropeptide Y (NPY)?  What are the effects of NPY on feeding?  What chemical inhibits the release of NPY?

c.   What is microdialysis?

d.   What are two means by which CCK inhibits feeding?  What are the effects of glucagon and GLP-1?

e.   What are two effects of orexin?

f.   Give one example of a group of people who demonstrate the relationship of genetic and environmental factors in the control of weight.  How important are exercise and restraint of eating?

g.   Compare the symptoms of anorexia nervosa with those of bulimia nervosa.

h. Describe the personality characteristics of many people with anorexia and their relatives.

i. What chemical differences are seen in bulimics, compared to other people. Can we determine whether these differences imply cause and effect relationships between the chemical and the disorder?

j. What evidence suggests that excessive eating in bulimia has some parallels with drug addiction?

## TRUE/FALSE QUESTIONS

_____ 1. Behavior can act as a negative feedback mechanism to correct homeostatic imbalances.

_____ 2. Poikilothermic animals are those that maintain almost constant temperature.

_____ 3. The POA/AH monitors its own temperature and that of the skin and spinal cord.

_____ 4. During illness, leukocytes produce interleukin-1, which elicits production of prostaglandins $E_1$ and $E_1$, which in turn stimulate the preoptic area to induce a fever.

_____ 5. Cells in the supraoptic and paraventricular nuclei send input to the OVLT concerning hypovolemic signals; the OVLT then releases vasopressin from the anterior pituitary.

_____ 6. Hypovolemic thirst and osmotic thirst are both relieved best by drinking pure water.

_____ 7. Aldosterone from the adrenal glands increases salt retention and salt hunger; its effect on salt hunger is increased by angiotensin II.

_____ 8. Renin from the kidneys splits off a portion of angiotensinogen, forming angiotensin I, which enzymes then convert to angiotensin II, which in turn constricts blood vessels and stimulates drinking.

_____ 9. Oral factors are sufficient to induce satiety.

_____ 10. The splanchnic nerve carries information about the nutrient content of the stomach.

_____ 11. CCK is a powerful stimulus to initiate eating.

_____ 12. Diabetics have high levels of glucose, but little is able to enter cells.

_____ 13. 6-OHDA lesions of axons passing through the lateral hypothalamus result in a specific loss of feeding.

_____ 14. Lesions of the ventromedial hypothalamus result in a voracious appetite that included even foods that were bitter or untasty and produc continued weight gain until the animals died.

_____ 15. Lesions of the ventromedial nucleus result in more, normal-sized meals; lesions of the paraventricular nucleus result in an unchanged number of larger meals.

_____ 16. Leptin is produced by fat cells and inhibits neurons that release neuropeptide Y (NPY).

_____ 17. NPY normally stimulates the paraventricular nucleus to produce satiety.

_____ 18. Orexin induces both satiety and sleepiness.

_____ 19. Some cases of obesity may be linked to a mutation in the melanocortin receptor.

_____ 20. People with bulimia nervosa tend to have high levels of peptide YY, low levels of CCK, and altered serotonin receptors.


## FILL IN THE BLANKS

1. Walter R. Cannon introduced the term _____ to refer to the biological processes that keep certain body variables within a certain range.

2. Animals whose body temperature matches that of the environment are referred to as

   _____.

3. The _____ _____/_____ _____ is the primary brain area that controls body temperature.

4. During illness leukocytes produce _____-__, which in turn stimulates the production of _____ _____ and ____, which result in an increase in body temperature.

5. The two kinds of thirst are _____ and _____.

6. The _____ is the main brain area that detects osmotic pressure.

7. Activity in the _____ and _____ nuclei result in the release of vasopressin from the _____ pituitary.

8. Salt hunger is stimulated by _____ from the adrenal glands and by _____.

9. _____ in the large veins detect low blood pressure and signal the hypothalamus to stimulate thirst and release vasopressin.

10. Low blood pressure also stimulates the kidneys to release _____, which results in the production of _____ from angiotensinogen in the blood.

11. The _____ nerve carries information about stomach distension; the _____ nerve carries information about the stomach's nutrient content.

12. The duodenum releases _____ (_____), which inhibits stomach emptying and also acts via the vagus nerve to promote satiety.

13. _____ facilitates glucose entry into cells; _____ promotes the release of glucose from the liver.

14. _____ axons passing through the lateral hypothalamus promote the initiation and reinforcement of learned behaviors.

15. Lesions of the _____ hypothalamus increase stomach motility and secretions, increase insulin and fat storage, and speed stomach emptying.

16. The _____ nucleus is important for ending meals.

17. _____ is a satiety signal produced by fat cells; it inhibits neurons that release _____ (_____).

18. Sibutramine, a new drug to treat obesity blocks the reuptake of _____ and _____.

## MATCHING ITEMS

_____ 1.   Poikilothermic

_____ 2.   Homeothermic

_____ 3.   POA/AH

_____ 4.   Vasopressin

_____ 5.   OVLT

_____ 6.   Osmotic thirst

_____ 7.   Hypovolemic thirst

_____ 8.   Renin

_____ 9.   Vagus nerve

_____10.   Splanchnic nerve

_____11.   Duodenum

_____12.   Lateral hypothalamus

_____13.   Ventromedial hypothalamus

_____14.   Paraventricular nucleus

_____15.   Leptin

_____16.   Bulimia nervosa

a.   Brain area that controls temperature

b.   Brain area that normally promotes eating

c.   Brain area that detects osmotic pressure

d.   Lesions → larger meals

e.   Lesions → more normal-sized meals per day

f.   Carries information about stomach distention

g.   Hormone from kidney → angiotensin II

h.   Releases CCK to inhibit stomach emptying

i.   Peptide hormone produced by fat cells

j.   Body temperature relatively constant

k.   Result of increased extracellular solutes

l.   Hormone → increases blood pressure, thirst

m.   Result of loss of blood, vomiting, heavy sweating

n.   Increased peptide YY, decreased CCK

o.   Body temperature similar to environment

p.   Carries information about nutrient content

## MULTIPLE-CHOICE QUESTIONS

1. Temperature regulation
   a.   is an example of a homeostatic mechanism.
   b.   is important in mammals and birds for increasing capacity for muscle activity.
   c.   maintains body temperature at levels that maximize the enzymatic properties of proteins.
   d.   all of the above.

2. The preoptic area monitors
   a.   only its own temperature.
   b.   only skin and spinal cord temperature.
   c.   both its own and skin and spinal cord temperature.
   d.   the temperature of internal organs via nerve input from those organs.

3. Behavioral means of temperature regulation
    a.  are the only means of temperature regulation in poikilotherms.
    b.  are the only means of temperature regulation in homeotherms.
    c.  do not become functional until adulthood.
    d.  are effective only for controlling temperature within the normal range, not to induce a fever.

4. Fever
    a.  is harmful and should always be reduced with aspirin.
    b.  is produced primarily by prostaglandins E1 and E2 acting on cells in the preoptic area.
    c.  is produced directly by bacteria acting on the preoptic area.
    d.  is especially high in baby rabbits, in response to infections.

5. Vasopressin
    a.  raises blood pressure by constricting blood vessels.
    b.  is also known as antidiuretic hormone, because it promotes water retention by the kidney.
    c.  is secreted from the posterior pituitary, as a result of control by the supraoptic and paraventricular nuclei of the hypothalamus.
    d.  all of the above.

6. The main reason that a salty meal makes us thirsty is that
    a.  excess salt in extracellular fluid produces cellular dehydration; such dehydration of cells in the OVLT results in osmotic thirst.
    b.  increased salt in extracellular fluid causes the fluid to enter OVLT cells, thus distending them and producing osmotic thirst.
    c.  increased salt in the blood causes the liquid portion of the blood to enter cells throughout the body, thus producing hypovolemia.
    d.  the salt enters cells in the OVLT and stimulates them directly.

7. The lateral preoptic area
    a.  controls hypovolemic, but not osmotic, thirst.
    b.  is the site of receptors for osmotic thirst.
    c.  receives input from the OVLT and controls drinking.
    d.  primarily responds to signals concerning dryness of the throat.

8. After its blood volume has been reduced, an animal
    a.  will drink more pure water than salt water of the same concentration as blood.
    b.  will drink more slightly salty water than pure water.
    c.  will not drink any more than usual, since both liquid and solute have been removed.
    d.  will drink only highly concentrated salt water.

9. Salt hunger
    a.  depends in part on aldosterone secreted by the adrenal glands.
    b.  is enhanced by angiotensin II.
    c.  is mediated by neurons in the nucleus of the tractus solitarius that are activated by aldosterone and angiotensin II.
    d.  all of the above.

10. Angiotensin II
    a. is secreted by the kidney.
    b. causes water to leave cells in the preoptic area and thereby stimulates osmotic thirst.
    c. stimulates the subfornical organ, which relays the information to the preoptic area, which in turn induces drinking.
    d. all of the above.

11. Which of the following is **not** likely to induce drinking?
    a. application of aldosterone to the lateral preoptic area
    b. application of angiotensin II to the subfornical organ
    c. low blood pressure signals from baroreceptors in the large veins
    d. a salty meal

12. In the stomach
    a. food is mixed with hydrochloric acid and enzymes for the digestion of protein.
    b. food is mixed with hydrochloric acid and enzymes for the digestion of carbohydrates.
    c. food is mixed with enzymes that aid the digestion of fats.
    d. absorption of food through the walls of the stomach occurs.

13. Lactase
    a. is the sugar in milk.
    b. is an intestinal enzyme for the digestion of milk.
    c. is abundant in almost all adult humans, but is lacking in adults of other mammalian species.
    d. is abundant in birds and reptiles, but is lacking in mammals.

14. Oral factors
    a. contribute to satiety but are not sufficient to determine the amount of food consumed.
    b. are irrelevant to satiety.
    c. are the single most important factor in inducing satiety.
    d. include only the taste of food.

15. If a cuff closes the outlet from the stomach to the small intestine
    a. the animal will not eat because of the trauma of the cuff.
    b. the animal will continue eating, since food must pass beyond the stomach to trigger satiety.
    c. the animal will eat a normal-sized meal and stop.
    d. the animal will eat a normal meal, wait for it to be absorbed through the walls of the stomach, and then eat again.

16. Splanchnic nerves
    a. carry information about the nutrient contents of the stomach.
    b. carry information about the stretching of the stomach walls.
    c. are stimulated directly by cholecystokinin (CCK).
    d. secrete CCK into the circulatory system.

17. CCK
    a. is produced by the duodenum in response to the presence of food there.
    b. works, in part, by closing the sphincter muscle between the stomach and duodenum, thus allowing the stomach to fill faster.
    c. is also produced in the brain, where it tends to decrease eating.
    d. all of the above.

18. Which of the following is true?
    a. Diabetes results from a deficit in glucagon.
    b. Obese people produce more insulin than do people of normal weight.
    c. Diabetic people produce more insulin than do non-diabetics.
    d. Glucose levels in the blood are elevated by insulin.

19. Insulin
    a. is secreted in response to low blood sugar.
    b. is released by the liver.
    c. is no longer secreted after VMH lesions.
    d. promotes entry of glucose into cells.

20. People with untreated diabetes eat more food because
    a. the vagus and splanchnic nerves are damaged.
    b. they store too much of their glucose, so it is unavailable for use.
    c. they excrete most of their glucose unused.
    d. their basal metabolic rate is too high.

21. Glucagon
    a. is high in the late autumn in migratory and hibernating species.
    b. is produced by the small intestine.
    c. stimulates the liver to convert stored glycogen to glucose for release into the blood.
    d. stimulates the liver to convert glucose to glycogen for storage.

22. Which of the following is true of lateral hypothalamic damage?
    a. It results in inactivity and decreased responsiveness to stimuli.
    b. At least some of the results are due to damage to axons passing through the area, rather than to cell bodies located there.
    c. At least some of the effects on eating are due to low levels of insulin and digestive juices.
    d. All of the above are true.

23. Obesity resulting from damage to the ventromedial hypothalamus and ventral noradrenergic bundle
    a. can be prevented by letting the animals eat only as much as they ate before the lesion.
    b. occurs because the stomach empties faster than usual and insulin secretion is increased.
    c. results from a dramatic increase in the palatability of all foods, resulting in overeating even of bitter or untasty food.
    d. results from eating much larger meals than usual, because of lack of satiety.

24. Which of the following is true of the paraventricular nucleus (PVN)?
    a. It is important for ending a meal.
    b. It is important for beginning a meal.
    c. NPY excites neurons in the PVN.
    d. Leptin increases eating by increasing NPY release in the PVN.

25. Leptin
    a. increases eating.
    b. is a neurotransmitter produced by the brain.
    c. is produced by fat cells.
    d. is reduced in quantity in overweight people.

26. Neuropeptide Y (NPY)
    a. is produced by fat cells and decreases feeding.
    b. directly increases metabolic rate.
    c. decreases fat storage by decreasing the production of leptin.
    d. inhibits activity in the PVN, thereby increasing meal size.

27. Microdialysis
    a. is a means of detecting the release of neurotransmitters.
    b. is a technique used primarily for damaging cell bodies while leaving axons intact.
    c. is a technique used primarily for damaging axons while leaving cell bodies intact.
    d. has been used to demonstrate that CCK is an important hunger signal.

28. Which of the following is true?
    a. Anorexics are frequently hardworking perfectionists.
    b. Bulimics have higher than normal levels of peptide YY (PYY).
    c. Bulimics have lower than normal levels of CCK and altered serotonin receptors.
    d. All of the above are true.

## Answers to True/False Questions

| | | | |
|---|---|---|---|
| 1. T | 6. F | 11. F | 16. T |
| 2. F | 7. T | 12. T | 17. F |
| 3. T | 8. T | 13. F | 18. F |
| 4. T | 9. F | 14. F | 19. T |
| 5. F | 10. T | 15. T | 20. T |

## Answers to Fill-in-the-Blank Questions

1. homeostasis
2. poikilothermic
3. preoptic area anterior hypothalamus
4. interleukin-1, prostaglandins $E_1$, $E_2$
5. osmotic, hypovolemic
6. OVLT
7. supraoptic, paraventricular, posterior
8. aldosterone, angiotensin II
9. Baroreceptors
10. renin, angiotensin II
11. vagus, splanchnic
12. cholecystokinin, CCK
13. Insulin, glucagon
14. Dopamine
15. ventromedial
16. paraventricular
17. Leptin, neuropeptide Y, NPY
18. norepinephrine, serotonin

## Answers to Matching Items

| | | | |
|---|---|---|---|
| 1. o | 5. c | 9. f | 13. e |
| 2. j | 6. k | 10. p | 14. d |
| 3. a | 7. m | 11. h | 15. i |
| 4. l | 8. g | 12. b | 16. n |

# Answers to Multiple-Choice Questions

| | | | |
|---|---|---|---|
| 1. d | 9. d | 17. d | 25. c |
| 2. c | 10. c | 18. b | 26. d |
| 3. a | 11. a | 19. d | 27. a |
| 4. b | 12. a | 20. c | 28. d |
| 5. d | 13. b | 21. c | |
| 6. a | 14. a | 22. d | |
| 7. c | 15. c | 23. b | |
| 8. b | 16. a | 24. a | |

**Please check the Exploring Biological Psychology CD-ROM**

## Diagram

Label the following areas:  preoptic area, posterior hypothalamus, lateral hypothalamus, ventromedial hypothalamus, paraventricular nucleus of the hypothalamus.

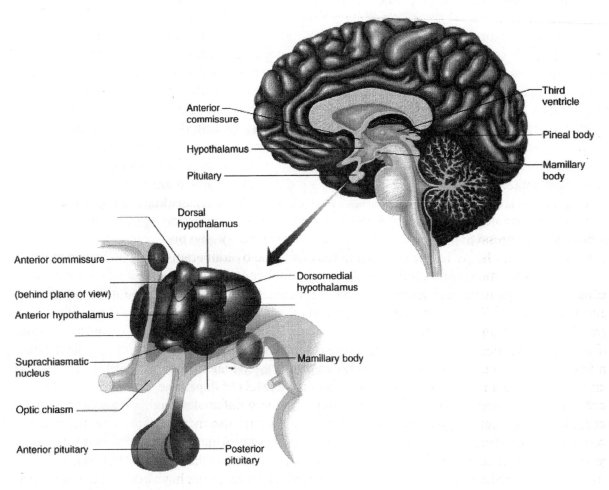

*Source: After Nieuwenhuys, Voogd, & vanHuijzen, 1988*

# 11

# REPRODUCTIVE BEHAVIORS

## INTRODUCTION

Hormones, released from endocrine glands, travel in the blood throughout the body. Because of their widespread effects they are useful for coordinating long-lasting effects. There are several classes of hormones, including protein or peptide hormones, steroids, thyroid hormones, and monoamines. The hypothalamus is the true master gland of the body, in that it controls the pituitary gland, which in turn controls the other endocrine glands. The pituitary is composed of two distinct glands. The posterior pituitary receives axons from two hypothalamic nuclei; when these neurons fire action potentials, oxytocin and vasopressin are released from the posterior pituitary into the blood. The anterior pituitary is controlled by blood-borne releasing and inhibiting hormones from the hypothalamus. It synthesizes and releases six hormones: adrenocorticotropic hormone (ACTH), thyroid-stimulating hormone (TSH), prolactin, growth hormone (GH, somatotropin), and two gonadotropins: follicle-stimulating hormone (FSH) and luteinizing hormone (LH). A negative feedback system maintains certain hormones within a set range.

Sex hormones have two distinct kinds of effects, depending on the stage of development at which they are present. The absence of androgens during an early critical period results in female-typical appearance and behavior, and androgens administered to a genetic female masculinize her genitals and behavior. However, a low level of estrogen must be present for differentiation of female brains. The SRY (sex-determining region on the Y chromosome) gene causes the primitive gonads to develop as testes and to secrete testosterone, which increases growth of the testes and Wolffian ducts (seminal vesicles and vas deferens). The testes also secrete Müllerian inhibiting hormone, which causes the female reproductive tract to regress. In the absence of the SRY gene, mammals develop as females. Their gonads differentiate into ovaries, their Müllerian ducts differentiate into oviducts, uterus, and upper vagina, and their Wolffian ducts regress. In rodents androgen exerts its masculinizing effects on behavior mostly by being converted, intracellularly, to estrogen. A female is not masculinized by her own and her mother's estrogen because it is bound to alpha-fetoprotein, which prevents it from entering cells. Hormones may also have organizing effects on the hypothalamus, on nerves and muscles that control the penis, and on nonsexual characteristics, such as body size, aggressiveness, parental behavior, life expectancy, and play patterns. Certain brain areas are relatively larger in one sex than in the other, and overall brain size is greater in males.

When sex hormones are administered during adulthood, they tend to activate whatever behavior patterns were organized during development. Estrogens enhance sensory responsiveness of the pubic area of female rats. The ventromedial nucleus and the medial preoptic area (MPOA) of the hypothalamus are important brain areas for the activational effects of hormones. Under the influence of sex hormones, neurons in the MPOA release dopamine, which enhances female-typical behavior in female rats and male-typical behavior in males. Castrated males produce dopamine in the MPOA but fail to release it in response to a female. Moderate levels of dopamine stimulate $D_1$ or $D_5$ receptors, which promote erection in males and receptivity in females; higher levels stimulate $D_2$ receptors and promote orgasm and ejaculation. Testosterone also increases men's sexual interest, and oxytocin may enhance sexual pleasure, especially at orgasm. Although decreases in testosterone generally decrease sexual activity, low testosterone is not always the source of impotence. Treatments that reduce testosterone production or block its receptors have been used to treat sex offenders.

In women and certain other female primates, menstrual cycles result from interaction between the hypothalamus, pituitary, and ovaries. Follicle-stimulating hormone (FSH) from the anterior pituitary stimulates the growth of ovarian follicles and the secretion of estrogen from the follicles. Increasing estrogen at first decreases the release of FSH, but near the middle of the cycle, it somehow causes a sudden surge of luteinizing hormone (LH) and FSH. These hormones cause an ovum to be released. They also cause the remnant of the follicle (the corpus luteum) to release progesterone, which causes the uterine lining to proliferate in preparation for implantation of a fertilized ovum. Progesterone inhibits release of LH; therefore, near the end of the cycle, all hormones are low, resulting in menstruation if fertilization does not occur. If the ovum is fertilized, estradiol and progesterone increase throughout the pregnancy. Combination birth-control pills contain estrogen, which suppresses the release of FSH early in the cycle, and progesterone, which inhibits the secretion of LH. Women's sexual interest is somewhat higher during the periovulatory period, but hormones are less important for women's sexual response than for females of other species. Sex hormones also affect women's preference for somewhat masculinized, as opposed to feminized, men's faces. Premenstrual syndrome is characterized by anxiety, irritability, and depression in the days preceding menstruation. It may result from low levels of allopregnanolone, a metabolite of progesterone that alters GABA receptors and thereby decreases anxiety.

Hormones also have activational effects on nonsexual behaviors. Testosterone enhances aggression in many species. Estrogen increases the number of dendritic spines in the hippocampus, which may be related to memory. It also increases the numbers of certain dopamine and serotonin receptors in the nucleus accumbens and several cortical areas; these areas are thought to control reinforcement and emotion. Estrogen also enhances verbal memory and fine motor control, but decreases performance on spatial tasks. Testosterone given to older men improved their spatial skills. However, hormonal effects on cognitive abilities are small, and their functional significance is not understood.

Parental behavior in rodents can be rapidly induced by hormonal patterns characteristic of the time of delivery. This suggests that the immediate maternal behavior that occurs with delivery may be under hormonal control. Oxytocin and prolactin appear to be especially important. Hormones increase activity in the medial preoptic area, which is important for parental behavior, as well as for temperature regulation, thirst, and sexual behavior. Repeated exposure to pups can induce parental behavior after about six days, even in females without ovaries. However, brain areas that respond to pheromones from the young animals initially suppress parental behavior; their activity is inhibited in the later phase, thereby allowing parental behavior to occur. Males of some mammalian species also contribute to the care of the young and may undergo hormonal changes that promote parental behavior. However, hormonal changes are not necessary for parental behavior in humans, except to permit a woman to nurse a baby.

There are a number of differences between men and women in some aspects of their sexual activities and in the qualities that they prefer in their mates. An evolutionary explanation for men's greater interest in short-term sexual relationships with many partners suggests that males typically seek to spread their genes, whereas females have a greater investment in a small number of offspring. However, females may also benefit from having multiple sexual partners, including greater fertility and a chance for a better mate. Women's use of odor in mate selection may provide clues at to the man's health and genetic compatibility. Women also seek good providers, especially in societies where women have little economic power. On the other hand men tend to seek younger partners, because they are more likely to be fertile. Studies of responses in hypothetical situations have suggested that men are more likely to be upset by sexual infidelity, whereas women are more upset by emotional infidelity. However, a study of people's responses to actual situations found that both men and women were more upset by emotional infidelity. The fact that similar sex differences are found in many cultures does not necessarily imply that there are genetic bases for them.

Humans are variable in their sexual development and gender identity. Early fetal gonadal structures differentiate in either a male or a female direction, depending on the presence or absence of the SRY gene. Some XY males have a mutation of the SRY gene, resulting in poorly developed genitals. Some XX females have an SRY gene translocated from their father's Y chromosome to an autosomal chromosome, which may result in some ovary and some testis tissue. If a female is exposed to excess androgen during the critical period for sex differentiation, she may develop structures intermediate between those of a normal female and a normal male. A similar condition may occur if a genetic male has low levels of testosterone or is unresponsive to it. Such individuals are called intersexes or pseudohermaphrodites. Most intersexes have been reared as females, since it is easier to feminize the genitals surgically than to masculinize them. However, the surgery often impairs genital sensation. A genetic male may develop a relatively normal female appearance and gender identity because of testicular feminization (androgen insensitivity), due to a lack of androgen receptors. In the Dominican Republic some genetic males lack an enzyme that converts testosterone to dihydrotestosterone. Because dihydrotestosterone is more effective than testosterone for masculinizing the genitals, these boys appeared to be girls early in life; however, they became masculinized by high levels of testosterone at puberty. They then developed male gender identity, which was consistent with their prenatal testosterone. It was not possible for a genetic male, whose penis was accidentally removed at birth, to develop a female identity, despite attempts by his parents to raise him as a girl. These cases suggest that prenatal hormones play an important role in determining gender identity, although environmental factors may have some influence.

Genetic factors may promote homosexual orientation in both men and women. Monozygotic (identical) twins of homosexuals are more likely to be homosexual than are dizygotic (fraternal) twins or other biological or adopted siblings. One study suggested that a gene that contributes to male homosexuality is on the X chromosome, and therefore is inherited from the mother; however, later studies did not replicate these results. A gene that increases homosexuality, and therefore decreases reproductive success, would be expected to be selected against in the course of evolution. However, it may be perpetuated through kin selection or by increasing the reproductive ability of the women who carry the gene. Homosexuality is not well correlated with hormone levels in adulthood. However, there is some evidence that low levels of prenatal testosterone, sometimes caused by stress, may predispose males to homosexuality in adulthood. In rats, similar stress effects appeared to be mediated by endorphins and were influenced by social experiences after birth. Some women whose mothers took diethylstilbestrol (DES) to prevent miscarriage may have increased bisexual or homosexual responsiveness. Some brain structures show sex differences in size. For some of these structures, including the anterior commissure, the suprachiasmatic nucleus, and the interstitial nucleus 3 of the hypothalamus, homosexual men have structures more similar in size to those of women than to those of heterosexual men. We do not know whether these differences are a cause or an effect of homosexuality, or indeed, if they are relevant at all.

## LEARNING OBJECTIVES

### Module 11.1  The Effects of Sex Hormones
1. Know the kinds of hormones and their receptors.
2. Understand the roles of the hypothalamus, anterior pituitary, and posterior pituitary in the control of hormone secretion.
3. Understand the roles of genes and hormones in the organization of physical and behavioral sex differences in mammals.
4. Understand the activating roles of hormones on reproductive behaviors and neurotransmitters.
5. Understand the hormonal processes that control women's menstrual cycles and pregnancy, including the effects of birth-control pills.

6. Know the endocrine influences on parental and other non-sexual behaviors.

## Module 11.1 Variations in Sexual Behavior
1. Be familiar with evolutionary interpretations of mate choice and jealousy.
2. Know the genetic and hormonal factors that can produce intersexes and other discrepancies in sexual appearance.
3. Understand the genetic and hormonal influences on gender identity and sexual orientation.


# KEY TERMS AND CONCEPTS

## Module 11.1 The Effects of Sex Hormones
1. Control of hormone release
   Endocrine glands
   Hormone
   > Chemical secreted by a gland, carried by blood
   > Coordinates long-lasting changes in multiple sites
   > Classes
   >> Protein and peptide hormones
   >>> Example: Insulin
   >>> Membrane receptors → second messenger system
   >> Steroid hormones
   >>> Two kinds of receptors
   >>>> Membrane receptors → second messenger system
   >>>> Cytoplasmic receptors → nucleus → gene expression
   >>> Derived from cholesterol
   >>>> Cortisol and corticosterone
   >>>> Androgens
   >>>> Estrogens
   >>>> Progesterone
   >>>> Anabolic steroids, including androstenedione
   >> Thyroid hormones
   >> Monoamines
   >>> Norepinephrine and dopamine
   Hypothalamus: True "master gland"
   Pituitary gland
   > Posterior pituitary
   >> Neurons in hypothalamus → axons to posterior pituitary → release oxytocin and vasopressin (antidiuretic hormone) into blood
   > Anterior pituitary
   >> Hypothalamus → releasing hormones or inhibiting hormones via blood to anterior Pituitary
   >> Adrenocorticotropic hormone (ACTH)
   >> Thyroid stimulating hormone (TSH)
   >> Prolactin
   >> Somatotropin (growth hormone, GH)
   >> Gonadotropins
   >>> Follicle-stimulating hormone (FSH)
   >>> Luteinizing hormone (LH)

258

2. Organizing effects of sex hormones
   Organizing effects
       Permanent change
       Sensitive stage of development
   Activating effects
       Temporary activation of a response
       May last longer than hormone remains in organ, but not indefinitely
   Sex differences in the gonads and hypothalamus
       Chromosomes
           Female: XX
           Male: XY
       Gonads: identical in very early stage
       Male (XY)
           SRY gene (sex region Y) → testes → testosterone →
           Wolffian ducts → seminal vesicles and vas deferens
           MIH (Müllerian inhibiting hormone) → degeneration of Müllerian ducts
           Penis, scrotum
       Female (XX)
           Ovaries (egg-producing organs)
           Müllerian ducts mature → oviducts, uterus, upper vagina
           Wolffian ducts degenerate
       Hypothalamus
           Medial preoptic hypothalamus
               Sexually dimorphic nucleus: Larger in males
           Cyclic pattern of hormone release in females
   Sensitive period for testosterone's effects
       Humans: Third and fourth months of pregnancy
       Rats: Last few days of pregnancy and first few postnatal days
       Masculinization of female rats by testosterone injections
       Low levels of sex hormones → female development
           Small amounts of estradiol necessary for brain differentiation
       Aromatization of testosterone to estradiol
           Alpha-fetoprotein: Protects some female mammals from estradiol
           Primates: Protected by metabolism of estradiol
           Estradiol injection → masculinizes female rodents
               Exceeds normal binding by alpha-fetoprotein or metabolism
   Sex differences in nonreproductive characteristics
       Body size, aggressiveness, life expectancy, infant care
       Excessive prenatal adrenal androgens in girls → male-typical toys and activities
       Women > men
           Increased density of neurons in language area of temporal lobe
           Larger corpus callosum relative to total brain size
       Men > women
           Overall size of cortex, but organized differently
           Apoptosis longer in females → fewer neurons

3. Activating effects of sex hormones
   Relationship to behavior
       Doves: Behavior → hormone change → behavior → hormone change, etc.
       Hormones → alter responsiveness of brain, peripheral structures to certain stimuli

Research using rodents
 Dependent on hormones
 Testosterone and its metabolites, dihydrotestosterone and estradiol → masculine behavior
 Estrogen followed by progesterone → feminine behavior
  Pudendal nerve: Tactile stimulation from pubic area to brain
  Ventromedial nucleus
  Medial preoptic area
   Sexually dimorphic nucleus: Exact importance unclear
   Stimulation → sexual behavior in rats
   Lesions → only mild deficits
   Dopamine
    Released in male MPOA in presence of female
    Facilitates copulation
    Males: Testosterone → release of dopamine in MPOA
     Castration → normal production of dopamine, but no release with female
    Females: Estradiol → release of dopamine in MPOA
    Moderate dopamine levels → $D_1$ and $D_5$ receptors → erection in male and
     receptivity in female
    Higher dopamine levels → $D_2$ receptors → Ejaculation and orgasm
Sexual behavior in humans
 Effects on men
  Correlation of testosterone levels and sexual excitement
  Oxytocin release during orgasm
  Impotence not always due to low testosterone
   Testosterone → nitric oxide in hypothalamus and penis → blood flow to penis
    Sildenafil (Viagra) → prolonged effect of nitric oxide
  Sex offenders: Reduce testosterone → reduced sexual activities
   Cyproterone: Blocks testosterone receptors
   Medroxyprogesterone: Inhibits gonadotropin and testosterone
   Triptorelin: Blocks gonadotropin and decreases testosterone and deviant behaviors
    more effectively than cyproterone or medroxyprogesterone
 Effects on women
  Menstrual cycle
  FSH (follicle stimulating hormone)
   Promotes growth of follicle, which nurtures ovum
   Increases secretion of estradiol by follicle
  Estradiol
   Decreases FSH, then causes surges of LH (luteinizing hormone) and FSH
  LH and FSH
   Release ovum
   Increase secretion of progesterone by corpus luteum (remnant of follicle)
  Progesterone
   Prepares lining of uterus
   Inhibits LH release
  Menstruation: Due to decreased hormone levels
  If pregnancy: Estrogen and progesterone increase
   Fluctuating activity at serotonin 5-$HT_3$ receptors → nausea
  Birth-control pills
   Combination pill
    Suppresses FSH and LH release

                  Thickens cervical mucus → sperm can't reach egg

                  Prevents ovum from implanting

            Periovulatory period

                Maximum fertility and sexual interest

                Preferred less feminized faces than during luteal phase or menstruation

            Premenstrual syndrome (premenstrual dysphoric disorder)

                Anxiety, irritability, depression in days before menstruation

                Estrogen and progesterone decrease, cortisol increases before menstruation

                    No difference in these hormones between women with and without PMS

                    Allopregnanolone (metabolite of progesterone)

                        Modifies GABA synapses → decrease anxiety

                        Low in women with PMS

Nonsexual behavior

    Testosterone: Increases aggression

    Estrogen

        Increases growth of dendritic spines in hippocampus

        Blocks apoptosis (decreases risk of Alzheimer's disease)

        Increases $D_2$ and $5HT_{2A}$ receptors in nucleus accumbens and cortex

            Increases sexual motivation, reinforcement, mood

        Monkeys: Estrogen → increased learning, memory, attention

        Humans: Estrogen → improves verbal fluency, memory, attention, manual dexterity

            Impairs spatial performance

        Menopause: Estrogen replacement

            Increased risk of heart attack, stroke, breast cancer

            Decreased risk of hip fractures, colorectal cancer


4.   Parental behavior

    Species differences

        Monkeys: Increased interest in babies as pregnancy progresses

        Rats: Less responsive late in pregnancy; after birth → very responsive

    Hormone-dependent early phase

        Oxytocin

        Prolactin

        Medial preoptic area and anterior hypothalamus

    Experience-dependent later phase

        Decreased response to pheromones

        Vomeronasal organ

    Paternal behavior

        Most species: No paternal behavior

        Species with paternal behavior: Father shows hormonal changes

            Testosterone: Increases near end of pregnancy, decreases after delivery

            Prolactin levels high after birth

    Hormones not necessary in humans


5.   In closing: Sex-related behaviors and motivations

    No need to understand purpose of behavior

        Sexual activity feels good

        Mother rat licks pups to get salt

# Module 11.2  Variations in Sexual Behavior

1. Evolutionary interpretations of mating behavior

    Interest in multiple mates

        Men: More interest in short-term sexual relations with multiple partners → spread genes

        Women: May sometimes gain from multiple partners

            Infertile mate; gifts; "trade up"

    What men and women seek in a mate

        Both prefer healthy, intelligent, honest, attractive mate

        Women

            Prefer acceptable odor: Sign of health, genetic compatibility

            Prefer good provider

        Men

            Prefer younger partner: Greater fertility

    Differences in jealousy

        Men: Hypothetically more upset by sexual infidelity

        Women: Hypothetically more upset by emotional infidelity

        Actual infidelity: Both men and women more upset at emotional infidelity

    Evolved or learned?

        Difficult to separate genetic influences from learned tendencies

    Conclusions

        Morality different from scientific questions


2. Determinants of gender identity

    Sex differences: Biological

    Gender identity: Sexual identification

        Human characteristic

    Intersexes

        Atypical chromosomes

            XY, with mutation of SRY

            XX, with translocated SRY from father's Y onto autosomal chromosome

        Atypical hormone pattern

            Excess androgens in females

                Toxic chemicals, including DDT

                Adrenal glands → excess testosterone and other androgens

                Antimiscarriage drugs → effects similar to testosterone's

            Insufficient testosterone or unresponsiveness to it in males

                Toxic chemicals, including DDT

                Mutation of testosterone receptors

        True hermaphrodites: Some testicular and some ovarian tissue

        Intersexes or pseudohermaphrodites: Intermediate appearance

            Previously: Usually reared as girls

            "Corrective" surgery destructive of sexual sensation

        Testicular feminization or androgen insensitivity

            XY genotype

            Lack of androgen receptors

            Female gender identity

        Discrepancies of sexual appearance

            Penis development delayed until puberty

                Decreased $5\alpha$-reductase 2 (enzyme that converts testosterone to dihydrotestosterone)

Dihydrotestosterone more effective in masculinizing genitals
Puberty → enough testosterone to masculinize penis
Accidental removal of the penis

3. Possible biological bases of sexual orientation
Genetics
Drosophila (fruit flies) with *fruitless* gene → males court only males
Greater similarity of orientation in monozygotic (identical) twins
Not clear if same factors influence both male and female homosexuality
Gene on X chromosome → increased male homosexuality
Not replicated in later studies
Evolutionary selection
May be perpetuated by kin selection: Not supported by one study
May increase reproductive success of women
Possible advantage to people heterozygous for the gene
Either too high or too low testosterone may predispose to homosexuality
Hormones
No consistent differences in adult hormone levels
Animal models
Decreased testosterone during early development of males → sexual interest in males
Excess testosterone in females → mounting other females
Some homosexual men look somewhat feminine
Others very masculine: Excess testosterone?
Finger length
Sex difference in ratio of index finger to ring finger
Homosexual men: Ratio hypermasculinized
Sex difference in responses to clicks
Lesbians: Responses similar to heterosexual men
Gay men: Responses hypermasculinized
Prenatal stress or alcohol
Endorphins → antitestosterone effects
Social experiences in male rats
Rearing in isolation or with only males → sexually responsive only to males
Rearing with males and females → sexually responsive to both sexes
Uncertain relationship in humans between stress and homosexual sons
Diethylstilbestrol (DES) in females → masculinization
Clicks in inner ear: heterosexual women > lesbian or bisexual women > heterosexual men
Brain anatomy
Anterior commissure
Larger in women and homosexual men
Suprachiasmatic nucleus (SCN)
Larger in homosexual than heterosexual men
Interstitial nucleus 3 of anterior hypothalamus
Larger in heterosexual men than in women and homosexual men
Differences not due to AIDS
Cause vs. effect
Functions unclear

4. In closing: We are not all the same
Biological understanding may increase acceptance of diversity

# SHORT-ANSWER QUESTIONS

**Module 11.1  The Effects of Sex Hormones**

1. *Control of hormone release*

   a. What is an advantage of hormonal communication, compared to communication by neurotransmitters?

   b. What are four types of hormones?  Give at least one example of each.

   c. What brain structure controls the pituitary gland?  How does control of the anterior and posterior pituitary differ?

   d. Which two hormones are released from the posterior pituitary?  Name the six that are released from the anterior pituitary.

   e. What is the secret to maintaining hormone levels within a relatively fixed range?

2. *Organizing effects of sex hormones*
   a. Distinguish between organizing effects and activating effects of hormones.




   b. What is the SRY gene? Describe the chain of events that result from its presence during development.




   c. What are Müllerian ducts? What are Wolffian ducts?




   d. What are two sex differences in the structure or function of the hypothalamus?




   e. Describe the effects of testosterone injections on female rats during the last few days before birth and the first few days after birth.




   f. What happens if a developing mammal is exposed to neither androgens nor estrogens during early development? Which hormone is required in low amounts for brain differentiation in females?

g. When is the critical period for testosterone's effects on rats? On humans?

h. By what mechanism does testosterone exert its effects on the hypothalamus in rodents?

i. Describe the effects of injections of large amounts of estrogen on female rodents during the critical period.

j. What is the role of alpha-fetoprotein?

k. What are some nonreproductive characteristics that may be influenced by prenatal hormones?

3. *Activating effects of sex hormones*
   a. Which hormones can restore male-typical sexual behavior following castration? What is the most effective hormone treatment for restoring female-typical behavior?

b. What is the pudendal nerve? What are estrogen's effects on its function?

c. What brain area may facilitate female-typical behavior in females and male-typical behavior in males?

d. What neurotransmitter in the MPOA stimulates male sexual activity? How does castration affect the release of that neurotransmitter in the MPOA?

e. What may be its role in the progression from the early stages of copulation, which require erection in males and the receptive posture in females, to the stage of orgasm?

f. Describe the relationship between testosterone levels and sexual activity in men. Which other hormone contributes to sexual pleasure?

g. Which two drugs have been used to treat sex offenders? What promising drug has more recently been used? What are the effects of these drugs?

h. List the chain of hormonal processes in the menstrual cycle.

i. What are the two effects of follicle-stimulating hormone (FSH)?

j. Rising levels of which hormone cause a sudden surge of LH and FSH near the middle of the cycle? What is the effect of the surge of LH and FSH on the ovum?

k. What is the corpus luteum, and what hormone does it release?

l. What are the effects of progesterone? Describe the levels of the major hormones shortly before menstruation.

m. How do combination birth-control pills work?

n.  Describe the effect of women's menstrual cycle on their preference for masculinized vs. feminized faces.

o.  Low levels of which metabolite of progesterone may be associated with premenstrual syndrome?  Which neurotransmitter does this metabolite affect?

p.  What nonsexual activational effects have been demonstrated for estrogen and testosterone?

4.  *Parental behavior*
    a.  Describe the roles of hormones and experience in parental behavior of rodents.

    b.  Which two hormones have been shown to promote maternal behavior in monkeys?  In rats?

    c.  What brain area is important for these hormonal effects?

d.  Describe the hormonal changes associated with parental behavior in male dwarf hamsters.

## Module 11.2  Variations in Sexual Behavior

1.  *Evolutionary interpretations of mating behavior*
    a.  What are some differences between men and women in mate preference?

    b.  Give an evolutionary explanation for each of these.

    c.  How did the results of studies of sex differences in jealousy differ when hypothetical vs. actual cases of infidelity were examined?

    d.  How certain can we be that sex differences that are fairly consistent across cultures have a genetic basis?

2.  *Determinants of gender identity*
    a.  What is an intersex?  What is the difference between a true hermaphrodite and an intersex?

b.  What are some developmental influences that may produce an intersex individual?

c.  Why have most intersexes been reared as females?

d.  How successful is the surgical treatment of intersexes?

e.  Describe the chromosomal pattern and the genital appearance of individuals with androgen insensitivity, or testicular feminization. What causes the unresponsiveness to androgen? What two abnormalities appear at puberty?

f.  Describe two situations in which children were exposed to the prenatal hormonal pattern of one sex and then reared as the opposite sex. What can we infer from these situations about the relative importance of early rearing experiences and hormones as determinants of gender identity?

3. *Possible biological bases of sexual orientation*
   a. Describe the evidence for a genetic predisposition towards homosexuality.

   b. What was the likely explanation for the increased incidence of homosexuality among maternal relatives of homosexual men? Has the early finding been replicated?

   c. Discuss the problems concerning evolutionary selection of any genes predisposing toward homosexuality.

   d. What are two possible explanations for the continued existence of those genes?

   e. Can hormone levels in adulthood account for sexual orientation? What is a more plausible hypothesis concerning hormonal influence on sexual orientation?

f.   Describe two studies suggesting that some homosexual men had unusually high testosterone levels during development.

g.   Describe the experiments on the effects of stress on sex differentiation of rats. What were their results?

h.   How may endorphins be implicated in the effects of stress? What other factor may influence the effects of prenatal stress?

j.   Summarize the evidence regarding possible prenatal stress effects on homosexual men.

k.   How strongly does prenatal diethylstilbestrol (DES) influence homosexuality in women?

l.   What are three brain structures that show a sex difference in size? In which direction is the size difference for each? How do homosexual men compare with heterosexual men and with women regarding the size of these structures?

m. Describe LeVay's evidence implicating the interstitial nucleus 3 of the hypothalamus in homosexuality.

n. If there is a consistent difference between homosexual and heterosexual men in the size of various brain nuclei, what can we conclude about the role of these nuclei in determining sexual orientation?

## TRUE/FALSE QUESTIONS

_____ 1. Some receptors for steroid hormones are in the cell membrane and activate second messenger systems similar to those of metabotropic neurotransmitters; others are in the cytoplasm, move to the nucleus when bound to hormone, and alter gene expression.

_____ 2. Anabolic steroids help to promote muscle growth, if combined with exercise, but may decrease testis size and increase breast growth and cholesterol levels, because of negative feedback on the anterior pituitary.

_____ 3. The anterior pituitary is composed of neural tissue; neurons in the hypothalamus send axons into the anterior pituitary, from which hormones are released into the general blood circulation.

_____ 4. Levels of some hormones are maintained within relatively constant ranges by a negative feedback system.

_____ 5. The Wolffian ducts are precursors to the internal female reproductive structures.

_____ 6. The SRY gene on the Y chromosome causes the primitive gonads to differentiate into testes, which secrete testosterone, which in turn leads to masculine development of the genitals and, either directly or through its metabolites, the brain.

_____ 7. The sexually dimorphic nucleus (SDN) of the hypothalamus is larger in females, because it generates a cyclic pattern of hormone release.

_____ 8. Female rodents are not masculinized by their own and their mother's estrogen because the aromatase enzyme rapidly converts it to progesterone.

_____ 9. Hormones activate behavior by altering the responsiveness of the brain and the genitals to various stimuli.

274

_____10. Moderate concentrations of dopamine in the MPOA of rats stimulate $D_1$ and $D_5$ receptors, which facilitate erections in males and sexually receptive postures in females.

_____11. Sildenafil (Viagra) promotes erections by increasing testosterone release.

_____12. Birth-control pills containing estrogen and progesterone prevent the mid-cycle surge of LH and FSH and also thicken the mucus of the cervix.

_____13. Hormones promote maternal behavior by increasing activity in the MPOA and anterior hypothalamus.

_____14. Testicular feminization occurs when the testes secrete large amounts of estrogen, rather than testosterone.

_____15. Some gay men may have inherited a gene on the Y chromosome, passed on to them from their father, that predisposed them to homosexuality.

_____16. Prenatal stress may alter brain development, in part, by increasing the release of endorphins, some of which cross the placenta and affect the fetus's hypothalamus.

_____17. The INAH-3 nucleus is larger in heterosexual men than in women and homosexual men.

## FILL IN THE BLANKS

1. Four classes of hormones are _____ and _____ hormones, _____ hormones, _____ hormones, and _____.

2. Two hormones released from the posterior pituitary are _____ and _____.

3. The gene that directs the primitive gonad to become a testis is the _____ gene.

4. The _____ ducts develop into the oviducts, uterus, and upper vagina.

5. The protein that binds estradiol in the blood of some immature animals, thereby protecting females from their own and their mother's estradiol, is _____-_____.

6. The enzyme that converts testosterone to estradiol is _____.

7. Sildenafil (Viagra) prolongs the effects of _____ _____ and thereby increases blood engorgement of the penis.

8. _____, a drug that blocks gonadotropin release, has been used to treat sex offenders.

9. Combination birth control pills work by preventing the surge of _____ and _____ that would normally release an ovum, and by _____ the _____ of the cervix.

10. High levels of estrogen improve women's performance on _____ tasks but worsens performance on _____ tasks.

11. A sudden surge of _____ and _____ around the time of birth increases maternal behavior by activating neurons in the _____ _____ _____ and _____ _____.

12. Men tend to prefer a _____ partner; women tend to prefer a mate who is a good _____.

13. A person who develops genitals intermediate between those of typical males and females is known as an _____.

14. People with an XY chromosome pattern but who lack androgen receptors and appear to be female have a condition known as _____ _____.

15. Delay of development of a penis until puberty can result from a genetic defect in the enzyme ____-_____, which converts testosterone into _____.

16. Evidence favoring a genetic predisposition to homosexuality includes the observation that the concordance rate for homosexuality among _____ twins is higher than that for _____ twins; however, these data also show environmental factors to be important, because the concordance rate is less than 100%.

17. Prenatal stress increases the release of _____ and of _____ hormones, which can impair masculine development of the brain.

18. The _____ is a brain nucleus that is larger in heterosexual men than in women and homosexual men. However, the interpretation of this finding is not clear.

# MATCHING ITEMS

_____  1.  ACTH, TSH, GH, FSH, LH, prolactin  a.  Binds estradiol in blood in development

_____  2.  Oxytocin, vasopressin  b.  Seminal vesicles, vas deferens

_____  3.  Anabolic steroids  c.  Testosterone → estradiol

_____  4.  Müllerian ducts  d.  Hormones from posterior pituitary

_____  5.  Wolffian ducts  e.  Increase muscle mass, decrease testes

_____  6.  Alpha-fetoprotein  f.  Hormones from anterior pituitary

_____  7.  Aromatase  g.  Oviducts, uterus, upper vagina

_____  8.  Dopamine in MPOA  h.  Testosterone → dihydrotestosterone

_____  9.  LH and FSH surge  i.  Releases ovum

_____  10.  Progesterone  j.  Facilitates male and female sex behavior

_____  11.  5α-reductase  k.  Larger in men than women and gay men

_____  12.  INAH-3  l.  Prepares uterus for embryo, inhibits LH

# MULTIPLE-CHOICE QUESTIONS

1.  Which of the following is true of the pituitary gland?
    a.  The anterior pituitary receives blood-borne releasing hormones from the hypothalamus.
    b.  The posterior pituitary receives blood-borne releasing hormones from the hypothalamus.
    c.  The anterior pituitary releases oxytocin and vasopressin into the blood.
    d.  The posterior pituitary releases ACTH, TSH, prolactin, GH, FSH, and LH into the blood.

2.  The SRY gene
    a.  is present on the X chromosome and is responsible for the tendency of mammals to become female, unless the gene's effects are overridden by high levels of testosterone.
    b.  is present on the Y chromosome and causes the gonads to differentiate into testes, which then secrete testosterone, which then masculinizes the organism.
    c.  has been linked to homosexuality.
    d.  is the major gene that directly specifies the size of certain brain structures.

3.  Wolffian ducts
    a.  are the precursors of the oviducts, uterus, and upper vagina.
    b.  are the precursors of the seminal vesicles and vas deferens.
    c.  are the precursors of the external genitals.
    d.  none of the above.

4. Sex differences in the hypothalamus include
    a. the sexually dimorphic nucleus of the medial preoptic area, which is larger in males.
    b. parts of the hypothalamus that generate a cyclic pattern of hormone release in females.
    c. both a and b.
    d. none of the above.

5. If a female rat receives testosterone injections during the last few days before birth or the first few postnatal days, then in adulthood
    a. she will exhibit neither masculine nor feminine sexual behavior.
    b. she will exhibit normal feminine sexual behavior in spite of the full masculinization of her genitals.
    c. she will exhibit normal feminine sexual behavior, and her genitals will appear fully feminine.
    d. her pituitary and ovary will produce steady levels of hormones rather than cycling in the normal manner.

6. A female pattern of development can be produced
    a. by giving a female mammal large amounts of estrogen during the sensitive period.
    b. in normal males by giving them estrogen in adolescence.
    c. in mammals of either sex by depriving the animal of testosterone during the sensitive period, although some estrogen is necessary for feminine differentiation of the brain.
    d. all of the above.

7. Which of the following is true?
    a. Testosterone's organizing effects occur throughout the entire period of gestation.
    b. Alpha-fetoprotein is the enzyme that converts testosterone to estradiol.
    c. Estradiol masculinizes the hypothalamus by being aromatized to testosterone.
    d. Testosterone masculinizes the hypothalamus of rodents largely by being aromatized to estradiol.

8. High levels of androgens during prenatal development
    a. cause female monkeys to display more rough and tumble play.
    b. will cause female rats to mount other females in adulthood.
    c. may contribute to choice of male-typical toys by girls.
    d. all of the above.

9. The sexually dimorphic nucleus (SDN) of the MPOA
    a. is larger in males than in females.
    b. is necessary for males to be able to perform any male-typical behavior.
    c. is the area that controls the production of testosterone.
    d. all of the above.

10. Activation of female sex behavior by hormones
    a. is most easily elicited by injections first of progesterone and then dihydrotestosterone in females whose ovaries were removed.
    b. may be mediated in part by increasing the area of skin that activates the pudendal nerve.
    c. is mediated by a decrease in stimulation of $D_1$ and $D_5$ dopamine receptors in the MPOA.
    d. is mediated by an increase in serotonin activity.

11. Dopamine in the MPOA of male rats
    a.  is released when a gonadally intact male is exposed to a receptive female.
    b.  is not released in normal amounts by castrated males.
    c.  may act through different receptors to promote erection first and then ejaculation.
    d.  all of the above.

12. Cyproterone, medroxyprogesterone, and a newer drug, triptorelin
    a.  are common treatments for impotence.
    b.  are common treatments for premenstrual syndrome.
    c.  can be used to decrease sexual fantasies and offensive sexual behaviors of sex offenders.
    d.  can be used to increase sexual interest in women.

13. The corpus luteum
    a.  is the remnant of the follicle, which releases progesterone.
    b.  releases estrogen during the early part of the cycle, which causes the pituitary to release a surge of progesterone at midcycle.
    c.  is the primary source of FSH.
    d.  is the primary source of LH.

14. FSH
    a.  is secreted from the uterus.
    b.  is secreted from the follicle.
    c.  stimulates the follicle to grow, nurture the ovum, and produce estrogen.
    d.  stimulates the follicle to grow and produce LH.

15. Combination birth control pills
    a.  contain both estrogen and progesterone.
    b.  suppress the release of FSH and LH.
    c.  thicken cervical mucus.
    d.  all of the above.

16. Which of the following is true?
    a.  The effects of sex hormones are limited to the control of reproductive behavior and the endocrine system.
    b.  Increases in estrogen may result in increased production of $D_2$ and $5HT_{2A}$ receptors in the nucleus accumbens and cortex, which have been implicated in mood and reinforcement.
    c.  Estrogen produces major enhancements in spatial performance.
    d.  Estrogen inhibits the growth of dendritic spines on neurons in the hippocampus, thereby preventing distracting stimuli from bothering a woman.

17. Premenstrual syndrome may be related to
    a.  low levels of allopregnanolone, a metabolite of progesterone that decreases anxiety by altering GABA receptors.
    b.  low levels of estrogen, coupled with high levels of progesterone.
    c.  low levels of progesterone, coupled with high levels of estrogen.
    d.  excessive testosterone.

18. Which is true concerning rodent parental behavior?
    a. Maternal behavior depends on hormones for the first few days after giving birth.
    b. Hormones continue to be the most important factor in eliciting parental behavior throughout the entire period of care of the young.
    c. The odor of newborn rat pups is naturally very attractive to female rats.
    d. Parental behavior is enhanced by lesions of the MPOA, since that area is concerned only with male sexual behavior, which would interfere with parental behavior.

19. Which of the following is true of mate selection?
    a. It is now clear that women are more jealous about their husbands' sexual infidelity, whereas men are more jealous of their wives' emotional infidelity.
    b. Men's odors may convey clues to their health and genetic compatibility.
    c. Women never have anything to gain from having more than one sex partner, since they can have only a limited number of pregnancies.
    d. Women tend to prefer more feminized faces during their periovulatory period than at other times.

20. Intersexes
    a. are extremely rare, no more than one in several million.
    b. usually have complete sets of both male and female structures.
    c. include genetic females who were exposed to elevated levels of androgens during fetal development.
    d. are usually genetic males who have been exposed to estrogens during fetal development.

21. Intersexes
    a. should always have surgical "correction" of their genitals immediately after birth.
    b. are sometimes resentful that surgical "correction" of their genitals destroyed sexual sensation and makes them feel violated.
    c. should be reared as males if they have an XY chromosome configuration, and as females if they have an XX configuration, regardless of the appearance of their external genitals.
    d. provide clear evidence that prenatal hormones are unimportant in gender identity.

22. Androgen insensitivity (testicular feminization)
    a. is characterized by normal testosterone levels, but a lack of androgen receptors.
    b. results in an individual who appears to be completely female but fails to menstruate at puberty and has no pubic hair.
    c. cannot be alleviated by giving injections of testosterone.
    d. all of the above.

23. Certain genetic males in the Dominican Republic
    a. lack the enzyme that converts testosterone to dihydrotestosterone.
    b. lack the enzyme that converts testosterone to estradiol.
    c. are usually reared as boys, but adapt easily to a feminine sexual identity when they begin to produce high levels of estrogen at puberty.
    d. are usually reared as girls, but are completely unable to adapt to their new male gender identity when high levels of testosterone at puberty cause growth of a penis.

24. A genetic predisposition to homosexuality
    a. may be carried by a gene on the X chromosome that promotes homosexuality in males, although the evidence is not consistent.
    b. may be carried by a gene on the Y chromosome that promotes homosexuality in males, although the evidence is not consistent.
    c. is now known to be controlled by the same genes in male and female homosexuals.
    d. has been disproven, since evolution strongly selects against any genes that would interfere with reproduction.

25. Male homosexuality
    a. is highly correlated with low levels of testosterone in adulthood.
    b. is highly correlated with high levels of estrogen in adulthood.
    c. may be associated with increased stress during prenatal development.
    d. may be redirected to heterosexuality by injections of testosterone in adulthood.

26. Diethylstilbestrol (DES)
    a. can be used in adulthood to change the sexual orientation of homosexual men.
    b. can be used in adulthood to change the sexual orientation of homosexual women.
    c. administered to mothers during pregnancy may slightly increase the likelihood of bisexuality or homosexuality in their sons.
    d. administered to mothers during pregnancy may slightly increase the likelihood of bisexuality or homosexuality in their daughters.

27. The interstitial nucleus 3 (INAH-3) of the anterior hypothalamus
    a. is larger in women and homosexual men than in heterosexual men.
    b. is smaller in women and homosexual men than in heterosexual men.
    c. is smaller in homosexual men than in either women or heterosexual men, primarily because the AIDS virus is known to kill neurons in that site more than in the rest of the brain.
    d. is now known to be the primary brain center that determines sexual orientation.

## Answers to True/False Questions

| | | | |
|---|---|---|---|
| 1. T | 6. T | 11. F | 16. T |
| 2. T | 7. F | 12. T | 17. T |
| 3. F | 8. F | 13. T | |
| 4. T | 9. T | 14. F | |
| 5. F | 10. T | 15. F | |

## Answers to Fill-in-the-Blank Questions

1. protein, peptide, steroid, thyroid, monoamines
2. oxytocin, vasopressin
3. SRY
4. Müllerian
5. alpha-fetoprotein
6. aromatase
7. nitric oxide
8. Triptorelin
9. LH, FSH, thickening, mucus
10. verbal, spatial
11. oxytocin, prolactin, medial preoptic area, anterior hypothalamus
12. younger, provider
13. intersex
14. testicular feminization

15. 5α-reductase, dihydrotestosterone
16. monozygotic (or identical), dizygotic
    (or fraternal)

17. endorphins, adrenal
18. INAH-3

## Answers to Matching Items

| | | | |
|---|---|---|---|
| 1. f | 4. g | 7. c | 10. l |
| 2. d | 5. b | 8. j | 11. h |
| 3. e | 6. a | 9. i | 12. k |

## Answers to Multiple-Choice Questions

| | | | |
|---|---|---|---|
| 1. a | 8. d | 15. d | 22. d |
| 2. b | 9. a | 16. b | 23. a |
| 3. b | 10. b | 17. a | 24. a |
| 4. c | 11. d | 18. a | 25. c |
| 5. d | 12. c | 19. b | 26. d |
| 6. c | 13. a | 20. c | 27. b |
| 7. d | 14. c | 21. b | |

**Please check the Exploring Biological Psychology CD-ROM.**

# Heat, Sex, and Gluttony

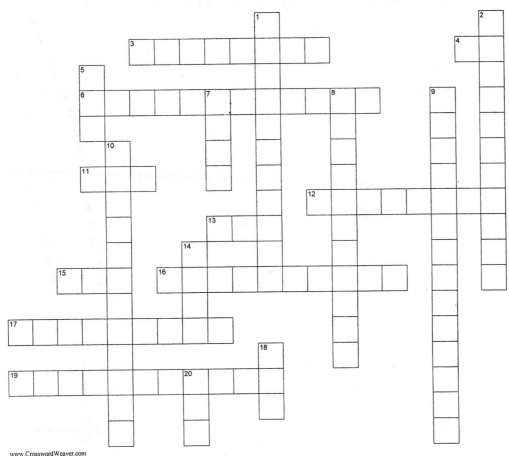

www.CrosswordWeaver.com

## ACROSS

**3** Initial segment of small intestine

**4** Chromosomal male

**6** Area of hypothalamus, lesion of which leads to obesity

**11** Gene on Y chromosome that initiates formation of testes (abbr.)

**12** Transmitter in MPOA that controls sexual behavior

**13** Hormone secreted by structure in 8 Down in response to the presence of food

**15** Syndrome characterized by irritibililty before menstruation (abbr.)

**16** Nerve sensitive to nutritive content of stomach

**17** Tract that differentiates into female internal genitals

**19** Tendency to maintain a variable within a set range

## DOWN

**1** Chemical produced by leukocytes that elicits a fever

**2** Type of thirst caused by loss of body fluids

**5** Brain area that produces vasopressin and that helps end a meal (abbr.)

**7** Brain area sensitive to osmotic stimuli (abbr.)

**8** Hormone produced by renin that signals hypovolemia

**9** Body temperature matching the environment

**10** Hormone produced by corpus luteum

**14** Brain area important for temperature regulation, sexual behavior, and parental behavior

**18** Hormone from anterior pituitary that stimulates egg to mature and follicle to produce estrogen (abbr.)

**20** Hormone from posterior pituitary that conserves water (abbr.)

283

# 12

# EMOTIONAL BEHAVIORS

## INTRODUCTION

Emotions require some level of consciousness; however, we can have an emotion without being aware of what caused it. Three areas of the cerebral cortex are strongly activated during emotional decision making—part of the prefrontal cortex, part of the cingulate gyrus, and the angular gyrus (in the posterior parietal lobe, adjacent to the temporal lobe). Damage to the prefrontal cortex results in a lack of emotions. People with such damage make stupid decisions, despite being able to predict the outcomes; they are also impulsive and fail to behave morally.

Activity of the autonomic nervous system, composed of the sympathetic and parasympathetic divisions, is associated with certain emotional states. For example, sympathetic activity prepares for vigorous or emergency activity. The parasympathetic system promotes digestion and conserves energy. Each situation requires a different combination of sympathetic and parasympathetic activity. There has been debate about the role of autonomic arousal in emotions. The James-Lange theory proposes that autonomic and skeletal activity occurs first, and emotions result from our perception of those responses. There is evidence for the importance of physiological responses in determining the intensity of emotions; however, it is possible to feel some blunted emotions, even after injuries that prevent autonomic responses.

Stress was defined by Hans Selye as the nonspecific response of the body to any demand made upon it. Vulnerability to certain diseases is affected by our behaviors and by stress and emotions. Excessive parasympathetic activity, after a period of intense stress, may cause some cases of ulcers and of voodoo death. Frequent hostility activates the sympathetic nervous system and may contribute to heart disease, whereas social support may decrease sympathetic activity and protect against heart disease. During stress, the hypothalamus directs the anterior pituitary to secrete ACTH (adrenocorticotropic hormone), which in turn stimulates the adrenal gland to secrete cortisol. Cortisol shifts energy metabolism to increase blood sugar and decrease synthesis of proteins, including the proteins necessary for immune function. Two important elements of the immune system are the B cells, which produce antibodies that attach to and inactivate specific antigens, and the T cells, which attack specific "foreign" cells or stimulate responses from other immune cells. Natural killer cells kill tumor cells and cells infected with viruses; their attacks are relatively nonspecific. Although brief stressors activate the immune system, chronic, uncontrollable stressors may depress its functioning and leave an individual more vulnerable to disease. Active coping and a sense of control may help strengthen the immune response. Prolonged stress, with its high cortisol levels, can also increase the vulnerability of hippocampal neurons. Furthermore, a vicious cycle develops, with hippocampal damage resulting in higher cortisol levels, which further damage the hippocampus. Post-traumatic stress disorder (PTSD) occurs in some people who have had traumatic experiences. They have flashbacks, nightmares, and exaggerated arousal to noises and other stimuli. We do not know why some people do, and others do not, succumb to PTSD. Those who do have been found to have a smaller hippocampus and low cortisol levels; however, a cause and effect relationship has not been established.

Aggression is complex and difficult to study. Increased aggressiveness is influenced by heredity and by prenatal influences, including maternal smoking during pregnancy. Testosterone is correlated with aggressiveness, although its effect is relatively weak. Stimulation of some brain areas can promote aggressive responses. Some people with temporal-lobe epilepsy have violent outbursts as a result of seizures that involve the amygdala. This tendency is referred to as intermittent explosive disorder. Antiepileptic drugs frequently control the epilepsy and the violence; however, for extremely violent individuals who were not helped by drugs, lesions of the amygdala have sometimes reduced the violence and/or the epilepsy. Low serotonin turnover may also be associated with aggressiveness in both animals and people. Turnover is inferred from levels of 5-HIAA, a serotonin metabolite. Low serotonin turnover was observed in mice that showed isolation-induced aggression and in monkeys that were naturally aggressive. Furthermore, the lack of serotonin 5-HT$_{1B}$ receptors was associated with excessive attack behaviors in mice. Low serotonin turnover in humans may be associated with impulsiveness, violent crimes, and suicide. However, low serotonin turnover is also associated with depression. Low serotonin turnover affects people differentially, worsening depression in those who are already depressed, increasing aggression in those with aggressive tendencies, and worsening impulsiveness in others.

Fear is a temporary experience, whereas anxiety is longer lasting. The basolateral and central nuclei of the amygdala are important for learned fear responses, including enhancement of the startle reflex. The amygdala receives input concerning pain, vision, and hearing. Its output to the hypothalamus controls autonomic responses; its output to prefrontal cortex influences interpretation of threat; and its connections to the central gray in the midbrain elicit the startle response. The amygdala is activated by emotional expressions and scenes, even if the person does not consciously recognize the picture. Damage to the amygdala reduces or eliminates fears and also impairs the interpretation of social signals. People with Urbach-Wiethe disease suffer atrophy of the amygdala and have a resultant loss of the experience or perception of fear.

Phobias are fears of specific objects or situations; panic disorder is characterized by extreme in unpredictable situations. Three repeats of a gene sequence on chromosome 15 have been linked to anxiety disorders and also to laxity of joints; people without anxiety disorder have only two repeats of that sequence. CCK (cholecystokinin) excites the amygdala and is also released in the prefrontal cortex in stressful situations. Injections of drugs that stimulate CCK receptors into the amygdala enhance the startle reflex, and drugs that block CCK type B receptors block anxiety. The main inhibitory transmitter in the amygdala is GABA; drugs that block GABA type B receptors produce panic. Anxiety is commonly treated with benzodiazepine tranquilizers. These drugs exert their effect at benzodiazepine binding sites on the GABA$_A$ receptor complex, thereby facilitating the binding of GABA to its own receptor at the complex. The binding of GABA increases the flow of chloride ions across the membrane and thereby inhibits neural activity. Alcohol also binds to the GABA$_A$ complex and facilitates GABA binding. An experimental drug can block the effects of alcohol on the GABA$_A$ complex and on behavior. However, this drug is not marketed because of its potential for misuse. Diazepam-binding inhibitor (DBI) is an endozepine (endogenous antibenzodiazepine). It is released by glia cells and blocks the effects of diazepam and other benzodiazepines, thereby increasing anxiety.

## LEARNING OBJECTIVES

### Module 12.1  What Is Emotion?
1. Understand the role of emotions in decision making and the brain areas that promote wise decision making.
2. Be able to describe the influences of the autonomic nervous system in emotions.
3. Know the components of the limbic system and the effects of damage or inactivation of limbic structures and of the right vs. left hemisphere on emotional responsiveness.

### Module 12.2  Stress and Health
1. Know the effects of emotions and of stress on psychosomatic disorders.

2. Know the components of the immune system and the effects of brief or prolonged stressors on immune function.
3. Be able to list the symptoms of post-traumatic stress disorder (PTSD) and describe the relation between size of hippocampus, cortisol levels, and vulnerability to PTSD.

## Module 12.3  Attack and Escape Behaviors
1. Know the genetic, environmental, and hormonal contributions to aggressiveness.
2. Understand the roles of brain abnormalities and serotonin turnover in aggressive behavior.
3. Understand the ways in which the amygdala promotes fear and anxiety.
4. Be able to explain the effects of anxiety-reducing drugs.


## KEY TERMS AND CONCEPTS

## Module 12.1  What Is Emotion?
1. Introduction
    Emotions as observable behaviors vs. feelings as private experiences
        Operational definition
        Require consciousness
            Absence seizure

2. Emotions and decision making
    Cortical areas that respond to emotion
        Part of prefrontal cortex
        Part of cingulate gyrus
        Angular gyrus (posterior parietal lobe adjacent to temporal lobe)
    Decision based on emotion; justify later
    "Gut feelings" based on autonomic responses, not identified consciously
    Prefrontal cortex damage → lack of emotions
        Stupid decisions, despite predicting outcomes
        No moral behavior
    Gambling task
        Damage to prefrontal cortex or amygdala → little or no emotion; choose riskier decks

3. Emotions, autonomic response, and the James-Lange theory
    Autonomic nervous system arousal
        Sympathetic nervous system→ vigorous, emergency activity
        Parasympathetic nervous system → digestion, conservation of energy
        Each situation → mixture of sympathetic and parasympathetic activity
    James-Lange theory: Autonomic arousal and actions before emotions
        Each emotion → different bodily response
    Is physiological arousal necessary for emotions?
        Cognitive vs. feeling aspects
            Prefrontal cortex: Responds differently to happy and frightened faces within 120 ms
                No time for feedback from body
            Pure autonomic failure
                Report cognitive aspects of emotions; decreased emotional intensity
            Locked-in syndrome
                Ventral brainstem damage → sensory input but no motor output

286

Mental alertness, total paralysis

Usually tranquil

Immediate cognitive component → autonomic and skeletal responses → feeling aspect

Is physiological arousal sufficient for emotions?

Small physiological differences among mild emotions → hard to differentiate

Panic disorder

Extreme sympathetic nervous system arousal → interpreted as fear

Smiling → increases happiness

Brain stimulation during surgery → laughter interpreted as emotion

James-Lange correct: Perception of bodily reactions → increases emotional intensity

4. Brain areas associated with emotion

Limbic system (border around brainstem)

Amygdala, cingulate cortex, hypothalamus, parts of somatosensory cortex, midbrain

Damage to cingulate cortex → decreases tension, anger

Inactivation of part of prefrontal cortex → decreases identification of anger

Insular cortex → disgust (taste cortex)

Right hemisphere more responsive than left

Both detecting and expression emotion

Left hemisphere → decreases detection and expression of emotion

Inactivating right hemisphere (Wada procedure) → recall facts, not emotions

More important for unpleasant emotions

Personality differences

Greater activity in left → outgoing, fun-loving

Greater activity in right → shy

5. In closing: Research on emotions

Emotions difficult to observe

Promising techniques

## Module 12.2  Stress and Health

1. Stress and the autonomic nervous system

Behavioral medicine: Effects on health of diet, smoking, exercise, stress

Stress: Nonspecific response of body to any demand made upon it

Hans Selye

Psychosomatic illnesses

Ulcers

More in rats **without** control of stressor

Prefrontal cortex damage → no ulcers in similar conditions

More in monkeys **with** control of stressor

Monkeys better at avoiding shocks → passive monkey → few shocks

Develop during rest periods between shock sessions

Rebound parasympathetic activation of stomach

Bacterium → increases risk, not major cause

Heart disease

More hostile facial expressions → more transient myocardial ischemias

Abnormal heartbeats predispose to heart attacks

Cause and effect not clear

Social support → decreased heart rate and blood pressure

Voodoo death and related phenomena
   Curt Richter's swimming rats
      Excessive parasympathetic activity
         Rescue → "immunizes" against future terror
      Most heart attacks: Excessive sympathetic arousal


2.  Stress and the hypothalamus-pituitary-adrenal cortex axis
   Slower than autonomic nervous system
   Hypothalamus → anterior pituitary: adrenocorticotropic hormone (ACTH) →
      Human adrenal cortex: cortisol (rat adrenal cortex: corticosterone) →
      Increased blood sugar and metabolism
      Useful in short term, harmful if prolonged
   The immune system
      Autoimmune disease
      Leukocytes
         Bone marrow, thymus, spleen, lymph nodes
         "Self" proteins
         Antigens
         Macrophages
         B cells
            Mature in bone marrow
            Plasma cells → antibodies
            B memory cells
        T cells
            Mature in thymus
            Cytotoxic T cells: Directly attack intruder
               Helper T cells: Stimulate response from other immune cells
     Natural killer cells: Relatively nonspecific in their targets
     Cytokines
         Example: Interleukin-1 (IL-1)
         Attack infections
         Peripheral cytokines → vagus nerve → hypothalamus and hippocampus →
            Release cytokines in brain → anti-illness behaviors
               Fever → viruses don't thrive
               Sleepiness → conserve energy
               Decrease appetite → deprive viruses of iron; save energy
  Effects of stress on the immune system
     Psychoneuroimmunology
     Inescapable, temporary stressors → response similar to illness
     Stressor → sympathetic system, HPA axis
     Brief stressors → brief activation of immune system
     Long-term stressors → decreased protein synthesis, including immune system proteins
        Sense of control helps
        High cortisol → hippocampal damage
           Decreased learning and memory
           Increased cortisol (vicious cycle)

3. Post-traumatic stress disorder (PTSD)
   Symptoms
      Flashbacks and nightmares
      Avoidance of reminders
      Exaggerated arousal in response to noises and other stimuli
   Vulnerability
      Small hippocampus (cause or effect?)
      Low cortisol levels → ill-equipped to combat stress?

4. In closing: Emotions and body reactions
   Which changes are symptoms and which are coping mechanisms?
   Social support → physiological effects or better care of themselves?

**Module 12.3 Attack and Escape Behaviors**
1. Attack behaviors
   "Play": Attack, escape
   Corticomedial amygdala
      Priming for further attacks
   Heredity and environment in violence
      Heritability
         Monozygotic = dizygotic in juvenile crimes
            Family, neighborhood more important than genes
         Monozygotic > dizygotic in adult crimes
            More control over environment → choice of friends, environment → violence
      Maternal smoking during pregnancy
         Effect compounded with complications during pregnancy
         Correlational, not causational effect
      Body size at age 3
      Combination: Biological parents with criminal record + adoptive parents with discord, depression, substance abuse, legal problems
   Hormones
      Male-female differences
         More crime in men 15-25 years of age: Highest testosterone levels
         Higher testosterone correlated with more violent acts
            Interpretation difficult
         Testosterone may → attend longer, respond more vigorously to conflict
   Brain abnormalities and violence
      Intermittent explosive disorder
         Outbursts of violent behavior with little provocation
      Temporal lobe epilepsy
         Hallucinations, lip smacking, repetitive acts, emotional behaviors
         Most people with temporal lobe epilepsy not violent
      Prefrontal cortex damage → general loss of inhibitions
   Serotonin synapses and aggressive behavior
      Nonhuman animals
         Social isolation of male mice → lower serotonin turnover, correlated with aggression
         5-HIAA (5-hydroxyindoleacetic acid): Measure of serotonin turnover
         Social isolation of female mice → no change in serotonin turnover or aggression
         Genetically aggressive mice: Lack of 5-HT$_{1B}$ receptors

Also develop cocaine addiction faster

Impulsive

Male monkeys: Low serotonin turnover correlated with high aggression, short lives

Possible evolutionary explanations

High-risk, high-payoff → sire many young

Heterozygotes → intermediate aggressiveness

Humans

Low serotonin turnover: Correlation with violent crimes or suicide

Unable to predict individual cases

Low tryptophan diet → increase in aggressiveness

Aspartame, maize (corn)

Low serotonin also linked to depression

Serotonin → suppress impulses

Individual differences in depression vs. aggression vs. impulsiveness worsened by low serotonin

2. Escape, fear, and anxiety

Fear, anxiety, and the amygdala

Startle reflex

Auditory input → cochlear nucleus of medulla → pons → tense muscles

Stronger if already tense

Studies in rodents

Pain, vision, hearing → basolateral, central amygdala

Output to hypothalamus → autonomic responses

Output to prefrontal cortex → interpretation

Output to midbrain central gray → pons → skeletal responses

Protozoan parasite → reproduce in cats → excrete eggs in feces → rats pick up eggs from ground → new parasites → damage rat's amygdala → lose fear → eaten by cat → reproduce in cat

Studies in monkeys

Amygdala damage →

Klüver-Bucy syndrome: Little fear or avoidance

Fall to bottom of social hierarchy

Increased friendliness

Similar to people taking tranquilizers

Studies in humans

Amygdala response: Fearful > happy > neutral expression

Social phobia: Angry, contemptuous > fearful expression

Amygdala response, even if not consciously recognized → autonomic responses

Amygdala damage →

Decreased fear expression or recognition (Urbach-Wiethe disease)

Inability to judge trustworthiness

Inability to shift attention to emotional stimuli

Process information with emotional meaning

Genetics of anxiety disorders

Phobia: Fear of specific object or situation

Panic disorder: Excessive fear in unpredictable situations

Genes on chromosome 15 → anxiety disorders and joint laxity

Three repeats of gene segment, rather than usual two

Not always consistent within one individual or parent to offspring (unstable segment)
Anxiety-reducing drugs
Transmitters in amygdala: CCK, excitatory; GABA, inhibitory
"Intruder" rats
CCK in prefrontal cortex → anxiety
CCK type B antagonist → no anxiety
CCK type A receptors → opposite effects (maybe), less abundant
CCK-stimulating drugs in amygdala → enhance startle reflex
GABA type B antagonist → panic
Benzodiazepines
Barbiturates: Habit forming, easy to take fatal overdose
Common benzodiazepine tranquilizers
Diazepam (Valium)
Chlordiazepoxide (Librium)
Alprazolam (Xanax)
$GABA_A$ receptor complex
Chloride channel → Hyperpolarize
Benzodiazepines, barbiturates, and alcohol → enhance GABA binding
Benzodiazepine effects
Amygdala, hypothalamus → decrease learned shock avoidance
Cerebral cortex, thalamus → sleepiness, decrease epilepsy, impair memory
Less perception of fear and anger in others
Diazepam-binding inhibitor (DBI), an endozepine: Endogenous antibenzodiazepine
Released mainly by glia cells
Alcohol as a tranquilizer
Cross-tolerance: Alcohol, benzodiazepines, barbiturates
Alcohol → increased flow of chloride ions through $GABA_A$ receptor complex
Antianxiety effects: Similar to benzodiazepines
Ro15-4313: Blocks effects of moderate amounts of alcohol on $GABA_A$ receptors and behavior
Not marketed because of potential for misuse


## SHORT-ANSWER QUESTIONS

### Module 12.1 What Is Emotion?

1. *Introduction*
   a. What is an operational definition? What can we infer about robots that show emotional behavior, according to an operational definition?

b. What is an absence seizure? Do people with absence seizures experience emotions during the seizure? What does this imply about consciousness and emotion?

2. *Emotions and decision making*
    a. Name the three cortical areas that respond to emotional stimuli.

    b. Describe the behavior of people with damage to the prefrontal cortex.

3. *Emotions, autonomic response and the James-Lange theory*
    a. What are the roles of the sympathetic and parasympathetic nervous systems?

    b. Describe the James-Lange theory of emotions.

c. Is physiological arousal necessary for emotions? What is the implication of the very rapid response of the prefrontal cortex to emotional stimuli?

d. Describe locked-in syndrome.

e. Describe panic disorder.

f. Describe the findings of the experiment in which subjects held a pencil between their teeth or with their lips.

g. Summarize the current understanding of the importance of physiological arousal for emotions.

4. *Brain areas associated with emotion*
   a. List the limbic system structures implicated in emotional responses.

   b. Describe the effects of damage to or inactivation of the cingulate cortex, the prefrontal cortex, and the insular cortex.

   c. What are the roles of the right and left hemispheres in the detection and expression of emotion?

**Module 12.2  Stress and Health**
1. *Stress and the autonomic nervous system*
   a. What is the main assumption of behavioral medicine?  What is a psychosomatic illness?

   b. What was Hans Selye's definition of stress?

c.  Describe the different findings regarding the importance of control of the stressor in producing ulcers in rats, compared to monkeys.

d.  When do ulcers form, relative to a period of stress?

e.  What may be the relative contributions of stress and a bacterium to the onset of ulcers?

f.  How important are hostile emotions and social support to heart disease?

g.  Describe Richter's experiment with swimming rats.

h.  What was the cause of death in Richter's rats?  Were wild or domesticated rats more likely to die?  What procedure averted death of the dewhiskered rats?

2. *Stress and the hypothalamus-pituitary-adrenal cortex axis*
   a.  Describe the steps in the control of cortisol secretion from the adrenal cortex.

   b.  What are the most important cells of the immune system?  Where are these cells produced?

   c   What are antigens?  How was the name "antigen" derived?

   d   What are the roles of B cells and of T cells?

   e   What is the role of macrophages?  Of natural killer cells?

   f   In what ways does the body react to temporary stressors similarly to illnesses?

g. What is the effect of short-term stress on the immune system?

h. Describe the evidence suggesting that long-term stress impairs the function of the immune system.

i. What are cortisol's major effects on blood sugar and metabolism? How does this affect the immune system?

j. Describe the vicious cycle that develops with high cortisol levels and the hippocampus.

3. *Post-traumatic stress disorder (PTSD)*
   a. What are the symptoms of posttraumatic stress disorder (PTSD)?

b. Is the hippocampus of people who suffer from PTSD likely to be larger or smaller than average? What can be inferred about cause and effect in this relationship? What may we infer about the relationship of low cortisol levels and vulnerability to PTSD?

## Module 12.3  Attack and Escape Behaviors
1. *Attack behaviors*
   a. What is one explanation of a cat's "play" behavior with its prey?

   b. What are the effects of stimulation of the amygdala on aggressive behavior? Which area of the amygdala is especially important for this effect?

   c. Describe the evidence for heritability of violence in adulthood, but not in childhood.

   d. What environmental risk factor is compounded with complications during pregnancy in determining predisposition toward violence?

e.   How strong is the correlation between testosterone levels and aggressive behavior? By what psychological effect may testosterone promote aggression?

f.   Describe intermittent explosive disorder. What physiological disorder may be linked to intermittent explosive disorder?

g.   What are the symptoms of temporal lobe epilepsy? Are most people with temporal lobe epilepsy violent? In which hemisphere is the greatest abnormality and loss of cells in those with violent tendencies?

h.   Describe the relationship between prefrontal cortex damage and aggressiveness.

i.   What transmitter abnormality appears to be associated with aggressive behavior? How can it be measured?

j. Describe the experimental evidence in mice for this relationship.

k. How was serotonin turnover related to behavior in male monkeys in a natural-environment study?

l. What evidence implicates low serotonin turnover in humans as a factor in aggressive behavior?

m. What dietary factors influence serotonin synthesis?

2. *Escape, fear, and anxiety*
   a. Why should researchers be interested in the startle response?

b.  What is a key brain area for learned fears?  What kinds of sensory input does it receive?
    Which two nuclei appear to be most important for conditioned fear responses?




c.  What are the main output connections of the amygdala?  What does each control?




d.  Describe the effects of a protozoan parasite on rats. How may the behavioral change lead to
    the reproduction of the parasite?




e.  What are the usual effects of amygdala damage?  Describe the Klüver-Bucy syndrome.




f.  What causes Urbach-Wiethe disease?  What are its symptoms?

g.  Describe the genetic abnormality that is implicated in anxiety disorders.  On which gene is the suspected sequence? How stable is the sequence within individuals and from parent to offspring?

h.  Name one excitatory and one inhibitory transmitter in the amygdala that have been implicated in the control of anxiety.

i.  What is the most common drug used to reduce anxiety?  What was a major problem with the use of barbiturates for anxiety?

j.  When a benzodiazepine molecule attaches to its binding site on the $GABA_A$ receptor, how is the binding of GABA affected?  What effect does this have on the flow of chloride ions across the cell membrane?

k.  What are the effects of benzodiazepines on the amygdala and hypothalamus? On the cerebral cortex and thalamus?

l. What is one endogenous chemical that affects the benzodiazepine receptors? Why is the term endozepine confusing? Which type of cell releases it?

m. What is the effect of alcohol on the $GABA_A$ receptor? What are the advantages and disadvantages of a drug that blocks alcohol's effects on the $GABA_A$ receptor? What is your opinion of the decision not to market the drug?

## TRUE/FALSE QUESTIONS

_____ 1. Students who viewed pictures of snakes or spiders very briefly showed a physiological reaction only if they could identify the object.

_____ 2. People with damage to their prefrontal cortex showed a lack of emotions and made stupid decisions, in spite of being able to predict the outcome of their actions.

_____ 3. Various situations call for different amounts and combinations of sympathetic and parasympathetic nervous system activity.

_____ 4. According to the James-Lange theory, our conscious identification of an emotion occurs first and instructs the autonomic nervous system to respond appropriately.

_____ 5. Three cortical areas that are very responsive in emotional situations are part of the prefrontal cortex, part of the cingulate gyrus, and the angular gyrus.

_____ 6. The right hemisphere is more responsive to emotions, especially unpleasant emotions, than is the left.

_____ 7. Rats that had control of the stressor had more ulcers than did the "yoked" control rats.

_____ 8. Ulcers form during the times of most intense stress; healing tends to occur during rest periods between the stressors.

_____ 9. Two kinds of T cells are cytotoxic T cells and helper T cells.

_____ 10. B cells of the immune system release cytokines that directly kill invading bacteria.

_____11. Brief stressors inhibit the immune system, and prolonged, intense stressors inhibit it even more.

_____12. High cortisol concentrations damage the hippocampus, resulting in memory problems and even higher cortisol concentrations than before.

_____13. People with PTSD have very high cortisol levels, because they are so frequently under a lot of stress.

_____14. Monozygotic twins show a greater concordance than dizygotic twins for juvenile crimes, but not for adult crimes.

_____15. Testosterone may increase aggressiveness by causing the individual to attend longer and respond more vigorously to conflict.

_____16. People with damage to the prefrontal cortex may be more aggressive because they have a general loss of inhibitions.

_____17. Low serotonin turnover in people is correlated with violent crimes and suicides.

_____18. Output from the amygdala to the hypothalamus controls skeletal responses.

_____19. People with Urbach-Wiethe disease show an increased tendency to panic disorder.

_____20. CCK is the main excitatory transmitter in the amygdala and tends to promote anxiety; GABA is the main inhibitory transmitter and tends to decrease anxiety.

_____21. Benzodiazepines directly open the chloride channel in the $GABA_A$ receptor, so that GABA is no longer needed. Therefore, it is easy to take a fatal overdose.

_____22. Alcohol, benzodiazepines, and barbiturates exhibit cross-tolerance; an individual that develops tolerance to one will show partial tolerance to the others.

## FILL IN THE BLANKS

1. People with damage to the _____ cortex or _____ showed little or no emotion and made riskier choices.

2. According to the _____-_____ theory, autonomic arousal and skeletal actions come first; our experience of emotion is the label we give to our responses.

3. Evidence for this theory is that people with locked-in syndrome are usually _____.

4. Structures that form a border around the brain stem and are associated with emotion are known as the _____ system.

5. A _____ increases the risk for ulcers but is not the main cause.

6. Frequent _____ increases the risk for heart disease, whereas social support decreases the risk.

7. Activation of the hypothalamus stimulates the anterior pituitary to produce _____, which in turn stimulates the adrenal cortex to secrete _____.

8. Blood cells that attack certain kinds of tumor cells and cells infected with viruses are called _____ _____ _____.

9. A _____ engulfs a bacterium and exposes the invader's antigens on its own surface.

10. _____, including interleukin-1, are released by T cells to combat infection and also to inform the brain that the body is ill.

11. PTSD victims tend to have a smaller _____ and, surprisingly, also have low levels of _____.

12. Stimulation of the _____ amygdala primes an animal for attack.

13. _____ _____ disorder is often associated with temporal lobe epilepsy, although most people with temporal lobe epilepsy are not violent.

14. Levels of _____ are a measure of serotonin turnover. Low serotonin turnover is associated with _____.

15. Monkeys with the _____-_____ syndrome, as a result of damage to the _____, show little fear or avoidance.

16. In humans the _____-_____ disease results in degeneration of the _____ and a resultant difficulty in expressing or recognizing _____.

17. The primary excitatory neurotransmitter in the amygdala is _____; the main inhibitory neurotransmitter is _____.

18. _____ bind to their own site on the $GABA_A$ receptor and enhance the binding of GABA; this tends to increase the flow of _____ ions.

## MATCHING ITEMS

_____ 1.  Prefrontal cortex damage     a.  Rebound of parasympathetic system after stress

_____ 2.  Panic disorder               b.  Leukocytes that mature in the thymus

_____ 3.  Ulcers                       c.  Extreme sympathetic activity interpreted as fear

_____ 4.  B cells                      d.  Make stupid decisions, no moral behavior

_____ 5.  T cells                      e.  Damages hippocampus

_____ 6.  Cytokine                     f.  Leukocytes that secrete antibodies

_____ 7.  Brief stressor               g.  Increases risk of anxiety disorder

_____ 8.  High cortisol                h.  Main inhibitory transmitter in amygdala

_____ 9.  Lack of 5-HT$_{1B}$ receptors   i.  Brief activation of immune system

_____ 10. 5-HIAA                       j.  Endogenous antibenzodiazepine

_____ 11. 3 repeats of gene on         k.  Released by T cells, fight infection, inform brain
          chromosome 15

_____ 12. CCK                          l.  Metabolite of serotonin

_____ 13. GABA                         m.  Main excitatory transmitter in amygdala

_____ 14. DBI                          n.  Genetically aggressive mice


## MULTIPLE-CHOICE QUESTIONS

1. Which of the following is true?
   a. A lack of emotions, as in people with prefrontal cortex damage, promotes rational decision making.
   b. The James-Lange theory proposed that physiological arousal is both necessary and sufficient for emotional experience.
   c. Responses based on "gut feelings" are almost always wrong.
   d. Sympathetic nervous system activity prepares the body for digestion and relaxation.

2. Which of the following cortical areas is **not** highly activated during emotional perceptions?
   a. Part of prefrontal cortex
   b. Part of cingulate gyrus
   c. Angular gyrus
   d. Occipital gyrus

3. People with "locked in syndrome"
   a. have ventral brainstem damage, which results in fairly normal sensory input, but almost no motor output.
   b. have little or no cognitive ability.
   c. express extreme panic at being unable to move.
   d. All of the above are true.

4. What is the current state of acceptance of the James-Lange theory?
   a. It is no longer thought to have any validity.
   b. It is correct in that physiological arousal is **necessary** for intense emotions, but incorrect in that physiological arousal is not **sufficient** to induce any emotions.
   c. It is incorrect in that physiological arousal is not **necessary** for intense emotions, but correct in that physiological arousal is in fact **sufficient** to induce emotions.
   d. It is largely correct in that physiological arousal is both necessary and sufficient to influence the intensity of our emotions.

5. The limbic system
   a. gets its name from the fact that it has many limbs branching in all directions.
   b. includes forebrain areas regarded as critical for emotion, which form a border around the brainstem.
   c. is especially important for higher cognitive functions that differentiate humans from other mammals.
   d. All of the above are true.

6. Which of the following is true?
   a. Damage to or inactivation of the cingulate cortex or part of prefrontal cortex increases the perception of anger.
   b. The insular cortex is important for feelings of disgust.
   c. Inactivation of the right hemisphere during the Wada procedure interferes greatly with the recall of facts but has little effect on the recall of emotion.
   d. People with greater activity in their right hemisphere tend to be more outgoing and loving.

7. Ulcers
   a. occurred more frequently in rats **without** control of the stressor.
   b. occurred more frequently in monkeys **with** control of the stressor
   c. developed during rest periods between shock.
   d. All of the above are true.

8. Voodoo death occurs only
   a. if a witch doctor has special powers.
   b. in very primitive societies.
   c. if the victim expects to die.
   d. in people with underactive parasympathetic nervous systems.

9. Curt Richter found that
   a. cutting off a rat's whiskers immediately before putting it into a tank of water resulted in its struggling frantically and then sinking suddenly to the bottom, dead.
   b. laboratory rats, but not the stronger wild ones, were most susceptible to the sudden death phenomenon.
   c. rats' whiskers are necessary for swimming, since removing them negated the otherwise helpful procedure of rescue training.
   d. All of the above are true.

10. Cortisol
   a. is secreted by the anterior pituitary gland.
   b. serves primarily to activate a sudden burst of "fight or flight" activity.
   c. serves primarily to decrease metabolic activity in order to save energy for later stresses.
   d. shifts energy away from synthesis of proteins, including those necessary for the immune system, and towards increasing blood sugar.

11. T cells
   a. are specialized to produce antibodies.
   b. mature in the thymus and either attack intruder cells or stimulate other immune system cells.
   c. engulf microorganisms and display antigen of the microorganism.
   d. are useless until they are activated by B cells.

12. Cytokines
   a. in the periphery activate receptors on the vagus nerve, which relays input to the hypothalamus and hippocampus, which then release cytokines themselves in the brain.
   b. help overcome typical illness symptoms, such as fever and sleepiness, after illness is over.
   c. increase appetite to urge the body to acquire more nutrients for fighting the illness.
   d. easily cross the blood-brain barrier, in order to coordinate peripheral and central effects.

13. Stress
   a. is by far the major factor in the activity of nonhuman animals' immune response; however, humans are not susceptible to stress effects.
   b. impairs the immune system from the first moments of the stressor's presence.
   c. produces a brief activation of the immune system, followed by inhibition of immune response if the stressor continues for a long time and is sufficiently intense.
   d. All of the above are true.

14. Prolonged high levels of cortisol
   a. make hippocampal neurons vulnerable to damage, which results in decreased learning and memory and also increased cortisol levels.
   b. lead to an increase in protein synthesis, which helps the immune system during long-term stressors.
   c. are found in almost all people with PTSD.
   d. All of the above are true.

15. PTSD
    a. occurs in almost all people who are subjected to traumatic experiences.
    b. includes symptoms of flashbacks, nightmares, avoidance of reminders, and exaggerated response to noises or other stimuli.
    c. is usually accompanied by a larger than usual hippocampus, because the memory of the trauma is so firmly established.
    d. All of the above are true.

16. Which of the following is true?
    a. Cats that "play" with their prey are really sadistically torturing the smaller animal.
    b. Increased aggressiveness can be elicited by stimulation of the corticomedial amygdala.
    c. There is greater evidence for heritability in juvenile crimes than in adult crimes.
    d. Smoking during pregnancy primarily increases the likelihood that the offspring will be arrested for nonviolent crimes, rather than violent crimes.

17. Which of the following is true?
    a. The correlation between testosterone and aggression in humans is real, but of modest size.
    b. Both genetics and environmental factors contribute to the predisposition to commit crimes and aggressive behaviors.
    c. Many people with damage to the prefrontal cortex have a tendency toward many socially inappropriate behaviors, including aggressiveness.
    d. All of the above are true.

18. Lesions of the amygdala
    a. usually produce difficulty in interpreting social stimuli as well as decreased aggressiveness.
    b. usually cause temporal lobe epilepsy.
    c. lead to a state that resembles panic disorder.
    d. usually result in decreased serotonin turnover.

19. Which of the following has **not** been implicated in aggressiveness?
    a. the corticomedial nucleus of the amygdala
    b. the entire hippocampus
    c. being a boy who was taller than usual at age 3
    d. maternal smoking during pregnancy

20. Temporal-lobe epilepsy
    a. is invariably associated with violence.
    b. is generally untreatable except by surgery.
    c. symptoms include hallucinations, lip smacking or other repetitive acts, and, in some cases, violence.
    d. can frequently be improved with antipsychotic drugs.

21. Which of the following is true?
    a. Mice with low levels of serotonin turnover are abnormally placid.
    b. Serotonin turnover has been found to be lower than normal in impulsive, aggressive humans.
    c. 5-HIAA is a drug that has been used successfully to treat uncontrollable violence.
    d. All of the above are true.

22. Which of the following is true?
    a.  Social isolation increased aggressiveness in female mice as much as in males.
    b.  A genetic lack of 5-HT$_{1B}$ receptors resulted in mice that were more aggressive, impulsive, and faster to develop addiction to cocaine.
    c.  Monkeys with low serotonin turnover had longer lifespans, because they killed off their competitors.
    d.  People who have a tendency toward aggressiveness should consume a lot of aspartame and maize (corn), in order to increase their serotonin synthesis.

23  Output from the amygdala to the hypothalamus controls
    a.  the intensity of sensory input to the organism.
    b.  the interpretation of potentially frightening stimuli.
    c.  skeletal movements of the startle response.
    d.  autonomic fear responses, such as increased blood pressure.

24. After damage, inactivation, or atrophy of the amygdala
    a.  a person has difficulty recognizing or portraying fearful expressions.
    b.  a rat no longer shows any startle reflex.
    c.  people with Urbach-Wiethe disease are unusually aggressive and fearful.
    d.  monkeys rise to the top of the social hierarchy, because they successfully threaten others.

25. Librium, Valium, and Xanax
    a.  are more habit-forming than barbiturates and more likely to lead to a fatal overdose.
    b.  are benzodiazepines.
    c.  act exclusively on CCK synapses.
    d.  All of the above are true.

26. The benzodiazepines
    a.  block GABA$_A$ synapses.
    b.  decrease the membrane's permeability to chloride ions.
    c.  attach to binding sites on the GABA$_A$ receptor complex, thereby facilitating GABA binding.
    d.  directly open chloride channels.

27. Which of the following is true?
    a.  Alcohol displaces benzodiazepines from their binding sites, thereby disrupting GABA transmission.
    b.  Endozepines, including diazepam-binding inhibitor (DBI), are actually endogenous antibenzodiazepines, which inhibit GABA transmission.
    c.  The most effective anti-anxiety drugs stimulate CCK receptors.
    d.  Alcohol produces its antianxiety effects by blocking chloride channels.

# Answers to True/False Questions

| | | | |
|---|---|---|---|
| 1. F | 7. F | 13. F | 19. F |
| 2. T | 8. F | 14. F | 20. T |
| 3. T | 9. T | 15. T | 21. F |
| 4. F | 10. F | 16. T | 22. T |
| 5. T | 11. F | 17. T | |
| 6. T | 12. T | 18. F | |

# Answers to Fill-in-the-Blank Questions

1. prefrontal, amygdala
2. James, Lange
3. tranquil
4. limbic
5. bacterium
6. hostility
7. ACTH, cortisol
8. natural killer cells
9. macrophage
10. Cytokines
11. hippocampus, cortisol
12. corticomedial
13. Intermittent explosive
14. 5-HIAA, aggressiveness
15. Klüver-Bucy, amygdala
16. Urbach-Wiethe, amygdala, fear
17. CCK, GABA
18. Benzodiazepines, chloride

# Answers to Matching Items

| | | | |
|---|---|---|---|
| 1. d | 5. b | 9. m | 13. h |
| 2. c | 6. k | 10. l | 14. j |
| 3. a | 7. I | 11. g | |
| 4. f | 8. e | 12. m | |

# Answers to Multiple-Choice Questions

| | | | |
|---|---|---|---|
| 1. b | 8. c | 15. b | 22. b |
| 2. d | 9. a | 16. b | 23. d |
| 3. a | 10. d | 17. d | 24. a |
| 4. d | 11. b | 18. a | 25. b |
| 5. b | 12. a | 19. b | 26. c |
| 6. b | 13. c | 20. c | 27. b |
| 7. d | 14. a | 21. b | |

**Please check the Exploring Biological Psychology CD-ROM.**

# 13

# THE BIOLOGY OF LEARNING AND MEMORY

## INTRODUCTION

Learning depends upon changes within single cells, which then work together as a system to produce adaptive behavior. Different kinds of learning and memory may rely on different neural mechanisms. Classical conditioning establishes a learned association between a neutral (conditioned) stimulus (CS) and an unconditioned stimulus (UCS) that evokes a reflexive response (UCR). As a result, the previously neutral stimulus comes to evoke a response (CR) similar to the reflexive response. Operant conditioning is the increase or decrease in a behavior as a result of reinforcement or punishment. Other forms of learning, such as bird song learning, may fall outside the categories of classical or operant conditioning.

Ivan Pavlov hypothesized that all learning is based on simple neural connections formed between two brain areas active at the same time. Karl Lashley tested this hypothesis by making various cuts that disconnected brain areas from each other and by removing varying amounts of cerebral cortex after rats had learned mazes or discrimination tasks. To his surprise, he found that no particular connection or part of the cortex was critical for any task. Lashley assumed that all learning occurred in the cortex and that all types of learning relied on the same physiological mechanism. Recent evidence suggests that certain subcortical nuclei may be important for specific types of learning and that several different neural mechanisms underlie different types of learning. For example, one simple type of conditioning, the eye-blink response, relies on the lateral interpositus nucleus of the cerebellum. The red nucleus, a midbrain motor center, is necessary for the motor expression of the eye-blink response, but not formation of the memory. Similar mechanisms appear to underlie eye-blink conditioning in rats and in humans.

Memory can be divided into several types: short-term vs. long-term, explicit vs. implicit, and declarative vs. procedural. Some short-term memories are consolidated rapidly into long-term memory; others are consolidated more slowly; most are not consolidated at all. Highly emotional events, which activate the sympathetic nervous system, are easily remembered. A major reason is that epinephrine in the periphery activates the vagus nerve, which relays activation to the brain stem, which in turn activates the amygdala. Cortisol is also released during stressful or exciting experiences; it, too, activates the amygdala, which enhances storage of emotional memories. However, prolonged or excessive stress, and its accompanying high cortisol level, impairs memory. Working memory is the temporary storage of information while we are using it. We may have separate neural mechanisms for storing auditory memory (a "phonological loop") and visual memory (a "visuospatial sketchpad"), as well as a "central executive" that directs attention and determines which items will be stored. The prefrontal cortex seems to be especially important for working memory. A common test of working memory is the delayed response task, in which one must respond to a stimulus presented a short time earlier. Neurons in the prefrontal cortex are active during the delay, and prefrontal damage impairs performance on delayed response tasks.

Information about memory has been obtained from studies of three major syndromes involving amnesia in humans. A main cognitive deficit in all three syndromes is the inability to form new long-term declarative or explicit memories. Declarative memory is memory that people can state in words, whereas procedural memory consists of motor skills. Explicit memory is deliberate recall of information that one recognizes as a memory; implicit memories can be detected as indirect influences on behavior, and do not require recollection of specific information. One syndrome results from hippocampal damage and is exemplified by the patient H. M., who had bilateral removal of the hippocampus to relieve incapacitating epilepsy. Following surgery, H. M. has suffered extensive anterograde amnesia and moderate retrograde amnesia; however, his working memory remains intact. The hippocampus is not the storage site for memories, since previously consolidated memories can still be retrieved; such memories depend on the cerebral cortex. The cases of H. M. and other patients with hippocampal damage suggest that the primary function of the hippocampus is to promote storage of declarative, explicit memory. Nonhuman animals with hippocampal damage show memory impairments on delayed matching tasks, which are somewhat similar to human declarative memory. In addition, they are impaired on tasks that measure spatial memory, suggesting a second hypothesis, that a major function of the hippocampus is spatial memory. Rats with hippocampal damage forget which arms of a radial arm maze they have already entered in search of food; they also forget the location of a platform submerged in murky water. Among related species of birds that live in different habitats, those that are most dependent on finding previously hidden food have the largest hippocampus. Humans also use their hippocampus to solve spatial problems. Apparently, some portions of the hippocampus code spatial information and others code nonspatial aspects. A third hypothesis is that the hippocampus is important for configural learning, in which the meaning of a stimulus depends upon other stimuli that are paired with it. Similarly, the hippocampus may bind together the various sites in the cortex that form a memory. However, hippocampal damage may also impair nonconfigural learning if it is complicated and difficult. A final theory of hippocampal function is that it regulates levels of adrenal hormones. Hippocampal damage results in high levels of cortisol in humans and corticosterone in animals, which in turn impair spatial memory.

A second human disorder, Korsakoff's syndrome, occurs almost exclusively in severe alcoholics and is characterized by apathy, confusion, confabulation (accepting guesses as if they were memories), and both retrograde and anterograde amnesia. It is caused by prolonged thiamine deficiency, which results in loss of neurons throughout the brain, especially in the mamillary bodies of the hypothalamus and the dorsomedial thalamus, which projects to prefrontal cortex. In addition to their deficit in explicit memory, Korsakoff's patients have difficulty recalling the temporal order of events.

The third human memory disorder is Alzheimer's disease, which is characterized by progressive forgetfulness, leading to disorientation, depression, restlessness, hallucinations, delusions, and loss of sleep and appetite. People with Down syndrome, who have three copies of chromosome 21, almost always get Alzheimer's disease if they survive into middle age. Mutations of genes on chromosome 14 or on chromosome 1 also result in early-onset Alzheimer's disease. Mutation of yet two other genes, on chromosomes 10 and 19, results in late-onset Alzheimer's disease. All of these mutations lead to the accumulation of amyloid deposits in the brain. Amyloid precursor protein is normally cleaved to form a smaller protein of 40 amino acids, amyloid beta protein 40 ($A\beta_{40}$), which probably has a useful function. In people with Alzheimer's disease, the precursor is cleaved to form a slightly larger protein consisting of 42 amino acids ($A\beta_{42}$), which accumulates and impairs the functions of neurons and glia. An abnormal form of tau protein, which forms part of the intracellular support structure of neurons, also accumulates in Alzheimer's patients. Amyloid deposits result in the accumulation of plaques, formed from degenerating axons and dendrites, and tangles, formed from degeneration of structures inside neurons. The brains of Alzheimer's victims reveal widespread neural degeneration, including the basal forebrain neurons that arouse the cortex. Alzheimer's disease can be temporarily alleviated by increasing levels of glucose, which not only supplies nutrition, but also increases insulin secretion, which somehow increases memory. Drugs that stimulate acetylcholine receptors or prolong acetylcholine release may also help. Antioxidants may guard against brain degeneration, and vaccination against $A\beta_{42}$ may someday be used to avoid Alzheimer's disease.

Donald Hebb suggested that the cellular basis for memory storage is increased effectiveness of specific synapses, brought about by continued activity in a self-exciting reverberating circuit. He showed that electroconvulsive shock administered during the period of consolidation impaired the transfer of short-term into long-term memory. However, sometimes this procedure also wiped out older memories, and some "forgotten" memories were later restored by reminders. Researchers now recognize intermediate stages between short-term and long-term storage. Furthermore, an enzyme, protein phosphatase 1, interferes with consolidation of memories of single experiences. Thus, we tend to remember only experiences repeated over time. Many researchers have studied the cellular mechanisms of learning in invertebrates, which have simple, well-defined nervous systems. Studies using Aplysia have demonstrated changes in identified synapses during habituation and sensitization. Long-term potentiation (LTP) is an increased synaptic responsiveness in cells of the mammalian hippocampus and other brain areas. LTP shows specificity, in that only the active synapses become strengthened. It also shows cooperativity, in which near simultaneous stimulation by two or more axons increases LTP. A third characteristic is associativity, which refers to the increased responsiveness to a weak stimulus as a result of its being paired with a strong stimulus. The opposite change, long term depression (LTD), occurs in both the hippocampus and cerebellum. It is a decreased responsiveness to a synaptic input that has been repeatedly paired with another input at low frequency. LTP depends on stimulation of two types of glutamate receptors. Stimulation of AMPA receptors depolarizes the neuron, thereby displacing the magnesium ions that normally block the ion channels of nearby NMDA receptors. As a result, the NMDA receptors are able to respond to glutamate, allowing both sodium and calcium ions to enter the cell. The calcium, in turn, activates certain chemicals and genes inside the postsynaptic neuron. These changes result in either increased responsiveness or increased numbers of AMPA receptors and increased dendritic branches. In addition, new NMDA receptors may be formed, cellular growth may be enhanced by neurotrophins, and new neurons may be generated. Finally, a retrograde neurotransmitter may increase the responsiveness of presynaptic terminals and cause them to produce GAP-43, a protein that facilitates growth and expansion of axons. Although stimulation of NMDA receptors is necessary for the establishment of LTP, activity of these receptors is not required for its maintenance. LTP and NMDA receptors may underlie the consolidation of memories and other forms of brain plasticity in the intact organism. During training LTP can be detected first in the hippocampus, and then 90 to 180 minutes later, it is detectable in parts of the cortex. Genetic alterations producing abnormal NMDA receptors or a lack of AMPA receptors result in impaired learning in mice, whereas alterations producing excess NMDA receptors result in better than normal memory. Other mice that overproduce GAP-43 also show enhanced ability to learn and solve problems. Ginko biloba and other "natural" drugs touted to enhance memory do increase blood flow and produce small benefits, but only in those with circulatory problems.

## LEARNING OBJECTIVES

### Module 13.1  Learning, Memory, Amnesia, and Brain Functioning

1. Know the differences between classical and operant conditioning and the terms used in each.
2. Be able to describe Lashley's search for the engram and his conclusions and why Richard Thompson's search arrived at a different conclusion.
3. Understand the factors that affect the consolidation of long-term memories and a current theory of working memory.
4. Be able to describe the theories of the function of the hippocampus in declarative memory, spatial memory, and configural learning and binding.
5. Know the symptoms and causes of Korsakoff's syndrome and Alzheimer's disease.

### Module 13.2  Storing Information in the Nervous System

1. Understand the mechanisms of habituation and sensitization in Aplysia.

2. Understand the roles of AMPA and NMDA receptors and of neurotrophins in long-term potentiation (LTP).


## KEY TERMS AND CONCEPTS

### Module 13.1  Learning, Memory, Amnesia, and Brain Functioning
1.  Localized representations of memory
    Classical conditioning
        Ivan Pavlov
        Conditioned stimulus (CS)
        Unconditioned stimulus (UCS)
        Unconditioned response (UCR)
        Conditioned response (CR)
    Operant conditioning
        Reinforcer
        Punishment
    Bird-song learning: Neither classical nor operant
    Lashley's search for the engram
        Engram: Physical representation of what has been learned
        Amount of damage, not location
            Equipotentiality: All parts of cortex contribute equally to complex behaviors
            Mass action: Cortex works as a whole
        Unnecessary assumptions:
            Cerebral cortex is the only site of the engram
            All kinds of memory are the same
    The modern search for the engram
        Richard F. Thompson
            Rabbit eye-blink response
            Lateral interpositus (LIP) nucleus of cerebellum: Site of conditioning
                Last structure in the circuit that had to be awake during conditioning
            Red nucleus: Motor expression
        Classical conditioning of eye-blink in humans
            PET scans: increased activity in cerebellum, red nucleus, and other areas
            Damage to cerebellum → impaired eye-blink conditioning

2.  Types of memory
    Short-term and long-term memory
        Donald Hebb
    Consolidation of long-term memories
        Reverberating circuit
            Theory: Electroconvulsive shock → disrupt reverberations that → long term memory
            Problem: Electroconvulsive shock sometimes wiped out much older memories
            Problem: Some "lost" memories later restored by reminders
        Intermediate stages between short- and long-term memories
        Protein phosphatase 1: Interferes with consolidation
            Massed practice: Protein phosphatase 1 accumulates → inhibits consolidation
            Distributed practice: Protein phosphatase 1 declines between trials → less interference
        Brain works harder to remember more recent events
        Emotional events easy to remember

Epinephrine → vagus nerve → brain stem → amygdala → hippocampus, cortex →
  memory storage
Cortisol
  Moderate amounts → amygdala, hippocampus → memory storage
  Excessive or prolonged → memory impairment
Damage amygdala: Emotional arousal does not enhance storage
A modified theory: Working memory
  Phonological loop: Stores auditory information
  Visuospatial sketchpad: Stores visual information
  Central executive: Directs attention and picks items for storage
  Delayed response task
    Dorsolateral prefrontal cortex → high activity during delay → working memory

3. The hippocampus and amnesia
   Amnesia: Memory loss
   Memory loss after hippocampal damage
     H. M.: Surgery for severe epilepsy
       Severe anterograde amnesia (loss of memory for events after surgery)
       Moderate retrograde amnesia (loss of memory for events shortly before surgery)
       Normal short-term or working memory
       Emotional placidity
       Impaired declarative memory: Ability to state memory in words
       Intact procedural memory: Development of motor skills
       Better implicit than explicit memory
         Explicit memory: Deliberate recall of information one recognizes as a memory
         Implicit memory: Influence of recent experience on behavior, even without
           realization one is using memory
   Theories of the function of the hippocampus
     Important for consolidation
       Well-consolidated memories stored in cortex
     The hippocampus and declarative memory
       Damage to the hippocampus in monkeys
         Delayed matching-to-sample test: Impaired
         Delayed nonmatching-to-sample test: Impaired
         Minor procedural changes: Variable results
         Episodic memories (memories of single events): Impaired
           Interpretation not clear
     The hippocampus and spatial memory
       Rats: Hippocampal neurons tuned to spatial locations
       London taxi drivers: Posterior hippocampus activated by answering spatial questions
       Damage to the hippocampus in rats
         Radial maze: Forget which arms they already tried
         Morris search task: Forget location of platform
       Closely related species that differ in spatial memory
         Clark's nutcracker: Most dependent on buried food
           Largest hippocampus
           Best performance on spatial tasks
         Pinyon jays: Moderately dependent on buried food
           Second largest hippocampus
           Second best performance on spatial tasks

Scrub jay and Mexican jay: Least dependent on buried food

Smallest hippocampus

Worst performance on spatial tasks

Some parts of hippocampus: Nonspatial aspects of task

The hippocampus, configural learning, and binding

Configural learning: Meaning of a stimulus depends on other stimuli

Hippocampal damage → impaired performance

Complicated nonconfigural learning: Also impaired

Hippocampus not necessary for configural learning, but assists

Theory: Hippocampus → quickly record single combination of stimuli

Cortex → detect repeated combinations

Hippocampus → Bind pieces of memory together; → map separate pieces

The hippocampus and adrenal hormones

Hippocampal damage→high levels of cortisol/corticosterone → impair spatial memory

4. Other types of brain damage and amnesia

Korsakoff's syndrome and other prefrontal damage

Wernicke-Korsakoff syndrome

Thiamine deficiency

Chronic alcoholics

Widespread loss of neurons, especially in:

Mamillary bodies of hypothalamus and

Dorsomedial thalamus (projects to prefrontal cortex)

Both anterograde and retrograde amnesia, apathy, confusion

Better implicit than explicit memory

Priming

Poor recall of temporal order of events

Confabulation

Alzheimer's disease

Memory loss, confusion, depression, restlessness, hallucinations, delusions, sleeplessness, loss of appetite

Better procedural than declarative memory

Better implicit than explicit memory

Genetic and nongenetic causes

Relationship to Down syndrome (3 copies of chromosome 21)

Mutations on chromosome 14 → 70% of early-onset Alzheimer's disease

Mutations on chromosome 1 → additional cases of early-onset disease

Mutations on chromosomes 10, 19 → late-onset disease

Cross-cultural differences

Yoruba people of Nigeria: Low-calorie, low-fat, low-sodium diet → low risk

Amyloid precursor protein → amyloid beta protein 40 ($A\beta_{40}$)

Alzheimer's disease: Amyloid beta protein 42 ($A\beta_{42}$, longer form, impairs function)

Plaques (degenerating axons and dendrites, in extracellular space)

Tau protein: part of intracellular support

Abnormal tau → tangles (degeneration within cell bodies)

Apolipoprotein E

Produced mostly by glia → growth of axons, dendrites,

Abnormal receptor → cell loss, inability to remove $A\beta_{42}$ molecules

Widespread atrophy
    Loss of acetylcholine neurons in basal forebrain → impaired attention, arousal
Prevention or alleviation
    Increase glucose → insulin secretion → enhance memory
        Type II diabetes → high insulin, few insulin receptors → low risk
    Stimulate acetylcholine receptors
    Block formation of $A\beta_{42}$
    Antioxidants
    "Vaccinate" with $A\beta_{42}$
        PDAPP mouse: Overproduce $A\beta_{42}$
        Inject young mice with a little $A\beta_{42}$ → immune attack → no Alzheimer's
What amnesic patients teach us
    Somewhat independent kinds of memory: Dependent on different brain areas

5. In closing: Different types of memory
    "Overall intelligence" as measured by IQ tests: Convenient fiction
    Different abilities: Different brain processes

## Module 13.2 Storing Information in the Nervous System

1. Blind alleys and abandoned mines
    Wilder Penfield: Each neuron stores particular memory
        "Memories" vague, not accurate
    G. A. Horridge: "Learning" in decapitated cockroaches
        Process slow, variable
    James McConnell and others: Transfer of memories by feeding or injecting "trained" RNA
        Variable results

2. Learning and the Hebbian synapse
    Simultaneous pre- and postsynaptic activity → increased synaptic efficiency

3. Single-cell mechanisms of invertebrate behavior change
    Aplysia as an experimental animal
        Plasticity
        Touch siphon, mantle, or gill → withdrawal response
    Habituation in Aplysia
        Decreased ability of sensory neuron to activate motor neuron
    Sensitization in Aplysia
        Increase in response to mild stimuli after more intense stimuli
        Facilitating interneuron
        Serotonin (5-HT)
        Presynaptic receptors → closing of potassium channels → prolonged action potential →
           more transmitter release
        Protein synthesis → long-term sensitization

4. Long-term potentiation in mammals (LTP)
    Brief but rapid series of stimuli → increased responsiveness for minutes, days, or weeks
    Characteristics
        Specificity: Only active synapses strengthened
        Cooperativity: Nearly simultaneous stimuli more effective than single stimuli
        Associativity: Pairing weak and strong inputs → enhanced later response to weaker one

Long term depression (LTD) in hippocampus and cerebellum
    LTD: Prolonged decrease in response to paired inputs presented at low frequencies
Biochemical mechanisms
    Actions at AMPA and NMDA synapses
        AMPA glutamate receptors
            Open sodium channels
        NMDA glutamate receptors
            Magnesium blockade of ion channel
            Removal of magnesium by depolarization
            Sodium and calcium influx into postsynaptic neuron
            Calcium → activation of genes and many chemicals →
            Increase in later responsiveness to glutamate
                CaMKII (α-calcium-calmodulin-dependent protein kinase II) activation →
                AMPA receptor adds phosphate group → more responsive to glutamate
                New AMPA receptors or old ones moved to better location
                "Silent" AMPA receptors become responsive
                New NMDA receptors
                Dendrite: New branches
        Release of neurotrophins → cellular growth
        Generation of new neurons
        NMDA receptors: Establish, not maintain, LTP
    Presynaptic changes
        Retrograde neurotransmitter → presynaptic neuron →
            Decrease threshold for action potentials
            Increase neurotransmitter release
            GAP-43 → growth, expansion of axons
    Consolidation of LTP
        LTP in hippocampus: Rapid storage
        Changes in cortex: 90 – 180 minutes later
        Contrasting studies
            Block NMDA receptors 1 – 2 weeks after training → prevent consolidation of
                long-term memories
            Block NMDA receptors 1 – 2 weeks after training → prolonged LTP, dendritic
                branching
            Interpretation: Block NMDA → later experiences can't override previous ones
LTP and behavior
    Mutation of gene for NMDA receptors → impaired LTP and memory
    Genes that → extra NMDA receptors → better than normal memory
    Lack of AMPA → impaired LTP and memory
    Similar effects of drugs on LTP and on memory
    Overproduction of GAP-43 → enhance learning
    Ginko biloba and other chemicals → increase blood flow → small benefits in those with
        circulatory problems

5.  In closing: The physiology of memory
    Complex behaviors: Large interacting network
    Requirement of memory: Record what we need to remember, not everything

## Module 13.1  Learning, Memory, Amnesia, and Brain Functioning

1. *Localized representations of memory*

   a. Describe the relationships among the conditioned and unconditioned stimuli and the unconditioned and conditioned responses in classical conditioning.

   b. Who discovered classical conditioning?  What were the conditioned and unconditioned stimuli in his experiments?  What was the unconditioned, and eventually the conditioned, response?

   c. What is the fundamental difference between classical and operant conditioning?  Define reinforcement and punishment in terms of operant conditioning.

   d. Why is bird-song learning difficult to classify?

   e. What is an engram?  What did Lashley discover in his search for the engram?

f. What two assumptions did Lashley make, that later investigators rejected?

g. What brain area was found by Richard F. Thompson to be important for classical conditioning of the eye-blink response in rabbits?

h. What area was important for the expression of the motor response, but not for the initial conditioning?

i. Which areas showed increased activity on PET scans during eye-blink conditioning in humans?

2. *Types of memory*
   a. Define short-term memory and long-term memory.

   b. How did Donald Hebb explain consolidation?

c.  What problems were encountered with the interpretation of experiments using electroconvulsive shock?

d.  What is protein phosphatase 1?  How do the effects of this enzyme explain the greater efficacy of distributed, as opposed to massed practice?

e.  Why may the inhibitory effects of protein phosphatase 1 be beneficial?

f.  In what two ways do exciting experiences enhance memory consolidation?

g.  What brain areas are stimulated by the amygdala after an emotional experience?  What is the effect of long term or excessive stress?

h.  What is working memory?  What are its three hypothesized components?

i. What brain area seems to be especially important for working memory? What is a common test of working memory?

3. *The hippocampus and amnesia*
   a. Why was H. M.'s hippocampus removed bilaterally? How successful was this treatment at relieving epilepsy? What were the other effects of the surgery?

   b. What is the difference between retrograde and anterograde amnesia? Which is more evident in H. M.?

   c. Distinguish between declarative and procedural memory. Which is impaired in H. M.? What is a test for procedural memory?

   d. Distinguish between explicit memory and implicit memory. What is one test of implicit memory?

e.  What seems to be the major function of the hippocampus? Why can we conclude that memories are not stored in the hippocampus itself? Where are well-consolidated memories stored?

f.  For what three types of memory is the hippocampus hypothesized to be important?

g.  Describe the delayed matching-to-sample and delayed nonmatching-to-sample tasks.

h.  Under what conditions does hippocampal damage impair performance on matching- or nonmatching-to-sample tasks?

i.  What type of memory is tested by the radial maze and the Morris search task? What two kinds of errors can rats make in the radial maze? Which type of error do rats make after damage to the hippocampus?

j. Describe the Morris search task. What deficits on this task are seen in hippocampally damaged rats?

k. Describe the relationship between birds' dependence on finding previously hidden food and the size of their hippocampus.

l. What is configural learning? Describe the likely role of the hippocampus in configural learning?

m. What is one hormonal change that is incurred following hippocampal damage? What is the effect of this change on spatial memory?

4. *Other types of brain damage and amnesia*
   a. What is the immediate cause of Korsakoff's syndrome? What are its symptoms? In what group of people does it usually occur?

b.    Which brain areas show neuronal loss in Korsakoff's syndrome?

c.    Describe the symptoms of Korsakoff's syndrome in terms of anterograde vs. retrograde amnesia and explicit vs. implicit memory. What is priming, and what type of memory can show priming effects?

d.    What symptoms do Korsakoff's patients have in common with patients with frontal-lobe damage? What additional symptom do Korsakoff's patients have?

e.    Describe the symptoms of Alzheimer's disease.

f.    Why are some cases of Alzheimer's disease thought to be related to a gene on chromosome 21? How does the chromosomal abnormality differ from that in Down syndrome?

g. What other chromosomes contain genes that have been linked to early-onset Alzheimer's disease? To late-onset Alzheimer's disease?

h. What is amyloid precursor protein? What are the two forms of amyloid beta protein? Which form is implicated in the formation of amyloid deposits?

i. What other protein is implicated in Alzheimer's disease? What is its normal function?

j. Which brain areas are atrophied in Alzheimer's disease? What physical signs are present in areas of atrophy?

k. What are two temporary means of alleviating Alzheimer's disease? What dietary factors may guard against Alzheimer's disease?

l. Describe the research on PDAPP mice.

m. What have we learned about memory from amnesic patients?

## Module 13.2 Storing Information in the Nervous System
1. *Blind alleys and abandoned mines*
    a. What did Wilder Penfield conclude from his brain stimulation experiments? What are some problems with his conclusion?

    b. Describe G. A. Horridge's experiments with headless cockroaches. Why was this experimental approach abandoned?

    c. Describe the experiments in planaria and rats that seemed to show transfer of training from one individual to another via RNA or protein. Why were these experiments abandoned?

2. *Learning and the Hebbian synapse*
    a. What is a Hebbian synapse? How is it related to classical conditioning?

3. *Single-cell mechanisms of invertebrate behavior change*
   a. Why should anyone be interested in the cellular mechanisms of habituation or sensitization in the lowly Aplysia?

   b. What possible mechanisms of habituation were ruled out? What mechanism does seem to account for habituation in Aplysia?

   c. How is sensitization produced experimentally in Aplysia?

   d. Describe the cellular events that explain sensitization in Aplysia. How does a decrease in potassium outflow increase transmitter release?

   e. How does long-term sensitization differ from the short-term variety?

4. *Long-term potentiation in mammals*
   a. How is long-term potentiation (LTP) produced? How long does it last? In what brain area was it first discovered?

b.    What is meant by specificity?  Cooperativity?  Associativity?

c.    What is long term depression (LTD)?  Where has it been observed?  How does it differ
      from LTP?

d.    Which transmitter stimulates both NMDA and AMPA receptors?  Why must AMPA
      receptors be stimulated, in addition to NMDA receptors, in order to produce LTP?

e.    Describe the sequence of events that follows the successful activation of NMDA receptors?

f.    What is CaMKII?

g.    List five changes in the postsynaptic neuron that contribute to LTP.

h.  Are NMDA receptors important for the establishment or maintenance of LTP?

i.  What is a retrograde neurotransmitter? What changes in the presynaptic terminal may contribute to LTP?

j.  What kinds of experiments have shown the relevance of NMDA receptors for establishing memories in intact organisms?

k.  What is GAP-43? What is the effect of a genetic mutation that results in overproduction of this protein?

l.  How beneficial is ginko biloba to memory? What is its mechanism of action? In what group of people is it beneficial?

## TRUE/FALSE QUESTIONS

_____  1.  In some classical conditioning experiments the UR resembles the UCR, and in other cases it does not.

_____  2.  Lashley proposed the principles of Equipotentiality and Mass Action.

_____ 3. Donald Hebb successfully showed that electroconvulsive shock completely prevented consolidation of new memories into long-term storage, but never affected older memories; furthermore, the "lost" memories could never be restored.

_____ 4. Protein phosphatase 1 interferes with consolidation of memories.

_____ 5. Emotional events are easy to remember because peripheral epinephrine inhibits protein phosphatase 1 in the brain and thereby facilitates memory storage.

_____ 6. During the delayed response task in monkeys, activity in the amygdala is especially high, because the amygdala is the main site for working memory.

_____ 7. H. M.'s major problems are severe retrograde amnesia and deficits in implicit memory.

_____ 8. The hippocampus may quickly record single combinations of stimuli and bind the pieces of memory together, whereas the cortex requires repeated presentation of those combinations in order to form long-term memories of them.

_____ 9. Korsakoff's syndrome is characterized by widespread loss of neurons, especially in the mamillary bodies of the hypothalamus and the dorsomedial thalamus.

_____ 10. People with Type II diabetes have high levels of insulin, which makes them especially susceptible to Alzheimer's disease.

_____ 11. Decapitated cockroaches show very impressive "learning" when injected with "trained" RNA from intact cockroaches.

_____ 12. Aplysia show sensitization when serotonin from a facilitating interneuron closes potassium channels on presynaptic terminals of sensory neurons, thereby prolonging the action potential and releasing more neurotransmitter.

_____ 13. The influx of magnesium through NMDA receptors triggers many intracellular changes that result in LTP.

_____ 14. Activation of CaMKII adds a phosphate group to AMPA receptors, thereby increasing their responsiveness.

_____ 15. Activation of NMDA receptors is necessary for both establishing and maintaining LTP.

_____ 16. One interpretation of the effects of blocking NMDA receptors 1 to 2 weeks after training is that such blocking prevents later experiences from overriding previous ones.

## FILL IN THE BLANKS

1. In _____ conditioning the individual's response determines the outcome; in

_____ conditioning the CS and UCS are presented independently of the

individual's behavior.

2. An _____ is the physical representation of what has been learned.

3. The _____ _____ _____of the cerebellum is the site of conditioning of the eye-blink response. The _____ _____ is required for motor expression of this response.

4. An enzyme that interferes with consolidation of memories is _____

_____ __.

5. During emotional situations peripheral epinephrine excites the _____ _____, which activates the brain stem, which in turn activates the _____, which relays the information to the _____ and _____ _____.

6. The _____ _____ stores auditory information; the

_____ _____ stores visual information; and the

_____ _____ directs attention and picks items for storage.

7. The deliberate recall of information one recognizes as a memory is _____ memory.

8. Damage to the hippocampus impairs _____ memory, _____ memory, and _____ learning.

9. Damage to the hippocampus results in prolonged high levels of _____ hormones, which in turn impair spatial memories.

10. _____ syndrome results from thiamine deficiency, which causes widespread loss of neurons, especially in the _____ _____ of the hypothalamus and the _____ thalamus, which projects to the prefrontal cortex.

11. Alzheimer's disease is characterized by _____, formed from degenerating axons and dendrites, and _____, resulting from abnormal _____ protein, which normally forms part of the intracellular support network.

12. Some possible means of preventing or alleviating Alzheimer's disease are increasing

_____ secretion, stimulating _____ receptors,

blocking the formation of A$\beta_{42}$, and including _____ in the diet.

13. The main difference between LTP and LTD is the _____ of stimulation of the

two inputs.

14. Stimulation of AMPA receptors is needed to remove the _____ ions that

normally block the ion channels of NMDA receptors.

15. LTP may cause the release of _____, which promote cellular growth.

16. A _____ neurotransmitter from the postsynaptic neuron to the

presynaptic neuron may decrease the threshold for _____ _____,

increase _____ release, and increase production of _____,

a protein that increases axon expansion.

17. Genes that result in extra _____ receptors or overproduction of _____ result in

better than normal learning and memory.

18. _____ _____ increases blood flow in people with circulatory problems

and thereby produces small increases in memory.

**MATCHING ITEMS**

| | | | |
|---|---|---|---|
| _____ | 1. | Bird song learning | a. Impairs consolidation |
| _____ | 2. | Mass action | b. Site of eye-blink conditioning |
| _____ | 3. | Lateral interpositus nucleus | c. Lashley: Cortex works as a whole |
| _____ | 4. | Protein phosphatase 1 | d. Moderate amounts → facilitate memory |
| _____ | 5. | Cortisol | e. Severe anterograde amnesia |
| _____ | 6. | Phonological loop | f. Neither classical nor operant conditioning |
| _____ | 7. | Dorsolateral prefrontal cortex | g. Responses tuned to spatial locations |
| _____ | 8. | H. M. | h. A$\beta_{42}$, abnormal Tau, plaques, and tangles |

| | | | |
|---|---|---|---|
| _____ 9. | Rat hippocampal neurons | i. | Stores auditory information |
| _____ 10. | Korsakoff syndrome | j. | Severe thiamine deficiency |
| _____ 11. | Alzheimer's disease | k. | Site of working memory |
| _____ 12. | Aplysia sensitization | l. | Stimulates growth, expansion of axons |
| _____ 13. | NMDA receptors | m. | Serotonin from facilitating interneurons |
| _____ 14. | GAP-43 | n. | Establish, not maintain, LTP |

## MULTIPLE-CHOICE QUESTIONS

1. In classical conditioning
   a. the meat used by Pavlov was the conditioned stimulus.
   b. the learner's behavior controls the presentation of reinforcements and punishments.
   c. a stimulus comes to elicit a response that may be similar to a response elicited by another stimulus.
   d. bird-song learning can be fully explained in terms of CS and UCS.

2. Ivan Pavlov believed that learning occurs when
   a. the connection between the CS center and the UCS center is strengthened.
   b. the connection between the CS center and the CR center is strengthened.
   c. the CS center takes over the UCS center's ability to elicit a UCR.
   d. cells in the UCS center degenerate and cells in the CS center branch diffusely.

3. Lashley successfully demonstrated that
   a. the lateral interpositus nucleus is the site of all engrams.
   b. all learning takes place in the cerebral cortex.
   c. the same neural mechanisms underlie all types of learning.
   d. none of the above.

4. The lateral interpositus nucleus of the cerebellum
   a. is important for the motor expression of eye-blink conditioning in rabbits, but not the actual conditioning.
   b. is important for the actual conditioning of the eyelid response.
   c. is more important for explicit than implicit memory formation.
   d. is an area that shows a great deal of damage in Korsakoff's syndrome.

5. Hebb's distinction between short-term and long-term memory
   a. was initially supported by data showing that electroconvulsive shock disrupted the reverberating circuits that stored short-term memories during the process of consolidation into long-term memories; however, problems later arose with those experiments.
   b. is supported by data showing that short-term memories are stored in the amygdala and long-term memories are stored in the lateral interpositus nucleus of the cerebellum.
   c. has been rejected by researchers because short-term and long-term memory merge so gradually that they are considered to be a single type of memory.
   d. has recently been attributed to Pavlov, instead of Hebb.

6. Experiments on consolidation have shown that
   a. protein phosphatase 1 is an important facilitator of consolidation.
   b. more brain activity may be required to remember recent events than those that were consolidated years ago.
   c. prolonged high elevations of cortisol levels are even more effective than brief moderate elevations for promoting memory storage.
   d. all of the above are true.

7. Epinephrine in the blood facilitates memory consolidation by
   a. causing circuits to reverberate.
   b. crossing the blood-brain barrier and activating epinephrine synapses in the hippocampus.
   c. stimulating the vagus nerve, which activates neurons in the brain stem, which stimulate the amygdala, which in turn stimulates the hippocampus and cerebral cortex.
   d. being converted into norepinephrine and then crossing the blood-brain barrier to activate synapses.

8. Working memory consists of
   a. a phonological loop.
   b. a visuospatial sketchpad.
   c. a central executive.
   d. all of the above.

9. The delayed response task for monkeys
   a. showed that visual memories are stored in primary visual cortex.
   b. showed that high activity in prefrontal cortex during the delay was correlated with successful performance on the task, suggesting that this area does store working memory.
   c. showed that cells in the prefrontal cortex are more important for initiating movement than for storing information about the stimulus.
   d. is no longer used as a test for working memory.

10. H. M.
    a. had his hippocampus removed because of his uncontrollable violence.
    b. acquired severe epilepsy as a result of the surgery.
    c. has a terrific memory for numbers but can learn no new skills.
    d. has more severe problems with declarative than with procedural memory.

11. Which of the following statements applies to H. M.?
    a. He has more severe anterograde than retrograde amnesia.
    b. He has more trouble with implicit than with explicit memory.
    c. His deficits show that the hippocampus is the storage site for all factual memories.
    d. All of the above are true.

12. Your memory of what you had for dinner last night is an example of
    a. explicit memory.
    b. implicit memory.
    c. procedural memory.
    d. short-term memory.

13. Priming is useful for
    a. producing memory consolidation.
    b. testing short-term memory.
    c. testing implicit memory.
    d. testing explicit memory.

14. Damage to the hippocampus produces impairment on tasks requiring
    a. declarative, explicit memory.
    b. configural learning and complicated nonconfigural learning.
    c. spatial memory.
    d. all of the above.

15. Damage to the hippocampus results in
    a. rats going down a never-correct arm of the radial maze.
    b. rats forgetting which arms they have already explored.
    c. inability to climb onto a platform in the Morris search task because of motor impairment.
    d. monkeys that cannot choose a nonmatching stimulus under any conditions.

16. Which of the following is true?
    a. Clark's nutcracker birds are very dependent on previously hidden food and have a large hippocampus.
    b. Mexican jays are also dependent on previously hidden food, but have a small hippocampus.
    c. The use of color memory in solving problems is a better predictor of hippocampal size than is dependence on previously hidden food.
    d. Hippocampal damage impairs performance on all tasks that use spatial memory, but does not impair any other tasks.

17 Korsakoff's syndrome
    a. occurs because alcohol dissolves proteins in the brain, thereby shrinking presynaptic endings.
    b. is caused by prolonged thiamine deficiency.
    c. results from damage primarily to the hippocampus.
    d. all of the above.

18. Patients with Korsakoff's syndrome
    a. have damage in the mamillary bodies of the hypothalamus and the dorsomedial nucleus of the thalamus, which projects to prefrontal cortex.
    b. have symptoms somewhat similar to those of patients with damage to the prefrontal cortex.
    c. have better implicit memory than explicit memory.
    d. all of the above.

19. Alzheimer's disease
    a. results from three copies of chromosome 21.
    b. results from a long history of excessive alcohol consumption.
    c. occurs much less frequently in the Yoruba people of Nigeria than in Americans, probably because of their low-fat, low-calorie, low-sodium diet.
    d. have too much apolipoprotein E, which is a particularly destructive chemical.

20. Patients with Alzheimer's disease
    a. have plaques and tangles in damaged areas of their brains.
    b. unlike H. M. and Korsakoff's patients, have more problems with implicit than explicit memory.
    c. have a nearly 100% probability of passing the disease on to their offspring.
    d. all of the above.

21. Which of the following is true concerning Alzheimer's disease?
    a. Amyloid precursor protein can be cleaved to produce amyloid beta protein 42 ($A\beta_{42}$), which accumulates in the brain and impairs the function of neurons.
    b. An abnormal form of the tau protein, which forms part of the intracellular support structure in neurons, also accumulates in Alzheimer's patients.
    c. Genes on chromosomes 21, 14, 1, 10, and 19 have all been implicated in either early- or late-onset Alzheimer's disease.
    d. All of the above are true.

22. Techniques for alleviating or preventing Alzheimer's disease include
    a. maintaining low levels of blood glucose, in order to decrease levels of insulin, which is destructive of neurons.
    b. eating a diet rich in antioxidants.
    c. giving drugs that block acetylcholine receptors or decrease acetylcholine release.
    d. injecting large amounts of $A\beta_{42}$ into the brains of aging people.

23. Donald Hebb proposed that
    a. a cellular basis of memory is the strengthening of synapses by simultaneous activity in the pre- and postsynaptic neurons.
    b. having two different axons stimulating a given dendrite at the same time is confusing to the dendrite and leads to long-term depression.
    c. short-term and long-term memory are the same thing.
    d. Hebbian synapses can explain operant, but not classical, conditioning.

24. Aplysia are studied because
    a. they are the intellectual giants of the ocean.
    b. they have simple nervous systems with large neurons that are virtually identical among individuals.
    c. they have the most complex brains of all invertebrates.
    d. we can automatically infer the principles of learning in complex vertebrates.

25. Habituation in Aplysia is the result of
    a. a decrease in the firing rate of a facilitating interneuron.
    b. a decrease in the firing rate of the sensory neuron.
    c. decreased ability of the sensory neuron to activate the motor neuron.
    d. muscle fatigue.

26. The mechanism mediating sensitization in Aplysia includes
    a. the release of dopamine from the sensory neuron onto the facilitating interneuron.
    b. the release of serotonin by the sensory neuron onto the motor neuron.
    c. release of serotonin by the facilitating interneuron onto the presynaptic terminals of sensory neurons → decreased potassium outflow in the sensory neurons → prolongation of transmitter release.
    d. synthesis of new proteins in short-term, but not long-term sensitization.

27. Long-term potentiation (LTP)
    a. was first discovered in Aplysia.
    b. results from increased inflow of magnesium through AMPA receptors.
    c. requires depolarization via NMDA receptors in order to allow calcium outflow through AMPA receptors.
    d. requires depolarization via AMPA receptors in order to dislodge magnesium ions from NMDA receptors.

28. LTP
    a. is very powerful but lasts only a few seconds.
    b. may result from increased responsiveness of AMPA receptors, increased numbers of AMPA or NMDA receptors, and/or increased dendritic branching.
    c. depends on NMDA receptors for its maintenance, but not for its establishment.
    d. may result from decreased sensitivity of the postsynaptic cell to the inhibitory transmitter glutamate.

29. Presynaptic changes in LTP
    a. are mediated by a retrograde neurotransmitter.
    b. may include a decreased threshold for action potentials and increased transmitter release.
    c. may include increased production of GAP-43, which stimulates expansion of axons.
    d. all of the above.

30. Which of the following is evidence for the relevance of LTP to behavior?
    a. Mutation of the gene for NMDA receptors impaired both LTP and memory.
    b. Genes that resulted in excess NMDA receptors also impaired both LTP and memory.
    c. Overproduction of GAP-43 impaired both LTP and memory.
    d. Ginko biloba is one of the best facilitators yet discovered for both LTP and memory.

## Answers to True/False Questions

| | | | |
|---|---|---|---|
| 1. T | 5. F | 9. T | 13. F |
| 2. T | 6. F | 10. F | 14. T |
| 3. F | 7. F | 11. F | 15. F |
| 4. T | 8. T | 12. T | 16. T |

## Answers to Fill-in-the-Blank Questions

1. operant, classical
2. engram
3. lateral interpositus nucleus, red nucleus
4. protein phosphatase 1
5. vagus nerve, amygdala, hippocampus, cerebral cortex
6. phonological loop, visuospatial sketchpad, central executive
7. explicit
8. declarative, spatial, configural
9. adrenal
10. Korsakoff's, mamillary bodies, dorsomedial
11. plaques, tangles, tau
12. insulin, acetylcholine, antioxidants
13. frequency
14. magnesium
15. neurotrophins
16. retrograde, action potentials, neurotransmitter, GAP-43
17. NMDA, GAP-43
18. Ginko biloba

## Answers to Matching Items

1. f
2. c
3. b
4. a
5. d
6. i
7. k
8. e
9. g
10. j
11. h
12. m
13. n
14. l

## Answers to Multiple-Choice Questions

1. c
2. a
3. d
4. b
5. a
6. b
7. c
8. d
9. b
10. d
11. a
12. a
13. c
14. d
15. b
16. a
17. b
18. d
19. c
20. a
21. d
22. b
23. a
24. b
25. c
26. c
27. d
28. b
29. d
30. a

**Please check the Exploring Biological Psychology CD-ROM.**

# Emotions and Memories

**ACROSS**

1 Type of memory that does not change from time to time

4 Researcher who studied type of learning in 17 Across

9 Disease with symptoms of impaired memory formation, plaques and tangles, and general neural degeneration

12 Type of leukocyte that produces antibodies

14 Nucleus in hypothalamus on which testosterone acts to promote aggression

17 Type of conditioning based on stimulus-stimulus associations

18 Researcher who searched for the engram

19 Hormone from anterior pituitary that stimulates the adrenal cortex (abbr.)

**DOWN**

2 Anatomical locus of memory, studied by researcher in 18

Across

3 Formation of long-term memories

5 Endozepine that increases anxiety (abbr.)

6 Site of neurons in interpositus nucleus that mediate eyeblink conditioning

7 Nutrient that promotes memory formation

8 Syndrome found in alcoholics in which memory consolidation is impaired

10 Brain structure that regulates cortisol and memory formation

11 Transmitter that may inhibit aggressiveness

13 Disorder produced by trauma, characterized by nightmares, avoidance, and flashbacks (abbr.)

15 Pioneer of stress research

16 5-____: major metabolite of serotonin, a measure of serotonin turnover (abbr.)

341

# 14

## LATERALIZATION AND LANGUAGE

### INTRODUCTION

Each hemisphere of the brain receives sensory input primarily from the opposite side of the body and controls motor output to that side as well. The hemispheres are connected by a large bundle of fibers, the corpus callosum, as well as several smaller bundles. In humans, the eyes are connected with the brain in such a way that the left half of each retina supplies input to the left hemisphere, and vice versa. Furthermore, the left half of each retina receives input from the right half of the visual field. Therefore, the right half of the visual field projects to the left hemisphere, and vice versa. The auditory system projects bilaterally, although the projection to the opposite side is stronger. This relationship has allowed researchers to test the roles of the two hemispheres in people whose corpus callosum had been severed in order to relieve epilepsy. Such studies have shown that the left hemisphere is specialized for language and details, whereas the right hemisphere is particularly adept at emotional expression and perception, complex spatial problems, and overall patterns. The enhanced perception of the "big picture" by the right hemisphere may derive from a stronger magnocellular projection to that hemisphere, whereas the stronger parvocellular projection to the left hemisphere may facilitate attention to details. In addition, happy emotions are more localized in the left hemisphere, and fear and anger, in the right. Split-brain people sometimes seem to have two "selves" occupying the same body. In these people each half of the brain processes information and solves problems more or less independently of the other, although cooperation can be learned, thanks to enhanced function of subcortical connections. Even in intact people, evidence for hemispheric specialization can be seen. One possible basis for the lateralization of language functions in the left hemisphere is that in 65 percent of people a portion of the left temporal lobe, the planum temporale, is larger on the left side than on the right. The size difference is apparent even shortly after birth, and is correlated with performance on language tests.

The corpus callosum matures gradually, and experience determines the survival of the axons that make the best functional connections through the corpus callosum. People born without a corpus callosum are different from those who had split-brain surgery in adulthood. They can verbally describe sensory input from either hand and from either visual field. They may rely on greater development of the anterior commissure and hippocampal commissure to convey information from one hemisphere to the other. In addition, each hemisphere develops connections to both sides of the body. About 10% of people are either left-handed or ambidextrous; most of them have mixed hemispheric control of speech, though the left is usually dominant. The corpus callosum is thicker in left-handers, especially those with left hemisphere dominance for speech. Although there may be hemisphere specialization, almost all tasks require cooperation by both hemispheres. Recovery of language ability after damage to the left hemisphere is variable and depends in part on age at the time of damage and also on the cause and suddenness of the damage. Early damage tends to result in greater reorganization of the right hemisphere for language, whereas any recovery in adulthood tends to be accomplished by reorganization of surviving parts of the left hemisphere. Rasmussen's encephalography progresses slowly and allows the opposite hemisphere to reorganize gradually.

Because new features evolve from older ones that may have served similar functions, researchers have studied the language abilities of our nearest relatives, the chimpanzees. A number of chimpanzees have been taught to communicate with their trainers, a computer, or each other using various nonspoken language systems. However, even after years of training, their linguistic abilities fall far short of those of young children. Bonobos (Pan paniscus, or pygmy chimpanzees) have shown the most impressive linguistic abilities among our primate relatives. They have learned by imitation, have used words to describe objects (as opposed to making a request) or to refer to a past event, and have created original sentences. In addition, some have learned to understand spoken English sentences. Dolphins and parrots also show some language-like abilities. Studies of nonhuman language abilities may provide insights about how best to teach language to brain-damaged or autistic people; they may also stimulate consideration of the unique versus shared abilities of humans and of the nature of language. Language may have evolved as a by-product of larger brains and increasing intelligence. However, neither absolute brain size nor brain to body ratio provides a reliable prediction of intelligence. Furthermore, some people with normal brains and intelligence have severely impaired language. Conversely, people with Williams syndrome have severe mental retardation and abnormally developed brains, but nearly normal language, social, and musical abilities. On some tests they even have better than average abilities. An alternative view is that language arose as an extra brain module. This view is supported by the ease with which children develop language. Indeed, if children do not learn some language when they are young, they will always be disadvantaged. However, much of the brain is involved in language processing, not just one or two new modules. Therefore, increasing intelligence may have occurred because of the growing importance of language for social interaction. In general, children learn new languages more easily than do adults, especially pronunciation and unfamiliar grammar. On the other hand, adults are better at memorizing vocabulary. If a second language is learned, it activates the same brain areas as the first language.

Paul Broca discovered that damage to an area of the left frontal lobe results in difficulties with language production and with the use of grammatical connectives and other closed-class grammatical forms. People with such damage can usually understand both written and spoken language better than they can produce it, although they do have difficulty understanding the closed class words that they have most trouble producing. Carl Wernicke, on the other hand, described a pattern of deficits almost the opposite of Broca's aphasia: poor language comprehension, anomia (difficulty finding the right word), but articulate (though frequently meaningless) speech. This syndrome results from destruction of an area in the left temporal lobe near the primary auditory cortex. Although "language areas" are specialized for language, they have other functions as well. The temporal lobe is important for declarative memories, including names and irregular verbs, and frontal lobe functions include procedural memories, such as rules for regular verbs.

Dyslexia, a reading disorder in otherwise normal people, may result from bilaterally symmetrical cortex, microscopic abnormalities, weak connections among areas of the left hemisphere, subtle hearing deficits, deficits in the magnocellular visual pathways, or differences in attention. There are many kinds of dyslexia, which have different underlying causes. Some dyslexics' reading ability may be improved by focusing on one word at a time.


## LEARNING OBJECTIVES

**Module 14.1 Lateralization of Function**
1. Be able to describe the visual and auditory connections to the hemispheres.
2. Know why some people have had their corpus callosum cut and how that operation affected their everyday lives and their ability to do conflicting tasks with their two hands.
3. Be able to describe the methods of testing hemispheric dominance for speech.
4. Be able to describe the functions of the right and left hemispheres.
5. Understand the relationship of handedness and language dominance and the anatomical differences between the hemispheres.
6. Know the mechanisms of recovery of speech after brain damage.

## Module 14.2  Evolution and Physiology of Language

1. Be able to describe the language abilities of common chimpanzees, bonobos, dolphins, and parrots.
2. Understand the problems with the hypothesis that language is a product of overall intelligence.
3. Understand the evidence for and against the development of language as a special module.
4. Know the symptoms and causes of Broca's aphasia and Wernicke's aphasia.
5. Be able to describe the symptoms of dyslexia and some contributing anatomical, physiological and functional factors.


## KEY TERMS AND CONCEPTS

## Module 14.1  Lateralization of Function

1. Connections
> Corpus callosum
> Anterior commissure
> Hippocampal commisure

    Lateralization


2. Visual and auditory connections to the hemispheres

    Right visual field → left half of both retinas → left hemisphere (and vice versa)
> Optic chiasm
> Small vertical strip in center of retina → both hemispheres

    Both ears → both hemispheres
> Opposite side stronger


3. Cutting the corpus callosum

    Decreases frequency of epileptic seizures

    Epilepsy: Repeated episodes of excessive synchronized neural activity
> Causes
>> Decreased release of GABA
>> Mutation of gene for GABA receptor
>> Trauma, infection, tumor, toxic substance
> Antiepileptic drugs
>> Block sodium flow across membrane
>> Enhance effects of GABA
> Surgical removal of focus (origin)
> Cut corpus callosum if more than one focus
>> Restricts seizures to one side
>> Decreases number of seizures

    Split-brain people or animals
> Independent control of two sides of body
> Abnormal behavior only if input is restricted to one side
> No problem with familiar tasks, new tasks difficult
> Can use two hands independently
>> Conflicting tasks: Cognitive, not motor problem for intact-brain people
>>> Easier if clear targets direct movement
> Left hemisphere: Speech comprehension and production
>> 95% of right-handers
>> 80% of left-handers

Some speech understanding in both hemispheres
Bilateral control of speech → stuttering in some people
Split hemispheres: Competition and cooperation
Hands do conflicting tasks
Learning to cooperate
Use of subcortical connections
Verbal task: One word to each hemisphere
Right hand drew input to left hemisphere
Left hand drew two pictures, but not combined concept
The right hemisphere
Understands simple speech
Emotional content of speech and facial expression, humor, and sarcasm
Left hemisphere damage → better detection of lying
Left hemisphere → interferes with right hemisphere emotional perception
Right hemisphere damage → monotone; can't understand emotional expression, humor, or sarcasm
Left hemisphere → feeling happiness
Right hemisphere → feeling fear and anger
Recognizes both pleasant and unpleasant emotions in others
Complex visual patterns, spatial relationships
Stronger magnocellular visual projection to right hemisphere
Stronger parvocellular visual projection to left hemisphere
"Big picture" of vision
Left hemisphere: Details
Hemispheric specializations in intact brains
Small differences
Difficulty doing two things at once when both depend on same hemisphere

4. Methods 14.1: Testing hemispheric dominance for speech
Wada test: Sodium amytal injected into carotid artery on one side of head
Dichotic listening task: Earphones → different words to the two ears at same time
Object naming latency test
Left hemisphere dominance → faster response to stimulus in right visual field and vice versa
Record brain activity during speech or listening to speech
PET, fMRI, electrical or magnetic evoked response
Some activity in non-dominant hemisphere

5. Development of lateralization and handedness
Anatomical differences between the hemispheres
Innate tendency to attend to language sounds
Planum temporale: Larger in left hemisphere
Left to right ratio: Correlation with language skills
Less ability to acquire language after early damage to left than to right
Maturation of the corpus callosum
Maturation over first 5 to 10 years
Survival of functional connections
Matures enough between ages 3 and 5 to compare stimuli between two hands
Development without a corpus callosum
Verbally describe stimuli in either hand

Each hemisphere: Connections to both sides of body
Anterior commissure
Hippocampal commissure
Posterior commissure
Handedness and language dominance
10% of people: Left-handed or ambidextrous
Prehistoric humans: 90% of pictures → tool or weapon in right hand
Other primates: Also right-handed, less so than humans
More than 95% of right-handed: Left hemisphere for speech
Most left-handers: Left hemisphere for speech, though some mixed control
Left-handers: Thicker corpus callosum
Recovery of speech after brain damage
Inactivation of hemisphere dominant for language → block speech
Age at time of left hemisphere damage
Adult: Remaining parts of left hemisphere reorganize
Young child: Right hemisphere gains language capacity
Variability in both young and old
Source of medical problem
Rasmussen's encephalopathy
Gradual degeneration of glia, neurons of one hemisphere
Epileptic seizures, deterioration of speech and memory
Remove damaged hemisphere → language recovers slowly
Gradual degeneration → right hemisphere reorganizes slowly

6. Avoiding overstatements
Complicated tasks: Both hemispheres

7. In closing: One brain, two hemispheres

## Module 14.2  Evolution and Physiology of Language
1. Nonhuman precursors to language
Productivity: Ability to produce new signals to represent new ideas
Common chimpanzees
Inability to speak
Ability to use visual symbols
Few original combinations: Little productivity
Symbols used to request, not describe
Limited comprehension of others' communications
Bonobos
Pan paniscus (pygmy chimpanzees)
Social order similar to humans'
Language ability of 2- to 2 ½-year-old child
Understand more than they produce
Name and describe without request
Request what they do not see
Refer to past
Creative requests
Early training by observation and imitation

Nonprimates
    Dolphins
        Respond to new combinations of words, if meaningful
    Parrots
        Speak, name, count, form concepts
Implications
    How to teach brain-damaged or autistic people
    Difficulty of defining language

2.   How did humans evolve language?
Language as a product of overall intelligence
    First problem: Unclear relationship between brain and intelligence
        Brain-to-body ratio
            Humans' not highest
            The chihuahua problem
    Second problem: People with full-sized brains and impaired language
    Third problem: Williams syndrome
        Mental retardation, skillful use of language
        Genes deleted from chromosome 7
        Abnormal development of posterior cerebral cortex, some subcortical areas
        Severe impairment in skills of living
        Normal abilities:
            Interpretation of facial expressions
            Social behavior
            Music
        Language: Variable, from near normal to spectacular
            Slow development
            Sometimes odd grammar
        Language not product of overall intelligence
Language as a special module
    Language acquisition device
    Ease of language development in most children
    Poverty of the stimulus argument:
        Children hear few examples of some grammatical structures they acquire
            Therefore, rules inborn
        But: Thousands of languages; can't be born knowing all
    *FOXP2* gene on chromosome 7: Mutation → impaired articulation, grammar
    Intelligence as a byproduct of language
Is there a critical period for language learning?
    Adults: Better at memorizing vocabulary
    Children: Better at pronunciation and unfamiliar grammar
    No age cutoff
    Second language: If mastered, same language areas as first language
    Some language: The earlier the better

3.   Brain damage and language
Broca's aphasia (nonfluent aphasia)
    Broca's area: Small part of left frontal cortex, near motor cortex
        Serious deficits only with more extensive damage
    Deficits in production and comprehension if meaning is difficult

Difficulty in language production
Articulation, writing, and gestures
Affects production of sign language
Omission of closed-class grammatical forms (prepositions, conjunctions, etc.)
Ability to speak open-class forms (nouns and verbs)
Problems comprehending grammatical words and devices
Still use normal word order for their language
Rely on inferences
Wernicke's aphasia (fluent aphasia)
Wernicke's area: Near auditory cortex
Articulate speech
Anomia: Difficulty finding the right word
Poor language comprehension, especially nouns and verbs
Structure and function: Difficult inferences
Other functions of "language areas"
Temporal lobe → declarative memories
Names, irregular verbs
Frontal lobe → procedural memories
Regular verbs
English → more work and brain activation than Italian

4. Dyslexia
Specific impairment of reading
Adequate vision and other academic skills
More common in boys than girls
More common in English readers than in more phonetic language readers
No single abnormality
Mild microscopic abnormalities
Bilaterally symmetrical cortex, especially planum temporale
Weak connections among areas in left hemisphere
Dysphonetic vs. dyseidetic dyslexics
Relatively unresponsive magnocellular system
Impaired perception of overall patterns and motion
Subtle hearing impairment
Difficulty distinguishing temporal order
Spoonerisms
Tapping rhythms
Converting vision to sound, vice versa
Differences in attention or strategy
Attend to letters far right of fixation point
Attend to several tasks at once
Treatment: Read one word at a time

5. In closing: Language and the brain
Language neither a simple by-product of intelligence nor independent of other functions

# SHORT-ANSWER QUESTIONS

**Module 14.1  Lateralization of Function**

1. *Connections*
   a. Name three connections between the two hemispheres.

2. *Visual connections to the hemispheres*
   a. To which hemisphere(s) does the right visual field project?  To which hemisphere(s) does the right half of both retinas project?  To which hemisphere(s) does the right eye project?

   b. To which hemisphere(s) does the right ear project? What ability requires this distribution of input?

3. *Cutting the corpus callosum*
   a. What is the corpus callosum?  Why is it sometimes severed in cases of severe epilepsy?  What are the effects of such an operation on overall intelligence, motivation, and gross motor coordination?

   b. What have we learned from split-brain humans concerning specialization of the two hemispheres?  Which tasks are best accomplished by the left hemisphere?

c. What is the basis for learned cooperation between the hemispheres in split-brain people?

d. What did the split-brain person draw with his right hand, when two different words were flashed to his right and left visual fields? What did he sometimes draw with his left hand? Could he combine information from his right and left visual fields to form a new concept?

e. Which functions are best performed by the right hemisphere?

f. Which emotions are associated with activity in the left hemisphere? The right hemisphere?

g. What is one simple task that can show hemispheric specialization in intact people? How large are the hemispheric differences in intact people?

h. Name four ways of testing hemispheric dominance for speech.

4. *Development of lateralization and handedness*
   a. What is the planum temporale and what is its significance for language?

   b. How early is the size difference in the left vs. right planum temporale apparent?

   c. What happens to the language ability of children who suffer damage to their left hemisphere in infancy?

   d. Compare the ability of 3-year-olds and of 5-year-olds to discriminate fabrics with either one hand or different hands. What can we infer from this about the development of the corpus callosum?

   e. In what ways are people who never had a corpus callosum different from split-brain people?

f.   Which other major axonal connections between the two hemispheres may compensate for the lack of a corpus callosum in people born without one?

g.   What percentage of right-handed people have left-hemisphere dominance for language? Describe the control of language in left-handed people.

h.   Is the corpus callosum thicker in right- or left-handed people?  What is the functional correlate of this increased thickness?

i.   How valid is the assumption that a given individual relies consistently on one hemisphere or the other?

j.   Describe Rasmussen's encephalopathy. Why does removal of the damaged hemisphere often result in slow, but surprisingly full recovery of language?

**Module 14.2  Evolution and Physiology of Language**

1.  *Nonhuman precursors of language*
    a.  What are some differences between the abilities of common chimpanzees and of humans to use symbols?

    b.  What was unusual about the ability of some bonobos to learn language?

    c.  In what ways do bonobos resemble humans more than common chimpanzees in language abilities?

    d.  What evidence is there that nonprimate species can learn language?

2.  *How did humans evolve language?*
    a.  Briefly discuss the proposal that our language may have developed as a by-product of overall intelligence.

b. How well do the correlations between intelligence and brain size or between intelligence and brain-to-body ratio hold up? How is this a problem for the view that language evolved as a product of large brains and intelligence?

c. Describe the pattern of abilities and disabilities in the family with a genetic mutation that produces language deficits. How is this a problem for the view that language evolved as a product of large brains and intelligence?

d. Describe Williams syndrome. How does this relate to the evolution of language as a product of general intelligence?

e. What is the main argument for the hypothesis that language evolved as an extra brain module? What is a problem with that hypothesis?

f. What is an alternative hypothesis regarding the evolution of language and intelligence?

g. Is there a critical period for language learning?  What are some ways of testing this idea?

3. *Effects of brain damage on language*
    a. Where is Broca's area located?

    b. Describe the effects of damage to Broca's area.  What are closed-class words?

    c. Locate Wernicke's area.

    d. Contrast the effects of damage to Wernicke's area with those of damage to Broca's area.

    e. What broader functions of the temporal and frontal lobes may partially explain the specializations of Wernicke's and Broca's areas?

4. *Dyslexia*
   a. What is dyslexia? How consistent are its symptoms?

   b. What are five possible biological causes of dyslexia?

   c. What is one method of improving the ability of dyslexics to read?

## TRUE/FALSE QUESTIONS

_____ 1. The right visual field projects to the left half of both retinas, and from there to the left hemisphere.

_____ 2. Similarly, the right *auditory* field projects to the left hemisphere, in order to be able to coordinate auditory and visual input to produce a coherent world view.

_____ 3. The primary causes of epilepsy are decreased release of glutamate and mutation of a gene for a glutamate receptor.

_____ 4. Split-brain people can perform familiar tasks with no problem and can use their hands independently to perform competing tasks, which is difficult for intact-brain people.

_____ 5. Speech is localized in the left hemisphere of 95% of right-handers and in the right hemisphere in 95% of left-handers.

_____ 6. There is a stronger magnocellular projection to the right hemisphere, which provides the basis for perception of complex visuo-spatial relations, and a stronger parvocellular input to the left hemisphere, which assists in processing of details.

_____ 7. The left-to-right ratio of size of the planum temporale is positively correlated with language ability.

_____ 8. Bonobo chimpanzees develop the language ability characteristic of human teenagers.

356

_____ 9. The "chihuahua problem" refers to the fact that these dogs eat all of their owners' tacos.

_____ 10. People with Williams syndrome are mentally retarded except in language, social, and musical abilities and ability to interpret facial expressions.

_____ 11. Broca's aphasia results from fairly extensive damage to Broca's area in the frontal lobe and cortical areas surrounding it, as well as some subcortical structures.

_____ 12. Wernicke's aphasia results in difficulty speaking and omission of closed-class words.

_____ 13. Dyslexia may have a variety of types and causes, including mild microscopic abnormalities, bilaterally symmetrical cortex, weak connections among areas in the left hemisphere, under-responsive magnocellular system, and subtle hearing impairment.

_____ 14. Dyslexics can sometimes be helped by trying to view a whole sentence at a time, rather than focusing on one word at a time.


## FILL IN THE BLANKS

1. The major connections between the hemispheres are the _____ _____,

   the _____ _____, and the _____

   _____.

2. The left visual field projects to the _____ half of both retinas, which then project to the

   _____ hemisphere.

3. Cutting the corpus callosum is an effective treatment for _____ when drugs or

   simpler surgery are ineffective.

4. The _____ test is used to test hemispheric dominance for speech; sodium amytal is injected into

   the carotid artery on one side of the head.

5. The _____ hemisphere is more important for expressing and understanding emotional

   content of speech and facial expression, humor, and sarcasm.

6. There is a stronger _____-cellular projection to the right hemisphere and a stronger

   _____-cellular projection to the left hemisphere.

7. The _____ _____ is an area in the temporal lobe that is larger on the left than the right side in most people.

8. _____ _____ produces gradual degeneration of glia and neurons in one hemisphere; as a result of increasing seizures the damaged hemisphere may be removed. If it is the left hemisphere that is removed in childhood, a surprising amount of language may be regained, because the gradual degeneration allowed the _____ hemisphere to be partially reorganized for language.

9. _____ chimpanzees can acquire ability to use visual symbols to name and describe (even when not requesting), to refer to the past, to request things they do not see, and to make creative requests.

10. Deletion of genes from chromosome ___ results in abnormal development of the _____ cerebral cortex and some subcortical areas of people with Williams syndrome.

11. _____ aphasia, also known as nonfluent aphasia, is characterized by difficulty in language _____ and in omission of _____-_____ grammatical forms.

12. _____ aphasia, also known as fluent aphasia, is characterized by articulate speech, combined with _____ (difficulty finding the right word) and poor comprehension of nouns and verbs.

13. Other proposed functions of "language areas" include a linkage of the temporal lobe with _____ memories, especially for names and _____ verbs, and of the frontal lobe with _____ memories, including the rules for _____ verbs.

14. _____ is a specific impairment of reading, together with adequate vision and other academic skills.

# MATCHING ITEMS

_____ 1. Split-brain people or animals     a. One word to left ear, another to right ear

_____ 2. Left hemisphere     b. Area larger in left than right temporal lobe

_____ 3. Right hemisphere     c. Major connection between hemispheres

_____ 4. Dichotic listening task     d. Specialized for spatial, emotional abilities

_____ 5. Corpus callosum     e. Independent control of two sides of body

_____ 6. Anterior commissure     f. Specialized for language, details

_____ 7. Planum temporale     g. Chimpanzees with good language skills

_____ 8. Productivity     h. Nonfluent aphasia, difficult closed-class words

_____ 9. Bonobos     i. Minor connection between hemispheres

_____ 10. Williams syndrome     j. Fluent aphasia, anomia

_____ 11. Broca's aphasia     k. Reading impairment, other skills OK

_____ 12. Wernicke's aphasia     l. Produce new signals for new ideas

_____ 13. Wada test     m. Normal language, retarded in other skills

_____ 14. Dyslexia     n. Test for hemispheric specialization

# MULTIPLE-CHOICE QUESTIONS

1. Severing the corpus callosum
    a. usually destroys language abilities.
    b. usually relieves the symptoms of epilepsy.
    c. has provided evidence that linguistic abilities reside largely in the right hemisphere.
    d. none of the above.

2. A person with a bisected brain
    a. can draw pictures and arrange puzzle pieces better with the left hand than the right.
    b. develops cooperation between the hemispheres because the corpus callosum grows back.
    c. performs very poorly on intelligence tests.
    d. all of the above.

3. The only way to restrict visual input to only the right hemisphere of a split-brain person is to
    a. flash it briefly to the left eye while the right eye is closed.
    b. flash it briefly to the right eye while the left eye is closed.
    c. flash it briefly in the left visual field while the person is looking straight ahead.
    d. flash it briefly in the right visual field while the person is looking straight ahead.

4. A split-brain person who sees a picture of an object in his left visual field usually
   a.  will be able both to point to the correct object with his left hand and to name it.
   b.  will not be able to pick out the object or to name it.
   c.  will be able to pick it out with his left hand, but will not be able to name it.
   d.  will be able to name it but not pick it out.

5. A split-brain person sees this picture flashed briefly on a screen while looking at a point in the middle of the screen.  He reports seeing
   a.  a woman.
   b.  a bearded man.
   c.  a meaningless hodge podge of lines, since the spatial perception center has been damaged.
   d.  one badly constructed face of two different people.

6. People with right-hemisphere damage
   a.  have trouble producing and understanding emotional facial expressions.
   b.  have trouble speaking with emotional expression and understanding others' vocal emotional expression.
   c.  have trouble with some complex visual and spatial tasks.
   d.  all of the above.

7. People with left-hemisphere damage
   a.  are generally very happy, because the intact right hemisphere is specialized for happiness.
   b.  perform better than chance in detecting lying.
   c.  easily begin to use the right hemisphere for language function.
   d.  all of the above.

8. Hemispheric specialization in intact people
   a.  has not been demonstrated.
   b.  can be shown but is small and inconsistent.
   c.  is consistent with that observed in split-brain people but is even more dramatic.
   d.  is the reverse of specialization in split-brain people.

9. Which of the following is true of the planum temporale?
   a.  Children with the biggest ratio of left to right planum temporale performed best on language tests.
   b.  It is larger in the right than in the left hemisphere for almost everyone.
   c.  It is equal in size in the two hemispheres at birth, indicating that maturation of language causes the size difference in adults.
   d.  All of the above are true.

10. What did Galin et al. discover when they asked 3-year-old and 5-year-old children to discriminate two fabrics?
    a.  The 3-year-olds were better than the 5-year-olds.
    b.  All children made fewer errors with their right hands than with their left.
    c.  All children made 90 percent more errors using different hands than when using the same hand.
    d.  Three-year-olds made 90 percent more errors using different hands than using the same hand, but 5-year-olds did equally well with one hand or two.

11. People who never had a corpus callosum
    a. are just like split-brain patients.
    b. can read words in either visual field and name objects that they touch with either hand.
    c. are especially fast at tasks requiring coordination of both hands.
    d. all of the above.

12. Which of the following is true of handedness and language dominance?
    a. Humans are the only species that show an arm preference.
    b. Right-handers have a thicker corpus callosum.
    c. Most left-handed people have language dominance in the right hemisphere.
    d. Most left-handed people have language dominance in the left hemisphere, but are more variable than right-handers.

13. Productivity
    a. refers to the ability to produce new language signals to represent new ideas.
    b. is a characteristic of communication systems of most mammals.
    c. refers to the ability to translate one signal into another.
    d. is only a means of increasing ones income, and has nothing to do with language.

14. Ordinary chimpanzees
    a. frequently use symbols in new, original combinations.
    b. frequently use symbols to describe scenes and events.
    c. have a social order much like that of humans.
    d. use symbols almost always to request, only rarely to describe.

15. Bonobos
    a. are unable to put symbols together in new ways to express new meanings.
    b. use symbols only to request objects.
    c. can understand spoken English sentences.
    d. have learned to speak English fluently.

16. Which of the following is a problem with the theory that human language evolved as a product of overall intelligence and larger brains?
    a. There is not a clear relationship between either brain size or brain-to-body ratio and intelligence.
    b. Some people have full-sized brains and normal overall intelligence, but have impaired language.
    c. Some people are severely retarded and have abnormal brain development, but have near normal language ability.
    d. All of the above are true.

17. People with Williams syndrome
    a. have severe difficulties with even simple grammatical rules.
    b. have good language abilities, but are retarded in nonlinguistic function.
    c. can draw beautifully, but cannot write.
    d. have almost total loss of Wernicke's area.

18. A patient has great difficulty in articulating words and a tendency to omit endings and abstract words, but less difficulty comprehending spoken and written words. The patient probably has damage in
    a. Broca's area.
    b. Wernicke's area.
    c. the corpus callosum.
    d. primary motor cortex controlling muscles of articulation.

19. A second patient has difficulty naming objects and understanding both spoken and written language; speech is fluent but not very meaningful. You suspect that the patient has damage in
    a. Broca's area.
    b. Wernicke's area.
    c. the anterior commissure and hippocampal commisure.
    d. left visual cortex and posterior corpus callosum.

20. Dyslexic people
    a. all have very similar symptoms, and all of the symptoms are limited to difficulties in visual perception.
    b. are sometimes helped by focusing on whole paragraphs at a time, rather than reading one word at a time.
    c. are more likely than normal readers to have a bilaterally symmetrical cerebral cortex, larger language-related areas in the right hemisphere than in the left, or relatively unresponsive magnocellular visual pathways.
    d. all of the above.

## Answers to True/False Questions

| | | | |
|---|---|---|---|
| 1. T | 5. F | 9. F | 13. T |
| 2. F | 6. T | 10. T | 14. F |
| 3. F | 7. T | 11. T | |
| 4. T | 8. F | 12. F | |

## Answers to Fill-in-the-Blank Questions

1. corpus callosum, anterior commissure, hippocampal commissure
2. right, right
3. epilepsy
4. Wada
5. right
6. magno, parvo
7. planum temporale
8. Rasmussen's encephalopathy, right
9. Bonobo
10. 7, posterior
11. Broca's, production, closed-class
12. Wernicke's, anomia
13. declarative, irregular, procedural, regular
14. Dyslexia

## Answers to Matching Items

| | | | |
|---|---|---|---|
| 1. e | 5. c | 9. g | 13. n |
| 2. f | 6. i | 10. m | 14. k |
| 3. d | 7. b | 11. h | |
| 4. a | 8. l | 12. j | |

## Answers to Multiple-Choice Questions

| | | | |
|---|---|---|---|
| 1. b | 6. d | 11. b | 16. d |
| 2. a | 7. b | 12. d | 17. b |
| 3. c | 8. b | 13. a | 18. a |
| 4. c | 9. a | 14. d | 19. b |
| 5. a | 10. d | 15. c | 20. c |

**Please check the Exploring Biological Psychology CD-ROM.**

## Diagram

Label the following areas related to language processing: Broca's area, Wernicke's area, Sylvian or lateral fissure, visual cortex.

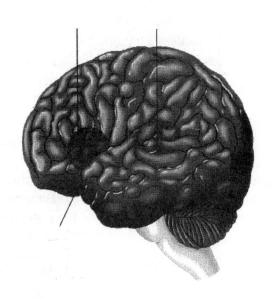

# Words and Brains

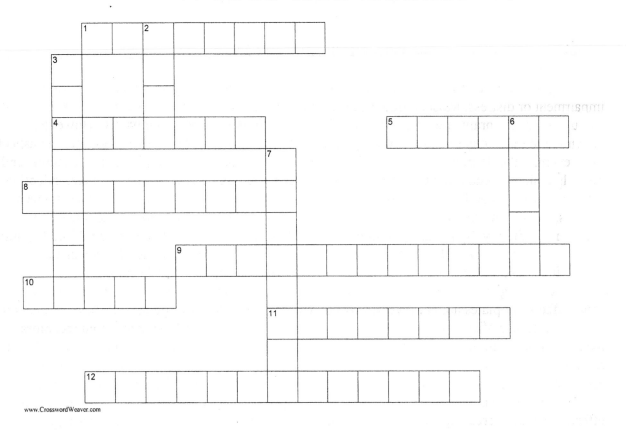

www.CrosswordWeaver.com

**ACROSS**

1 Syndrome with mental retardation but skillful language
4 Ability that right hemisphere specializes in
5 Chimpanzee with surprisingly good language ability
8 Planum ____: cortical area larger in left hemisphere than right
9 Type of visual system neuron projecting mostly to right hemisphere and promoting perception of visual motion
10 Feeling promoted by left hemisphere
11 Corpus _____, the major brain commisure
12 Type of visual system that projects mostly to left hemisphere and promotes language and perception of details

**DOWN**

speech

2 Hemisphere specialized for speech
3 Reading disorder in otherwise normal people
6 Man who discovered brain area that supports fluent speech and use of connectives
7 Man who discovered brain area that supports naming and understanding

364

# 15

# PSYCHOLOGICAL DISORDERS

## INTRODUCTION

Substance abuse is a maladaptive pattern of substance use leading to clinically significant impairment or distress. Most abused drugs and most reinforcing activities, including electrical self-stimulation of the brain, are linked to dopamine release in the nucleus accumbens. However, dopamine in the nucleus accumbens may be more related to activational or attention-getting aspects of an event, rather than its rewarding effects. Stimulant drugs, such as amphetamine, cocaine, and methylphenidate (Ritalin), either increase the release of dopamine or block its reuptake. Nicotine acts on nicotinic acetylcholine receptors to increase dopamine release in the nucleus accumbens. Opiates, such as morphine and "endogenous morphines" (endorphins), increase the release of dopamine indirectly, by inhibiting inhibitory GABA neurons that would otherwise inhibit dopamine release. Low doses of MDMA ("ecstasy") increase dopamine release; higher doses increase serotonin release as well, but also destroy axons that release dopamine and serotonin.

Several drugs do not depend on dopamine synapses for their reinforcing effects. For example, some effects of opiates are not reversed by dopamine antagonists. Marijuana and other cannabinoids mimic the effects of anandamide or 2-AG, neurotransmitters that bind to cannabinoid receptors located primarily in the hippocampus, basal ganglia, and cerebellum. Stimulation of cannabinoid receptors also inhibits activity at serotonin 5-HT$_3$ synapses that produce nausea. Hallucinogenic drugs, such as LSD and mescaline, bind to serotonin receptors, especially the 5-HT$_{2A}$ subtype.

Alcohol is the most commonly abused drug. Alcohol inhibits brain activity through general effects, such as decreasing sodium influx and expanding neuronal membranes, and also by decreasing serotonin activity, facilitating responses at GABA$_A$ receptors, blocking glutamate receptors, and increasing dopamine activity. There are two major types of alcoholism. Type I alcoholism is less dependent on genetics, develops gradually, and is equally common in women and men. Type II alcoholism has a stronger genetic basis, a rapid, early onset, and a great preponderance of men. Type II alcoholics have low serotonin turnover and a history of impulsivity and violence. There is a genetic contribution to alcoholism. Monozygotic twins have a higher concordance rate than do dizygotic twins. Biological children of alcoholics have a higher risk of alcoholism, especially the sons of alcoholic fathers. Several genes are weakly correlated with alcoholism. Antabuse (disulfiram) is used to treat alcoholism; it inactivates acetaldehyde dehydrogenase, the enzyme that converts acetaldehyde (the toxic metabolic product of alcohol) to acetic acid (a source of energy). A person who drinks after taking Antabuse will become sick. However, many persons who use Antabuse never drink, and therefore never become ill; they use Antabuse as a daily reminder not to drink alcohol. Some factors that may mediate the genetic predisposition to alcoholism include less intoxication from small to moderate amounts of alcohol and greater than average relief from tension after drinking alcohol. In addition, alcoholics tend to have a smaller than normal amygdala in the right hemisphere. Gambling and other habitual behaviors have much in common with alcoholism and other forms of substance abuse. Therefore, the addiction is not specific to the drug, but to the user.

Depression is typified by episodic sadness and helplessness, lack of energy, feelings of worthlessness, suicidal ideas, sleep disorders, and lack of pleasure. While the cause of depression is not fully understood, a number of possible factors have been identified. There may be a genetic component to depression, especially for severe, long-lasting depression beginning before age 30. However, no single gene has been found to have a strong link to depression. Women are at greater risk for depression than are men, although hormone levels are not strongly correlated with depression. Traumatic experiences may trigger depression in people who had already suffered some depression; however, they do not cause long-lasting depression in those who were not predisposed. Abnormal hemispheric dominance is sometimes associated with mood disorders. Happiness in normal people is associated with activation of the left prefrontal cortex, whereas depressed people have lower metabolic activity in the left, and increased activity in the right prefrontal cortex. Depression may occasionally be caused by exposure to a virus at some point in life. The Borna virus predisposes people to various psychiatric difficulties, perhaps including depression.

Most drugs that improve affective disorders act in one of three ways: blocking reuptake of monoamines (tricyclics), inhibiting monoamine oxidase (monoamine oxidase inhibitors, or MAOIs), or blocking reuptake of only serotonin (selective serotonin reuptake inhibitors, or SSRIs). Fluoxetine and other SSRIs have fewer side effects than do the tricyclics. Several atypical antidepressants have other mechanisms of action. Bupropion inhibits reuptake of dopamine and, to some extent, norepinephrine. Venlafaxine inhibits reuptake of serotonin and, to a lesser extent, norepinephrine and dopamine. Nefazodone blocks serotonin type 2A receptors and weakly inhibits serotonin and norepinephrine reuptake. St. John's wort is an herb and is not regulated by the Food and Drug Administration. Its effects are variable but similar to those of SSRIs; however, it may also contribute to more rapid breakdown of beneficial drugs. A major problem with the transmitter hypothesis is that drugs affect transmitter levels almost immediately but exert noticeable effects on mood only after two or three weeks. A possible explanation is that brain-derived neurotrophic factor is released with dopamine. To the extent that antidepressants increase dopamine release, they would also increase release of this peptide. There is evidence that the effectiveness of antidepressants is mediated by brain-derived neurotrophic factor, which increases the size of parts of the hippocampus and cerebral cortex that shrink during depression. In addition to treatment by drug therapy, mood disorders are sometimes treated with electroconvulsive therapy (ECT), sleep alterations, or bright lights. ECT is particularly useful for patients who are unresponsive to antidepressants or who are suicidal and need rapid relief. Memory loss that is sometimes associated with ECT is minimized by administering the ECT only to the right hemisphere. ECT increases the numbers of $D_1$ and $D_2$ receptors in the nucleus accumbens and decreases the number of norepinephrine receptors. Sleep-deprivation therapy is based on observations that depressed persons enter REM sleep much sooner than normal persons, as though their body temperature rhythms were phase-advanced. A regimen of earlier bedtimes following one sleepless night decreases the amount of REM sleep, as do antidepressant drugs.

Depression can occur as either a unipolar or a bipolar disorder. A unipolar disorder is one in which an individual varies between normal mood and depression. Bipolar disorder, or manic-depressive disorder, is characterized by cycles of depression and mania. During their manic phase, people are restless, uninhibited, excitable, impulsive, self-confident, and apparently happy. In bipolar I disorder there is a full-blown manic phase; in bipolar II disorder the manic phase is milder and is referred to as hypomania. Manic-depressive cycles may last a year or only a few days. Bipolar disorder has been linked to genes on several chromosomes; however, the specific genetic influences are not understood. Lithium is effective in treating bipolar I disorder, and if taken regularly, prevents relapse into either mania or depression. Valproic acid and carbamazepine are effective treatments for bipolar II disorder; they increase activity at GABA synapses, whereas lithium does not. All three drugs block the synthesis of inositol; however, there is no documented abnormality in inositol in bipolar patients. Both lithium and valproic acid block synthesis of arachidonic acid, which is produced during brain inflammation. One additional treatment for bipolar disorder is to stay in bed for 10 hours per night in a darkened, quiet room.

Seasonal affective disorder (SAD) occurs mostly in areas where nights are long in the winter. SAD patients may have phase-delayed sleep and temperature cycles, unlike other depressed people. Exposure to bright lights is usually an effective treatment for SAD. This treatment may affect serotonin synapses and circadian rhythms.

Schizophrenia is an illness in which emotions are "split off" from the intellect. Its positive symptoms include a psychotic cluster (hallucinations and delusions) and a disorganized cluster (inappropriate emotions, bizarre behaviors, and thought disorder). Negative symptoms include deficits in social interaction, emotional expression, speech, and working memory. The main problem may be disordered thoughts, which result from abnormal connections between the cortex, thalamus, and cerebellum. Approximately 1 percent of the US population suffer schizophrenia at any given time. Schizophrenia is less common in the Third World, where fewer people live in crowded cities and where their extended families care patiently for schizophrenic relatives. The incidence of schizophrenia appears to be decreasing worldwide, for unknown reasons.

Much evidence favors a genetic predisposition to schizophrenia. It is more common in monozygotic than in dizygotic twins of schizophrenics and is more common in biological relatives than in adopted relatives of schizophrenics. Also, adopted children have a higher concordance with their biological than their adoptive parents. Genetics cannot completely explain the occurrence of schizophrenia, however, since the concordance rate for monozygotic twins is not 100 percent. Also, there may be greater similarity in the prenatal environment in monozygotic than dizygotic twins, since they usually develop in a single placenta, and in dizygotic twins, compared to non-twin siblings. One confounding factor in many genetics studies is that biological parents of schizophrenics are more likely to engage in unhealthy habits, including smoking and drinking, that could impair prenatal development. Some studies have found genes with possible links to schizophrenia, but no strong link. Perhaps several genes on different chromosomes may predispose people to schizophrenia and may interact with environmental factors.

The neurodevelopmental hypothesis suggests that schizophrenia results from abnormal early development of the brain. Difficulties surrounding birth or during early or middle pregnancy have been linked to increased incidence of schizophrenia. These include complications during delivery, low birth weight, starvation during pregnancy, Rh incompatibility, and fevers due to viral infections during middle pregnancy. A number of minor brain abnormalities have been found in the brains of schizophrenics. Prefrontal and temporal cortex, hippocampus, and amygdala are smaller than usual; the ventricles are larger; the left hemisphere is smaller and less active. The area of most consistent abnormalities is the dorsolateral prefrontal cortex, one of the latest brain areas to mature. Schizophrenics have fewer synapses there and less activation during working memory tasks. In addition, neurons are smaller and less ordered. Because there is no evidence of neuronal loss in adulthood, it is thought that the brain abnormalities result from early developmental factors. Since the most affected brain areas are those that mature slowly, the behavioral problems may not emerge until long after the damage occurred. However, neurons may continue to shrink, rather than die, in adulthood.

Antipsychotic drugs, including phenothiazines (chlorpromazine: Thorazine) and butyrophenones (haloperidol: Haldol), block dopamine receptors. Furthermore, some symptoms of schizophrenia can be temporarily experienced by people who take large doses of drugs that stimulate dopamine synapses. On the basis of such observations it has been hypothesized that schizophrenia occurs because of excess activity at dopamine synapses. There are a number of problems with this hypothesis. First, neuroleptic drugs block dopamine receptors almost immediately, but take two or three weeks to produce therapeutic benefits. In addition, there is no consistent evidence of abnormally high levels of dopamine or its metabolites in schizophrenics, although there may be altered ratios of specific types of dopamine receptors. A second hypothesis is that there may be a deficit in glutamate activity, especially in the prefrontal cortex. Schizophrenics release less glutamate in prefrontal cortex and hippocampus than do other people, and glutamate has effects that are frequently opposite to those of dopamine. Therefore, any problem observed could be due either to insufficient glutamate or excess dopamine. Phencyclidine (PCP) inhibits NMDA glutamate receptors, produces both positive and negative symptoms similar to schizophrenia, and impairs prefrontal cortex function. It also produces little psychotic response in preadolescents and produces a long-lasting relapse in recovered schizophrenics. A drug that stimulates one type of metabotropic glutamate receptor blocks the behavioral effects of PCP in rats. Finally, the amino acid glycine stimulates a co-transmitter site on the NMDA receptor and increases the effectiveness of other antipsychotic drugs, especially on negative symptoms. Cycloserine has similar effects and crosses the blood-brain barrier more easily than does glycine.

The decision to administer neuroleptic drugs has been complicated by their potentially severe side effects. The most troublesome effect is tardive dyskinesia, which consists of tremors and other involuntary movements. This condition develops gradually and may result from receptor supersensitivity, although the exact mechanism is not understood. Recent advances in research have led to the use of new atypical antipsychotic drugs (such as clozapine), which appear to control schizophrenia without causing tardive dyskinesia. These drugs block $D_4$ dopamine receptors, with little effect on $D_2$ receptors. Clozapine also blocks serotonin $5-HT_{2A}$ receptors and relieves negative, as well as positive, symptoms. Clozapine's major side effects are increased risk of diabetes and an impaired immune system.

## LEARNING OBJECTIVES

### Module 15.1 Substance Abuse
1. Understand the relation of dopamine in the nucleus accumbens to motivation or surprise and why dopamine does not seem to be related directly to pleasure.
2. Know the effects of stimulant drugs, nicotine, opiates, marijuana, and LSD on transmitters.
3. Know the physiological effects of alcohol and the effects of Antabuse on alcohol metabolism.
4. Be able to describe the evidence for a genetic contribution to alcoholism.

### Module 15.2 Mood Disorders
1. Know the symptoms of depression and the evidence for a genetic contribution to depression.
2. Understand the possible roles of hormones, abnormalities of hemispheric dominance, and viruses in the onset or worsening of depression.
3. Be able to describe the short-term and long-term mechanisms of action of antidepressant drugs.
4. Understand the mechanisms of action of psychotherapy, electroconvulsive therapy, and altered sleep patterns.
5. Be able to describe the symptoms of bipolar disorder and the possible contributions of genetics and an abnormally large amygdala.
6. Know the mechanisms of action of drugs used to treat bipolar disorder.
7. Be able to describe seasonal affective disorder and a possible cause and a treatment for it.

### Module 15.3 Schizophrenia
1. Be able to describe the negative and positive symptoms of schizophrenia.
2. Know the conditions resembling schizophrenia, with which it may be confused, and the demographic factors related to schizophrenia.
3. Be able to describe the evidence for a genetic contribution to schizophrenia.
4. Understand the evidence for the neurodevelopmental hypothesis.
5. Be able to describe the evidence for the dopamine hypothesis of schizophrenia.
6. Be able to describe the evidence for the glutamate hypothesis of schizophrenia.
7. Know the undesired effects of antipsychotic drugs and the newer drugs that minimize these effects.

# KEY TERMS AND CONCEPTS

## Module 15.1  Substance Abuse

1. Synapses, reinforcement and drug use
   Substance abuse: Maladaptive pattern of substance use leading to clinically significant
   impairment or distress
   Electrical self-stimulation of the brain
   James Olds and Peter Milner
   Self-stimulation of the brain
   Nucleus accumbens
   Role of dopamine: Pleasure vs. motivation or surprise
   Drug addicts: Work hard for drug, even if tolerance decreases "high"
   Less dopamine response to food if stimulus predicts its delivery
   Drugs and reinforcement
   Events that → dopamine release in nucleus accumbens
   Informative events, positive or negative
   But, classical conditioning → dopamine release
   Does not require attention
   Almost all addicting drugs
   Sexual excitement
   Video game playing
   Men viewing attractive women's faces during fMRI
   Attractive men's faces → *decreased* dopamine release
   Ibogaine → decreased reinforcement value of drugs in nucleus accumbens
   Also decreased reinforcement value of everything else
   Craving not simply withdrawal effect

2. Common drugs and their synaptic effects
   Stimulant drugs
   Produce excitement, alertness, elevated mood, decreased fatigue, increased motor activity
   Amphetamine → release of dopamine via reversal of transporter
   Also blocks synapses that inhibit dopamine release
   Cocaine → blocks reuptake of dopamine, norepinephrine, and serotonin
   Prolongs effects
   Dopamine more important
   Rebound "crash"
   Dopamine washed away before more can be synthesized
   Excess dopamine stimulates inhibitory autoreceptors → negative feedback →
   decreased release
   Tolerance
   Dynorphin released with dopamine → counteracts reinforcing effects of cocaine
   Less dopamine released
   Each reinforcement → less effective
   Methylphenidate (Ritalin): Blocks reuptake of dopamine and increases serotonin release
   Gradual onset and offset
   Attention deficit disorder (ADD)
   Dopamine effect → improved attention
   Serotonin effect → calming of activity
   May decrease risk for later drug abuse
   Dopamine: Mostly inhibitory, may decrease "noise"

369

Cocaine use → long term disruption of brain function
    Increased risk of stroke, epilepsy, and memory impairments
MDMA ("ecstasy")
    Low dose → stimulates dopamine release
    High dose →
        Stimulation of serotonin release → hallucinations
        Destruction of dopamine, serotonin axons → later depression, Parkinson's disease
    May damage memory
Nicotine (nicotinic acetylcholine receptors)
    Increases dopamine release in nucleus accumbens
    Long term use → less responsive to reinforcing events
    Antidepressant drugs may help smokers quit
Opiates
    Morphine, heroin, methadone
        If used for pain relief, rarely addicting
    Endorphins (*endo*genous m*orphines*)
        Increase dopamine release indirectly, by inhibiting GABA release
        Also act independently of dopamine
        Block norepinephrine release from locus coeruleus → decrease stress response, impair
            memory
Marijuana (cannabinoids, related to $D^9$-tetrahydrocannabinol, $D^9$-THC)
    Relieve pain, nausea, glaucoma
    Intensify sensory experiences, make time seem to pass slowly
    Memory impairments
    Fat soluble → slow release → moderate withdrawal symptoms
    Cannabinoid receptors widespread in animal kingdom, except insects
    Cannabinoid receptors in hippocampus, basal ganglia and cerebellum
        Few in medulla → little chance of fatal overdose
    Anandamide: Endogenous cannabinoid
    2-AG (sn-2 arachidonylglycerol): also binds to cannabinoid receptors
    Receptors on presynaptic terminals → inhibit release of glutamate, GABA
        Neither stimulant nor depressant
        Decrease brain damage from stroke
        May → LTD (inhibit memory)
    Inhibits nausea by inhibiting $5-HT_3$ receptors
    "Slow passage of time" shown in rats
Hallucinogenic drugs (LSD, mescaline)
    Stimulate $5-HT_{2A}$ receptors

3.  Alcohol and alcoholism
    Alcoholism (alcohol dependence): Cannot quit or control the amount consumed
    Physiological effects
        Inhibits flow of sodium and expands membrane surface
        Decreases serotonin activity
        Facilitates $GABA_A$ receptor
        Blocks glutamate receptors
        Increases dopamine activity
    Genetics
        Type I (or Type A) alcoholism
            Less dependence on genetics

Develops gradually
Fewer genetic relatives are alcoholic
Men and women about equally affected
Generally less severe
Type II (or Type B) alcoholism
Stronger genetic basis
Rapid, early onset
Overwhelmingly men
More severe
More associated with criminality
Low serotonin turnover: Strong genetic basis
History of impulsive and violent behaviors
Alcohol increases impulsiveness
Monozygotic twins → greater concordance for alcoholism than dizygotic twins
Biological children of alcoholics → greater risk of alcoholism
But mothers drank during pregnancy
Several genes weakly correlated with alcoholism
Alcohol metabolism and Antabuse
Ethyl alcohol → acetaldehyde → acetic acid
Acetaldehyde dehydrogenase
Abnormal gene → metabolize acetaldehyde more slowly → illness after alcohol
Antabuse (disulfiram): Antagonizes acetaldehyde dehydrogenase → illness after alcohol
Moderately effective
Supplement to alcoholic's commitment to quit
Risk factors for alcohol abuse
Genetic predisposition
Sons of alcoholic fathers
Less than average intoxication after small to moderate amount of alcohol
More than average relief from tension after alcohol
Brain abnormalities: Smaller amygdala in right hemisphere
Person high in sensation-seeking → heavy drinking

4.  In closing: Drugs and behavior
Similarities among addictions
Not just the pharmacological properties of the substance
Addiction not in the drug, but in the user

## Module 15.2  Mood Disorders
1.  Major depressive disorder
May be caused by hormonal problems, head injuries, brain tumors, other illnesses
Co-morbid with substance abuse, anxiety, schizophrenia, Parkinson's disease
Symptoms
Sad and helpless for weeks
No energy, feel worthless, contemplate suicide
Trouble sleeping, concentrating
Little pleasure from sex or food
Cannot imagine being happy again
Incidence
Twice as common in women as men
Any time from adolescence to old age

5% of adults in United States each year: "Clinically significant" depression

Genetics

    Adopted children similar to biological parents

    Severe, long-lasting depression before age 30 → greater genetic factor

        Stronger effect if affected relatives were women

    No single gene

Life events

    Interaction between heredity and environment

        Traumatic experiences

Hormones

    Episodic, not constant

    Stress → cortisol release

        Helpful in short term, harmful if prolonged

    Postpartum depression

        Hormones aggravate depression in vulnerable women

            Decrease estradiol and progesterone → depression

    Increase estradiol → relieve depression in menopausal women

    Increased incidence in women not just due to increased reporting

    No strong correlation with hormones

Abnormalities of hemispheric dominance

    Happy mood: Increased activity in left prefrontal cortex

    Depression: Decreased activity in left and increased in right prefrontal cortex

    Right-hemisphere damage → manic

Viruses

    Borna disease

Antidepressant drugs

    Accidental discoveries of psychiatric drugs

        Disulfiram (Antabuse): Helps people avoid alcohol

            Originally used in manufacture of rubber

        Bromides: Treatment for epilepsy

            Originally thought to reduce sexual drive, masturbation

        Today: Evaluate new drugs in test tubes or tissue samples

    Tricyclics

        Decrease reuptake of catecholamines or serotonin → longer in synapse

        Imipramine (Tofranil)

        Also block histamine and acetylcholine receptors and some sodium channels → side
            effects

    MAOIs

        Block monoamine oxidase → monoamines broken down more slowly

        Phenelzine (Nardil)

    Selective serotonin reuptake inhibitors (SSRIs)

        Similar to tricyclics, but selective for serotonin

        Fluoxetine (Prozac), sertraline (Zoloft), fluvoxamine (Luvox), citalopram (Celexa) and
            paroxetine (Paxil or Seroxat)

        Fewer side effects

    Atypical antidepressants

        Bupropion (Wellbutrin)

            Inhibits reuptake of dopamine and, to some extent, norepinephrine

            Does not affect serotonin reuptake

Venlafaxine

    Inhibits reuptake mostly of serotonin

    Somewhat inhibits reuptake of norepinephrine, slightly that of dopamine

Nefazodone

    Specifically blocks serotonin type 2A receptors

    Weakly blocks reuptake of serotonin and norepinephrine

St. John's wort

    Herb, not regulated by FDA

    Effects similar to SSRIs, but variable

    Increases effect of enzyme that breaks down toxins and beneficial drugs

Delayed effects of antidepressants

    Decrease sensitivity of postsynaptic receptors

    Stimulate autoreceptors → decrease release

Exactly how do antidepressants work?

    Problem of time course

        Rapid effect on synapses

        Effects on behavior: Two to three weeks

            In contrast: methylphenidate (Ritalin) for attention deficit disorder

                Effects on synapses and behavior peak at 60 minutes

    Brain-derived neurotrophic factor

        Released with dopamine

        Increased with repeated use of antidepressants

        Parts of hippocampus and cerebral cortex

            Decrease in size during depression

            Restored with antidepressant drugs

Other therapies

    Psychotherapy/cognitive therapy

        Increases metabolism in brain areas similarly to antidepressants

        Effects last longer, but require more time to be effective

        2/3s of patients respond to drugs, psychotherapy, or both

    Electroconvulsive therapy (ECT)

        Used for patients who do not respond to drug therapy or who are suicidal

        Works faster than drugs

        Administered every other day for two weeks

        Used with muscle relaxants or anesthetics

        Side effect: memory loss; minimized with shock to right hemisphere only

            Right-hemisphere activity or left-hemisphere underactivity → unpleasant mood

        Half are depressed again within six months

        Increases $D_1$ and $D_2$ receptors in nucleus accumbens

        Decreases postsynaptic norepinephrine receptors

        Variety of other effects

        Repetitive transcranial magnetic stimulation

    Altered sleep patterns

        Depressed: REM within 45 minutes, not 80 minutes

            Have trouble staying asleep, drowsy during day

        Therapy

            Stay awake all night → fastest improvement

                Especially effective in those with low dopamine turnover, mild thyroid

                    abnormalities, hyperactive prefrontal cortex

            Effective only until next night's sleep

Combine with earlier bedtime → effective for at least a week

Sleep deprivation or rescheduling → decrease REM

So do antidepressants

2.  Bipolar disorder

Definitions

Unipolar disorder: One extreme – vary between normal and depression

Bipolar disorder: Manic-depressive disorder

Mania: Restlessness, excitement, laughter, self-confidence, rambling speech, loss of inhibitions

Full-blown mania: Bipolar I disorder

Hypomania: Bipolar II disorder

Cycle length: Days to a year

Glucose metabolism: Higher than normal in mania, lower than normal in depression

Larger than normal amygdala

Genetics

Greater similarity in monozygotic > dizygotic twins and in biological > adoptive relatives

Apparent linkage to genes on several chromosomes

Treatments

Lithium salts

May have toxic side effects

Effective for bipolar I disorder

Other drugs

Valproic acid (Depakene, Depakote), carbamazepine

Effective for bipolar II disorder

How do drugs relieve bipolar disorder?

Increase activity at GABA synapses

Valproic acid, carbamazepine do

Lithium does not

Block synthesis of inositol

Membrane formation, transport of fats, precursor to second messenger

All three drugs block synthesis

But no known abnormality of inositol in bipolar patients

Block synthesis of arachidonic acid

Produced during brain inflammation

Blocked by lithium, valproic acid

Counteracted by polyunsaturated fatty acids (abundant in seafood)

Stay in bed 10 hours per night

3.  Seasonal affective disorder (SAD)

Common where nights are long in winter

SAD: Phase-delayed sleep and temperature rhythms, unlike other depressed people, who are phase-advanced

Bright lights, especially in morning

May affect serotonin synapses

May affect circadian rhythms

4.  In closing: The biology of mood swings

Brain structure and chemistry → alter reactions to events

Experience alters brain

**Module 15.3 Schizophrenia**
1. Characteristics
   Deteriorating function in everyday life; some combination of hallucinations, delusions, thought
      disorder, movement disorder, and inappropriate emotional expressions
      Dementia praecox
      Not multiple personality
   Behavioral symptoms
      Negative symptoms: Behaviors that are absent, but should be present
         Deficits in social interaction, emotional expression, speech, and working memory
         More stable, less responsive to treatment
      Positive symptoms: Behaviors that are present, but should be absent
         Sporadic occurrence
         Psychotic cluster: Delusions and hallucinations
            Increased activity in thalamus, hippocampus, and cortex
         Disorganized cluster: Inappropriate emotions, bizarre behaviors and thought disorder
            Difficulty with abstract concepts
      Main problem: Disordered thinking
         Abnormal connections between cortex and thalamus and cerebellum
      Acute onset → greater probability of recovery than with chronic onset
   Differential diagnosis of schizophrenia
      Conditions resembling schizophrenia
         Mood disorder with psychotic features
         Substance abuse
         Brain damage
         Undetected hearing deficits
         Huntington's disease
            Catatonic schizophrenia → motor and psychological abnormalities
         Nutritional abnormalities
            Deficiency of niacin, vitamin C
            Allergy to milk proteins, wheat gluten, other proteins
   Demographic data
      Approximately 1% of US population: Schizophrenia at any given time
         Gradual decline in prevalence
      Reported 10-100 times more often in United States and Europe than in Third World
         More common in crowded cities
            More crowded cities in developed world
         Expressed emotion by care-givers → hostile expressions → aggravation of condition
            More traditional cultures: Large extended family; more patience
      Diagnosed at earlier age in men than women, though lifetime prevalence is similar
         Protective effect of estrogen?
      Childhood-onset: much less common
         Identifiable genetic abnormalities
         Gradually increasing and more severe brain damage
      Older father → increased risk of schizophrenia


2. Genetics
   Twin studies
      Greater concordance for monozygotic (50%) than dizygotic (15-20%) twins
         Heredity not the only factor
            Greater similarity of prenatal environment (monozygotic twins: single placenta)

Dizygotic twins: Same genetic resemblance as siblings, but higher concordance
Adopted children who develop schizophrenia
    Greater concordance with biological than adoptive parents
    Biological mother → genes + prenatal environment
        Poor nutrition; smoke, drink; poor medical care
Efforts to locate a gene: No strong links
    Possible problems
        Inaccurate diagnoses
        Complex combinations of genes
    Schizophrenia not a single-gene disorder

3.    The neurodevelopmental hypothesis
    Argument for:
        Several early brain abnormalities linked to later schizophrenia
        People with schizophrenia: numerous small brain abnormalities originating early in life
        Plausible that early brain abnormalities → adult behavioral abnormalities
    Prenatal and neonatal environment
        Poor nutrition, premature birth, low birth weight, delivery complications
        Rh-positive child of Rh-negative mother→ immunological rejection
            Later-born boys with Rh incompatibility → schizophrenia, hearing & mental problems
        Season of birth effect
            Winter births → higher risk
            Only in non-tropical climates
            Especially strong effect in people with schizophrenia but no schizophrenic relatives;
                those born in large cities
        Viral epidemics
            Influenza in fall → later schizophrenia in babies born in winter
            Fever in mother slows cell division, high fever kills cells
    Mild brain abnormalities
        Smaller prefrontal cortex, temporal cortex, hippocampus, amygdala
            Especially in left hemisphere
            Enlarged ventricles
            Especially in those with complications during pregnancy or birth
            Areas that mature most slowly most affected: Dorsolateral prefrontal cortex
            Fewer synapses in prefrontal cortex
        Memory and attention deficits
            Similar to those with temporal or prefrontal cortex damage
            Poor working memory
        Microscopic level
            Smaller cell bodies, especially in hippocampus and prefrontal cortex
            Disorderly cell arrangement
        Lateralization
            Larger right hemisphere
            Lower activity in left hemisphere
                More likely left-handed
        Brain abnormalities not due to antipsychotic drugs
            Alcohol abuse by schizophrenics → damage to cerebellum
        Brain damage may not be progressive
            Brain abnormalities similar in older and younger patients
            No glial cell proliferation or activation of genes for repair

Cells may shrink but not die
Early development and later psychopathology
    Prefrontal cortex: Slow maturing
    Neurodevelopmental hypothesis: Plausible, not firmly established

4.   Methods 15.1 The Wisconsin card-sorting task
    Measures functioning of prefrontal cortex
    Deck of cards sorted first by one rule, then by a different (conflicting) rule
    Schizophrenia or damage to prefrontal cortex → difficulty shifting to the new rule

5.   Neurotransmitters and drugs
    The dopamine hypothesis: Excess activity at certain dopamine synapses
        Antispychotic (neuroleptic) drugs: Block postsynaptic dopamine receptors
        One fourth of schizophrenics:  No benefit from drugs
            Phenothiazines
                Chlorpromazine (Thorazine)
            Butyrophenones
                Haloperidol (Haldol)
            Correlation between clinically effective dose and dose needed to block dopamine
                receptors
        Drugs that can provoke schizophrenic symptoms
            Substance-induced psychotic disorder
                Hallucinations and delusions: Positive symptoms
            Amphetamine, methamphetamine, cocaine → increase activity at dopamine synapses
                LSD → effects at serotonin synapses; increases activity at dopamine synapses
        Problems with the dopamine hypothesis
            Time course of drugs
                Affect synapses quickly
                Effects on behavior build up over 2 to 3 weeks
            Approximately normal levels of dopamine and its metabolites
            Dopamine receptors
                Low $D_1$ and $D_2$ receptor density
                High $D_3$ and $D_4$ receptor density
                Variability of results
        Additional support for the dopamine hypothesis
            Schizophrenia → twice as many $D_2$ receptors occupied as normal
            Greater $D_2$ activation in prefrontal cortex → greater cognitive impairment
    The glutamate hypothesis
        Deficient activity at certain glutamate synapses, especially in prefrontal cortex
        Relationships between dopamine and glutamate: Opposing effects
            Dopamine inhibits glutamate release
            Glutamate excites neurons that inhibit dopamine release
            Glutamate excites neurons that dopamine inhibits
        Measurements of glutamate
            Schizophrenia → less glutamate release in prefrontal cortex and hippocampus
                Also fewer glutamate receptors
        The effects of phencyclidine (PCP, "angel dust")
            Inhibits NMDA glutamate receptors
            Positive and negative symptoms similar to schizophrenia
            Impairs prefrontal cortex function, including dopamine synapses

PCP and ketamine → little psychotic effect in preadolescents
PCP → long-lasting relapse in people recovered from schizophrenia
LSD, amphetamine, and cocaine → only temporary symptoms
Drugs that enhance glutamate activity
Too much glutamate → toxic effects
LY 354740 → selective stimulation of one type of metabotropic glutamate receptor
Blocks behavioral effects of PCP in rats
Prevents PCP's disruption of prefrontal cortex activity
Glycine: Co-transmitter at NMDA glutamate receptors
Increases effectiveness of glutamate
Increases effectiveness of antipsychotic drugs, especially for negative symptoms
Cycloserine: → similar effects; crosses blood-brain barrier more easily
The search for improved drugs
Antipsychotic drugs → decrease mesolimbocortical activity → beneficial effects
Decrease activity of dopamine neurons that control movement → undesired effects
Tardive dyskinesia: Tremors and other involuntary movements
May result from denervation supersensitivity
May last for years after quitting drug
Atypical antipsychotics
Clozapine
Blocks $D_4$ receptors
Briefer or less intense blockade of $D_2$ receptors
Also blocks serotonin 5-$HT_2$ receptors
Increases glutamate release
Effective on negative, as well as positive, symptoms
Side effects: Increased risk of diabetes; impaired immune system

6.  In closing: The fascination of schizophrenia
Search for pattern among many clues and false leads


## SHORT-ANSWER QUESTIONS

**Module 15.1 Substance Abuse**
1.  *Synapses, reinforcement and drug use*
a.  How were the brain mechanisms of pleasure and reinforcement discovered?



b.  Which brain area is especially important for reinforcement and addiction? What is the effect of dopamine on neurons there?

c.  Is dopamine release always associated with pleasure?  What evidence suggests that other processes are more closely associated with dopamine release in the nucleus accumbens?

2.  *Common drugs and their synaptic effects*
a.  What is the effect of amphetamine on synapses?

b.  Compare the effects of cocaine with those of amphetamine.  What are the similarities and differences?

c.  Why do amphetamine and cocaine users frequently report a "crash" a couple of hours after taking the drugs?

d.  How does dynorphin affect cocaine use?

e.  Why is methylphenidate (Ritalin) usually not abused?

f.   What are the physiological effects of MDMA ("Ecstasy")?

g.   What is the basis of nicotine's reinforcing effects?  Is stimulation of all types of acetylcholine receptors reinforcing?

h.   What is an endorphin?  What is the derivation of its name?

i.   How do opiates increase the release of dopamine?

j. What is the main psychoactive chemical in marijuana?  Why do marijuana users not experience a sudden "crash" several hours after taking the drug, as do amphetamine and cocaine users?

k.   Which two endogenous brain chemicals bind to cannabinoid receptors?  How might marijuana decrease nausea?

l.   Where in the brain are cannabinoid receptors located?  Why do large doses of marijuana not threaten breathing or heartbeat?

m.   What are cannabinoids' effects on GABA and glutamate synapses?  How might this affect brain damage after a stroke?

n.   Which receptor does LSD stimulate?  Can we explain the effects of LSD on behavior?

3.   *Alcohol and alcoholism*
     a.   What are two effects of alcohol on membranes?  What type of receptor is made more responsive by alcohol?  Which other two types of synapses are affected?

     b.   List the differences between Type I and Type II alcoholism.

     c.   Turnover of what neurotransmitter has been linked to Type II alcoholism?  What other behavioral characteristic is associated with low turnover of that neurotransmitter?

d.  Describe the evidence for a genetic risk factor for alcoholism.  How strong is that evidence?

e.  Describe the metabolism of alcohol.

f.  What is the biochemical effect of Antabuse?  What is its physiological effect when combined with alcohol use?

g.  How may Antabuse work, in addition to its physiological effect?

h.  What are two characteristics of sons of alcoholics that may predispose them to alcoholism?

**Module 15.2  Mood Disorders**
1.  *Major depressive disorder*
    a.  List the symptoms of major depression.

b. What is the evidence for a genetic predisposition for depression?

c. Are men or women more vulnerable to depression? What may be the role of hormones in depression?

d. What seems to be the role of traumatic experiences in the onset of episodes of depression?

e. What patterns of hemispheric dominance have been associated with happy moods in normal people? What is the pattern in depressed people?

f. What is Borna disease? What evidence links it to depression?

g. Name three groups of antidepressant drugs and explain how each exerts its effects.

h.  Why is fluoxetine (Prozac) preferred over the tricyclics and the monoamine oxidase inhibitors?

i.  What are atypical antidepressants? For whom are they used?

j.  How effective is St. John's wort in relieving depression? Which class of antidepressants produces effects similar to those of St. John's wort? What is one potential problem with the use of St. John's wort?

k.  Explain the problem of the time course of drugs' effects on neurotransmitters and their effects on depressive symptoms. What are some of the delayed effects of antidepressants?

l.  What neurotrophin is produced as a result of repeated use of antidepressants? In which brain areas is it produced?

m.  How is electroconvulsive therapy (ECT) applied today? How is this an improvement over practices in the 1950s?

n. For which two groups of patients is ECT most often used?

o. What are the advantages and disadvantages of ECT?

p. What are the effects of ECT on neurotransmitter receptors? What newer treatment is similar to ECT?

q. How does the onset of REM sleep differ in depressed people, compared to nondepressed individuals? How may this be related to body temperature cycles?

r. What change in sleeping schedules has been found to alleviate depression? How long do the benefits last?

2. *Bipolar disorder*
   a. What is the difference between unipolar and bipolar disorder? What is another term for bipolar disorder?

b.  Describe the symptoms of mania. What is hypomania? What is the difference between bipolar I and bipolar II disorder?

c.  Describe the pattern of glucose metabolism in the two extreme conditions of bipolar I disorder. What additional brain abnormality has been reported?

d.  What can we say about genetic factors in bipolar disorder?

e.  What is the most effective therapy for bipolar disorder? What can we say about its mode of action?

f.  What other drugs are used to treat bipolar disorder? What are three possible mechanisms by which these drugs achieve their effects?

3. *Seasonal affective disorder (SAD)*
    a.  What is seasonal affective disorder?  How is it treated?




    b.  How are the sleep and temperature rhythms of SAD patients different from those of other depressed patients?




## Module 15.3  Schizophrenia
1. *Characteristics*
    a.  What is the origin of the term schizophrenia?




    b.  What are the negative symptoms of schizophrenia?  How stable are they?




    c.  What are the two clusters of positive symptoms of schizophrenia?  How stable are they?




    d.  What is the overall incidence of schizophrenia?  Does this incidence vary among ethnic groups and sexes?

e. How does the prevalence of schizophrenia today compare with that of the mid-1900s? Give two reasons why Third World countries might have a lower incidence of schizophrenia than do the developed countries.

2. *Genetics*
   a. What evidence from twin studies suggests a genetic basis for schizophrenia? What are concordance rates?

   b. What other factor may explain the greater concordance for monozygotic over dizygotic twins and for dizygotic twins over non-twin siblings?

   c. What evidence from adoption studies suggests a genetic basis for schizophrenia? What is another interpretation of that evidence?

   d. What can we conclude about the role of genetics in schizophrenia?

3. *The neurodevelopmental hypothesis*
    a. What three lines of evidence suggest that schizophrenia may result from abnormalities in the early development of the brain?

    b. What specific prenatal and neonatal conditions have been associated with increased risk for schizophrenia?

    c. In which season of birth is there a slightly greater likelihood of developing schizophrenia? What factor may account for this effect?

    d. What brain abnormalities have been linked with schizophrenia?

    e. Which brain areas have been most strongly implicated? What are some psychological functions of those areas? Do schizophrenics show impairment of those functions?

    f. Why do researchers believe that these abnormalities resulted from developmental effects, rather than from gradual brain damage in adulthood?

g. How might one explain the late onset of schizophrenic symptoms, if the brain damage occurred during early development?

4. *Neurotransmitters and drugs*
   a. What is the dopamine hypothesis of schizophrenia? What are the main lines of evidence favoring it?

   b. What are two chemical families of antipsychotic (neuroleptic) drugs that have been in wide use for many years? What is their major effect on receptors?

   c. Which drugs can induce a state similar to schizophrenia? What is their major mechanism of action?

   d. What are two problems with the dopamine hypothesis?

e.   What other neurotransmitter has been hypothesized to be abnormal in schizophrenia? What are three types of interactions between these two neurotransmitters?

f.   Why may blockade of dopamine receptors have beneficial effects, if the original problem is deficient glutamate?

g.   What is phencyclidine? What are its effects on receptors? What are its psychological effects?

h.   What kinds of evidence suggest an abnormality in glutamate release or receptors?

i.   Why would it be unwise to administer glutamate to schizophrenic people? What kind of drug has been found to block the behavioral effects of PCP in rats?

j.   What is glycine? How does it affect NMDA receptors? What were the clinical findings concerning glycine or cycloserine?

k.  What is tardive dyskinesia? How rapid is its onset?  What drug effect may account for it?

l.  What is one atypical antipsychotic drug?  What are its effects on receptors and neurotransmitter release?

m.  What is a major advantage of atypical antipsychotic drugs?   What are their negative side effects?

## TRUE/FALSE QUESTIONS

_____ 1.  Electrical stimulation of the brain is usually reinforcing only if it activates dopamine release, especially in the nucleus accumbens.

_____ 2.  Dopamine release in the nucleus accumbens is now thought to be synonymous with pleasure: It always occurs with pleasant stimuli and never with unpleasant stimuli.

_____ 3.  One factor that leads to tolerance to drug effects is the co-release of dynorphin with dopamine; the dynorphin counteracts the effects of dopamine.

_____ 4.  Methylphenidate has been shown to increase the likelihood of later drug abuse.

_____ 5.  Nicotine stimulates one type of glutamate receptor.

_____ 6.  Endorphins increase dopamine release indirectly and also have effects independent of dopamine.

_____ 7.  Marijuana activates cannabinoid receptors primarily located in the hippocampus, basal ganglia and cerebellum.

_____ 8.  Endogenous neurotransmitters that activate cannabinoid receptors are known as endorphins.

_____ 9. Alcohol inhibits the flow of sodium across membranes, decreases serotonin activity, facilitates the $GABA_A$ receptor, and increases dopamine activity.

_____ 10. Type II alcoholism is associated with low serotonin turnover, impulsivity, and a relatively strong genetic basis.

_____ 11. Antabuse (disulfiram) stimulates acetaldehyde dehydrogenase, thereby decreasing the effects of alcohol.

_____ 12. During depression there is decreased activity in the left hemisphere and increased activity in the right hemisphere.

_____ 13. Tricyclic antidepressants work by inhibiting monoamine oxidase, which would otherwise metabolize the monoamine neurotransmitters.

_____ 14. St. John's wort is an especially effective antidepressant that has no bad side effects.

_____ 15. Brain-derived neurotrophic factor is released with dopamine and may mediate the effects of antidepressant drugs.

_____ 16. ECT increases $D_1$ and $D_2$ receptors in the nucleus accumbens.

_____ 17. Bipolar disorder is usually treated with the same drugs as are used for unipolar depression.

_____ 18. Arachidonic acid is a neurotransmitter that increases dopamine release.

_____ 19. Negative symptoms of schizophrenia include deficits in social interaction, emotional expression, speech, and working memory.

_____ 20. The neurodevelopmental hypothesis is supported by evidence that the prefrontal and temporal cortex, the hippocampus, and the amygdala are smaller in schizophrenics, but there are no signs of damage in adulthood, such as increased glia cells and expression of genes that promote repair.

_____ 21. Support for the dopamine hypothesis includes the observations that schizophrenics have much higher levels of dopamine and its metabolites and that the time courses of neuroleptic drugs on dopamine synapses and on clinical symptoms are similar.

_____ 22. Glycine is a co-transmitter at glutamate synapses and increases the effectiveness of glutamate.

_____ 23. The glutamate hypothesis states that dopamine and glutamate have the same effects on postsynaptic neurons.

_____ 24. Atypical antipsychotics, unlike typical ones, relieve negative as well as positive symptoms.

# FILL IN THE BLANKS

1. Almost all addictive drugs increase the release of _____ in the _____ _____.

2. _____ is released with dopamine and counteracts the effects of dopamine, thereby contributing to tolerance.

3. Methylphenidate usually is not addictive because its onset and offset are _____.

4. MDMA ("ecstasy") in high doses stimulates release of _____ and destroys _____ and _____ axons.

5. Nicotine stimulates nicotinic _____ receptors.

6. Marijuana stimulates _____ receptors; endogenous transmitters that stimulate the same kinds of receptors are _____ and _____.

7. Alcohol decreases _____ activity, facilitates _____ receptors, blocks _____ receptors, and increases _____ activity.

8. The enzyme that metabolizes acetaldehyde to _____ _____ is _____ _____.

9. Happy moods are associated with _____ activity in the _____ hemisphere.

10. Atypical antidepressants include _____, _____, and _____.

11. _____-_____ _____ _____ is released with dopamine and is increased with repeated administration of antidepressants.

12. ECT and _____ _____ _____ stimulation work faster than drugs but may cause memory loss, which can be lessened by administration only to the _____ hemisphere.

13. Three drugs used to treat bipolar disorder are _____ _____, _____ _____, and _____.

14. _____ _____ is produced during brain inflammation and is blocked by lithium and valproic acid.

15. Seasonal affective disorder is often associated with phase-_____ sleep and temperature rhythms, unlike other depressed people.

16. Positive symptoms of schizophrenia are grouped into a _____ cluster and a _____ cluster; the main problem is _____ _____.

17. Brain abnormalities in schizophrenia include smaller _____ and _____ cortex, _____, and _____, especially in the _____ hemisphere.

18. Currently used antipsychotic drugs block _____ _____ receptors or increase the effectiveness of _____.

19. Tremors and other involuntary movements that result from prolonged use of neuroleptic drugs are referred to as _____ _____.

20. _____ is an atypical antipsychotic that blocks _____ receptors more than _____ receptors and also blocks _____ receptors.

# MATCHING ITEMS

_____ 1. Amphetamine

_____ 2. Dynorphin

_____ 3. MDMA

_____ 4. Anandamide

_____ 5. Disulfiram

_____ 6. History of impulsiveness and violence

_____ 7. Fluoxetine (Prozac)

_____ 8. Bupropion (Wellbutrin)

_____ 9. Phase-advanced diurnal rhythm

_____ 10. Phase-delayed diurnal rhythm

_____ 11. Lithium salts

_____ 12. Haloperidol (Haldol)

_____ 13. Phencyclidine (PCP)

_____ 14. Tardive dyskinesia

_____ 15. Glycine

_____ 16. Clozapine

a. Endogenous cannabinoid

b. Inhibits acetaldehyde dehydrogenase

c. Atypical antidepressant

d. Atypical antipsychotic

e. Destroys dopamine and serotonin axons

f. Tremors, involuntary movements

g. Associated with typical depression

h. Associated with SAD

i. Associated with Type II alcoholism

j. Typical antipsychotic

k. Enhances effect of glutamate

l. An SSRI antidepressant

m. Reverses dopamine transporter

n. Treatment for bipolar I disorder

o. Counteracts dopamine's effects

p. Blocks NMDA glutamate receptors

## MULTIPLE-CHOICE QUESTIONS

1. Addictive drugs
   a. inhibit certain cells in the nucleus accumbens.
   b. release dopamine in the nucleus accumbens.
   c. have neural effects similar to those of naturally reinforcing behaviors.
   d. all of the above.

2. Amphetamine
   a. stimulates the release of dopamine by reversing the dopamine transporter and by blocking synapses that inhibit dopamine release.
   b. stimulates the release of endorphins by reversing the endorphin transporter and by blocking synapses that inhibit endorphin release.
   c. directly stimulates nicotinic receptors.
   d. directly stimulates glutamate receptors.

396

3. Cocaine
   a. blocks reuptake and enzyme degradation of glutamate, thus prolonging its effects.
   b. blocks reuptake of dopamine, norepinephrine, and serotonin, thus prolonging their effects.
   c. is absorbed into fat and released slowly, thereby preventing a "crash" a few hours later.
   d. all of the above.

4. Methylphenidate (Ritalin)
   a. is frequently abused because it acts rapidly when taken in pill form, producing a sudden rush of excitement.
   b. inhibits certain kinds of glutamate receptors.
   c. inhibits reuptake of dopamine and increases serotonin release.
   d. is used to treat opiate addiction.

5. Nicotine
   a. stimulates nicotinic acetylcholine receptors and thereby increases dopamine release.
   b. blocks nicotinic receptors and thereby increases dopamine release.
   c. blocks dopamine receptors and thereby increases acetylcholine release.
   d. stimulates dopamine receptors directly, and thereby produces reinforcement.

6. Opiates
   a. block receptors that are stimulated by endorphins.
   b. inhibit GABA neurons and thereby increase dopamine release.
   c. inhibit dopamine neurons and thereby increase GABA release.
   d. are especially addictive when taken for medical reasons.

7. Marijuana
   a. stimulates cannabinoid receptors located primarily in the brain stem; it thereby interferes with breathing.
   b. blocks endorphin receptors.
   c. is very likely to produce a "crash" a couple of hours after its ingestion.
   d. mimics the effects of the endogenous neurotransmitters anandamide and 2-AG.

8. LSD
   a. stimulates the release of norepinephrine and dopamine.
   b. blocks most serotonin receptors.
   c. stimulates $5\text{-}HT_{2A}$ receptors.
   d. blocks the synthesis of serotonin.

9. Alcohol
   a. inhibits the flow of sodium across the membrane.
   b. expands the surface of membranes.
   c. makes $GABA_A$ receptors more responsive.
   d. all of the above.

10. Type II alcoholism
    a. has a stronger genetic basis than does Type I.
    b. develops gradually over the years.
    c. affects men and women about equally.
    d. all of the above.

11. Low serotonin turnover is associated with
    a. Type II alcoholism.
    b. impulsivity.
    c. a strong genetic basis for alcoholism.
    d. all of the above.

12. Acetaldehyde dehydrogenase
    a. is the generic name for Antabuse.
    b. controls the rate of conversion of acetic acid, a toxic product of alcohol metabolism, into acetaldehyde, a source of energy.
    c. controls the rate of conversion of acetaldehyde, a toxic product of alcohol metabolism, into acetic acid, a source of energy.
    d. if present in high levels, would make us feel very ill after drinking alcohol.

13. Which of the following is true?
    a. Sons of alcoholics experience less than average relief from tension after drinking alcohol; therefore, they have to drink more for the same effect.
    b. Antabuse acts primarily as a supplement to the alcoholic's commitment to stop drinking.
    c. Sons of alcoholics show greater than average intoxication after drinking a small to moderate amount of alcohol.
    d. Sons of alcoholics tend to have an unusually large amygdala in the right hemisphere.

14. Which of the following is **not** a common symptom of major depression?
    a. sleeping for at least 10 - 12 hours per night
    b. sadness and helplessness
    c. lack of energy
    d. little pleasure from sex or food

15. Which of the following is true of depression?
    a. A gene on chromosome 11 is now known to be the cause of most cases of depression.
    b. Hormonal changes before menstruation or after childbirth can cause depression, even in women without a biological predisposition to that disorder.
    c. Since no specific genetic abnormality has been discovered, it is now commonly agreed that depression does not have any genetic basis.
    d. It is likely that several genes increase the risk for some sort of disorder, including depression, substance abuse, and anxiety disorder.

16. Depression is frequently associated with
    a. increased activity in the left, and decreased activity in the right prefrontal cortex
    b. decreased activity in the left, and increased activity in the right prefrontal cortex.
    c. increased activity in the right, and decreased activity in the left temporal cortex
    d. decreased activity in the right, and increased activity in the left temporal cortex.

17. Research on Borna disease suggests that
    a. a virus causes an autoimmune attack on the brain.
    b. any illness that causes a fever also causes major depression.
    c. a virus may be one cause of depression.
    d. the viruses that infect animals cannot infect humans.

18. Which of the following is **not** a type of antidepressant drug?
    a.   monoamine oxidase inhibitors
    b.   tricyclics
    c.   serotonin reuptake inhibitors
    d.   dopamine receptor blockers

19. Which of the following is true?
    a.   The effects of drugs on transmitter systems are immediate, but their effects on depression are delayed for one to two weeks.
    b.   The effects of drugs on transmitter systems are delayed for one to two weeks, but their effects on depression are immediate.
    c.   Depression results from having excessive activity of all the monoamine transmitters.
    d.   The major effect of fluoxetine is to block serotonin receptors.

20. Repeated use of antidepressant drugs
    a.   results in decreased sensivity of postsynaptic receptors.
    b.   stimulates autoreceptors and thereby decreases further release.
    c.   increases production and release of brain-derived neurotrophic factor in parts of the hippocampus and cerebral cortex.
    d.   all of the above.

21. Electroconvulsive therapy (ECT)
    a.   is effective because it confuses patients, and they forget their depressing thoughts.
    b.   is rarely used anymore because of its bad reputation.
    c.   increases the numbers of $D_1$ and $D_2$ receptors in the nucleus accumbens.
    d.   must be administered to the left hemisphere, which produces loss of language ability.

22. Depressed people
    a.   enter REM sleep more slowly than do normal people.
    b.   are sometimes helped by an earlier bedtime, in phase with their declining body temperature.
    c.   have their symptoms worsened by exposure to transcranial magnetic stimulation.
    d.   all of the above.

23. Bipolar disorder is characterized by
    a.   cycles between depression and normal moods.
    b.   cycles between depression and mania.
    c.   a smaller amygdala than normal.
    d.   higher glucose metabolism in the brain during depression, and lower activity during mania.

24. Lithium
    a.   is more effective than valproic acid and carbamazepine for bipolar I disorder.
    b.   is extremely safe because it is so simple.
    c.   is helpful for depression but not for mania.
    d.   all of the above.

25. People with seasonal affective disorder (SAD)
    a.   become more depressed during winter because of the cold.
    b.   are frequently helped by sitting in hot sauna baths for an hour or more each day.
    c.   show phase-advanced sleep and temperature rhythms, similar to other depressed people.
    d.   are frequently helped by exposure to bright lights for an hour or more each day.

26. Schizophrenia
    a. is characterized by multiple personalities.
    b. refers to a split between the emotions and the intellect.
    c. is rarely misdiagnosed because its symptoms are so clearly distinctive.
    d. is typically first diagnosed in the elderly.

27. Which of the following is true of the positive symptoms of schizophrenia?
    a. They are usually associated with increased neural activity in the medulla, the visual cortex, and the dorsolateral prefrontal cortex.
    b. They include deficits in social interactions, emotional expression, and speech.
    c. They consist of a disorganized cluster, including inappropriate emotions, bizarre behaviors, and thought disorder, and a psychotic cluster, including delusions and hallucinations.
    d. They are more stable over time than are the negative symptoms.

28. The prevalence of schizophrenia
    a. is declining, for unknown reasons.
    b. is higher in Third World countries because of increased stress there.
    c. is higher in women than in men.
    d. is fairly easy to study, since schizophrenia is one of the easiest disorders to diagnose.

29. Which of the following provides some support for a genetic basis for schizophrenia?
    a. Adopted children have a higher concordance rate with their adoptive than biological kin.
    b. The concordance rate for schizophrenia is greater for dizygotic than for monozygotic twins.
    c. The concordance rate for schizophrenia is greater for monozygotic than for dizygotic twins.
    d. Mutation of a gene on chromosome 7 has been shown to cause schizophrenia.

30. A problem with the conclusion that schizophrenia has a genetic basis is that
    a. common prenatal factors may at least partially explain the greater concordance rate of monozygotic over dizygotic twins, and of dizygotic twins over non-twin siblings.
    b. common prenatal factors, such as smoking, drinking, and other poor health habits, may at least partially explain the increased concordance rate of biological parents, compared to adoptive parents, of schizophrenics.
    c. both a and b are true.
    d. none of the above is true.

31. Research on possible causes of schizophrenia has demonstrated that
    a. a prenatal viral infection may cause fever, which results in impaired brain development.
    b. several studies have converged on a single gene as the primary cause of schizophrenia.
    c. conflicting messages from parents are a major cause of schizophrenia.
    d. the season-of-birth effect occurs more often in the tropics, where diseases are harder to control.

32. Studies of the brains of schizophrenics have revealed that
    a. they have shrunken ventricles.
    b. their prefrontal and temporal cortex, hippocampus, and amygdala are smaller, especially in the left hemisphere.
    c. they have more abnormalities in rapidly maturing areas than in slowly maturing areas such as dorsolateral prefrontal cortex.
    d. they have a large proliferation of glia cells and expression of genes activated during repair, indicating that much of the damage was caused during adulthood.

33. Drug-induced psychosis
    a.  is usually permanent and causes a full-blown state of schizophrenia, complete with auditory hallucinations.
    b.  is caused by drugs that block dopamine receptors.
    c.  is caused by drugs that increase the stimulation of dopamine receptors.
    d.  is caused by drugs that stimulate glutamate receptors.

34. Which of the following is not an effective neuroleptic drug?
    a.  haloperidol
    b.  chlorpromazine
    c.  amphetamine
    d.  clozapine

35. According to the dopamine hypothesis of schizophrenia, people with schizophrenia have
    a.  excessive activity at dopamine synapses.
    b.  deficient activity at dopamine synapses.
    c.  glutamate in neurons that should release dopamine.
    d.  dopamine in neurons that should release glutamate.

36. A problem with the dopamine hypothesis is that
    a.  neuroleptic drugs improve schizophrenic symptoms before they have a significant effect on dopamine synapses.
    b.  people with schizophrenia have nearly normal levels of dopamine and its metabolites.
    c.  densities of all types of dopamine receptors are higher in people with schizophrenia, whereas they would be expected to be lower.
    d.  amphetamine, cocaine, methamphetamine, and LSD increase activity at dopamine receptors, but are among the best treatments for schizophrenia, suggesting that excess dopamine activity cannot be a cause of that disorder.

37. Which of the following is true?
    a.  PCP is an atypical neuroleptic drug that treats schizophrenia by stimulating glutamate receptors.
    b.  Since there is too much glutamate in the brains of schizophrenic people, a good way to improve their symptoms is to block glutamate receptors.
    c.  Glycine interferes with the binding of glutamate to NMDA receptors, thereby worsening schizophrenic symptoms.
    d.  In many brain areas, dopamine inhibits glutamate release, or glutamate stimulates neurons that inhibit dopamine release, or glutamate excites neurons that dopamine inhibits.

38. Tardive dyskinesia
    a.  recedes completely once all traces of antipsychotic drugs have left the body.
    b.  usually occurs soon after beginning antipsychotic drug treatment.
    c.  may result from denervation supersensitivity of dopamine receptors in the basal ganglia.
    d.  develops because of decreased numbers of dopamine receptors in the basal ganglia.

39. Atypical antipsychotic drugs
    a.  include haloperidol and chlorpromazine.
    b.  decrease dopamine activity primarily in the mesolimbocortical system.
    c.  decrease dopamine activity primarily in the basal ganglia.
    d.  should be avoided because they produce more tardive dyskinesia than typical neuroleptics.

40. Clozapine
    a. blocks dopamine $D_4$ receptors more than $D_2$.
    b. also blocks serotonin 5-HT$_2$ receptors.
    c. has undesirable side effects, including increased risk of diabetes and impaired immune system.
    d. all of the above.

## Answers to True/False Questions

| | | | |
|---|---|---|---|
| 1. T | 7. T | 13. F | 19. T |
| 2. F | 8. F | 14. F | 20. T |
| 3. T | 9. T | 15. T | 21. F |
| 4. F | 10. T | 16. T | 22. T |
| 5. F | 11. F | 17. F | 23. F |
| 6. T | 12. T | 18. F | 24. T |

## Answers to Fill-in-the-Blank Questions

1. dopamine, nucleus accumbens
2. Dynorphin
3. gradual
4. Serotonin, dopamine, serotonin
5. acetylcholine
6. cannabinoid, anandamide, 2-AG
7. serotonin, GABA$_A$, glutamate, dopamine
8. acetic acid, acetaldehyde dehydogenase
9. increased, left
10. bupropion, venlafaxine, nefazodone
11. Brain-derived neurotrophic factor
12. repetitive transcranial magnetic, right
13. lithium salts, valproic acid, carbamazepine
14. Arachidonic acid
15. delayed
16. psychotic, disorganized, disorganized thinking
17. prefrontal, temporal, hippocampus, amygdala, left
18. D$_4$ dopamine, glutamate
19. tardive dyskinesia
20. Clozapine, D$_4$, D$_2$, 5-HT$_2$

## Answers to Matching Items

| | | | |
|---|---|---|---|
| 1. m | 5. b | 9. g | 13. p |
| 2. o | 6. i | 10. h | 14. f |
| 3. e | 7. l | 11. n | 15. k |
| 4. a | 8. c | 12. j | 16. d |

## Answers to Multiple-Choice Questions

| | | | | | |
|---|---|---|---|---|---|
| 1. d | 8. c | 15. d | 22. b | 29. c | 36. b |
| 2. a | 9. d | 16. b | 23. b | 30. c | 37. d |
| 3. b | 10. a | 17. c | 24. a | 31. a | 38. c |
| 4. c | 11. d | 18. d | 25. d | 32. b | 39. b |
| 5. a | 12. c | 19. a | 26. b | 33. c | 40. d |
| 6. b | 13. b | 20. d | 27. c | 34. c | |
| 7. d | 14. a | 21. c | 28. a | 35. a | |

**Please check the Exploring Biological Psychology CD-ROM.**

# Drugs, Moods, and Psychoses

www.CrosswordWeaver.com

**ACROSS**

**1** Co-discoverer of reward sites in the brain

**4** Abused drug that blocks reuptake of dopamine, norepinephrine, and serotonin

**5** Wisconsin ____-sorting task: a test for damage to prefrontal cortex

**8** Drug that inhibits reuptake of serotonin and is used to treat depression (abbr.)

**9** Disorder in which moods vary between mania and depression

**11** Positive symptom of schizophrenia

**12** Transmitter that may be deficient in schizophrenia

**14** Endogenous cannabinoid

**16** Brain-derived _____ factor, released with dopamine, promotes recovery from depression

**17** Neurotransmitter whose receptors are blocked by antipsychotic drugs

**19** Season when schizophrenics are somewhat more likely to be born

**20** Drug that inhibits reuptake of monoamine transmitters and is used to treat depression

**DOWN**

**2** Peptide released with dopamine that counteracts the reinforcing effects of cocaine

**3** Treatment for bipolar I disorder

**6** Prefrontal cortex area that matures slowly and has deficits in schizophrenia

**7** Receptor facilitated by alcohol

**8** Disorder most common in regions where nights are long in winter (abbr.)

**10** Atypical antipsychotic

**13** _____ acid, product of metabolism of acetaldehyde

**15** Type of glutamate receptor, blockage of which gives symptoms of schizophrenia

**18** Treatment for depression that works more quickly than drugs (abbr.)

403

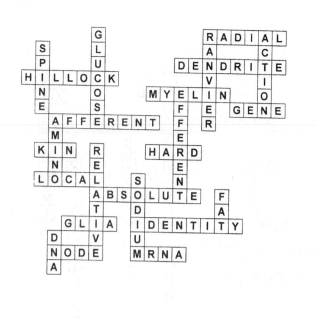

Genes, Neurons and Behavior

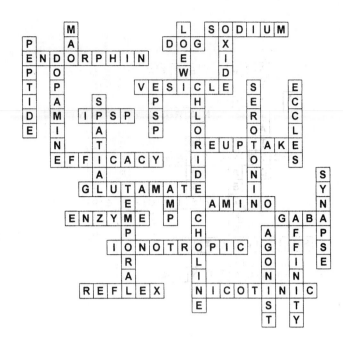

Synaptic Symphony

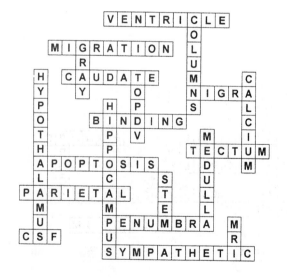

Brain Parts and Development

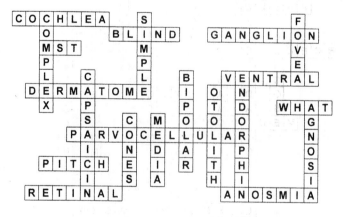

Sensational Senses

404

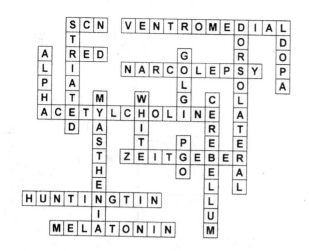

Doing and Dreaming

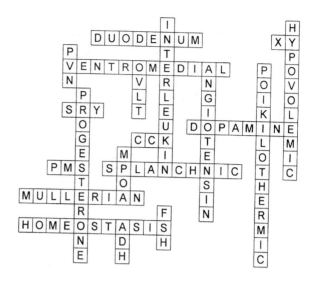

Heat, Sex, and Gluttony

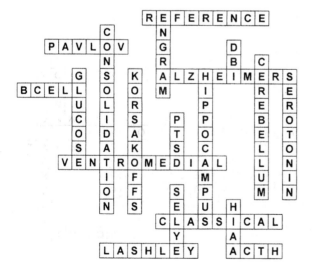

Emotions and Memories

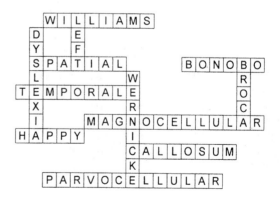

Words and Brains

405

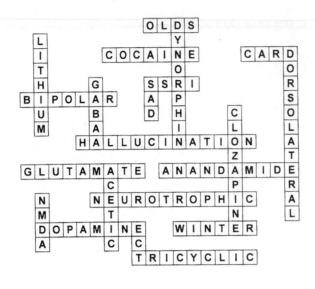

Drugs, Moods, and Psychoses